OBJECTS OF POVERTY

OBJECTS OF POVERTY

MATERIAL CULTURE IN BRITAIN FROM 1700

Edited by Joseph Harley and Vicky Holmes

BLOOMSBURY ACADEMIC
LONDON • NEW YORK • OXFORD • NEW DELHI • SYDNEY

BLOOMSBURY ACADEMIC

Bloomsbury Publishing Plc, 50 Bedford Square, London, WC1B 3DP, UK
Bloomsbury Publishing Inc, 1385 Broadway, New York, NY 10018, USA
Bloomsbury Publishing Ireland, 29 Earlsfort Terrace, Dublin 2, D02 AY28, Ireland

BLOOMSBURY, BLOOMSBURY ACADEMIC and the Diana logo are trademarks
of Bloomsbury Publishing Plc

First published in Great Britain 2025

Copyright © Joseph Harley and Vicky Holmes, 2025

Joseph Harley and Vicky Holmes have asserted their right under the Copyright,
Designs and Patents Act, 1988, to be identified as Editors of this work.

For legal purposes the Acknowledgements on p. xv constitute an
extension of this copyright page.

Cover design by Chris Bromley
Cover images © Svyatoslav, photohampster, Oksava, Scott Donkin, djumandji,
Tetiana and Brian Donovan via Adobe Stock and by Emily Cockayne

All rights reserved. No part of this publication may be: i) reproduced or transmitted in any form, electronic or mechanical, including photocopying, recording or by means of any information storage or retrieval system without prior permission in writing from the publishers; or ii) used or reproduced in any way for the training, development or operation of artificial intelligence (AI) technologies, including generative AI technologies. The rights holders expressly reserve this publication from the text and data mining exception as per Article 4(3) of the Digital Single Market Directive (EU) 2019/790.

Bloomsbury Publishing Plc does not have any control over, or responsibility for, any third-party websites referred to or in this book. All internet addresses given in this book were correct at the time of going to press. The author and publisher regret any inconvenience caused if addresses have changed or sites have ceased to exist, but can accept no responsibility for any such changes.

A catalogue record for this book is available from the British Library.

A catalog record for this book is available from the Library of Congress.

ISBN: HB: 978-1-3503-6818-7
PB: 978-1-3503-6817-0
ePDF: 978-1-3503-6820-0
eBook: 978-1-3503-6819-4

Typeset by Newgen KnowledgeWorks Pvt. Ltd., Chennai, India
Printed and bound in Great Britain

For product safety related questions contact productsafety@bloomsbury.com.

To find out more about our authors and books visit www.bloomsbury.com
and sign up for our newsletters.

CONTENTS

List of figures   viii
List of tables   xii
List of contributors   xiii
Acknowledgements   xv
Preface   xvi

Introduction   1
    Joseph Harley and Vicky Holmes

PART I OBJECTS OF SUSTENANCE

1   Bread: The matter that mattered most   17
     Carl Griffin

2   Global goods to pauper provisions under the old poor law:
     Evidence from overseers' vouchers, 1765–1834   27
     Peter Collinge

3   'Full of saloop with fire under it': Teaware, saloop stalls and warmth
     on the streets of Georgian London   39
     Freya Purcell

PART II OBJECTS OF HOME

4   From cradle to grave? The enduring afterlife of the egg box in
     Victorian London   53
     Vicky Holmes

5   From improvised to subsidised safety: Fireguards   65
     Jonathan Reinarz and Shane Ewen

6   Coal in the bath: Poverty, modernity and the welfare state
     in post-war Britain   75
     Michael Lambert

Contents

PART III CRAFTED OBJECTS

7 Creativity in poverty: British sailors' craft in the long nineteenth century   89
   Maya Wassell-Smith

8 Buttons for whistles in the late Victorian, early Edwardian era:
   Unbranded calls   105
   Emily Cockayne

9 Makeshift dolls and working-class childhood, c. 1880–1930   115
   Emily Cuming

PART IV OBJECTS OF CHILDHOOD

10 Toys for the poor, c. 1700–1918   131
    Ken Sneath

11 'Models of needlework': A needlework sample book from the
    Dublin Female Orphan House, c. 1860–90   141
    Eliza McKee

12 Fragmentary findings: A Victorian school needlework sample   157
    Vivienne Richmond

PART V LIVING OBJECTS

13 The poor's best friend? Dog ownership and companionship
    in England, c. 1780–1880   169
    Joseph Harley

14 'Up with the Hen House': Chickens, coops and class identity in British
    Municipal Cottage Estates, 1920–50   187
    Lesley Hoskins and Rebecca Preston

PART VI MONETARY OBJECTS

15 'Was much Reduced and had been under the necesity to Pawn
    his Cloaths': Parish payments to redeem pawned goods in London
    in the long eighteenth century   203
    Samantha Williams

16 'No Money Value': The Salvation Army social work tokens in the late nineteenth century — 219
Flore Janssen

17 The purses of the poor: Money, autonomy and everyday life in Victorian and Edwardian England — 231
Julie-Marie Strange

VII WORKHOUSE OBJECTS

18 Going to bed in the workhouse: Facilities, practices and implications in the 1790s — 247
Alannah Tomkins

19 Scraps and samplers: The form and function of textile artefacts in the nineteenth-century workhouse — 261
Karen Thompson, Peter Jones and Steven King

20 Investigating all they possessed: Depredation, damage and defiance in the vagrant ward from 1834 to 1900 — 275
Megan Yates

VIII OBJECTS OF INJURY AND DEATH

21 'Ought I Not to Have Been Grateful?': Wooden legs as military charity, 1800–1850s — 289
Caroline Louise Nielsen

22 Medical objects: The sick poor and their relief in the long nineteenth century — 301
Steven King and Peter Jones

23 Inscription gravestones: Poverty and commemoration in the late nineteenth century — 311
Rebecca Senior

Subject index — 323

FIGURES

3.1	Detail of anonymous, *Five Criers on a Single Sheet*, c. 1780–90	40
3.2	M. Egerton, *Street Breakfast*, 1825	42
4.1	Front of a tradesman shop from Henry Mayhew's *London Labour and the London Poor*, Vol 1 (1861), p. 73	54
4.2	Photograph of the interior of a Salvation Army shelter, c. 1890s	57
4.3	Photograph of the interior of the Salvation Army metropole on Burne Street, London, c. 1896	58
4.4	Paul Renouard's sketch of the Whitechapel shelter after a visit with *Graphic* journalist F. W. Robinson not long after its opening	59
4.5	Excerpt from the *Islington Gazette*, 31 January 1894, p. 3	59
4.6	A baby sleeping in a converted egg box	60
7.1	Ship's biscuit painted by an unknown sailor, c. 1890s	91
7.2	*Jack's Christmas Present* frontispiece, Robert Barnes, *The British Workman*, December 1867	95
7.3	*The Feathered Builders and Their Homes* frontispiece, engraved by J. Knight after Harrison Weir, *The British Workman*, June 1863	96
7.4	Woolwork picture embroidered by Andrew Andrews, 1863	97
7.5	Woolwork picture embroidered by Andrew Andrews, c. 1860	98
7.6	Farmyard frontispiece, engraved by J. Knight after Harrison Weir, *The British Workman*, July 1858	99
7.7	Retired sailor selling woolwork pictures, 1899	100
8.1	An 'unbranded' whistle made from two plain brass uniform buttons alongside a similar button	106
8.2	Barometer made around the late Victorian period from reused wooden and brass objects	107
8.3	The button back-stamp	108
8.4	A type of police whistle illustrated in *The Boy's Own Paper* (1887)	108
8.5	Whistle made from two King's Royal Rifles Corps uniform buttons	109
8.6	A sweetheart brooch made from a British Royal Navy tunic button, the button was made by Firmin & Sons, London	112
9.1	Doll made of a ninepin by a poor child in London	116

Figures

9.2	Mutton bone doll, *c.* 1900	117
9.3	Shoe doll, *c.* 1905	118
9.4	Emma Brownlow, *The Sick Room*, oil on canvas, 1864	119
9.5	Illustration from Mrs H. M. Stanley (Dorothy Tennant), *London Street Arabs*, 1890	120
9.6	Illustration from an advert for Louise Chandler Moulton's *Bedtime Stories* included in *Aunt Jo's Scrap-Bag*	121
11.1	A darning sampler worked on canvas with yellow and green thread produced by Annie Marshall and dated 1890	146
11.2	A miniature dress with smocking detail around the neckline, lace trimming around the neckline and cuffs of the sleeves, and three rows of four horizontal pleats on the skirt	147
11.3	A miniature white shirt with four panels of vertical lacework on either side of the centre front. A miniature white shirt collar. A religious sampler worked in red thread	149
11.4	Crochet edging sampler with five rows of crochet trimming. Two crocheted place mats with frayed trim	150
11.5	A miniature lace bonnet with two strings for fastening	151
12.1	(a) Annie Sawden's sample, front side; (b) Annie Sawden's sample, reverse side	158
12.2	A plain-sewing sampler, incorporating a button and buttonholes, worked by a London schoolgirl in 1888	162
13.1	William Hogarth, *The Four Stages of Cruelty*, 1751	171
13.2	Portrait of June Mark, pauper/seasonal farm worker, eighty-four years old, *c.* 1833	177
13.3	Portrait of Bet Mattock, widowed pauper, eighty-two years old, *c.* 1862	178
13.4	Portrait of John Mattock, pauper/colt breaker, seventy-one to seventy-two years old, *c.* 1851–2	179
13.5	John Wilkins, gamekeeper, *c.* 1892	182
14.1	The *Feathered World* Poultry House, 1939	193
14.2	*The Borough of Southgate Municipal Tenants Handbook*, 1950	195
14.3	Backyards photographed by the London County Council in Southwark before clearance in 1913 for the Tabard Gardens Estate	196
14.4	A. P. Thompson, 'Poultry', in C. H. Middleton (ed.), *War Time Allotments, Daily Express*, 1940, p. 99	196
15.1	Draft trade card of William Purse, pawnbroker	204

Figures

15.2	Two men are standing behind the counter of a pawnbroker's shop in London, examining some articles of clothing which have been brought in to pawn, etching by George Cruikshank, 1836	206
15.3	Sums paid by the parish to redeem pledges in three London parishes, 1695–1808	208
16.1	The collection of Salvation Army Social Work tokens (M54)	220
16.2	Extract on remuneration in City Colonies, from *Orders and Regulations for Social Officers of the Salvation Army*, 1898	223
16.3	Illustration of Battersea Wharf Elevator, from the *Darkest England Gazette*, 31 March 1894, p. 2	224
16.4	Illustrations of first-, second- and third-class tokens from Battersea Wharf City Colony, from the *Social Gazette*, 19 November 1898, p. 3	224
17.1	Stocking purse, *c.* 1880	233
17.2	Pouch purse, *c.* 1910	234
17.3	Clasp purse, *c.* 1900	235
17.4	Seed purse, *c.* 1900	240
18.1	Engraving by Thomas Rowlandson, showing a wooden bed frame and the physical presence of bedbugs, 1793	252
19.1	*Oliver Twist Asking for More*, George Cruikshank, 1838	262
19.2	Four of the five balls found at the former Mitford and Launditch workhouse, Norfolk	265
19.3	Deconstructed ball from the former Mitford and Launditch workhouse, Norfolk	266
19.4	Initial findings of investigation into textiles contained in the Mitford and Launditch workhouse ball	266
19.5	Section of a sampler by Lorina Bulwer	269
19.6	Section of a sampler by Lorina Bulwer	270
19.7	Appliqué figures on a panel by Lorina Bulwer	271
20.1	A widely shared image of a 'typical vagrant', 1887	278
21.1	Henry Heather Bigg. Simple wooden leg	292
21.2	I. Cruikshank, An old sailor with wooden leg and a man with no arms drinking in a tavern, 1791	293
22.1	Empty bottle found at Cerne Abbas workhouse, Dorset	303
22.2	Allen and Hanbury Double Truss	306
23.1	View of 'Guinea Grave Row', Beckett Street Cemetery, Leeds	312
23.2	Inscription gravestone 22699, Beckett Street Cemetery, Leeds	315

Figures

23.3	View of inscription graves, Beckett Street Cemetery, Leeds	317
23.4	Inscription gravestone 22825, Beckett Street Cemetery, Leeds	317
23.5	View of inscription graves, Beckett Street Cemetery, Leeds	318
23.6	Cemetery Chapel and view of inscription grave path, St George's Field, University of Leeds, 2023	319

TABLES

2.1	Overseers' Vouchers and Sample Parishes in Cumberland and Staffordshire, 1769–1836	29
2.2	Prices of Groceries Supplied to Parishes in Cumberland and Staffordshire, 1782–1836	31
15.1	Types of Clothing Redeemed and Sums Paid by the Parish Authorities in Three London Parishes, 1695–1808	210
20.1	Most Common Entries for Vagrants in the Stourbridge Admissions Register, 1870–86	282

CONTRIBUTORS

Emily Cockayne, Associate Professor of Cultural History, School of History and Art History, University of East Anglia, UK

Peter Collinge, Honorary Visiting Research Fellow, School of Humanities, Keele University, UK

Emily Cuming, Senior Lecturer in English Literature, School of Humanities and Social Science, Liverpool John Moores University, UK

Shane Ewen, Professor of History, School Humanities and Social Sciences, Leeds Metropolitan University, UK

Carl Griffin, Professor of Historical Geography, School of Global Studies, University of Sussex, UK

Joseph Harley, Senior Lecturer in History, School of Humanities and Social Sciences, Anglia Ruskin University, Cambridge, UK

Vicky Holmes, Adjunct Assistant Professor in History, Notre Dame London, The University of Notre Dame (USA) in England, UK

Lesley Hoskins, Independent Scholar, London, UK

Flore Janssen, Assistant Professor in Comparative Literature, Department of Languages, Literature and Communication, Utrecht University, the Netherlands

Peter Jones, Postdoctoral Research Fellow, School of Arts and Humanities, Nottingham Trent University, UK

Steven King, Professor of Economic and Social History, School of Arts and Humanities, Nottingham Trent University, UK

Michael Lambert, Research Fellow, Lancaster Medical School, Faculty of Health and Medicine, Lancaster University, UK

Eliza McKee, Fulbright Scholar, Glucksman Ireland House, New York University, USA

Caroline Louise Nielsen, Senior Lecturer in History and Heritage, Faculty of Arts, Science and Technology, University of Northampton, UK

Rebecca Preston, Blue Plaques Historian, English Heritage, London, UK

Freya Purcell, Project Curator, Museum of Hartlepool, UK

Contributors

Jonathan Reinarz, Professor of the History of Medicine, Department of Health Sciences, University of Birmingham, UK

Vivienne Richmond, Independent Textile Researcher, UK

Rebecca Senior, Impact and Evaluation Manager, the Courtauld Institute of Art, Paul Mellon Centre for Studies in British Art, London, UK

Ken Sneath, Former Assistant Director of Studies, Economic History, Peterhouse College, University of Cambridge, UK

Julie-Marie Strange, Professor of Modern British History, Department of History, Durham University, UK

Karen Thompson, Senior Lecturer, Kelvin Centre for Conservation and Cultural Heritage Research, University of Glasgow, UK

Alannah Tomkins, Professor of Social History, School of Humanities, Keele University, UK

Maya Wassell-Smith, Assistant Curator of Art/CDA PhD candidate, Royal Museums Greenwich, UK

Samantha Williams, Professor of Social History, Institute of Continuing Education and Girton College, University of Cambridge, UK

Megan Yates, Independent Researcher, Leicester, UK

ACKNOWLEDGEMENTS

During the final leg of our last edited collection, we joked that we might give it another year or two before embarking on another. However, before *The Working Class at Home* even came to press, we struck upon the idea of exploring poverty through objects. In the midst of the pandemic, we put out a call for papers for an online conference hosted by Anglia Ruskin University which revealed a clear appetite for work into the material lives of the poor. The events of the conference, questions from the audience and each paper have collectively helped to inspire us to take the idea forward to book form. We would like to thank each of you who participated in the conference.

Thanks are due to the contributors in this volume. As with any edited collection, there have been swings and changes in the authors over the past three years. Eleven have been with us since the start, while others joined us when we were writing the proposal and some even joined us in the final stretch. Each have written excellent chapters and helped to make our jobs as editors all the more satisfying. We would also like to thank the many organisations who have kindly allowed us to reproduce images of their collections here and bring the objects of the poor further to life.

Finally, we extend our thanks to each other. Finding such a great writing/editing partnership is rare, though for now, we shall head down differing paths as we venture onto new projects ...

Joe Harley and Vicky Holmes, August 2024

PREFACE

Objects of Poverty is the first volume dedicated to analysing the material culture of poverty in British history from 1700 to the present. The book examines the history of poverty through the objects 'owned' by the poor and those crafted, repurposed or simply encountered by them. It shows how these objects, or the absence of them, offers critical new insights into the experience of being impoverished.

This collection brings together leading and emerging scholars who draw on a wide array of 'objects of poverty' from those that survive today, ranging from dolls to whistles to textile samples, to those that have long since gone and now only exist in visual and written sources. The contributors trace the importance of materiality in eighteenth century and modern life, covering objects connected to sustenance, home, the makeshift, childhood, animals, money, workhouses, and injury and death. In its twenty-three chapters, the book provides a detailed exploration of the history of poverty in Britain. All the chapters are based on original research and make a new contribution to the literature, but are written so that all can engage with them, from history enthusiasts to students to established academics across multiple disciplines.

INTRODUCTION
Joseph Harley and Vicky Holmes

In recent decades, the study of history through objects has become a well-established and stimulating area across historical disciplines. From Neil MacGregor's landmark *A History of the World in 100 Objects* to historians studying pockets, pots and pans, ornaments and clothing, such works have begun to rewrite our understanding of the past. However, the objects encountered by the poor have remained opaque, under-researched and neglected, creating a significant gap in our understanding of the material cultures of the past. The history of poverty has always been the story of material dearth – a history of objectlessness rather than wealth and of defining the poor by the objects that they do not possess. Yet, as new research is beginning to uncover, a history of poverty is also a story of possession. In the following twenty-three chapters, we continue to address this sizeable gap through the lens of material culture. Turning our focus to the items used and owned by the poorest in society, expanding our understanding on both what an object is and where we find it, our book offers new perspectives on poverty, both by those who experienced it and by those who sought to document, alleviate or even punish the deprived.

Drawing on a range of historical sources, the contributors discuss a selection of 'objects of poverty' connected to sustenance, home, the makeshift, childhood, animals, money, workhouses, and injury and death. The book demonstrates how objects, or a lack thereof, allow us to understand the experience of impoverishment from new and exciting perspectives. The chapters reveal that the poor were a creative, pragmatic and resourceful group worthy of extensive study through material culture. Their lives might be one of relatively few objects, of constantly trying to acquire or get by without the things they could not afford, but understanding their material lives is vital to our understanding of poverty, past and present. Of course, the objects included in our collection are just a fraction of those that were part of their daily lives. Nevertheless, our book serves as a significant starting point to the material culture of poverty, laying the groundwork for new research into this fascinating area of study. The chapters in this volume are based on original research and make a new contribution to the literature but are written so that all can engage with them, from history enthusiasts to students to established academics across multiple disciplines.

Historians, objects and poverty

Over the past forty years, scholarship on middle-class and elite material culture has burgeoned. We now have vast knowledge about their homes, ranging from the country estate to the townhouse, the immense array of household objects they possessed, the incredible variety of attire they wore and even the minute intricacies of their shopping habits. However, poverty and its link to the material world has rarely been subject to sustained research in various histories including welfare, class and even the standard of living debate, for such work is implicitly (and sometimes explicitly) concerned with what the poor *did not* have rather than what they had. For example, seminal works such as Sidney and Beatrice Webbs's vast research on the poor laws and E. P. Thompson's *The Making of the English Working Class*, along with Peter Townsend's study of poverty in the UK in the 1970s, are staples of any poverty historian's bookshelf.[1] Yet, the material nature of poverty – both objects encountered and possessed – is conspicuously absent across thousands of pages. Of course, each writer had their own objectives and priorities, so it is unfair to criticise them for what they have not done as opposed to what they have done. Nonetheless, poverty was (and is) *so* intrinsically linked to objects that all studies should be much more conscious of the roles items play in people's lives.

Recent research on the poor has brought objects into view more than previous generations of writers. Historians examining the homes of the poor in the 'long' eighteenth century (*c.* 1680–1830), such as Peter King, Craig Muldrew and Joseph Harley, have revealed, through the use of pauper and probate inventories, that poverty did not necessarily equate to people owning little and that a great many owned new objects, such as novel cooking items, mirrors and timepieces.[2] Moving forward in time, through autobiographies and oral testimonies, Anna Davin's seminal work on growing up poor in late-nineteenth- and early-twentieth-century London notes no less than fifty objects – from the mundane to the makeshift – that made up the close-quartered homes of London's poorer population, indicating that even in slums interiors were far from sparse, as is often depicted in contemporary writings and illustrations.[3] While such acute poverty has declined in the UK since the birth of the welfare state, poverty is still present. The inability to acquire enough food and fuel is a daily struggle for millions of working families today, as noted repeatedly by charities and in media reports.[4] However, when we consider changes to the domestic sphere, we see that the past seventy years have brought unprecedented access to a vast range of consumables, from televisions to microwaves to washing machines to smartphones. As Avner Offer argues in his summary of these many consumer changes, during 'the course of the twentieth century, the luxuries of the rich have become necessities for all'.[5]

The material culture of the poor has emerged in the work of historians turning to archaeological findings. To name but one example, when the Museum of London Archaeology (MOLA) dug down into two privies sealed during late-nineteenth-century sanitary improvements in the slums of Limehouse, they uncovered 131 separate items 'unwanted or no longer of use' discarded by generations of inhabitants. Analysed by Alastair Owens and a team of researchers, a series of 'mundane, if not banal' items were located, revealing vital glimpses into the rhythms and realities of everyday life among London's poorer population. Other items from the excavations – such as a decorative rolling pin and many tea goods – were far from 'banal' and reveal as many questions as they do answers about individual lives, especially when the fragmented objects appear as less usual.⁶

Clothing has been a particularly fruitful research area for understanding experiences of poverty. Work by John Styles, Beverly Lemire and Alison Toplis has been pivotal in showing how, despite much desperation, the variety, quality and availability of ordinary and poor people's clothing increased from the eighteenth century. Even when people had little recourse to acquire clothing, people could attain decent attire through employers or charities (involuntary consumption) or make themselves appear fashionable inexpensively by adding a few buttons or ribbons.⁷ Letters written by paupers seeking relief reveal how applicants felt about and used their apparel to negotiate welfare during the old and new poor laws. Many would highlight how they were almost naked 'for want of clothes' or how they were unable to go into service without 'respectable' attire to force officials into action.⁸ Vivienne Richmond, a contributor to this collection, has explored the centrality of clothing to the experience of poverty during the nineteenth century. In doing so, Richmond demonstrates how studying objects provides valuable insights into a section of society that we still have much to learn about.⁹ Work into the twentieth century has continued this trend, such as Cheryl Roberts's study on how young working-class women in the 1930s navigated fashion through second-hand clothing markets to the arrival of clothing catalogues and consumer credit.¹⁰

The material lives of the poor emerge among the evidence of their encounters with institutions. Several writers – some of whom feature in this collection – have researched the material realities of life in workhouses, especially during the old poor law (1601–1834). Alannah Tomkins, for instance, studied food and material surroundings in urban workhouses to argue that such institutions were 'not decisively comfortable', but nor were they 'the repositories of squalor and neglect depicted by the most pessimistic contemporaries'.¹¹ Research underway at Gressenhall workhouse in Norfolk is analysing some 1,000 objects found onsite buried underground to determine how material life changed across distinct periods of welfare during *c.* 1777–1948.¹² The poor were also resident in other institutions. Jane Hamlett has used material culture to access the experience of living in the institution, including those spaces occupied by the poor, such as common lodging houses and public asylums.¹³ In such asylums, which bourgeoned during the nineteenth century, material surroundings were closely monitored and controlled for safety purposes. Yet, they were also designed to create the comfortable and cheerful atmosphere of the middle-class home, for it was believed that this particular type of domesticity and domestic routine would aid their treatment. As such, patients, as documented by Cara Dobbing, formed bonds with physical objects, both large and small, and in some cases, found a sense of home among these material goods.¹⁴ Much of the literature on almshouses has focused on the architecture of the buildings. However, recent studies have revealed that although conditions could vary considerably between one building and another, there could be many material advantages to having an almshouse place, such as greater access to food, fuel and furniture.¹⁵

The work noted above represents only a few examples of how material culture has started to enter into studies of the poor. Though relatively few in number, this research

Objects of Poverty

is beginning to reveal new findings and ways of understanding the lives of those living in poverty. For example, by looking at clothing, we can now grasp the identities, feelings and priorities of the poor, as well as how others viewed and judged them. Research on the material surroundings of workhouses reveals how, despite the best intentions of legislators to make such buildings basic and unappealing, poor residents could be creative and exercise their agency to make the best of their living situations. Our book adds to this literature and represents a significant milestone in the material culture of poverty in Britain.

Defining poverty

So, what is poverty? Who were the poor? In its simplest terms, the poor in this collection are defined as people who lacked resources such as, most obviously, money, as well as basics including food and fuel and a bed to sleep in, clothes to dress their families or a roof over their heads. The poor encompassed nearly everybody's ancestors in some shape or form. As Patrick Joyce argues, we are all 'ultimately the children of peasants'; it has only been since the end of the Second World War when peasants have gone from being the majority to the minority of the population.[16]

Historically, then, the poor were a colossal group, but this does not mean they were a homogenous mass who were all alike. To truly understand poverty beyond simple terms, we must see poverty in broader and less static terms. As one of the co-editors and contributors Harley has argued previously, the poor were 'a large, complicated and constantly changing section of the population'.[17] They were a group with many subsections – almost in hierarchical form – in which people could be placed in different segments as health, work, age, family circumstances and a host of other factors changed in or out of their favour. At the very bottom of this scale, there are those who lived in abject poverty who might be homeless and lacking any means to acquire the basic necessities of life, especially food and shelter. They relied on begging, welfare or charity for their very existence. Sitting above the line of abject poverty were those who could barely afford shelter and food, surviving through low, often irregular, earnings alongside economy of makeshifts, such as pawning and selling what material possessions they had to make ends meet. At the top of this scale, you have those who survived on relatively low but regular earnings that just covered the basic necessities of life. Some of these people might have even had access to land or a back garden for growing vegetables and rearing animals for subsistence.[18]

To complicate things, people did not neatly and statically sit within one of these clusters. Everybody's circumstances were unique, and there was considerable overlap between the groups, with people moving between these different sections throughout their lives. This move might be a positive change resulting from hard work, a serendipitous inheritance, marrying well, meeting a generous employer or simple good luck. But it might also be negative, with poverty spiralling out of control from an act of God, a creditor calling in a debt, being sacked, a medical emergency or a landlord putting up the rent. People might be poor from the simple process of growing up and getting old.[19] As Seebohm Rowntree argued in 1901, people often went through desperate times at different points of their lives according to the 'life-cycle of poverty'. This model, though perhaps a little too neat and crude,[20] illustrates how people might be more impoverished during particular periods, such as when they were young and their parents struggled to support the children or when their earnings dropped in old age.[21] The birth of the welfare state after the Second World War has undoubtedly provided people with more of a safety net. However, it still remains true to this very day that, throughout the UK, many children grow up in poverty and numerous pensioners face the choice between heating and eating during the winter.[22]

With this broad definition of poverty, our book encompasses a wide range of 'poor' people, including vagrants, the institutionalised, people in receipt of charity and welfare, and manual workers such as agricultural labourers and industrial employees, as well as the disabled and women who for swathes of history were much disadvantaged. We encounter the experiences (and even voices) of not only the perpetually poor but also those who fell briefly or suddenly into poverty or, at the very least, had it lurking around the corner. We do not see the poor as one collective mass of bodies but as separate individuals making their way through life.

Defining material culture

Since the 1970s, scholars from a range of fields have turned to studying objects, from which there now exists much theorisation and numerous definitions of 'material culture'.[23] In setting out this book to be as accessible as possible, we use a simple definition of material culture that is broad and inclusive of various methodologies. Simply put, material culture is taken here to mean the study of people and their connections to objects, and not just those they possessed but those they handled, used, borrowed, stole or made, as well as their thoughts and emotional and sensory connections with the objects. This list is far from exhaustive and nor should it ever be: researchers are continually coming up with new questions and ways of studying people and objects. But in essence, if the research involves people and their interactions with objects in some form, it is considered as material culture.

The contributors to this volume use objects that survive today, ranging from dolls to whistles to textile samples, and also the objects recorded in visual and written sources. Paintings, photographs and sketches – and the items depicted therein – as well as the items noted in first-hand sources such as autobiographies and letters, and objects recorded in the words of people on the peripheries of poverty, including journalists, social commentators and governmental actors, are all utilised in this collection. Of course, this is partly due to necessity as the number of surviving objects is much smaller than the items of the middle and upper classes, but more so than this, driven by our inclusive definition of material culture, we want poverty and objects to be studied much more closely and doing this requires a broad range of sources. By taking this approach

Objects of Poverty

and focusing on the poor, the ephemeral and makeshift is much more central here than we would usually see in museum exhibits and other material culture books. Likewise, our book moves away from more showy and ostentatious items in other ways by considering 'living' (or once living) objects that were central in the experience of poverty, from the food on their plates to the canine companions by their sides.

Each chapter deals with a partial, opaque and, quite often, enigmatic picture pieced together through the available evidence. Like with any method of historical study, researching the poor's material culture requires a certain level of speculation and conjecture, especially when it comes to studying those who left few accounts themselves. Nonetheless, the benefits far outweigh the disadvantages. Objects were used by the poor in similar ways to wealthier people, who have been studied much more extensively. Yet they also served different and sometimes unique functions to indigent populations. To the poor, objects could be a means through which they might be deemed destitute enough to receive charitable assistance or be sources of ridicule from those who thought they knew better. Objects gave people options, helping them to alleviate suffering and were often their most important form of recourse as they fell deeper into poverty. They, ultimately, helped people to have – or feel like they had – some agency and choice. Moreover, the study of objects is not always a story of possession when it comes to the poor. Often it was one of encounters as both persons and objects came and went through their lives, for objects were not just owned and used by the poorer population, they were created, borrowed, exchanged, repurposed and pawned. This book, then, is the story of the many roles that objects had in the poor's lives.

Scope and structure

The objects of poverty examined in this collection span an almost 300-year period of British history and, in doing so, covers three distinct periods in the history of poverty: the old poor law (1601–1834), the new poor law (1834–1948) and the rise of social insurance and welfare in the twentieth century. The old poor law of 1601, though varying regionally and locally in its administration, was relatively flexible and could be a benevolent form of relief, offering people pensions and cash payments, as well as medical support and clothing to meet individual needs. However, in the late eighteenth century, as the population increased and the strain on the ratepayer's purse was more acutely felt, resentment towards the poor burgeoned. What followed was the passing of the new poor law in 1834, designed to deter, if not punish, people from seeking relief through the increased use of workhouse. The dawn of the twentieth century brought about a change in perceptions towards the poor and in their treatment by authorities. There were a range of reforms under the 1900s Liberal government to reduce the number of those living in poverty, providing a safety net through old-age pensions, national insurance and free school meals. In 1945, Labour won a landslide election to bring about the 'birth' of the welfare state. The landscape of Britain changed within a few short years as reformers sought to eradicate want, disease, ignorance, squalor and idleness through the founding of the National Health Service, the introduction of family allowances and many other new provisions. Several chapters in this collection engage with how the state, but also how charitable organisations which grew from the nineteenth century, viewed and treated those living in poverty at these various junctures.

The various spaces inhabited by the poor, including homes, institutions and public spaces such as streets and cemeteries, are covered in this collection. Not only does the research explore the London poor, but many of the contributors venture beyond the boundaries of England's metropolises as far as Dublin prior to the founding of the Irish Free State. The chapters do not just include cities and towns, for even by 1851, only 54 per cent of the population lived in urban locales,[24] and, as is well acknowledged, poverty could be prevalent among rural populations, especially during times of agricultural depression. This collection highlights the regional, even local, variations in the experience of poverty and the objects they encountered. Types of food and fuel, for instance, varied regionally, and although workhouses were widespread, encounters with them differed between populaces. Similarly, the options people had available to alleviate their problems, such as philanthropic societies, varied widely. In cities, for example, people did not need to go far for some of their material needs, such as a warm drink or a night's bed in one of several shelters provided by Salvation Army or other religious institutions.

This edited collection is divided into eight parts. The first part – Objects of Sustenance – examines perishable objects consumed by the poor. Bread was central to labouring diets in every part of the country. As Carl Griffin's chapter argues, the humble loaf was 'the matter that mattered most'. It was central to people's survival, but it also became the object that defined the experience and culture of being poor, a marker of dignity and even something worth protesting and fighting over. Peter Collinge's chapter on pauper provisions under the old poor law explores the extent to which imported global goods such as tea, rice, spices and tobacco found their way into workhouse supply chains and the mouths of the poor. What Collinge reveals is that, despite contemporary complaints about the extravagance and wastefulness of the parish authorities, workhouse inmates seldom encountered global goods except where imported goods were cheaper than their domestic counterparts. The final chapter in this section takes us onto the streets of Georgian London and to the material culture of hot beverages. Freya Purcell moves away from the well-trodden topics of tea and coffee to bring to our attention saloop (a creamy beverage typically made from orchid roots) and the eighteenth-century saloop stall. There, the labouring poor would gather for a moment's rest and a warm, comforting beverage.

The second part, Objects of Home, furthers our understanding of the domestic lives of the poor and how society sought to tackle problems associated with poverty. Vicky Holmes examines the duality of the egg box as an object of poverty. Large, wooden and rectangular, these boxes were transformed from commercial objects to makeshift beds, providing many of the poorest in London a semblance of structure and home. However, having been seen as a symbol of poverty throughout much of the Victorian period, this simple box came to be viewed as a poverty solution. Jonathan Reinarz and

Objects of Poverty

Shane Ewen's chapter explores an object largely absent from the homes of the poor but strongly associated with the ills of poverty for over a century: the fireguard. Reinarz and Ewen document how burns-related injuries and deaths were frequently attributed to the absence of fireguards and a shift in responsibility regarding accident prevention from parents to manufacturers and councils. Coal, once a symbol of national prosperity, became – as Michael Lambert discusses – increasingly associated with poverty in post-war Britain. Contemporaries wrote about the 'coal in the bath': the belief that if you gave the unwashed masses decent housing, they would use the bath to store coal. Exploring this image, Lambert demonstrates how such a prejudice underpinned restrictions and rations of the material benefits of the welfare state.

Crafted and makeshift objects are the focus of Part III. Taking to the seas, Maya Wassell Smith's chapter explores the centrality of craftwork among British sailors during the nineteenth century, how it shaped their identity and how, when they returned to land facing homelessness on a meagre pension, their crafting skills obtained in service provided them with a source of income. Emily Cockayne's chapter takes us among the hubbub of the poor. The whistle, seen as an object of authority used to control the poor in various settings, is revealed by Cockayne to demonstrate the frugality and ingenuity of the poor through their recycling of buttons into whistles. Finally, Emily Cuming's chapter explores how examining crafted objects – even those of the most rudimentary form – opens a window into understanding poverty. In this case, dolls cobbled together from old shoes and even potatoes reveal the resourcefulness of those living in poverty and how play and imagination can prevail even in the direst of circumstances.

Following Cuming's chapter on dolls, Part IV explores childhood through objects of play and education. Ken Sneath surveys the range of toys poor children encountered across two centuries, revealing a thriving market, including shop-bought tin penny toys, marbles and simple wooden trains. Yet his findings highlight that play among the poor did not necessarily require manufactured toys or any expenditure. With space in the home hard to come by, children would spill out onto the streets where all that was needed was a stick, chalk or a few stones for play. The other two chapters in this section examine the childhood experiences of poverty through educational objects, namely needlework sample books. Having located in the archives a rare example of a mid- to late-nineteenth-century needlework sample book from a female orphan house, Eliza McKee unravels the experience of the female orphans through the sewing specimens and miniature clothing they produced during their stay. As well as uncovering the needlework and dressmaking skills of the orphans, their gendered education and the intention behind their training, McKee causes us to reflect on the emotive nature of such samples. Vivienne Richmond's chapter then moves on to disentangle a needlework sample book – a button and buttonhole, hand-stitched onto a piece of calico and labelled 1896 – produced by a Victorian elementary schoolgirl that found its way into the bargain bin of an antique store. Rescued by an eagle-eyed student, Richmond traces the idealised goals of school leaders with the actual classroom experience of poor schoolgirls, shedding light on the politics of class and gender and the juxtaposition between ancient craft skills and new industrial technologies.

Adding to the growing literature on pets and other animals, Part V, Living Objects, considers the roles of animals in the lives of the poor. Dogs were 'functional' objects in the eighteenth and nineteenth centuries in the sense that they fulfilled a wide range of purposes such as hunting, controlling vermin and even entertainment in dog fights. However, as Joseph Harley's chapter argues, dogs were also objects of affection by at least the late eighteenth century. In many cases, they were the poor man's best friend. Moving into the twentieth century, Lesley Hoskins and Rebecca Preston's chapter exposes through the humble hen and chicken coop the tensions between the 'slum' poor and the authorities who rehoused them in municipal cottage estates. The chicken coop had long been associated with the poverty of the slums, so to prevent this taint from carrying into their new homes, local authorities sought to regulate poultry-keeping. However, Hoskins and Preston's findings demonstrate that former slum residents were not so willing to give up a way of life that was so closely tied to their class identity.

Monetary Objects, Part VI of the book, considers the currencies of poverty from the eighteenth century to the Edwardian era. The first two chapters consider two alternative currencies that were used by the poor: pawning and tokens. As is well understood, pawning was a vital way in which people made ends meet for much of the period covered by this book. Samantha Williams's chapter expands our understanding of this practice by revealing how the clothing provided for the poor through welfare was pawned in times of hardship. Surprisingly, rather than the officials being irate by this practice and refusing to help the pauper further, parishes appear to have been more pragmatic, choosing instead to redeem the pawned goods, effectively meaning that the pauper was granted relief twice. Flore Janssen discusses the Salvation Army's own internal economy in the form of metal tokens. While acknowledging the absence of sources documenting the experiences of those paid in tokens, Janssen demonstrates how these tokens represent dependence on charity but also a route out of poverty. Despite extensive studies on working-class economies, the role of the purse has remained obscure. This risks, as argued by Julie-Marie Strange, perpetuating middle-class Victorian moralists' ideals regarding the poor and their lack of money. Opening the purse, Strange brings a new understanding of the everyday experiences of money among the poor and how purses can be linked to ideas of respectability, independence and character, as well as anxiety, stigmatisation and dependency.

Part VII takes us behind the doors of the institution that epitomised poverty throughout much of the past three centuries: the workhouse. Beds have garnered much interest in recent years, including those slept upon by the poor. Adding to this lively discussion, Alannah Tomkins analyses the beds found in fifty-nine workhouses in England at the close of the eighteenth century. Tomkins argues that while the beds in the workhouse were similar to that which the pauper might experience in their own homes, the institutional bed lacked the security, privacy and autonomy that came with domestic slumber. Karen Thompson, Peter Jones and Steven King explore an embroidered sampler created by an inmate of Great Yarmouth workhouse and five roughly constructed 'balls' found at the Mitford and Launditch workhouse in Gressenhall, Norfolk. Through close analysis, Thompson, Jones and King explore the construction and potential use of these objects, shedding light on the material culture of the workhouse poor and proposing a future research agenda for similar 'poverty objects'. Megan Yates concludes the section by taking a fresh look at the Victorian vagrant through their personal possessions. Alongside the clothing that for the vagrant provided social capital, a means of rebellion and a physical marker of their destitution, Yates shows how tobacco pipes, knives and other small objects helped to form their identities as vagrants.

The final part of this book focuses on the objects of poverty encountered in times of injury and death. Before the introduction of National Insurance in 1911, the injured and sick had limited options but to turn to charity or the parish when their conditions forced them into the depths of poverty. In the case of Sergeant Thomas Jackson, the protagonist in Caroline Nielsen's chapter, the wooden 'peg leg' he received after losing his limb in action not only marked him out as a veteran but as a recipient of public charity for the rest of his life. However, in later life, Jackson's artificial leg also presented him with the means to alleviate his financial distress, as he sat to document his story that would come to be sold in his lifetime. In the following chapter, Steven King and Peter Jones investigate the everyday medical treatments of the dependent poor through two objects: a discarded bottle of tonic mixture and a truss used to improve the mobility of individuals suffering from a hernia. By examining these two relatively ordinary items, King and Jones uncover a side of medical care for the poor that was flexible, expansive and even customised to meet the individual needs of those who used the poor law. When those in poverty finally succumbed to injury or sickness, it meant, for many, a pauper funeral – a death that was marked in the ground or on the surface by no objects at all. However, as Rebecca Senior's chapter discusses, where families could spare small amounts, such a humiliation could be avoided by purchasing an inscription gravestone shared by multiple people. In understanding these 'final' objects, Senior reveals the agency exercised by the poor when it came to commemorating their loved ones.

Each chapter provides the reader with a detailed understanding of many of the essential objects of the poor in various spaces, places and periods. Taken together, these chapters allow us to track the lives and experiences of poverty, quite literally, from the cradle to the grave. The study of poverty through the lens of material culture provides a pivotal and necessary perspective into poverty. In examining the objects owned, utilised, repurposed or simply encountered by the poorest in society, we gain new insights into what mattered to people and the experience of impoverishment across three centuries of history. The history of poverty is not a story of material dearth but rather, as this book reveals, a tale marked by creativity, resourcefulness and resilience.

Notes

1   Sidney and Beatrice Webb, *English Poor Law Policy* (New York: Longmans, Green, 1910); Sidney and Beatrice Webb, *English Local Government from the Revolution to Municipal Corporations Act*, vol. 7: *English Poor Law History*, Parts I–III (London: Longmans, 1927–9); E. P. Thompson, *The Making of the English Working Class* (London: Penguin, [1963] 1991);

Peter Townsend, *Poverty in the United Kingdom: A Survey of Household Resources and Standards of Living* (Berkeley: University of California Press, 1979).

2   Peter King, 'Pauper Inventories and the Material Lives of the Poor in the Eighteenth and Early Nineteenth centuries', in Tim Hitchcock, Peter King and Pamela Sharpe (eds), *Chronicling Poverty: The Voices and Strategies of the English Poor, 1640–1840* (Basingstoke: Palgrave Macmillan, 1997), pp. 155–91; Craig Muldrew, *Food, Energy and the Creation of Industriousness: Work and Material Culture in Agrarian England, 1550–1780* (Cambridge: Cambridge University Press, 2011); Joseph Harley, *At Home with the Poor: Consumer Behaviour and Material Culture in England, c. 1650–1850* (Manchester: Manchester University Press, 2024).

3   Anna Davin, *Growing Up Poor: Home, School, and Street in London, 1870–1914* (London: Rivers Oram Press, 1996), pp. 45–61.

4   Such as the charities National Energy Action, Fuel Poverty Action, Trussell Trust, Feeding Britain and FoodCycle. Examples of media reports include 'Energy Bills: Half of UK Households Face Fuel Poverty, EDF Warns', *BBC News*, 23 August 2022. https://www.bbc.co.uk/news/business-62643934 (accessed 18 June 2024); Russell Hope, 'Fuel Poverty: More Than 465,000 UK Households Will Suffer This Winter, Research Suggests', *Sky News*, 22 January 2024. https://news.sky.com/story/fuel-poverty-more-than-465-000-uk-households-will-suffer-this-winter-research-suggests-13053804 (accessed 18 June 2024).

5   Avner Offer, 'Consumption and Affluence, *c.* 1870–2010', in Roderick Floud, Jane Humphries and Paul Johnson (eds), *The Cambridge Economic History of Modern Britain. Vol 2: 1870 to the Present*, 2nd edn (Cambridge: Cambridge University Press, 2014), p. 205.

6   Alastair Owens, Nigel Jeffries, Karen Wehner and Rupert Featherby, 'Fragments of the Modern City: Material Culture and the Rhythms of Everyday Life in Victorian London', *Journal of Victorian Culture*, 15:2 (2010): pp. 212–25. Other examples of archaeological remnants being used to study the poor's material culture include Alastair Owens and Nigel Jeffries, 'People and Things on the Move: Domestic Culture, Poverty and Mobility in Victorian London', *International Journal of Historical Archaeology*, 20:4 (2016): pp. 804–27; Katherine Fennelly, *An Archaeology of Lunacy: Managing Madness in Early Nineteenth-Century Asylums* (Manchester: Manchester University Press, 2019); Charlotte Newman and Katherine Fennelly, *Poverty Archaeology: Architecture, Material Culture and the Workhouse under the New Poor Law* (Oxford: Berghahn Books, 2023); Liz Jackson, 'St Pancras: Excavation Sheds New Light on Notorious Workhouse', *BBC News*, 15 November 2023. https://www.bbc.co.uk/news/uk-england-london-67425926 (accessed 25 June 2024).

7   Such as John Styles, *The Dress of the People: Everyday Fashion in Eighteenth-Century England* (New Haven: Yale University Press, 2007); Beverly Lemire, *Fashion's Favourite: The Cotton Trade and the Consumer in Britain, 1660–1800* (Oxford: Oxford University Press, 1991); Beverly Lemire, *Dress, Culture and Commerce: The English Clothing Trade before the Factory, 1660–1800* (Basingstoke: Palgrave Macmillan, 1997); Beverly Lemire, *The Business of Everyday Life: Gender, Practice and Social Politics in England, c. 1600–1900* (Manchester: Manchester University Press, 2005); Alison Toplis, *The Clothing Trade in Provincial England 1800–1850* (London: Routledge, 2011).

8   Such as Steven King, '"I Fear You Will Think Me Too Presumtuous in My Demands but Necessity Has No Law": Clothing in English Pauper Letters, 1800–1834', *International Review of Social History*, 54:2 (2009): pp. 207–36; Peter Jones, '"I cannot keep my place without Being Deascent": Pauper Letters, Parish Clothing and Pragmatism in the South of England, 1750–1830', *Rural History*, 20:1 (2009): pp. 31–49.

9   Vivienne Richmond, *Clothing the Poor in Nineteenth-Century England* (Cambridge: Cambridge University Press, 2013).

10 Cheryl Roberts, *Consuming Mass Fashion in 1930s England: Design, Manufacture and Retailing for Young Working-Class Women* (Cham, Switzerland: Palgrave Macmillan, 2022).
11 Alannah Tomkins, *The Experience of Urban Poverty, 1723-82: Parish, Charity and Credit* (Manchester: Manchester University Press, 2006), pp. 36-78. Also see Susannah R. Ottaway, *The Decline of Life: Old Age in Eighteenth-Century England* (Cambridge: Cambridge University Press, 2004), pp. 247-76; Joseph Harley, 'Material Lives of the Poor and Their Strategic Use of the Workhouse during the Final Decades of the English Old Poor Law', *Continuity and Change*, 30:1 (2015): pp. 71-103; Newman and Fennelly, *Poverty Archaeology*.
12 Grant no AH/Z000262/1, Arts and Humanities Research Council, 'Material Life in the Workhouse: Gressenhall Workhouse, Norfolk, 1777-1948', Collaborative Doctoral Training Grant. Grant holder Joseph Harley.
13 Jane Hamlett, *At Home in the Institution: Material Life in Asylums, Lodging Houses and Schools in Victorian and Edwardian England* (Basingstoke: Palgrave Macmillan, 2015).
14 Ibid., pp. 16-37; Cara Dobbing, 'Pauper Lunatics at Home in the Asylum, 1845-1906', in Joseph Harley, Vicky Holmes and Laika Nevalainen (eds), *The Working Class at Home, 1790-1940* (Cham, Switzerland: Palgrave Macmillan, 2022), pp. 193-211; Fennelly, *Archaeology of Lunacy*; Mary Guyatt, 'A Semblance of Home: Mental Asylum Interiors, 1880-1914', in Susie McKellar and Penny Sparke (eds), *Interior Design and Identity* (Manchester: Manchester University Press, 2004), pp. 48-71.
15 Alannah Tomkins, 'Retirement from the Noise and Hurry of the World? The Experience of Almshouse Life', in Joanne McEwan and Pamela Sharpe (eds), *Accommodating Poverty: The Housing and Living Arrangements of the English Poor, c. 1600-1850* (Basingstoke: Palgrave Macmillan, 2011), pp. 263-83; Angela Nicholls, *Almshouses in Early Modern England: Charitable Housing in the Mixed Economy of Welfare 1550-1725* (Woodbridge: Boydell Press, 2017), pp. 138-87; David Hussey and Margaret Ponsonby, *The Single Homemaker and Material Culture in the Long Eighteenth Century* (Abingdon: Ashgate, 2012), pp. 191-200.
16 Patrick Joyce, *Remembering Peasants: A Personal History of a Vanished World* (London: Allen Lane, 2024), p. xi.
17 Harley, *At Home with the Poor*, p. 4.
18 Joseph Harley, 'Consumption and Poverty in the Homes of the English Poor, c. 1670-1834', *Social History*, 43:1 (2018): esp. pp. 101-3.
19 Ibid., pp. 101-3; Harley, *At Home with the Poor*, pp. 55-83.
20 For example, Barry Reay, *Rural Englands: Labouring Lives in the Nineteenth Century* (Basingstoke: Palgrave Macmillan, 2004), pp. 81-2; Samantha Shave, 'The Dependent Poor? (Re)constructing the Lives of Individuals "On the Parish" in Rural Dorset, 1800-1832', *Rural History*, 20:1 (2009): pp. 67-97.
21 Seebohm B. Rowntree, *Poverty: A Study of Town Life*, 3rd edn (London: Macmillan, [1901] 1902).
22 See note 4.
23 This literature is summarised well and succinctly in Karen Harvey, 'Introduction: Historians, Material Culture and Materiality', in Karen Harvey (ed.), *History and Material Culture: A Student's Guide to Approaching Alternative Sources*, 2nd edn (London: Routledge, 2018), pp. 1-26.
24 Susie Steinbach, *Understanding the Victorians: Politics, Culture and Society in Nineteenth-Century Britain*, 3rd edn (London: Routledge, 2023), pp. 14-15.

Further reading

Gerritsen, Anne, and Giorgio Riello (eds). *Writing Material Culture History* (London: Bloomsbury, 2015).

Hannan, Leonie, and Sarah Longair. *History through Material Culture* (Manchester: Manchester University Press, 2017).

Harley, Joseph, Vicky Holmes and Laika Nevalainen (eds). *The Working Class at Home, 1790–1940* (Cham, Switzerland: Palgrave Macmillan, 2022).

Harley, Joseph. *At Home with the Poor: Consumer Behaviour and Material Culture in England, c. 1650–1850* (Manchester: Manchester University Press, 2024).

Harvey, Karen (ed.). *History and Material Culture: A Student's Guide to Approaching Alternative Sources,* 2nd edn (London: Routledge, 2018).

Hitchcock, Tim, Peter King and Pamela Sharpe (eds). *Chronicling Poverty: The Voices and Strategies of the English Poor, 1640–1840* (Basingstoke: Palgrave Macmillan, 1997).

McEwen, Joanne, and Pamela Sharpe (eds). *Accommodating Poverty: The Housing and Living Arrangements of the English Poor, c. 1600–1850* (Basingstoke: Palgrave Macmillan, 2011).

Styles, John. *The Dress of the People: Everyday Fashion in Eighteenth-Century England* (New Haven: Yale University Press, 2007).

PART I
OBJECTS OF SUSTENANCE

CHAPTER 1
BREAD: THE MATTER THAT MATTERED MOST
Carl Griffin

Introduction

Richard Richardson, who, as we stated in our last, was found dead on the downs, in the parish of Alceston [Alciston, Sussex], is supposed to have fallen a sacrifice to fatigue and want. He was in the habit of going every morning to the distance of four miles from home to work, at 12s. per week. On the fatal day he got up at his usual hours, and was about to start for his destination without taking any victuals with him – for all the food he possessed in the world consisted only of a three-penny loaf, and which he would fain have left for his family, as it was the only article of subsistence in the house, and he had no money or credit, and had been refused, as we understand, parochial support, when his wife, by repeated solicitations, induced him, though most reluctantly to accept the loaf, with which at length he departed. On his return, at night, it is supposed, he sunk exhausted, as he was found lifeless on the downs, with the loaf, almost untouched, in his bag, intending no doubt, to restore it to his half-starved wife and six children. The verdict returned was 'Died by the visitation of God.'[1]

Whatever the absolute truth of Richardson's death – the report suggesting a hint of dramatic license – his untimely demise at the age of 42 speaks to a series of profound truths about the parlous state of the poor in rural England in the early nineteenth century. Richardson and his family were born into a country no longer directly impacted upon by famine, but famine-like conditions still sporadically gripped the country – notably in 1740, 1766, 1795 and 1800–1 – while abject, grinding hunger and even starvation remained an occasional reality and an ever-present fear for Richardson and others like him.[2] His wages were pitiable and, as we will see, insufficient to meet even his family's barest subsistence. The Dorset labourer was worse off still, locked in a desperate spiral that would make their wages fall to a wretched national low of six shillings a day in the late 1820s and early 1830s.[3] As the long-standing wars against France ceased, both rural and industrial economies fell into a deep recession. Farmgate and commodity prices collapsed as demand fell – with there being no mobilised forces to equip and feed – and many international markets reopened, leading to greater competition. Moreover, the recently demobilised soldiers flooded the labour markets, the extra supply of labour acting to drive down wages. If food prices fell – at least before the Corn Laws were passed in March 1815[4] – then both the demand for labour and wages fell faster still. At the same time, the poor rate payers of rural parishes sought to try to reduce the costs of welfare payments (poor relief), while farmers' incomes were in fast retreat, at the very point when rural workers increasingly turned to poor relief to supplement inadequate wages or cover them and their families during periods of worklessness.[5] In this perfect storm, the contents of Richardson's bag – that three-penny loaf, probably weighing just over 1lb – assumed an extraordinarily deep political and cultural potency. In that moment of leaving the family home that fateful August morning, Richardson's life, and the future of his dependents, was dictated by that solitary loaf of bread – mixed, leavened and baked flour, yeast, salt and water probably purchased from a baker rather than baked at home, with home baking a practice supposedly in sharp decline in the south by 1800.[6]

Whatever the precise realities behind the report, the story vividly shows how bread was more than matter to the labouring poor – it was their future, their survival and their bodily dependence. But the perishable nature of bread means that its material archive relates not to loaves themselves but to the making and marketing of bread. Otherwise, beyond myriad weights, measures and ovens preserved and displayed in museums, the remnant mills dotted about the rural and urban landscape provide the most powerful reminder of how important the making and consumption of bread was in the age of the industrial revolution. Even representations of bread in the form of paintings of everyday life in the period are few. What follows, then, examines this central and complex place of bread in the lives of poor rural workers. The chapter starts by exploring bread, the household and everyday life, before going on to examine the culture of bread and bread cultures, and ends with a consideration of the centrality of bread to popular protests, to charity and to the poor laws, paying particular attention to so-called bread scales that tied poor relief to the price of bread.

Bread, the household and everyday life

In the early decades of the eighteenth century, there was a marked regional difference in the dietary habits (and preferences) of bread consumption, with 'pure' white wheaten – finely sifted and free from bran – bread favoured in the south. In the north, coarser brown breads and mixed breads – often including rye and barley – dominated bread consumption. By the middle of the eighteenth century, as Adrian Randall has noted, a slight but continuing shift in consumption patterns was occurring, with absolute preferences for fine white bread now also true of many labouring and industrial families in the midlands and even parts of the north.[7] By the 1790s, as a respondent to the *Annals of Agriculture* related of Lincolnshire working families, 'People like to eat wheaten bread of the finest sort; though a great many, of all descriptions, use rye and barley bread'.[8]

Richardson's loaf would have likely been of this increasingly desired white 'finest sort', but it is important, though, not to underestimate regional differences. In the north and, to a lesser extent, the midlands, labouring and industrial families benefitted from a richer, more varied diet of pottages and soups – these often including the cheapest cuts of meat, or bacon, if the household could afford it – porridges and puddings, peas and potatoes, as well as various mixed breads.[9] To the southern labourer, large parts of the standard mixed northern diet were considered to be an affront to their dignity: potatoes being seen as food for pigs, a sign of the final desperation, a famine food. Brown and mixed breads were thought by southern workers to be 'purgative and relaxing', an affront to their *right* to purchase white wheaten bread, the consumption of the finest bread not just habitual and a matter of flavour but linked to labouring dignity and self-respect.[10]

During the food crises of the 1790s and early 1800s, attempts to get workers in the rural south to deviate from white bread met with either refusal or open protest. For example, in November 1795, labourers at Monkton in the Isle of Thanet (Kent) went on strike as a consequence of a proposal made by the parish poor law officers to mix one-third barley meal in their bread, reducing its primacy as white bread. They demanded flour be sold at a shilling a gallon, beans for their hogs at three shillings a bushel, and that their wages be increased from 1s 6d to 2s a day.[11] When the Making of Bread Act came into force on 24 March 1801 – stipulating that millers could only make wholemeal flour in response to a poor wheat harvest – it soon became known as the Brown Bread Act. Tellingly, in radical and satirical circles this popularly loathed Act gained the telling epithet of the Poison Act.[12] Radicals even mocked King George III as 'Brown George'. Protests in the south and east were no less blunt, being particularly intense in Surrey and Sussex.[13] Millers (and the cloths they used to 'dress' wholemeal flour) were particular targets. For instance, at St Leonard's Forest (Sussex) a group of women cut to pieces the cloth a miller was using to dress the hated brown flour and threatened to return and destroy the rest of his if necessary.[14] Complaints to magistrates figured on the taste of the brown bread, one Surrey magistrate concurring that it was 'disagreeable', and as being 'utterly incompetent to support them under their daily labour, & as productive of bowelly complaints to them and to their children in particular'.[15]

Alimentary complaints ultimately were a function of the absolute reliance of the labourers of the south and east on, as Sir Frederick Eden – in his survey of the 'state of poor' in the early 1790s – commented, an 'unvarying meal of dry bread and cheese from week's end to week's end'.[16] Even cheese might give way in the most parlous states of times to a diet exclusively based on bread (and beer). According to David Davies's study of the condition of the Berkshire labourer in the late 1780s and early 1790s, during non-crisis years 59 per cent of the average household expenditure (excluding rent) was spent on the necessities to make bread.[17] For those unable to find (or afford) the fuel to bake their own bread, or without access to communal ovens, the proportion spent on bakers' bread would be higher still. Thus, outside of the harvest (when wages were higher) and allowing a typical two shillings a week for rent, of the remaining 48d from Richardson's weekly wages, if Davies's calculations were accurate, some 28d would have been spent on bread. But a three-penny loaf – that in Richardson's bag on that fateful day – would only sustain a working adult for a day. For the typical six-day working week, Richardson would need to spend 15d on himself alone, thus 28d might be enough to keep him and wife in bread for the week but would be totally inadequate to feed his growing family,[18] let alone pay for additional expenditure such as clothes and shoes. His case was typical. Without additional means of support – whether from wages from other members of the household, charity, poor relief or crime – many labouring households in the final decades of the eighteenth and early decades of the nineteenth centuries could not even afford sufficient daily bread to stay alive.

Whatever the actual proportions, there was, as Eden noted, a 'remarkable difference' between the percentage of income spent on all foods between the southern and northern labourer. Given that northern workers spent far less of their income on food and had a more diverse diet than their southern brethren – this, as noted above, a result of customs and habits as much of what cereals, pulses and legumes were grown nearby – it figures that the proportion of income spent on bread by the northern labourer was rather lower than that spent by Richardson and his southern kin.[19] Further, those living in rural areas of relative 'isolation', as Peter Greaves has put it, and supported by a 'peasant-style culture' – the northern and upland areas – had access to a broader range of cheap foodstuffs and thereby had a more nutritious diet and lower mortality rates.[20] Whatever the regional differences, bread was the staple food of the English labourer and would remain so well into the twentieth century.

Bread cultures/cultures of bread

Bread was not just the matter of life but it also gave meaning to life. Indeed, many aspects of European culture are threaded through with references to bread. Linguistically, the record of what we might usefully call not just the culture of bread but a culture based on bread is extraordinarily rich. 'Breadwinner' – a term originally relating to the means of earning a living, before also assuming the current understanding of a person whose earnings support the household – dates back to the early seventeenth century. By the late eighteenth century, the term 'bread and butter' had been coined to refer to matters of an everyday nature, bread again providing a ready metaphor for the most basic stuff of life.[21] Poor workers' religious and imaginative lives were threaded through with bready symbolism and allegory. Taking communion in the Protestant faith – as Richardson would have done – rested on the belief that the sacramental bread was invested with Christ's sacrifice. Every Sunday Richardson, and much of his rural community rich and poor alike, would also have recited the words 'Give us this day our daily bread' from the Lord's Prayer. This collision of spiritual and material needs being a reminder that if the Christian faith was rooted in the principle that 'man cannot live by bread alone', bread ultimately provided the material grounding for faith. If the word love figured 280 times in the King James Bible, bread featured 330 times. Yet ultimately, to draw on Piero Camporesi's study of food cultures in early modern Europe, bread rather than religion remained the opiate of the poor.[22]

Beyond religion, the culture of bread was underwritten by a complex web of laws and policy pronouncements that attempted to regulate the making and sale of bread (and flour). Such enactments were in part motivated by a paternalistic wish to protect the poor but also to prevent the poor from becoming, to draw on an Italian label for the culture of bread dependence, the rioting bread-crazy (*matta panes*). E. P. Thompson, in a hugely influential article, outlined a particular code of beliefs and reciprocal action around the retailing of foodstuffs, with a particular emphasis upon bread and flour, rooted in Tudor legislation designed to protect poor consumers. Magistrates had a duty to make sure that foodstuffs were being retailed fairly (using correct weights and measures; not having been adulterated; and not fouled or soured) and sold without market manipulation at a 'fair' rather than 'artificially' inflated price. Poor consumers were thus protected by their social 'betters' and were, as is always the case in paternalist systems, duly expected to keep to their side of the script by deferentially and courteously behaving and submissively keeping in their place. This, as Thompson labelled it, 'moral economy' was rooted in shared values, thus when one side of the triangulation – magistrates; farmers, dealers, millers, bakers and retailers; and poor consumers – failed to uphold the social compact, it collapsed, with food riots as a means of the poor attempting to enforce the fair marketing of bread (and other produce) in a collective, muscular way.[23] Or to put it another way, somebody like Richardson might expect that in return for his dutiful labouring and for good behaviour, his social betters might at least keep him and his family in bread.

Many of the policies to protect poor consumers – for example, the Tudor Books of Orders, issued in times of crisis, which outlined strict orders around getting food to market and ensuring it was marketed directly to consumers[24] – were first legislated for in the medieval or early modern periods. However, by 1700 much of this paternalist policy was under challenge by the increasing primacy of the market in political thought, something that filtered through into everyday marketing practice. The medieval Assize of Bread (and Ale) regulated the price and weight of bread in relation to the price of wheat. Varying and set locally,[25] the Assize fell into disuse in most locales during the latter decades of the eighteenth century – although it continued to be set in London – only to be attempted to be revived during food crises. Likewise, by the eighteenth century, earlier laws against the market manipulations of forestalling (the selling of foodstuffs before they had got to market or before the market had opened), regrating (buying and selling on in the same or nearby market) and engrossing (buying up and hoarding large quantities of usually grain to force up prices) were increasingly flouted. The laws against forestalling and regrating were repealed in 1772, although this was subject to a later legal challenge during the subsistence crisis of 1800.[26] What unambiguously remained in place throughout the eighteenth and into the nineteenth centuries was a set of statute laws that strictly prohibited the adulteration of bread (and other foodstuffs) and selling short weights and measures, unscrupulous millers and bakers subject to bother stiff penalties and popular opprobrium.[27] Attempts to standardise measures – grain being sold not by weight but by measure – were also met by stiff popular opposition by poor consumers in the belief that 'their' customary measure was to be replaced by new, smaller measures.[28]

Charity, poor relief and protest

Given the susceptibility of grain prices (and thus the price of flour and bread too) to rapid inflation in consequence of poor harvests, or even the threat of a poor harvest, poor consumers were left in a perilous position. Given that bread was the staple of most labouring diets, consumption could only fall so low before starvation – as Richardson's tragic case so graphically shows – so all other things were sacrificed first. We know that for many of the poorest members of society their first port of call in difficult times was to the parish poor law authorities to request additional poor relief. 'Pauper letters', typically letters from those resident elsewhere to the parish responsible for their support requesting relief, often speak to this awful bread-bound predicament. As John Balls, then living in Maldon and writing to his home parish of St Botolph's in Colchester, pleaded in March 1828:

> I am very Sorry that I am under the Nessesity of Troubling you. but our Trade is so bad that We have little or Nothing to Do Since I was at Colchester. and we realy are in Great Distress and Cannot Get Work enough for Nessasary Food and Oblidge to go without Bread or any thing frequently by the Day tolgeter, we would not have troubled You but Hunger is so very Sharp.[29]

But not all calls for support, as had been the case for Richardson thirteen years earlier, resulted in poor relief being given.

Other routes to secure their daily bread might also be available. In such parlous times, Andrew Charlesworth and Adrian Randall have suggested that rural workers might be able to procure corn at below market rates from their employers, or could pilfer from their stores, and while both options are probably overplayed, rural residents undoubtedly had more options than their urban cousins.[30] One way in which the wretched dependence of urban workers was in part mitigated was through charity. For example, the raising of a charitable subscription to provide bread (or flour) to the poor at subsidised prices or instead offer soup, potatoes and rice was as much a feature of food crises as was the resort to riot.[31] Many more modest rural charities – often funded by individual bequests – provided their aid in the form of bread. These 'bread charities', often detailed on benefaction boards in parish churches, tied support to church attendance, the giving of the bread a highly public performance during church services, in deference to the cost of charitable bread.[32]

Perhaps the most notorious bread-bound policy innovation in the face of grinding need was the so-called Speenhamland scheme, otherwise known as bread scale. Although similar schemes had a slightly longer history, the meeting at Speenhamland, Berkshire, in May 1795 – in response to rapid and sustained increases in the price of corn (and hence bread) in early 1795 – popularised bread scales. The Speenhamland scheme regulated minimum household incomes according to the number (and age) of children and set against the price of bread in the locality: the variance between household wages and the set baseline income given in poor relief. Bread scales quickly became embedded in the welfare regimes of the cornland counties, although initial humane intentions were often being manipulated by farmers who cut wages in the knowledge that the broader community of ratepayers in the parish would be responsible for making up the difference. The link to the price of bread remained, but scales, especially after 1815, were in effect no longer about making bread affordable. Instead, the scales solidified a longer-term shift in making wages rather than the price of bread the key nexus of labouring conflict.[33] Whatever this shift, in many parishes, including in the southern and eastern cornlands, poor relief was given 'in kind' in the form of bread or tokens to be spent at a certain shop or bakers. And in those parishes which relieved some or all of their poor in a poorhouse or workhouse, bread often formed the major part of the calorific intake of the inmates: the grim routine of institutional life punctuated by bread for breakfast, lunch and dinner. When the new poor law of 1834 dictated that all who claimed poor relief were to be supported in large, multi-parish workhouses, this monotonous bready diet was critical to the deterrent aspect of the new law. In short, the diet of the workhouse was to be less full and wholesome than that of an 'independent' labourer.[34]

Charity and poor relief undoubtedly helped stave off absolute destitution for many households, but neither solved the problem of market failures and the sense of injustice generated by market manipulation. The response for many during periods of food crises, often prompted by, if not exclusively caused by, harvest failures, was to engage in food rioting. Indeed, the major food crises of the period (as detailed above) were all met by waves of food rioting in market towns and major urban centres alike. Almost all food riots were a response to the authorities failing (or being unable) to prevent market manipulation or a failure to prevent grain and other foodstuffs from being exported out of the locality to meet demand elsewhere. Most crowd actions were either an attempt to get the magistrates to intervene or directly targeted the hoarders and exporters of grain, or greedy dealers, millers and bakers. The powerful political symbolism of the simple loaf was often mobilised in the riots to make a simple point: women and men parading with loaves of bread speared on the end of sticks. This was a common way of warning the authorities that direct action would be taken if they did not act, the impaled bread a graphic reminder of what was at stake. Likewise, blood-soaked loaves left about the city (as at Bristol in 1800) were a visceral threat that blood might be spilt if bread was not made affordable.[35] The emphasis was not then on 'cheap' bread – rare were the occasions when grain or bread was stolen – but on fairly priced food. When food rioters did take food, almost invariably, they 'paid' what price they thought it should be sold at.[36]

Conclusions

While food riots continued sporadically in some locales into the middle of the nineteenth century, the collective actions against the 'Brown Bread Act' and market town food riots in early 1801 were the last major wave of collective action over access to food. Wages rather than bread became the locus of popular protest. This is not to say that bread, and its cultural potency and powerful symbolism, no longer figured in the protests of the poor. Threatening letters sent to employers and poor law authorities often invoked the established discourse of the affordable loaf. Similarly, political reformers used the rhetoric of the 'big loaf' to advance their arguments to a broader plebeian constituency: one Luddite ballad represented the machine-breaking movement as 'hunting a loaf'. It is also telling that a series of rural protests in East Anglia in 1816 were marked by the refrain 'Bread or Blood'.[37] More telling still were the series of protests throughout towns and cities in 1815 against the introduction of the Corn Laws in which the language of the 'small loaf' was often invoked – sometimes in the form of small loaves being paraded – as the consequence of prices being kept artificially high by limiting imports. The same language, symbolism and rituals were also threaded through the protests and claims of the Anti-Corn Law League of the late 1830s and 1840s.[38] Even Chartism, that working-class social movement for parliamentary reform, was often perceived to be rooted in, if not reducible, to 'bread and butter' politics, a hope that an extension of the vote to working men would lift them from the threat of hunger.[39] For all the while the poor could afford little more than bread, the loaf remained the matter that mattered most, the object that defined the experience and culture of being poor.

Notes

1. *Hampshire Courier*, 28 August 1815.
2. On these dynamics, see Carl Griffin, *The Politics of Hunger: Protest, Poverty and Policy in England, c. 1750–c. 1840* (Manchester: Manchester University Press, 2020).
3. On the parlous state of the Dorset labourer, see Carl Griffin, 'The Culture of Combination: Solidarities and Collective Action Before Tolpuddle', *Historical Journal*, 58:2 (2015): p. 476.
4. The Corn Laws of 1815 were designed to protect the income of farmers (and landowners who could charge higher farm rents) by preventing the importation of all cereals below certain prices. This meant that prices for corn – and hence bread – were kept higher than they would be if cheaper imports were allowed. This was a disastrous and unpopular move for poor consumers and subject to considerable popular opposition. See: James Wordie, 'Perceptions and Reality: The Effects of the Corn Laws and Their Repeal in England, 1815–1906', in James Wordie (ed.), *Agriculture and Politics in England, 1815–1939* (Basingstoke: Palgrave, 2002), pp. 33–60.
5. On these dynamics, see Roger Wells, 'Social Protest, Class, Conflict and Consciousness, in the English Countryside 1700–1880', in Mick Reed and Roger Wells (eds), *Class, Conflict and Protest in the English Countryside, 1700–1880* (Stroud: Alan Sutton, 1990), pp. 121–214.
6. On the decline of 'cottage' baking, see William Cobbett, *Cottage Economy* (London: W. Clement, 1822), esp. part III. On contrary evidence, see Joseph Harley, 'Domestic Production and Consumption in English Pauper Households, 1670–1840', *Agricultural History Review*, 69:1 (2021): pp. 25–49.
7. Adrian Randall, *Riotous Assemblies: Popular Protest in Hanoverian England* (Oxford: Oxford University Press, 2006), p. 213.
8. *Annals of Agriculture*, XXIV, 1795, pp. 122, 127, 280.
9. Frederick Eden, *The State of the Poor: Or, a History of the Labouring Classes in England, from the Conquest to the Present Period*, vol. 1 (Cambridge: Cambridge University Press, [1797] 2011), pp. 496, 497–533.
10. Rebecca Earle, *Feeding the People: The Politics of the Potato* (Cambridge: Cambridge University Press, 2020), pp. 140–3; Eden, *State of the Poor*, vol. 1, p. 526; Roger Wells, *Wretched Faces: Famine in Wartime England, 1793–1801* (Stroud: Allan Sutton, 1988), pp. 219–29.
11. *Kentish Chronicle*, 1 December 1795.

12 The Making of Bread Act 1800, 41 Geo. III, c.16; E. P. Thompson, 'The Moral Economy of the English Crowd in the Eighteenth-Century', *Past and Present* 3 (1971): p. 82.
13 Wells, *Wretched Faces*, pp. 219–29.
14 *Sussex Weekly Advertiser*, 9 February 1801.
15 The National Archives, Home Office, 42/61, folios 118–120, Thomas Turton, Lingfield, to Home Secretary Duke of Portland, 7 February 1801.
16 Eden, *State of the Poor*, vol. 1, pp. 496, 497–533.
17 David Davies, *The Case of Labourers in Husbandry Stated and Considered* (London: C. G. & J. Robinson, 1795).
18 We know that Richardson fathered six children, although we cannot be sure how many children were dependent upon him at the time of his death.
19 Eden, *State of the Poor*, vol. 1, pp. 496–7.
20 Peter Greaves, 'Regional Differences in the Mid-Victorian Diet and Their Impact on Health', *Journal of the Royal Society of Medicine*, 9:3 (2018): pp. 1–6.
21 'Breadwinner', n. and 'bread and butter', adj. *Oxford English Dictionary Online*. March 2023. Oxford University Press. https://www.oed.com/view/Entry/22890?redirectedFrom=bread+and+butter (accessed 28 April 2023).
22 Piero Camporesi, *Bread of Dreams: Food and Fantasy in Early Modern Europe* (Chicago: University of Chicago Press, 1996); Paul Warde, *The Invention of Sustainability: Nature and Destiny, c. 1500–1870* (Cambridge: Cambridge University Press, 2018), pp. 17–18.
23 Thompson, 'Moral Economy'.
24 Paul Slack, 'Books of Orders: The Making of English Social Policy, 1577–1631', *Transactions of the Royal Historical Society*, 30 (1980): pp. 1–22.
25 James Davis, 'Baking for the Common Good: A Reassessment of the Assize of Bread in Medieval England', *Economic History Review*, 57:3 (2014); pp. 464–502.
26 On these laws and their history in the eighteenth and early nineteenth centuries, see Randall, *Riotous Assemblies*, pp. 69–121; and, Douglas Hay, 'The State and the Market in 1800: Lord Kenyon and Mr Waddington', *Past & Present*, 162 (1999): pp. 101–62.
27 John Burnett, 'The Baking Industry in the Nineteenth Century', *Business History*, 5:2 (1963): pp. 98–108.
28 Richard Sheldon, Adrian Randall, Andrew Charlesworth and David Walsh, 'Popular Protest and the Persistence of Customary Corn Measures', in Adrian Randall and Andrew Charlesworth (eds), *Markets, Market Culture and Popular Protest in 18th Century Britain and Ireland* (Liverpool: Liverpool University Press, 1996), pp. 25–45.
29 Thomas Sokoll (ed.), *Essex Pauper Letters, 1731–1837* (Oxford: Oxford University Press, 2006), p. 354.
30 Andrew Charlesworth and Adrian Randall, 'Morals, Markets and the English Crowd in 1766', *Past and Present*, 114 (1987): p. 202.
31 For the role of charity during the 1790s and 1800s crises, see Wells, *Wretched Faces*, pp. 288–314.
32 Steve Hindle, *On the Parish? The Micro-Politics of Poor Relief in Rural England c.1550–1750* (Oxford: Oxford University Press, 2004), esp. pp. 149–54.
33 Griffin, *The Politics of Hunger*, pp. 85–129.
34 On which see Samantha Shave, *Pauper Policies: Poor Law Practice in England, 1780–1850* (Manchester: Manchester University Press, 2017), esp. pp. 56–110; Griffin, *The Politics of Hunger*, pp. 130–76.
35 Steve Poole, 'Scarcity and the Civic Tradition: Market Management in Bristol, 1709–1815', in Randall and Charlesworth, *Markets, Market Culture and Popular Protest*, p. 107.

36 On these dynamics, see: Thompson, 'The Moral Economy'; Wells, *Wretched Faces*; John Bohstedt, *The Politics of Provisions: Food Riots, Moral Economy, and Market Transition in England, c. 1550–1850* (Farnham: Ashgate, 2010).
37 Derby Local Studies Library, box 15, 'Hunting a Loaf', Broadsheet Collection, cited in Kevin Binfield, *Writings of the Luddites* (Baltimore, MD: John Hopkins University Press, 2004), pp. 135–6; A. J. Peacock, *Bread or Blood: A Study of the Agrarian Riots in East Anglia: 1816* (London: Victor Gollancz 1965), pp. 77, 79.
38 Griffin, *The Politics of Hunger*, pp. 55–82; Masahiro Konishi, 'Free Trade without Words: Popular Public Rituals and Corn Law Repeal in the Early 1840s', *History*, 108 (2023): pp. 87–107.
39 For the best study of Chartist thought, see Malcolm Chase, *Chartism: A New History* (Manchester: Manchester University Press, 2013).

Further reading

Bohstedt, John. *The Politics of Provisions: Food Riots, Moral Economy, and Market Transition in England, c. 1550–1850* (Farnham: Ashgate, 2010).
Camporesi, Piero. *Bread of Dreams: Food and Fantasy in Early Modern Europe* (Chicago: University of Chicago Press, 1996).
Eden, Frederick. *The State of the Poor: Or, a History of the Labouring Classes in England, from the Conquest to the Present Period*, 3 vols. (Cambridge: Cambridge University Press, [1797] 2011).
Griffin, Carl. *The Politics of Hunger: Protest, Poverty and Policy in England, c. 1750–c. 1840* (Manchester: Manchester University Press, 2020).
Randall, Adrian. *Riotous Assemblies: Popular Protest in Hanoverian England* (Oxford: Oxford University Press, 2006).
Sheldon, Richard, Adrian Randall, Andrew Charlesworth and David Walsh. 'Popular Protest and the Persistence of Customary Corn Measures', in Adrian Randall and Andrew Charlesworth (eds), *Markets, Market Culture and Popular Protest in 18th Century Britain and Ireland* (Liverpool: Liverpool University Press, 1996), pp. 25–45.
Thompson, E. P. 'The Moral Economy of the English Crowd in the Eighteenth-Century'. *Past and Present*, 3 (1971): pp. 76–136.
Wells, Roger. *Wretched Faces: Famine in Wartime England, 1793–1801* (Stroud: Allan Sutton, 1988).

CHAPTER 2
GLOBAL GOODS TO PAUPER PROVISIONS UNDER THE OLD POOR LAW: EVIDENCE FROM OVERSEERS' VOUCHERS, 1765-1834

Peter Collinge[1]

Introduction

In October 1744, a workhouse accommodating fewer than five people opened in the rural parish of Greystoke, between Keswick and Penrith in the historic county of Cumberland in northwest England. The workhouse's monthly expenditure, as recorded in overseers' accounts, show the provision of a bland and monotonous diet. In the two years to September 1746, the accounts record 485 purchases, of which 310 (64 per cent) cover just five items: milk (n. 158), bread (n. 47), butter (n. 46), oatmeal (n. 31) and cheese (n. 28). Tobacco, purchased on sixty-seven occasions in half or one-ounce amounts, is the only imported product recorded, but this may have been destined for the workhouse master rather than the inmates.[2] Notwithstanding how those in receipt relief outside of the workhouse (outdoor relief) spent their money, on the evidence of the overseers' accounts, Greystoke's poor barely participated in the growing consumer market for global comestibles, what may be termed as ephemeral 'objects of poverty'. The picture does not change when looking at overseers' vouchers; the collective name given to the itemised bills and receipts drawn up between goods and service providers and those responsible for the administration of the poor laws at parish level.[3] On just one occasion does an imported foodstuff appear in these records, with surgeon Wilkin Irving prescribing oranges to a sick pauper.[4]

The evidence from Greystoke raises two questions regarding global goods and pauper provisions under the old poor law. First, for those in receipt of poor relief, particularly workhouse inmates, what comestibles from Britain's expanding empire and global markets were purchased on their behalf? Second, under what circumstances were such products consumed? To address these questions, this chapter explores the purchases of global groceries made by the overseers of the poor in Cumberland (now part of Cumbria) and Staffordshire in the Midlands between 1769 and 1834.

Objects of Poverty

Contexts and sources

The provision of imported consumables to those in receipt of poor relief was determined primarily at parish level by four, often overlapping, factors: price; perceived need, including illness, childbirth, infirmity and old age; occasions, including funerals and feasts; and work, such as spinning, picking oakum or gardening. What is evident is that rather than evidence of profligacy or emulation, as the eighteenth century turned into the nineteenth, the consumption of cheaper imports was an outward manifestation of increasing poverty among the poor and attempts by parish authorities to control spending and stretch their limited resources.[5] Indeed, as domestic cereal and grain prices rose in periods of poor harvests, notably in the 1790s, the essential staples of the diets of paupers and the labouring poor began to shift to include global commodities.[6] Across England, the social commentator Frederick Morton Eden reported that following price increases during the 1790s, the consumption of cereals, malt, bread and beer had given way to tea and spirits.[7]

Global products were, of course, not new to British diets in the eighteenth century. What was different, and part of the reason that imported goods filtered their way into the diets of the poor was the scale on which they became available. This was the consequence of the combined impact of improved production and preservation techniques and storage facilities, transport and distribution networks, and changing levels of credit and taxation.[8]

Research by historians, including Jon Stobart, Erika Rappaport and others, has explored the relationship between empire and the availability and distribution of global groceries.[9] Stobart found that by the 1770s, groceries accounted for over one-third of British imports; a decade earlier, tea, sugar and treacle were regarded as important components of labourers' diets.[10] As the availability increased, spices – once considered exotic luxuries for the wealthy – became 'mundane store cupboard staples' for the majority, while treacle became the 'favourite fare of the rural population'.[11] Yet, what was available outside the workhouse was not necessarily available within. Carole Shammas, Alannah Tomkins, and Jeremy Boulton and Romola Davenport have long been attuned to the fact that under the old poor law, monotonous institutional diets of ale, broths, bread, cereals, cheese, milk and meat, relieved occasionally by treats, is an over-simplification.[12] Tomkins, for instance, observes that in the mid-eighteenth century, standard workhouse fare at St Mary's workhouse in Shrewsbury and St Michael le Belfrey in York was supplemented by regular, rather than occasional, additions of treacle, sugar and tobacco.[13]

Establishing what workhouse inmates were provided with and when is clouded by absences and silences in source material. These include published menus, known as workhouse dietaries, and overseers' accounts of parish expenditure. Dietaries nominally specified what inmates were fed each week but are often brief and lacking in detail. The dietary for Lichfield St Mary, for example, lists a daily breakfast of milk pottage, while dinner alternated between meat and vegetables and broth and cold meat. Supper each day consisted of bread and cheese.[14] From dietaries alone it is impossible to determine whether what was listed was actually provided, nor whether diets were supplemented from other sources (including workhouse gardens as in the case of Lichfield), nor the quality or quantity of what was on offer. Except in instances like Greystoke, where the workhouse was very small, overseers' accounts tend to categorise and aggregate expenditure. Subheadings of 'groceries' could include grains, oils, alcoholic and non-alcoholic beverages, pickles and dairy products, and washing items like soap and ash balls, alongside imported goods.[15] To fill in some of these blanks, the chapter draws on overseers' vouchers from selected parishes in Staffordshire, including the market towns of Uttoxeter and Wednesbury, the village of Tettenhall and the cathedral city of Lichfield. The Cumberland sample includes the rural villages of Dalston and Skelton and the market town of Brampton.

The sample of 118 vouchers itemises 3,128 goods (Table 2.1). Of these, 1,594 were for consumables imported from Britain's empire and the wider global community. There are, however, some caveats. No parish has a complete run of vouchers for the timeframe covered. Lichfield St Mary's vouchers, for example, survive for the 1820s and 1830s only. Meanwhile, parishes in Cumberland often contracted out the management of their poor for several years at a time and vouchers do not exist during these periods. Some vouchers refer simply to 'goods supplied' rather than line-by-line itemisation. The sample does not include all the businesses that supplied comestibles in each parish. Nevertheless, the vouchers show the simultaneous purchase of a range of global products by individual parishes from multiple suppliers; sometimes in very small quantities or on just a single occasion.

Table 2.1 Overseers' Vouchers and Sample Parishes in Cumberland and Staffordshire, 1769–1836

	County	Date	No. of vouchers in sample	Total no. of items listed	No. of imported consumables listed	No. of workhouse inmates (1804)
Brampton	Cumb.	1818–20	5	453	246	28
Dalston	Cumb.	1834–8	3	330	75	1
Skelton	Cumb.	1784–9	7	69	24	0
Lichfield St Mary	Staffs.	1822–31	35	1,089	638	42
Tettenhall	Staffs.	1835–6	12	35	90	40
Uttoxeter	Staffs.	1769–1834	33	687	395	52
Wednesbury	Staffs.	1778–1804	23	423	125	40
Total			118	3,128	1,594	203

Objects of Poverty

Global goods

All seven parishes in the sample purchased tea and tobacco; six purchased sugar and treacle; and five, pepper. Four bought rice and three, coffee. Of the items bought less frequently, Lichfield and Uttoxeter purchased wine, citrus and dried fruits, brandy and ginger. Lichfield also bought port, rum and cardamom, while Uttoxeter purchased cloves, Jamaica pepper and nutmeg. In contrast, in Cumberland, other than pepper, none of the three parishes purchased imported spices.

The principal sources of these groceries show the extent of the global trade in the mid- to late-Georgian age. Until the 1840s when Indian teas became available, most tea came directly from China.[16] All the parishes listed black tea, probably bohea, the cheapest and poorest quality available, but Lichfield, Uttoxeter and Wednesbury also show evidence of green tea or mixed tea purchases.[17] Sugar and tobacco came from America and the West Indies and rice from America, notably Carolina. The best coffee came from Arabia and Turkey and increasingly from plantations in Southeast Asia and the West Indies. Pepper came from Asia, including Southwest India, and cloves and nutmeg from the spice islands of Maluku in Indonesia. Ceylon (now Sri Lanka) produced the finest quality cinnamon. Asia remained the main source for ginger and nutmeg, but supplies also came from Jamaica. Europe supplied wine, port and brandy, while those countries bordering the Mediterranean produced citrus and dried fruits. Oranges first arrived in Europe from China along Portuguese trading routes in the late fifteenth century.[18] Many of these goods came through the ports of London, Liverpool and Bristol, but molasses, rum and sugar from the West Indies and wines from the Iberian Peninsula also found their way into Britain through the port of Whitehaven in Cumberland. Few of these imports, however, were purchased by the county's workhouses in any significant quantities.

Price

Table 2.2 shows illustrative grocery prices in Cumberland and Staffordshire between 1782 and 1836.[19] Although broadly similar, they were subject to variation between parishes and fluctuated according to war, conditions at sea, harvest failures and changes in duty. Notably, tea made regular appearances in the vouchers only following the Commutation Act (1784), which reduced the tax on tea from 119 per cent to 12.5 per cent. Despite its appearance in six parishes, treacle – common to many workhouse diets – was only quantitatively significant to Wednesbury and Uttoxeter.[20]

Shammas notes that rice was used by institutions and labourers from the early eighteenth century because of its relative cheapness in comparison to cereals, a situation that only intensified as the century progressed.[21] Like so many other global consumables, however, the presence of rice in institutional diets is patchy. In the mid-eighteenth century, for example, rice was a recurrent component of the workhouse diet at St Michael le Belfrey in York, while at St Martin's in the Fields in London, rice comprised an insignificant aspect of inmates' diets for the majority of the century.[22]

Table 2.2 Prices of Groceries Supplied to Parishes in Cumberland and Staffordshire, 1782–1836

Product	Brampton 1818–20	Dalston 1834	Skelton 1786–88	Lichfield St Mary 1823–6	Tettenhall 1836	Uttoxeter 1827	Wednesbury 1782–91
Tea	2 oz 1s	—	2 oz 7d	2 oz	1s	½ lb 3s–3s 6d	½ lb 2–3s
Sugar	1 lb 10d	—	1 lb 6d	¼ lb 2d	—		1 lb 6–10d
Treacle	2 lbs 1s	1 lb 3d	1 lb 3d	6 lbs 2s 6d	—	36 lbs 12s	1 lb 4d
Rice	n/a	1 lb 4 d	—	1 lb 5d	—	1 lb 3d	3 lb 10½d
Tobacco	1 oz 4d	—	2 oz 3d	1 oz 3d	—	1 lb 4s	1 lb 2s–3s
Pepper	2 oz 6d	2 oz 4d	—	2 oz 6d	—	2 oz 4d	2 oz 4d
Ginger	—	—	—	2 oz 2d	—	2oz 3d	—
Brandy	—	—	—	pint 2s	—	—	—
Port	—	—	—	pint 3s	—	—	—

Rice first appears in the accounts of St Mary's workhouse in Lichfield in the 1730s, but even in the early nineteenth century, when the workhouse population was around forty, the amounts purchased were small compared to beef and oatmeal.[23] In the 1820s, eight out of nine Lichfield grocers supplying the parish itemised rice in their bills.[24] One such supplier was Elizabeth Dawes. In October 1823, when Dawes supplied 9 lbs of rice and 5 lbs of Carolina rice each at 5d per pound (a price consistent with other suppliers in the town), rice cost the same as 1 lb of beef.[25] With no price differential, beef purchases remained high and rice low. Between March and May 1824, for instance, Ann Hill, one of a number of Lichfield's butchers, supplied 214 lbs of beef to the workhouse.[26] Although its workhouse population was similar to Lichfield, a different situation emerged in Uttoxeter. Rice was supplied to the workhouse in 1769, but this did not feature consistently in overseers' vouchers until the nineteenth century. This followed changes in American production and processing techniques, notably the introduction of the steam-powered rice mill, which brought prices down.[27] Uttoxeter's rice came from several suppliers. In 1827, Michael Clewley delivered 140 lbs of rice at 3d per lb.[28] In August 1830, Ralph Bagshaw and Sons supplied 90 lbs of rice, and in January and October 1832 supplied 160 lb on each occasion.[29] Here, at least, it appears that orders for rice came at the expense of beef. In the year ending March 1822, the workhouse had purchased 8,770 lbs of beef.[30] In the eight months to March 1832, the amount purchased totalled a more modest 1,383½ lbs. Over the decade, beef prices remained relatively static at around 5d per pound, so the purchase of rice represented a cost-saving measure for the parish, rather than an indulgence.

Substantial amounts of sugar – used to flavour puddings and porridge-like dishes – reached workhouse inmates before tea. Usually, sugar was itemised simply as sugar. Lichfield's and Uttoxeter's vouchers, however, are occasionally more specific in listing loaf, lump, moist or raw sugar, without specifying the uses to which they were put. In 1769, Joseph Chell supplied 17 lbs of sugar at 5d per pound and 5 lbs at 6d to Uttoxeter.[31] The same year, Ralph Smith supplied 23 lbs of sugar at 5d per pound and 8 lbs at 6d per pound.[32] Other than price, there was nothing to determine the nature or quality of the sugar supplied. In both instances, however, the cheaper option was preferred.

Perceived need: Sickness, lying-in, infirmity and old age

The provision of imported consumables to the poorest in society fed into contemporary anxieties about extravagance and wastefulness under the old poor law. Critics, including Jonas Hanway in his 1756 publication *An Essay on Tea*, complained of the deleterious effects of tea on consumers, the nation and the pockets of the poor. Contemporary commentators, however, often failed to recognise that as the cost of wheat and barley rose and labouring families found it increasingly difficult to cook for themselves, drinking heavily sugared tea was symptomatic of impoverishment rather than evidence of profligate spending.³³ Partly to avoid such accusations, many parish authorities and workhouses, including Kendal workhouse in Westmorland (now in Cumbria), nominally restricted the consumption of tea and coffee to cases of medical need, illness or infirmity. Unless on medical or infirmity grounds, the consumption of distilled spirits in institutions, including workhouses, was expressly excluded by the Gin Act (1751). Such limitations, however, were irregularly enforced. Illness, childbirth, infirmity and old age were occasions when workhouse inmates often received additional attention in the form of extra food and drink allowances. The provisions, aimed at offering comfort and alleviating suffering, included tea and sugar, port, wine, brandy and citrus fruits, and the more common beer, ale and gin.

In the early eighteenth century, tea, coffee and tobacco were all enthusiastically promoted for their medical or health-giving properties. They were believed to eradicate or relieve scurvy, gout, rheumatism, fevers, toothache, indigestion, constipation, dropsy and nightmares. By mid-century such claims were on the wane.³⁴ There is no specific voucher that references tobacco being supplied in instances of illness, childbirth, infirmity or old age. In popular imagination, however, the medical benefits and comfort afforded by tea lasted well into the nineteenth century.

Determining precisely the use to which some items were put can be hazardous. Rice, cinnamon and sugar were used in puddings, but the same ingredients were also used to make rice water. Pepper was added to meats and soups, while dried fruits could be added to frumety (a wheat and milk porridge) and puddings. Sago, making a single appearance in the sample, could be added to gruel.³⁵ Vouchers and accounts, however, do occasionally itemise specific provisions for the sick and those lying-in separately to the same items listed for more general consumption. In 1769, Rebecca Basfort, an ill inmate of Uttoxeter workhouse, received wine, minced pie, biscuits, pikelets, apple pie and a pint of brandy.³⁶ Between April 1818 and September 1819, Brampton grocer Sarah Oliver itemised 2 oz of tea and 1 lb of sugar for the sick on five separate occasions. These are outnumbered, however, by the forty-five and fifty-five occasions when tea (in 2-oz to 4-oz amounts) and sugar (in ½ lb to 1¾ lbs amounts), respectively, were itemised in the same timeframe.³⁷ In Dalston, the overseers' accounts for 30 September 1821 record 'Tea Sugar Ale & bread for a woman lying in & Jonⁿ Clark poorly'.³⁸ A bill settled in 1828 by Lichfield's overseers, headed 'For the use of the sick poor', listed 1½ pints of rum, two pints of brandy and half a pint of gin.³⁹ Again, in Lichfield, between 1830 and 1832, biscuits, gin, brandy, wine, port, rum and oranges 'for the sick' were ordered on several occasions.⁴⁰ They also supplied brandy and port to named individuals identified as ill or sick, including widow Elizabeth Waltho, who received biscuits, two pints of gin, lemons and a pint of brandy.⁴¹ Waltho may also have been the same person for whom lemons were purchased over four consecutive weeks in October 1830. In Tettenhall, in the mid-1830s, the overseers provided tea and wine 'for the poor that are sick'.⁴² The overseers of Brampton purchased rum in 1817, as did the overseers of Papcastle (Cumberland) in 1822, while John Chatterton supplied Uttoxeter with oranges and lemons in 1833, but whether for the sick or not is unknown.⁴³

Objects of Poverty

Work, funerals, regular allowances and feasts

Aside from medical need, the occasions when imported goods were supplied to those in receipt of poor relief ranged from mundane and regular allowances to 'rewards' for work and 'treats' at funerals and feasts. Frederick Morton Eden noted that at Farnham workhouse (Surrey), the usual breakfast alternated between onion pottage, and bread and broth. Female inmates were also allowed bread if they were fortunate enough to have friends to provide tea and sugar for them, although Eden offers no explanation as to why this was the case, nor specifies whether this was an additional allowance.[44] In the 1790s, Wednesbury's overseers purchased tobacco or shag tobacco each month, usually in 1 lb amounts.[45] Lichfield and Uttoxeter also purchased tobacco across the year. The regularity of these purchases illustrates that, despite nominal restrictions – St Mary's workhouse, Carlisle, for instance, forbad inmates from smoking in bedrooms – smaller workhouses routinely issued tobacco and sometimes as a reward for work.[46]

Workhouses repeatedly attempted to establish work schemes, such as spinning, picking oakum or gardening.[47] Despite being promoted for their ability to reduce institutional costs, few made any substantial profit. Consequently, they have traditionally been regarded as failures. This was either the consequence of a lack of zeal or aptitude on the part of those tasked with their management or simply because the majority of inmates had neither the capacity nor skills to contribute. Tomkins, however, reminds us that the schemes had functions other than profit including to enable inmates to earn a meagre income or reward, to impose discipline on participants or to act as a deterrent to those seeking relief. They were also of significance to local businesses.[48] In the 1790s, Eden reported that in Halifax 'women are permitted to spin, in order to enable themselves to purchase tea'.[49] In this instance, the tea was probably purchased from the workhouse, but the supply would have come from a local grocer. In the 1804 parliamentary *Abstract of Returns*, Dalston, Skelton and Tettenhall declared no 'money earned by labour of the poor towards their maintenance' in their workhouses. In the 1830s, however, three men in Tettenhall received tobacco and beer in return for work in the workhouse garden.[50] The source of Uttoxeter's £43 14s 3½d and Wednesbury's £17 3s 6d income is unstated, but both had gardens, and by the mid-1820s, Uttoxeter also had a brickworks. Brampton's £3 17s 0d came from 'old women employed in spinning factory lint'. Fifteen years later, Sarah Oliver itemised tea and sugar for spinners and tailors, indicating both the longevity of the scheme and the nature of the rewards given.[51] Lichfield's income of £60 5s 11d came from the production of blankets, but the workhouse paid its washing women in ale or cash.[52] On this evidence, workhouse inmates accessed only a very limited range of global consumables in return for work-based activities.

Funerals were occasions when the parish poor were often given extra provisions, including bread, cheese and ale. The extent to which imported goods were consumed on such occasions, however, is obscured by vouchers that refer to funeral expenses with little or no further detail. In 1779, Brampton paid for 'sundry spirits got for Hugh Cummins funeral', but on other occasions itemised rum, ale and brandy for funerals, including those of James Stott and his child.[53] In the same location, tobacco was supplied for a funeral in 1786 and brandy and ale for the funerals of Jane Hoodless in 1792 and 'Wears Wife' the following year.[54] In Skelton, separate bills of expenses, itemising bread, cheese, butter, tea, sugar, cake spice and tobacco, were drawn up for the funerals of men, women and children. In 1788, the provisions for Jane Peacock's funeral included sugar, tobacco and tea.[55]

There are scant references to purchases relating specifically to feasts or celebrations. In 1831, ale was purchased in Lichfield for the coronation of William IV and for Christmas Day.[56] The use of some items can be inferred from purchase dates. In December 1826, Uttoxeter's overseers purchased 6 lbs each of currants and raisins, 12 lbs of sugar, and ¼ lb of clove pepper and the same again in December 1829.[57] The dates suggest that the goods were used for something akin to plum pudding or Twelfth Cakes, eaten at Epiphany. John Mollard's recipe for Twelfth Cakes in *The Art of Cookery* (1802), for example, included sugar, currants, cinnamon, cloves, mace, nutmeg and candied orange or lemon; his recipe for plum pudding included raisins, currants, almonds, candied orange and lemon, nutmeg, sugar and brandy. Such treats, however, were rare in all seven parishes.

Conclusion

Workhouse inmates had access to ephemeral 'objects of poverty' in the form of imported groceries, but it was a restricted range for the most part. This may seem surprising, particularly in the westcoast county of Cumberland with its ready access to ports, but can be accounted for by the county's widespread practice of contracting out poor relief (resulting in fewer vouchers) and a history of less generous provision under the old poor law. Global goods either augmented existing provision for the poor or were consumed under specific circumstances. Only where a price differential existed did the products of empire and global trade begin to supplant more traditional fare. On the evidence presented here, and contrary to oft-repeated claims by contemporaries, it would be inaccurate to conclude that by the mid-1830s such goods had percolated down to workhouse inmates on a generous or even consistent basis.

Notes

1 The initial research into overseers' vouchers was funded by AHRC Project Reference: AH/R003246/1: Small bills and petty finance: co-creating the history of the Old Poor Law. Lead Research Organisation: Keele University.
2 Cumbria Archive Centre, Carlisle (hereafter CACC) PR5/43, Greystoke Poor Account Book, 1740–1812.
3 CACC PR 5/53–54, Greystoke Overseers' Vouchers, 1763–1837; PR5/67A–M, Greystoke Overseers' Vouchers, 1774–1837.
4 CACC PR5/54/12, Wilkin Irving, 5 August 1828.
5 Lizzie Collingham, *The Hungry Empire: How Britain's Quest for Food Shaped the Modern World* (London: Bodley Head, 2017), p. 94.

6 Carole Shammas, 'The Eighteenth-Century English Diet and Economic Change', *Explorations in Economic History*, 21:3 (1984): p. 259.
7 Frederick Morton Eden, *The State of the Poor*, vol. 2 (London: J, Davis, 1797), p. 60 and vol. 3, pp. 729, 847.
8 Collingham, *Hungry Empire*, p. 118.
9 Jon Stobart, *Sugar and Spice: Grocers and Groceries in Provincial England 1650–1830* (Oxford: Oxford University Press, 2013); Collingham, *Hungry Empire*; Erika Rappaport, *A Thirst for Empire: How Tea Shaped the Modern World* (Princeton: Princeton University Press, 2017); Markman Ellis, Richard Coulton and Matthew Mauger, *Empire of Tea: The Asian Leaf That Conquered the World* (London: Reaktion, 2015); Troy Bickham, *Eating the Empire: Food and Society in Eighteenth-Century Britain* (London: Reacktion, 2020).
10 Stobart, *Sugar and Spice*, p. 48.
11 Collingham, *Hungry Empire*, pp. 76, 86.
12 Shammas, 'Eighteenth-Century English Diet'; Alannah Tomkins, *The Experience of Urban Poverty, 1723–82: Parish, Charity and Credit* (Manchester: Manchester University Press, 2006), pp. 61–5; Jeremy Boulton and Romola Davenport, 'Food, Drink and Diet in the Georgian Workhouse: St Martin-in-the-Fields, 1725–1830', 82nd Anglo-American Conference of Historians, Senate House, London (13 July 2013).
13 Tomkins, *Urban Poverty*, pp. 61–5.
14 Eden, *The State of the Poor*, vol. 3, p. 652.
15 Shammas, 'Eighteenth-Century English Diet', p. 265.
16 There was a thriving trade in smuggled tea until the passing of the Commutation Act in 1784.
17 For example, Staffordshire Record Office (hereafter SRO) D483/6/1/9/1/16/4, Samuel Addison, 27 May 1790; D3891/6/31/22, Lydia West, 1826; D3891/6/39/5/4, Lewis Hall, 1832. Uttoxeter purchased 'tea' on forty occasions, green tea on seven and mixed tea on four.
18 Alan Davidson, *The Oxford Companion to Food* (Oxford: Oxford University Press, 1999), p. 558.
19 Some items have no quantities, others have prices aggregated with other goods.
20 For example, SRO D4383/6/1/9/3/199, Saml. Addison, July 1793; D3891/6/31/14, H. West, 10 August 1827.
21 Shammas, 'Eighteenth-Century English Diet', p. 259.
22 Tomkins, *Urban Poverty*, pp. 61–5; Boulton and Davenport, 'Food, Drink and Diet', n.p.
23 SRO LD20/6/1, Lichfield St Mary, Overseers' Accounts, 6 December 1733.
24 For example, SRO LD20/6/6, no item nos., John Budd, 31 March 1825; Thomas Woodward, 6 October 1825.
25 SRO LD20/6/6, no item no., Elizabeth Dawes, 6 October 1823.
26 SRO LD20/6/6, no item nos., Ann Hill, 1 April and 29 June 1824.
27 Collingham, *Hungry Empire*, p. 109; SRO LD20/6/1, Lichfield St Mary, Overseers' Accounts, 6 December 1733; D3891/6/31/5, Ralph Smith, November 1769.
28 SRO D3891/6//31/7, Michael Clewley, 5 May 1827.
29 SRO D3891/6//35/2/11, Ralph Bagshaw and Sons, 26 August 1830; D3891/6/39/8/1, Ralph Bagshaw and Sons, 8 April 1832; D3891/6/39/6/12, Ralph Bagshaw and Sons, 30 November 1832.
30 SRO D3891/6/8, Uttoxeter Parish Bills Account Book, 1821–4.
31 SRO D3891/6/30/23/2, Jos Chell, 1 June 1769.
32 SRO D3891/6/31/5, Ralph Smith, November 1769.
33 Collingham, *Hungry Empire*, pp. 94–5.
34 Jessica Hanser, 'Teatime in the North Country: Consumption of Chinese Imports in North-East England', *Northern History*, 49:1 (2012): p. 71; Bickham, *Eating the Empire*, p. 30.
35 Peter Higginbotham, *The Workhouse Cookbook* (Stroud: History Press, 2008), pp. 20, 31, 89.

36 SRO D3891/6/30/21, Wm Prince to Abrm Booth for Workhouse, November 1769.
37 CACC PR60/21/13/5/124, Sarah Oliver, 8 January 1819. 1 lb of tea was sufficient to make approximately 200 cups: Hanser, 'Teatime in the North Country', p. 57.
38 CACC SPC 44/2/26, Dalston Overseers' Account Book, Ledger E, 1820–36.
39 SRO LD20/6/6/160b, Wm Wildey, 12 August 1828.
40 For example, SRO LD20/6/7/131, M. Slater, 2 October 1830; LD20/6/7/436, Sundrys for St Mary's workhouse, 1 January–25 March 1832; LD20/6/7/437, John Page, 25 March 1832; LD20/6/7/438, John Page, 25 January 1832.
41 SRO LD20/6/7/134, P. Burton, 4 January 1831; LD20/6/7/166, Thos Baker 29 September–31 December 1830; LD20/6/7/291, John Page, 5 October 1831; LD20/6/7/237, John Page, 17 July 1831.
42 SRO D571/A/PO/72/5j, Overseers' Vouchers, December 1835–January 1836.
43 CACC PR60/21/13/5/65, Thos Bell, 10 December 1817; SPC110/1/3/2/3/112, J. Richardson, 22 June 1822SRO, John Chatterton, 22 July 1833.
44 Eden, *State of the Poor*, vol. 3, p. 716.
45 For example, SRO D4383/6/1/9/3/221, Samuel Addison, 30 January 1799.
46 Eden, *State of the Poor*, vol. 2, p. 55; Tomkins, *Urban Poverty*, p. 64.
47 See, Peter Collinge, '"He shall have care of the garden, its cultivation and produce": Workhouse Gardens and Gardening, 1780–1835', *Journal for Eighteenth-Century Studies*, 44:1 (2021): pp. 21–39.
48 Alannah Tomkins, 'Bricks, Brickmaking and the Economies of the Old Poor Law: Staffordshire, 1750–1834', *Midland History*, 49:1 (2024): pp. 97, 99–100.
49 Eden, *State of the Poor*, vol. 3, p. 822.
50 SRO D571/A/PO/72/7e and D571/A/PO/72/7g, Tettenhall Overseer's Vouchers, 28 May and 25 June 1835.
51 CACC PR60/21/13/5/124, Sarah Oliver, 8 January 1819.
52 *VCH Staffordshire*, vol. 14, p. 89; SRO LD20/6/6/95, Jane Godwin, 29 March 1825; LD20/6/6/27, Chas Houldcroft, 18 June 1822.
53 CACC PR60/21/13/1/13/16 and PR60/21/13/1/12/31, Payments above the Weekly Allowance, 1779.
54 CACC PR60/21/13/1/12/31, Payments above the Weekly Allowance, May 1779; PR60/21/13/2/64, Thos Allen, 12 October 1786; PR60/21/13/3/26, Thos Bell, 7 October 1792–26 March 1793.
55 CACC PR10/V/13/14, Jane Peacock's funeral, 8 March 1788.
56 SRO LD20/6/7/291, John Page, 5 October 1831; LD20/6/7/350, John Page, 27 December [1831].
57 SRO D3891/6/31/22, Lydia West, 23 December 1826; D3891/6/34/10/12, Lewis Hall, 23 December 1829.

Further reading

Bickham, Troy. *Eating the Empire: Food and Society in Eighteenth-Century Britain* (London: Reacktion, 2020).
Collinge, Peter. '"He shall have care of the garden, its cultivation and produce": Workhouse Gardens and Gardening, 1780–1835'. *Journal for Eighteenth-Century Studies*, 44:1 (2021): pp. 21–39.
Collinge, Peter, and Louise Falcini. *Providing for the Poor: The Old Poor Law, 1750–1834* (London: Royal Historical Society/University of London Press, 2022).
Collingham, Lizzie. *The Hungry Empire: How Britain's Quest for Food Shaped the Modern World* (London: Bodley Head, 2017).

Ellis, Markman, Richard Coulton and Matthew Mauger. *Empire of Tea: The Asian Leaf That Conquered the World* (London: Reaktion, 2015).

Rappaport, Erika. *A Thirst for Empire: How Tea Shaped the Modern World* (Princeton: Princeton University Press, 2017).

Shammas, Carole. 'The Eighteenth-Century English Diet and Economic Change'. *Explorations in Economic History*, 21:3 (1984), pp. 254–69.

Stobart, Jon. *Sugar and Spice: Grocers and Groceries in Provincial England 1650–1830* (Oxford: Oxford University Press, 2013).

Tomkins, Alannah. *The Experience of Urban Poverty, 1723–82: Parish, Charity and Credit* (Manchester: Manchester University Press, 2006).

CHAPTER 3
'FULL OF SALOOP WITH FIRE UNDER IT':
TEAWARE, SALOOP STALLS AND WARMTH ON
THE STREETS OF GEORGIAN LONDON
Freya Purcell

Introduction

In 1792, the radical and author Thomas Spence made his way from Newcastle to London.[1] A former teacher and son of a net- and hardware-maker, Spence spent his life trying to spread his message of political and social reform.[2] Skilled at marketing, Spence used different techniques, including making promotional material such as political tokens to spread his message of the rights he believed labouring people were entitled to, such as universal suffrage (including for women), the abolishment of land ownership and the creation of a society where children would grow up free from poverty. In London, hundreds of miles from where he started, Spence used another tool to engage people with his ideas. Having piled his stall, nestled in an alley, with tracts and missives, Spence carried one other item to tempt people to linger and give him their attention: a piping hot drink called saloop.[3]

Much has been written by historians about the conversable worlds of tea and coffee. For example, Brian Cowan has argued that coffeehouses allowed for new spaces of discussion.[4] However, while the labouring sort did enjoy these spaces, they were dominated by the middling sort and the elite. So what fuelled the days and discussions of the labouring poor? Where did the labouring poor tend to go? This chapter explores another space they frequented and asks: What can we learn about the labouring poor's experience through examining the saloop stall?

But first, what was the drink at the centre of the stall, saloop? While tea, coffee and chocolate have all left their mark on British culture and on histories of drink, saloop is a less familiar substance to Western audiences. Saloop was a creamy beverage typically made from orchid roots and a variety of other ingredients, including milk or water and sugar or spices. Originally, saloop was imported from the Anatolia region (in what is modern-day Türkiye, where it is still enjoyed) at the end of the seventeenth century. It became popular over the Georgian period until its use declined at the beginning of the nineteenth century.[5] During this period, people started to substitute the imported root with other ingredients, such as native roots including hyacinth, snowdrops and domestic orchids. These domestic sources were easily foraged and cheaper than the imported

Objects of Poverty

variety and so made the drink available to the new audiences of the labouring poor. Therefore, it is not surprising that when we study the records of the later eighteenth century, it is within the company of the labouring sort that saloop was most often enjoyed. The drink was consumed at street stalls, an inversion of the common trends of other contemporary hot drinks, often consumed either at home or in other enclosed spaces such as the tea garden or coffeehouse. Instead, sellers like Spence moved the new material culture associated with hot drinks out onto the open street, and together with their customers, they forged a new consumption space. This space was one that, unlike coffeehouses, was dominated not by the middling sort and the elite but by the labouring poor, and it was shaped by their experiences and needs.

How can we understand the stall?

From the 1740s, saloop stalls became more widespread on London's street corners and steps. While no concrete references to the number of stalls are available for the period, it is clear that they burgeoned from the growing frequency of references to them in the court records of the Old Bailey, as well as in literary and visual sources such as newspapers, prints and the writings of social commentators.[6] Each of these sources brings its own challenges, biases and limitations, but through this jigsaw of sources we can start to better understand these spaces.

One key source for this chapter is prints, such as that shown in Figure 3.1. These are crucial to understanding these spaces as they frequently capture details of material

Figure 3.1 Detail of anonymous, *Five Criers on a Single Sheet*, c. 1780–90. Source: © London Metropolitan Archives (City of London), p7513470.

40

culture that were deemed unimportant to record in written text. However, while these prints are potentially valuable sources, they were not created in a vacuum. Artists like Thomas Rowlandson and William Henry Pyne – artists and social observers of their time – who captured the stalls were unlikely to be attendees of these spaces themselves, instead approaching the stalls as outsiders looking for inspiration. Even less likely to attend the stalls were the middling and elite audience who bought the prints, whose purchasing power Rowlandson and other artists would want to appeal to. We can see, then, the attitudes of these outsiders colouring these prints like ink, whether in the idyllic, rosy cheeks of Payne's market seller or in how M. Eagerton depicts the customers of the saloop stall as crude as they 'saucer' their saloop (drinking from the saucer and not the cup). Only by acknowledging these factors and the prints' complexity as a source can we start to consider them as evidence.

The value of these prints for studying the material culture of poverty often lies in the minutiae they captured: objects and information often not seen as significant enough to record either in text or in historic collections. Few aspects of the stall survive today, the notable exemption being the type of ceramic cup that customers used, which survives in the archaeological record.[7] An item that was crucial to the functioning of the stall was the tea urn, yet none are known to have survived to today. Elite counterparts are still held in the collections of country houses and museums such as the Victoria and Albert Museum, yet the typical urns used by street sellers are not preserved in this way. They were not seen as worthy of being held in such collections. Instead, their value was as economic tools. It is likely that when they were no longer useful on the stall, they served one final economic purpose: being sold or melted down for scrap.

Tools of the trade

Certain tools were key to the stalls' success and existence. Without utensils such as tea urns, cups and even tables, the stall could not function, so each morning these items had to be carried through streets and set up. This was an arduous task that faced sellers such as Anne Hall – one that could not be managed alone – and she required her husband's and daughter's help to carry the equipment she needed.[8] Unfortunately, we know nothing more about Anne Hall's daily life besides her presence as a saloop seller on London's streets recorded in one Old Bailey session paper. Yet, by combining such snapshots with other sources such as the images in Figure 3.1, we can start to understand the saloop stall, its functions and wares, and how it crafted a space for working Londoners.

Another object crucial to the stall's success was the ceramic dishes for customers to drink from. A breakfast stall with dishes stacked, as depicted in Figure 3.2, gives us a sense of what these ceramics might have looked like. With no disposable cups to be found during this period, sellers would bring their own dishes to serve saloop. The period saw the development of a wide range of ceramic goods from the high-end Wedgewood and imported ceramics that graced elite homes to a plethora of domestically produced wares that catered to the middling and labouring classes. In fact, the century saw ownership

Figure 3.2 M. Egerton, *Street Breakfast*, 1825. Source: © London Metropolitan Archives (City of London), q8035015.

of goods expand across the social classes, as Joseph Harley has found.[9] Several factors contributed to this rise, including increased affordability due to changing production methods. Materials such as earthenware and techniques like printing and moulding allowed producers to reduce costs and cater to an audience far beyond the elite.[10] And should a brand new set remain outside the saloop seller's budget, there were various fellow street sellers and second-hand traders, often operating on a barter system, from whom goods could be procured.

Spaces such as the saloop stall allowed labouring Londoners to experience material goods before purchasing them for themselves. Ceramics such as earthenware were popular throughout the victualling trades, and, as Sarah Richards has highlighted, Londoners would have been exposed to an array of new goods as they ate outside the home.[11] Being carted across London and handled by all sorts, the dishes on the stalls were exposed to rough wear and tear, and saloop stall owners would likely have turned to cheap suppliers such as second-hand dealers. This would have resulted in a hotchpotch of patterns and colours as different sets were mixed together. However, by being exposed to this array of materials, poorer audiences could develop their material knowledge before purchasing their own cup or bowl. Saloop stalls, then, provided a low-cost entry into exploring these wares, as saloop was priced at only a few pennies. The space of the saloop stall reminds us of the importance of transient relationships with the material world in the early modern period – that an understanding of the material culture of poverty should not be limited to ownership and whatever objects were recorded in wills, which often listed only the most treasured items given to named recipients.

Similarly, it is hard to trace the presence of the most essential tool on the stall – the tea urn – when we examine wills and similar sources. As Nancy Cox and Karin Dannehl's *Dictionary of Traded Goods and Commodities* suggests, there was a great deal of overlap between the names and functions of different items of teaware, and many terms, such as 'tea kettle', 'boiler' and 'urn', were used interchangeably.[12] From examining visual records, tea urns were typically metal containers with a large body to hold the liquid and a tap at the base for immediate serving of the saloop. As stated before, urns were economic tools and not treasured personal items, so they were more likely to be melted for scrap or pawned than passed on. Given the challenge of locating this object in written and legal sources, a researcher must turn to other material to better understand its presence on the stall and how the labouring sort used it.

When examining the visual depictions of the stall, such as in Figures 3.1 and 3.2, we get a clearer picture of the tea urn. Here, the full image of the urn is visible and these prints depict a crucial part of it: the brazier that kept it warm (in the figures, this is visible just below the urns' main body: the horizontal bars with the dark shading in between). Elsewhere, in other prints, we see further evidence of these small portable fires, from flames that creep up the sides of the urn in William Henry Pyne's depiction of a saloop stall to the bellows for tending the fire at the feet of Rowlandson's saloop seller. Taken together, these elements provide a visual clue as to the presence of heat emanating from the stall, acting as the glue for this unique consumption space, for the heat of the urn would warm not only the saloop but the space around it, including the seller and all the customers.

Warmth and the cold streets of London

The warmth of the urn would have been crucial to sellers and customers on the cold street. It would have been 1.00 am when Sarah Anderson rose to sell saloop, and it would be many more hours till the sun rose to warm the streets. It may seem strange that Anderson would be out so early, but the curfew of the seventeenth century and earlier periods had lost its sting. As J. M. Beattie notes, with the development of theatres, tea gardens and other places of late-night entertainment, the culture of the nocturnal streets had changed.[13] Further, as Charlie Taverner has shown in his history of street food, while at the start of the seventeenth century some hawkers were still being arrested for selling at night, by the second half of the century these arrests petered out.[14] Saloop was warm and affordable: qualities that would have been popular both in the early morning or at night, whether it was a warm repast for those at the end of an evening's entertainment, comfort for those who found themselves without lodgings that night, or fuel for those who worked early and unfriendly hours, such as carters. Each of these examples can be found in the Old Bailey papers, and each of these customers would have likely welcomed Anderson and the warmth her saloop and her brazier would bring.

We cannot underestimate the importance of the heat to the saloop stall's audience. Street sellers such as Anderson, who carried a portable brazier on her stall, would have likely used charcoal to heat their braziers: as the historian Sara Pennell has argued, the fuel's lightness made it perfectly portable.[15] It can easily be imagined that warming hearths could be a source of comfort and community when alight.[16] The heat from the brazier would help to keep people warm while away from their hearths on the cold London streets. As the social reformer Henry Mayhew observed in his description of the saloop stall, warmth was central to the stall's success and its sociable atmosphere. Mayhew emphasised the poverty of the stalls' customers and how they appreciated the warmth of the drink and space, whether the chimney sweep who would stand numbly, barefoot, with his 'smoking hot' cup of saloop or the 'tattered' coachman who nursed his cooling cup.[17] Joining the warmth, customers might stop and forge their own sociable space on the street.[18] Perhaps this was why the radical Thomas Spence kept a saloop urn on his stall: to tempt those who could not read but most needed to hear his works. Here, drawn by the warm drink they cradled in their borrowed cup, customers might stay and share ideas.

Warmth was key to the saloop stall space; indeed it was the essential function of the tea urn more generally. The differences in design between those urns depicted in prints and those that survive in elite collections highlight an important lesson about the material culture of the labouring poor: that while they may have engaged in the same activity as the elite, they did not merely replicate their culture but adapted it to their own needs. When examining elite tea urns, it appears that warmth is a utility but not a priority, as the active heat source of the brazier in older models was later sacrificed to allow for a more fashionable shape. What was a valuable sign of taste in middling homes did not have the same importance on the public street and was simply impractical. Instead, sellers retained the old-fashioned braziers that allowed them to heat both the saloop and the street. These differences highlight how varied goods of the early modern period were and what existed beyond what we see in collections, from large silver tea sets that cost hundreds of pounds to humble copper tea urns that cost much less and have now been lost. Anderson and London's other sellers did not simply mimic the elites, they adapted wares to better suit their wants and needs.

Sellers, identity and material culture

The saloop seller's business was more ephemeral than that of fixed shops, as at the day's end the stall would be packed up and carried back home. However, the stalls were no less a business than any of the physical shops that surrounded Hall's or Spence's stalls. As Taverner argues, street sellers were keen business operators developing their own in-depth business knowledge and identity.[19] The investment in material goods for the stall, such as the urn and other wares, would potentially act to reinforce this sense of self – a material representation of the sellers' professional identities. Within the Old Bailey papers and the fragments of statements that exist by those who were saloop sellers, it certainly is possible to see such a professional identity emerge. Sellers such as Sarah Anderson, Hannah Shepard and others describe their business as primarily selling saloop. Little information is provided about these women in the Old Bailey save for their statements, and without other additional identifiers like age it is hard to trace them in records. What we know is their testimony and that they were economic agents in the London streets often working unsocial hours when many genteel folk had retired. Indeed, Shepard goes as far as to describe herself as a 'saloop-woman'.[20] It is clear that these sellers saw their saloop business as part of their core professional identity.

Many people who operated a saloop stall were labouring-class women who carved out their own professional and economic space on the London streets. Some saloop sellers were men, not least Thomas Spence and William Miller, who proudly proclaimed in the Old Bailey that his 'business [wa]s to sell saloop'.[21] However, it seems that overall, sellers were noticeably more likely to be women; in the seventeen cases where the gender of the seller is noted in the Old Bailey papers, twelve were women.[22] This is admittedly a very slim sample, but this supposition is further supported by the popular prints of the time, with prints such as Figures 3.1 and 3.2, among others, frequently showing older labouring women working the stalls.

Women may have been well represented in street selling trades because this role afforded them flexible work which could fit around their other duties, such as childcare. These women were economic agents, building and operating for years at a time within the busy streets of London, on its steps and street corners. Mary Griffiths, for instance, identifying herself to the Old Bailey, plainly said: 'I live in a court in the Minories and sell saloop, which I have done for many years'.[23] The presence of sellers like Mary Griffiths or Hannah Sheppard, who worked for years in the same spots, reminds us that the lives of labouring women (and indeed women generally) do not fit into neat stereotypes. Through their activities, these women were active agents in the streetscape, shaping its experience with their stalls.

A space for the labouring poor

The women who sold saloop were not the only members of the labouring sort at the stall, for, as noted above, the labouring poor were the primary consumers of the drink. Tradespeople were often depicted as stall attendees. Figure 3.1 is no exception, the dress of two figures revealing their professions: a hairdresser with his scissors tucked neatly into his apron, while the dark leather apron of his companion is the sign of a cobbler or blacksmith. A similar assortment of characters can be seen in Figure 3.2, from the jolly tradesman with the ruler in his apron to the dustman arriving in his strange black hat. Similarly, when the writer Pierce Egan chose to depict the various characters of London and their spaces in his 1821 comic novel *Real Life in London*, it was dustmen whom he chose to cluster around the saloop stall.[24] Throughout the depictions of the saloop stall we see watchmen, chimney sweeps and market sellers – as varied a collection of people as you would find in eighteenth-century London. Little unites these figures apart from the fact that they worked for their living in professions that would not be considered genteel or polite.

But how authentic are these depictions? If we go beyond the artist's imagination to legal records, what evidence can we find of who attended the stall? Despite the limited pool of evidence, it appears that the depictions of Figures 3.1 and 3.2 are representative. Where the customer's trade is described, they are often of the labouring sort. Their jobs are humble, such as basket-maker William Moss or Constable Samuel Cooper (a job which was often low-paid if at all). They were people like Edmund Law, a carter who stopped at a saloop stall next to the carter's yard before he started his rounds.[25] While we must be wary of caricature when using prints as sources, the evidence of the Old Bailey papers seems to confirm that the saloop stall was a space attended by the labouring sort as they sought a brief respite in their busy lives.

Indeed, unlike other consumption spaces that might serve various people, the saloop stall seems to have been branded in the minds of elite Londoners as a space for the labouring poor. One 1864 columnist reflected on the long-gone saloop stalls and how gauche it was to drink on the street.[26] Similarly, in the anti-abolition poem *No Abolition of Slavery*, James Boswell used saloop to mock members of the labouring sort who called for the abolition of slavery, using the drink to emphasise their poverty to his audience.[27] Among the half-baked arguments Boswell had against the abolition of the slave trade was that the poor in Britain had it worse than those enslaved. Further, he felt that those labouring-class Britons who did object to slavery should be mocked and dismissed as the uneducated, emotional 'rabble'. The image of the poor cobbler drinking his saloop and expressing sympathy for the enslaved is meant as a cruel joke:

> See in a stall three feet by four,
> Where door is window, window door,
> Saloop a hump-back'd cobler drink;
> 'With him the muse shall sit and think;'
> He shall in sentimental strain,
> That negroes are oppress'd, complain.
> What mutters the decrepit creature?
> The Dignity of Human Nature![28]

In Boswell's eyes, the cobbler is a figure of both pity and derision. In his tiny dwelling with his 'hump-back', he represents the abject poverty in Britain, who mimics the conversations held at coffeehouses but has only the poor man's hot drink, the cheap saloop, as an accompaniment. His poverty and his ignorance about how bad he has it are meant to be the very reason we should dismiss his naive and 'sentimental' arguments about slavery. Every line of Boswell's description is meant to reinforce the cobbler's low class and lack of gentility. Boswell's choice to have him drink saloop (and not beer or tea) is no accident: it is yet one more element to reinforce his poverty, and one that Boswell felt confident his audience would identify.

It is clear that by the end of the century, the saloop stall was firmly a labouring-class space both in practice and in the popular imagination. Whether someone was drawn to the stall out of need (such as the basket maker William Moss, who stopped at a stall when locked out of his lodging) or for pleasure (such as the thieves David Milton and John Cossey, who stopped at the stall as part of a night out), the low cost of the drink made it accessible, unlike many other social and consumption spaces.[29] While coffeehouses and tea gardens might charge a fee, the saloop stall provided no such barrier. Instead, it afforded a space for the labouring poor to come together, to take respite in the warmth of the brazier and chat. As Pennell has argued, such shared consumption spaces provided a break in routines and allowed people to come together and form common identities.[30] This chapter has shown that one of the attractions the stall held for the labouring sort was its physical warmth, but perhaps it offered another type of warmth – a space of brief companionship amid the London bustle.

Conclusion·

The title of this chapter comes from a line in the Old Bailey papers in a case regarding saloop. As Sarah Anderson headed out in the very early hours of the morning, her kettle or urn was stolen from her step. After William Box recovered it, he described it to the court as 'full of saloop and fire under it', in seven words managing to conjure a sense of warmth and taste.[31] In many ways, the scene described in the Old Bailey papers is mundane, something that happened across London streets in the Georgian period. Yet it touches on what was interesting about saloop stalls and how they can help us to understand the labouring experience of London and material culture. Poor labouring Londoners adapted these new goods to their own needs, taking goods like Anderson's tea urn out of the spaces they were designed for and onto the street. The use of these wares on the street, whether owned by the seller or experienced momentarily by the customer, highlights how much the new material culture related to hot beverages had permeated society. It is such momentary and fleeting moments that make up so much of our own daily lives, and that the historian must be open to when researching: moments such as the importance of a warm brazier on a cold London street and how that would have been experienced. Women like Sarah Anderson who went out on cold mornings helped shape the city streets, contributing to their routines and sensory experiences. In return, their roles as saloop sellers seems to have helped shape their own identities. Historians such as Taverner have done fantastic work examining the lives of street sellers, but there is much more to be done, and many more stories to be examined. Saloop stalls were very much a labouring space, from the customers who visited to the owners who served on them. They were recognised as such – a fact that likely contributed to their demise, as they could not adapt and bring in new audiences when coffee and tea became more commonly consumed at the end of the period.

This chapter has only just scratched the surface of the saloop stall; there is much more to be uncovered. By examining these mundane spaces that made up so much of daily experience, we can learn more about the past, whether in the lives of labouring women or the experience of material culture. These small histories can help us to piece together the broader story of poverty. Such spaces that belonged to the labouring sort existed throughout London and the United Kingdom, and while they may not have been recorded in the same ways as coffeehouses or tea gardens, we can understand them and the early modern labouring experience by using more expansive research methods. Whether this is using material culture, as the chapters in this volume have demonstrated, or using sensory history to view old sources through a new lens, the possibilities are many.

Notes

1. The research for this chapter draws on my dissertation 'The Ephemeral Saloop Stall: 'Examining the Stall, the Seller and Space in Georgian London, 1700–1820', produced during my MA in the History of Design with the V&A/RCA. For further information, also see my article 'Time and Space in a Dish: Examining the Relationship between Materiality and Space in the Early Modern Saloop Stall', *History of Retailing and Consumption* 8:11 (2023): pp. 1–21.
2. British Library Add MS 27808(307), 'The Memoir of Thomas Spence', in Eneas Mackenzie, *MacKenzie's History of Newcastle* (1826).
3. Alastair Bonnett and Keith Armstrong, *Thomas Spence: The Poor Man's Revolutionary* (London: Breviary Stuff Publications, 2014), p. 54; P. M. Ashraf, *The Life and Times of Thomas Spence* (Newcastle upon Tyne: Frank Graham, 1983), pp. 46–7.
4. Brian Cowan, *The Social Life of Coffee: The Emergence of the British Coffeehouse* (London: Yale University Press, 2011), p. 124.
5. The earliest mention is in John Peachie, *Some Observations Made upon the Root Called Serapias, Imported from Turkey* (London, 1694); later reference is made in the papers of the East India Company, IOR/C/141, recording its imports up until 1789.
6. For a more detailed assessment of the sources, see Purcell, 'Time and Space in a Dish', pp. 1–21.
7. Jaqui Pearce, 'Consumption of Creamware', in Tom Walford and Roger Massey (eds), *Creamware and Pearlware Re-examined* (Beckenham: English Ceramic Circle, 2007), pp. 242–51.
8. Old Bailey Proceedings (hereafter OBP) t17780916-13, Trial of Joseph Ruff, April 1754, www.oldbaileyonline.org (accessed 3 May 2024).
9. Joseph Harley, *At Home with the Poor: Consumer Behaviour and Material Culture in England, c. 1650–1850* (Manchester: Manchester University Press, 2024) .
10. David Baker, 'Creamware in Context', in Walford and Massey (eds), *Creamware and Pearlware*, p. 31.
11. Sarah Richards, *Eighteenth-Century Ceramics* (Manchester: Manchester University Press, 1999), p. 155.
12. 'Tea – Tea Ware', in Nancy Cox and Karin Dannehl (eds), *Dictionary of Traded Goods and Commodities 1550–1820* (Wolverhampton: University of Wolverhampton, 2007), British

History Online, www.british-history.ac.uk/no-series/traded-goods-dictionary/1550-1820/tea-tea-ware (accessed 2 May 2024).

13   J. M. Beattie, *Policing and Punishment in London, 1660–1750: Urban Crime and the Limits of Terror* (Oxford: Oxford University Press, 2001), p. 172.
14   Charlie Taverner, *Street Food: Hawkers and the History of London* (Oxford: Oxford University Press, 2023).
15   Sara Pennell, *Birth of the English Kitchen, 1600–1850* (London: Bloomsbury, 2017), p. 126. Further, Henry Mayhew notes the use of charcoal braziers at a saloop stall in his Henry Mayhew, *London Labour and the London Poor* (Oxford: Oxford University Press, 1861), p. 160.
16   Harley, *At Home with the Poor*.
17   Mayhew, *London Labour*, p. 160.
18   Ibid.
19   Taverner, *Street Food*, pp. 41, 53.
20   OBP t17920215-7, Trial of John Lewis, Robert Pearce, February 1792. www.oldbaileyonline.org (accessed 17 May 2024), OBP t17840526-43, Trial of Joeseph Levy, May 1784, www.oldbaileyonline.org (accessed 3 May 2024).
21   OBP t17830723-122, Trial of William William Law, July 1783, www.oldbaileyonline.org (accessed 17 May 2024).
22   Purcell, 'Time and Space in a Dish', p. 284.
23   OBP t17770514-29, Trial of John Gibson, May 1777, www.oldbaileyonline.org (accessed 3 May 2024).
24   Pierce Egan, *Real Life in London* (London: Methuen, 1905), pp. ii, 250–2.
25   OBP t17830723-122, Trial of William William Law, July 1783; OBP t18090517-17, Trial of William Jones, Moses Fonseca, May 1809 (accessed 17 May 2024); OBP t18230115-97, Edmund Law, Thomas Webb, January 1823, www.oldbaileyonline.org (accessed 17 May 2024).
26   Aleph, 'City Scraps: Early Breakfast Stalls and Coffee Shops', *London City Press*, 5 March 1864, p. 3.
27   James Boswell, *No Abolition of Slavery, or, the Universal Empire of Love, a Poem* (London: R. Faulder, 1791), p. 11.
28   Ibid., p. 11.
29   OBP t18090517-17, Trial of William Jones, Moses Fonseca, May 1809; OBP t18021201-98, Trial of David Milton, John Cossey, December 1802, www.oldbaileyonline.org (accessed 17 May 2024).
30   Sara Pennell, '"Great Quantities of Gooseberry Pye and Baked Clod of Beef": Victualling and Eating Out in Early Modern London', in Paul Griffiths and Mark Jenner (eds), *Londinopolis: Essays in the Cultural and Social History of Early Modern London c. 1500–c. 1750* (Manchester: Manchester University Press, 2000), pp. 228–49.
31   OBP t17840526-43, Trial of Joeseph Levy, May 1784, www.oldbaileyonline.org (accessed 17 May 2024).

Further reading

Kelley, Victoria. *Cheap Street: London's Street Markets and the Cultures of Informality, c. 1850–1939* (Manchester: Manchester University Press, 2019).
Owens, Alastair, Nigel Jeffries, Karen Wehner and Rupert Featherby. 'Fragments of the Modern City: Material Culture and the Rhythms of Everyday Life in Victorian London'. *Journal of Victorian Culture*, 15:2 (2010): pp. 212–25.

Objects of Poverty

Pennell, Sara, '"For a Crack or Flaw Despis'd": Thinking about Ceramic Durability and the "Everyday" in Late Seventeenth- and Early Eighteenth-Century England', in Tara Hamling and Catherine Richardson (eds), *Everyday Objects: Medieval and Early Modern Material Culture and Its Meanings* (Farnham: Ashgate, 2010), pp. 27–40.

Pennell, Sara. '"Great Quantities of Gooseberry Pye and Baked Clod of Beef": Victualling and Eating Out in Early Modern London', in Paul Griffiths and Mark Jenner (eds), *Londinopolis: Essays in the Cultural and Social History of Early Modern London c. 1500–c. 1750* (Manchester: Manchester University Press, 2000), pp. 228–49.

Taverner, Charlie. *Street Food: Hawkers and the History of London* (Oxford: Oxford University Press, 2023).

Withington, Phil. 'Where Was the Coffee in Early Modern England?', *Journal of Modern History*, 92:1 (2020): pp. 40–75.

PART II
OBJECTS OF HOME

CHAPTER 4
FROM CRADLE TO GRAVE? THE ENDURING AFTERLIFE OF THE EGG BOX IN VICTORIAN LONDON

Vicky Holmes[1]

Introduction

One late summer evening in 1858, neighbours were going about their business on Little Windmill Street, Soho, when they saw that egg merchant Francois Bryselbout had yet to shut up for the night. Concerned, they entered his shop and made their way into the room where Francois lived – a space 'bare of furniture' – where they found Francois lying dead in an egg box. However, Francois had not simply fallen down dead into one of the boxes of his trade: this was where he made his bed, covered only by 'a quantity of rags'. And, indeed, just a few weeks before, Bryselbout's wife died in 'the same strange kind of bed'. The shop itself was full of 'chests and baskets of egg, which [the coroner's court determined] put an end to any conjecture that [he] had died from absolute want'. Nonetheless, the inquest revealed the Bryselbouts lacked any material wealth beyond their stock-in-trade.[2]

The egg boxes in which the Bryselbouts slept are far from what we know as egg boxes today. Constructed from sturdy wood for transportation to the city, these boxes could measure up to six feet in length. Such was their size that tradespersons were fined if the boxes were left on the footpaths fronting their shops. Hornsey grocer and provision merchant David Murray Grieg was summoned before the Highgate Petty Sessions 'for obstructing the free passage of the footway by placing three empty egg boxes outside his shop' (as can be seen in Figure 4.1) and ordered to pay costs of 5s 6d.[3] At the more extreme end of these prosecutions, 22-year-old John Eaton faced five days imprisonment (or a five-shilling fine) after causing an obstruction on Moreton Street, Pimlico, as he walked along carrying an egg box.[4] Impractical to return to their origins, these large boxes – as accounts of fires in the newspaper reveal – would soon fill every nook and cranny of the tradesperson's shop and outbuildings. For instance, when the fire brigade arrived at the general stores of a Whitechapel provision merchant, they found their way blocked, 'The arch was crammed with empty egg boxes and other flammable material'.[5] The question, then, was what to do with a surplus of egg boxes?

Surprisingly, perhaps to our modern understanding, egg boxes still held value even without their fragile cargo. Advertisements in local newspapers reveal that these 'empty'

Figure 4.1 Front of a tradesman shop from Henry Mayhew's *London Labour and the London Poor*, Vol 1 (1861), p. 73. The box on the right side of the picture, lying upturned on the footway to serve as a produce stand, is one of the few illustrations depicting the larger types of egg boxes in circulation.

boxes could be sold – sometimes in their hundreds – from around four to six pence per unit. The Elms provision store in Limehouse ran the following advertisement in the *East End News*: 'LARGE Quantity of EGG BOXES for sale, from 4d. each',[6] while J. Sainsbury of Kilburn, advertising in *Hendon & Finchley Times*, was selling 'EMPTY Egg Boxes 6ft. long, suitable for Florists and others 6s. dozen' (6d each).[7] Of course, neighbours that came knocking might only be charged a fraction of that price. A provisions dealer in Bethnal Green, for instance, charged a local wood dealer, a man known to him, just 3d for an empty egg box.[8] There is no account of whether they would be given freely, but we know they held such value to the tradesperson that the theft of one of these boxes could result in prosecution. In November 1895, 'a young fellow' named James Blees (Bleeze) was found guilty of stealing an empty egg box, valued at 6d, from a grocer's yard. Despite being his first offence, he was sentenced to seven days hard labour for his crime.[9] Aside from wood dealers, florists and thieves who else sought out these empty boxes?

For as long as food and other consumables have been transported, those living in poverty have made use of these commercial containers, providing boxes such as the egg box and other crates with a domestic afterlife. In isolation, the Bryselbout's 'strange' beds might be seen as a one-off, only used by Francois and his wife because the egg boxes were already at their disposal. However, it is undoubtedly the case that the Bryselbouts made a few pence here and there in selling these wooden boxes to their poorest neighbours to roughly repurpose in their own homes. Or, indeed, if James Blees had been passing his shop, snatched up to be crafted into something else entirely new as Blees and his father were carpenters by trade. Our understanding of commercial boxes and crates as an object of poverty is not entirely new. In their respective discussions of the experiences of the Victorian poor, Anna Davin and Vivienne Richmond provide evidence of poverty-stricken households populating their home with a range of discarded or sold-on commercial boxes and crates, such as orange and soap boxes that were 'used for cupboards, chairs and cradles, or their dismantled planks put up as shelves'. Similarly, tobacco boxes could be constructed into a makeshift chest of drawers.[10] Drawing on Victorian newspapers – including their advertisements, reports of crimes and inquests, as well as the musing of journalists and social investigators – this chapter focuses on the egg box not just as an object of poverty utilised by only the poorest in society but also as an object that came to be promoted by middling classes – namely coroners, religious organisations, and schools for mothers – as a solution to some of the evils that blighted those living in poverty.

A signifier of poverty

When the middle classes – in their various guises – entered the homes of those in absolute poverty, they were often confronted by an absence of domestic possessions. Instead, they might have stumbled over commercial boxes and crates, which, as well as making cheap firewood when coal could not be afforded, could serve as the family's furniture. The Wood's Bermondsey home – 'a wretched den' – was one example of many that epitomise the scenes witnessed by London's courts and other visitors. With their father out of work on account of ill health, the family depended on the kindness of neighbours to put food on their plates. They also turned to theft: the Woods situation came to light when their 'poorly clad' thirteen-year-old son appeared before Southwark Police Court in 1891, charged with stealing a German sausage valued at 1s 6d (in which the *Weekly Dispatch* titled the report: 'Hungry'). By the time of their son's crime, it appears that the family had pawned or sold nearly all of their possessions – a typical recourse for people facing the temporary loss of the breadwinner's wage – for when 'a gentleman' visited the Woods's home, he found: 'The furniture of the room consisted of an old egg-box and one chair, and up stairs the only bedding for the whole of the family was three sacks filled with straw'. Moved by the family's plight, the magistrate gave the mother money from the court's poor box.[11] Arthur Sherwell witnessed similar scenes as he undertook a census of the poor of West London at the turn of the century. Coming across one family, unable to pay their rent and on the brink of eviction, he found:

> The woman was 'keeping guard,' afraid to go out lest the landlord, who was watching, should take possession. The only furniture in the room was an egg-box, a chair with no back, a kettle, and a saucepan in which the woman was cooking some cods' heads for their dinner.[12]

Frustratingly, neither the 'gentleman' nor Sherwell stated how these egg boxes were used as furniture. However, evidence of use can be found in A. S. Krause's *Starving*

Objects of Poverty

London – his account of a three-week sojourn among London's destitute in the 1880s serialised in the *Globe* newspaper. Upon entering the Warren Street home of Mrs Hall, Krause found 'an empty egg box, which, placed upside down, serves as a table'. Notably, aside from an iron pail and a truss of straw, the egg box was the only piece of furnishing in the twelve-foot by nine-foot room that was Mrs Hall's home, for 'everything [had] been pawned' when her husband found himself out of work. Learning that the family faced eviction, Krause himself arranged new lodgings and a bedstead to replace the truss of straw that served as the bed.[13]

Other accounts in the newspapers at the time reveal further use of the egg box as a bed. Laid flat, the slumbering occupant could nestle within the egg box's sides, as Bryselbout and his wife did, while upturned, the egg box could serve as the base to a bed. For example, in the winter of 1898, when a police constable entered the loft over a disused stable that served as the family home of 43-year-old carman, William Laycock, and 33-year-old charwoman, Johanna Fleharty, 'the furniture consisted only of an old and dirty mattress and a few rags spread on an egg box'.[14] One newspaper report even reveals that the egg box bedstead could accommodate additional sleepers in people's abodes. The Steels ran a bakery on High Road, Stamford Hill, with at least one live-in employee. Yet, while the master bakers slept comfortably in the confines of their home, no such provision was made for their young journeyman, Thomas Dracey, who was made 'to sleep on an egg box in a shed at the rear of the premises'. This discomfort led him to abscond from his employers with some of their money in his pocket, which Dracey claimed at Tottenham Police Court was due to him in wages.[15]

The most commonly noted use of egg boxes in the homes of those in poverty was as a cot or a cradle. A report in the *Eastern Post*, June 1871, stated that among the mothers of the Golden Lane slum in the City of London, egg boxes were 'a popular kind of cradle'.[16] Most of these egg boxes would have been the shorter form, sufficient enough to accommodate a solitary infant, but in some cases, the longer egg boxes – with a partition – could house two slumbering infants.[17] Yet, neglect was also strongly associated with the egg box.[18] When cases of baby farming or paternal neglect came before the courts, the egg box cot served as tangible evidence that a child was not adequately cared for. In May 1890, Eliza Hamerton, a woman living apart from her husband, was sent to gaol for three months after being found guilty of neglecting her children. However, the evidence presented suggests her only crime was poverty:

> When the police went to the Prisoner's address on another charge they found the children almost naked, and overrun with vermin, and with no food in the house but a little sugar. A lame child was lying in an old egg box, and another was on two stinking mattresses without bed-clothes. The place was horribly filthy, and in one of the mattresses the police found 45 pawn-tickets, mostly for articles of children's clothing.[19]

Indeed, so ubiquitous was the egg box as a symbol of neglect and poverty that Charles Dickens's *Hard Times* (1854) character, the professed self-made man Mr Bounderby, told in his rags-to-riches story of being abandoned by his mother and brought up by his abusive grandmother, 'who kept [him] in an egg-box'. Yet, at around the same time of Hamerton's prison sentence, the egg box as an object of poverty began to be reframed as an object that had the potential to resolve, if not at least alleviate, some of the problems of poverty that plagued London's poorer population.

A poverty solution

When the Salvation Army opened its shelters in the late nineteenth century in response to the growing number of unemployed and homeless sleeping on London's streets or its notorious lodging houses, they relied on subscriptions and the goodwill of others to secure buildings and beds. Thus, thrift was essential. In its second male shelter, opened in 1889, on the premises of a three-storey warehouse in St John's-gate, Clerkenwell, all 250 of the beds were four-sided boxes – just long and wide enough to accommodate a working man – containing 'a mattress of American cloth, stuffed with seaweed, and a curious sheepskin apron, serving as a coverlet' (Figures 4.2 and 4.3). Unfortunately, with no direct documentary evidence from the Salvation Army archives as to the purchasing of these boxes, we cannot be sure of the exact origins of these boxes. However, one reporter stated in *Lloyd's Weekly Newspaper* that after visiting the Clerkenwell shelter, he found the beds to 'resemble substantial egg boxes'.[20] Given the ubiquitous egg boxes and

Figure 4.2 Photograph of the interior of a Salvation Army shelter, *c.* 1890s. Image Courtesy of the Salvation Army International Heritage Centre.

Objects of Poverty

Figure 4.3 Photograph of the interior of the Salvation Army metropole on Burne Street, London, c. 1896. Image Courtesy of the Salvation Army International Heritage Centre.

their resale in large volumes during this period, it is not a stretch to conclude that the Salvation Army did utilise the larger egg boxes in some of their shelters.[21]

Similarly, at Hanbury Street women's shelter in Whitechapel, another 250 beds were supplied, many of which fit the above description – although it was here that they appear to have acquired their moniker of 'coffin beds' (Figure 4.4).[22] However, despite this morbid nickname, there is little evidence that egg boxes were ever used to bury London's poor. Certainly, as in Figure 4.5, anecdotal tales of bodies buried in egg boxes might have titillated the newspaper reader, but such a suggestion was promptly dismissed when it came to the question of pauper burials. When one juror at an 1869 London coroner's inquest suggested that an egg box would make a 'good' coffin for the poor, he was rebuffed for his recommendation.[23] Just over six years later, in a debate over pauper burials, it was remarked that the poor law 'Guardians should draw the line at egg boxes'.[24] Although, one cannot help but wonder whether the Bryselbouts – whom we met at the beginning of the chapter – were buried in the egg boxes that had served as their beds.

We know that egg boxes, albeit in their smaller form, were present in the Salvation Army's day-creches adjoining the women's shelters. Here, for a small fee, working mothers could leave their infants and children between 8.00 am and 8.00 pm to earn money for a night in the shelter and begin to work their way out of poverty.[25] These creches were, like the shelters, substantial, and the economy was essential in their construction. The Hanbury Street shelter reportedly accommodated up to 250 babies during the day, and

Figure 4.4 Paul Renouard's sketch of the Whitechapel shelter after a visit with *Graphic* journalist F. W. Robinson not long after its opening. Responding to a statement on the wall – 'ARE YOU READY TO DIE?', Robinson stated that the women 'look[ed] as though they were dead already; the unsightly receptacles for the sleepers are strangely like open coffins – open graves, in which they can repose and rest in peace for a while'. *The Graphic*, 27 February 1892. Image Courtesy of the International Salvation Army Heritage Centre.

> OBSERVATIONS, BY THE RAMBLER..in a story told me by a Holloway costermonger the other day. He had not the means to pay for the orthodox funeral, and did not care to have his partner buried by the parish. So he procured an egg-box, which he painted black, placed his dead wife in it, nailed up the case, and lifting the primitive coffin and its contents on to a barrow, pushed it up to Highgate Cemetery.

Figure 4.5 Excerpt from the *Islington Gazette*, 31 January 1894, p. 3.

the egg box provided an affordable solution to providing so many cots. Mother Webb's own account of setting up one such creche stated: 'We begged a lot of egg-boxes, and I had them well scrubbed out and covered with chintz – people's faded chair-covers do well for this – and made some little mattresses to fit, and bed-clothes; they really looked very well' (Figure 4.6). Meanwhile, upturned egg boxes formed much of the creche's seating.[26] Yet, it was not just the Salvation Army that could see the benefits of the egg box cot. Despite the disdain shown towards slum mothers' use of egg boxes as cots for

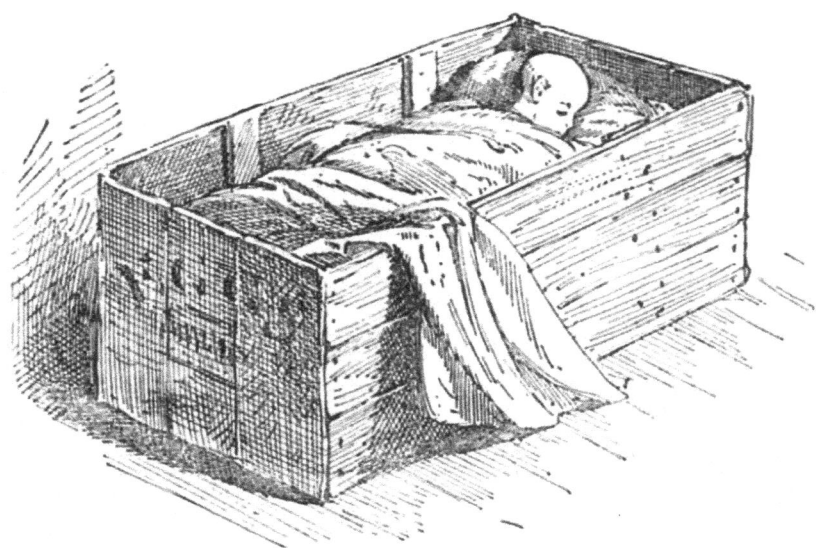

Figure 4.6 A baby sleeping in a converted egg box in an article entitled 'Slum Babies' in the Salvation Army publication *All the World*, September 1888, p. 302. Image Courtesy of the Salvation Army International Heritage Centre.

much of the period, by the 1890s, the egg box – along with its other commercial cousins, the orange box and banana crate – began to be hailed as a practical solution to what was considered 'one of the great problems of the day' among the poorer classes in London and other urban areas: infantile mortality from overlaying (accidental smothering).[27]

Among the high infant mortality experienced by the poor, those deaths that occurred while sleeping alongside their mothers were all too easily attributed to overlaying by medical men who could not proffer any other explanation. Such a determination was undoubtedly shaped by the middle-class ideals of separation that infants and children did not belong in the parental bedroom but 'safely' confined to their nurseries. Thus, the assumption was often made that if an infant died in the parental bed, then the child must have been overlaid. Both the medical men and the coroner's courts investigating cases of infant death were aware that the poorer woman's purse would not stretch to the provision of an actual cot or cradle and instead called for these women – they believed to be 'ignorant' if not careless in their care of infants – to seek alternatives to bedsharing such as the egg box. For example, in 1893, when a coroner's inquest was held in Lewisham to determine what had caused the death of the eleven-week-old infant found in the bed of his parents, joiner Samuel Millgate and his (unnamed) wife, Dr A. T. Todd White concluded from an external examination that 'the death was due to suffocation, the deceased being well nourished and healthy'. In his rider to the parents, the deputy coroner took a hard-line against the Millgates, giving the advice that was repeated by coroners across England at this time:

The coroner characterised the matter as one of gross carelessness, and stated that he considered that the parents should be called upon to pay the cost of the inquest. He expressed his disapproval of the habit of parents having children sleeping with them. The children should sleep in cots; if cots were too expensive, egg boxes could be procured at 6d. a piece.[28]

Likewise, the coroner covering the district of Finchley in the late 1890s stated he held 'a very large number of inquests upon children who die whilst in bed with their parents, and he always tells the mother to procure an egg or orange box and use it for a cradle … as it is so easy for them to get smothered'.[29] Of course, we now know that the occurrence of these deaths was often wildly exaggerated in the press – the mean annual death rate per million of the population of London for the period 1891–1900 from 'suffocation in bed' was just 139.44[30] – and, in light of advanced medical understanding today, it is also understood that even many of this number were likely to have been wrongly attributed.[31]

Nonetheless, hearing the coroners' calls, Schools for Mothers – established by middle- and upper-class women and public health physicians in London and across Britain – swung into action to provide a practical solution to preventing deaths from supposed overlaying. These schools aimed to educate poorer mothers on various matters of childrearing, including reducing their 'ignorance' regarding child sleeping practices. Among their various 'mothercraft' activities, these schools demonstrated how mothers could transform a commercial box into a domesticated cot. Notably, the schools favoured the cheaper, although less sturdy, two-penny banana crates.[32] A report in the *London Daily News* in August 1907 regarding the newly established St Pancras School for Mothers describes in detail how to construct one of these 'convenient cradles' from a banana crate:

> A box direct from the fruiterer, with nails sticking out and laths broken is produced. A couple of minutes with a hammer results in the box being put to rights; a few more minutes, and the box is lined and cushioned with things common to any working-class home. The banana box changes into a child's cot in an amazingly short time, and there is nothing to suggest its humble origin.[33]

The school even went on to sell repurposed banana crate cots at a shilling each, although the success of this venture is not reported.[34]

The sturdier egg box, however, had not entirely fallen out of favour by the 1900s. Popular's Health Visiting Association appears to have favoured the egg box, demonstrating at one event a model of a cot fashioned from an egg box that cost just 9d.[35] The packaging placed in the box to protect the eggs also had its uses. In July 1904, at the Sanitary Congress in Glasgow, Miss Isabel G. Smith's 'hints on the management of infants' stated that as well as 'Egg boxes and banana boxes, suitably draped with washable material, ma[king] useful cradles … the shaving in which the eggs came packed from abroad, hay, fine straw, or chaff could [be] sewn in a clean tick' for bedding.[36]

Conclusion

On its journey through Victorian London, the humble egg box was transformed from an object of commerce to an object of poverty. Built to transport eggs into the city, these often unusually large boxes found a new purpose among London's poorest slum dwellers. In exploring such a transition, we have expanded our understanding of the 'economies of makeshift' beyond what was left behind at the pawnshop, revealing how the very poor created a semblance of home as they struggled to maintain the roof over their heads. However, the egg box's story is not just contained to the experience of poverty. As an object transformed, the egg box provides further insight into the attitudes towards and attempts to alleviate poverty during this period. Various institutions recognised the egg box – among other boxes and crates – as an affordable solution that allowed them to support or 'educate' women living in poverty. Yet, as the egg box transformed into the egg carton we know today, its place in the story of poverty came to pass.

Notes

1. I would like to thank Joe Harley, Helen Sword and members of WriteSPACE live writing studio for their feedback on this chapter and Steven Spencer for his research on the Salvation Army's use of egg boxes.
2. *Morning Advertiser*, 5 July 1858, p. 3.
3. *Islington Gazette*, 16 November 1897, p. 2.
4. *Westminster & Pimlico News*, 25 October 1890, p. 3.
5. *London Evening Standard*, 24 January 1894, p. 6; *Croydon Times*, 11 October 1882, p. 2; *Finchley Press*, 25 March 1899, p. 2.
6. *East London News & London Shipping Chronicle*, 26 May 1871, p. 4.
7. *Hendon & Finchley Times*, 4 August 1893, p. 4; *London Daily Chronicle*, 24 October 1868, p. 3.
8. *Tower Hamlets Independent*, 1 February, 1896, p. 7.
9. *Croydon Times*, 23 November 1895, p. 3.
10. Anna Davin, *Growing Up Poor: Home, School, and Street in London, 1870–1914* (London: Rivers Oram Press, 1996), p. 49; Vivienne Richmond, *Clothing the Poor in Nineteenth-Century England* (Cambridge: Cambridge University, 2013), p. 158.
11. *Weekly Dispatch*, 1 February 1891, p. 11. For more information on the court's poor box, see Jennifer Davis, 'A Poor Man's System of Justice: The London Police Courts in the Second Half of the Nineteenth Century', *Historical Journal*, 27:2 (1984): pp. 309–35.
12. Arthur Sherwell, *Life in West London: A Study and a Contrast* (London: Methuen, 1901), p. 10.
13. *Globe*, 23 February 1886, p. 3.
14. *Daily Telegraph & Courier*, 4 January 1899, p. 9.
15. *Middlesex Gazette*, 20 September 1890, p. 3.
16. *Eastern Post*, 10 June 1871, p. 4.
17. *Daily News*, 12 August 1881, p. 6.
18. The most infamous of these cases is documented in James Greenwood, *Seven Curses of London* (London: S. Rivers, 1869), pp. 55–7.
19. *London Evening Standard*, 29 May 1890, p. 1.
20. *Lloyd's Weekly Newspaper*, 20 January 1889, p. 12.

21 Ibid.; Salvation Army, *The 'Darkest England' Social Scheme: A Brief Review of the First Year's Work* (London: Salvation Army Printing and Publishing Depts., 1891), pp. 5–21, 120–6.
22 *Lloyd's Weekly Newspaper*, 20 January 1889, p. 12; *The Graphic*, 27 February 1892, pp. 276–7.
23 *Tower Hamlets Independent*, 13 February 1869, p. 6.
24 *Islington Gazette*, 25 August 1876, p. 2.
25 Robert Sandall, *The History of the Salvation Army*, vol. 3 (London: Thomas Nelson & Son, 1955), p. 2
26 Ibid.; *All the World*, September (monthly), p. 303.
27 *British Medical Journal*, 24 September 1904, pp. 753–5.
28 *Sydenham, Forest Hill & Penge Gazette*, 8 July 1893, p. 5; *Kentish Mercury*, 7 July 1893, p. 2.
29 *Finchley Press*, 14 May 1898, p. 2.
30 *British Medical Journal*, 24 September 1904, p. 754.
31 Elizabeth de G. R. Hansen, '"Overlaying" in 19th-Century England: Infant Mortality or Infanticide', *Human Ecology*, 7 (1979): pp. 333–52.
32 For more information on the evolution of England's schools for mothers, see Carol Dyhouse, 'Working-Class Mothers and Infant Mortality', in Charles Webster (ed.), *Biology Medicine and Society 1840–1940* (Cambridge: Cambridge University Press, 2002), pp. 73–98 and Jane Lewis, *The Politics of Motherhood* (London: Croom Helm, 1980), pp. 89–113.
33 *London Daily News*, 8 August 1907, p. 6. A photograph of such a construction can be seen in *The Sphere*, 26 December 1908, p. 4.
34 Lewis, *The Politics of Motherhood*, p. 98; Dyhouse, 'Working-Class Mothers', p. 76.
35 *Tower Hamlets Independent*, 16 January 1909, p. 3.
36 *Sheffield Evening Telegraph*, 29 July 1904, p. 4.

Further reading

Davin, Anna. *Growing Up Poor: Home, School, and Street in London, 1870–1914* (London: Rivers Oram Press, 1996).

Dyhouse, Carol. 'Working-Class Mothers and Infant Mortality', in Charles Webster (ed.), *Biology Medicine and Society 1840–1940* (Cambridge: Cambridge University Press, 2002).

Lewis, Jane. *The Politics of Motherhood* (London: Croom Helm, 1980).

Richmond, Vivienne. *Clothing the Poor in Nineteenth-Century England* (Cambridge: Cambridge University Press, 2013).

CHAPTER 5
FROM IMPROVISED TO SUBSIDISED SAFETY: FIREGUARDS
Jonathan Reinarz and Shane Ewen

Introduction

When it comes to the history of fire, the homes of the poor were the focus of prevention campaigns in the Victorian period. Not entirely unfounded, the material culture of burns and scalds in poor homes at this time included common items which posed potential fatal hazards, such as candles, paraffin lamps, kettles and wash tubs. Other objects regularly appeared in reports documenting attempted rescues, including clothing, carpets and blankets, which were used to smother the flames of burns victims, who were often the elderly, but even more frequently children under the age of ten. A preoccupation of contemporary publications, such hazards have been neglected in studies of health in the home.[1] While hazards and remedies evolved with technological and medical innovations since Victorian times, one object – albeit a largely absent one – in the homes of the poor remained a consistent feature of accident reports and became ever more rooted in debates around fire prevention by the end of the nineteenth century: the fireguard.

Despite the variety of domestic fire hazards, the most prominent was the hearth. In the homes of the poor, the hearth – particularly in Victorian and Edwardian England – was the heart of the family home, due to the warmth it generated, and as a means of cooking and washing. Yet, young children – unaware of fire's dangers – could easily find their clothing ignited or topple a pan of hot water when playing too close to the fire. Unsurprisingly, burns or scalds occurring in poorer homes were a consistent feature of accident reports throughout this period, with absent fireguards often noted as a contributory factor. This absence fuelled debates around fire prevention and an outcry for poorer householders to invest in a fireguard to avoid further domestic deaths.

By the mid-nineteenth century, a rising chorus of calls emerged for the proliferation of fireguards in the homes of the poor, starting with local coroners who used newspapers to communicate on fatal burns injuries coming before their courts. By the close of the first decade of the twentieth century, legislation intended to prevent such unnecessary deaths was introduced by politicians who primarily sought to encourage poorer households to purchase fireguards. Despite countless reminders of fireguards' benefits from at least the 1850s, change came only with the Children's Act (1908), which introduced fines if fatal fires were found to result from an unguarded fireplace. The implementation of fines,

Objects of Poverty

however, varied: while some magistrates punished parents for their negligence, others argued that losing a child was punishment enough.

Over successive decades, further newspaper reports and research undertaken by staff at newly established regional burns units, such as Glasgow and Birmingham, renewed the case for the use of fireguards, seeking to shift the burden from poor families to manufacturers, and discussions moved into medical publications. Despite some legislative success, the traditional open fire remained unguarded. In this chapter, we trace the place of fireguards in the homes of Britain's poor and their centrality to fire safety campaigns over approximately a century of burns-prevention campaigning. In so doing, we follow a particular object of the poor through coroners' inquests, local newspaper reports, medical publications, published reports and correspondence among fire prevention campaigners.

Early cases

By the 1830s, the British press regularly reported accounts of violent deaths, including burns and scalds.[2] Reports of burns injuries, initially revolving around middle-class sociability and the theatre, gradually diversified to include the homes and workplaces of the poor. Reports of domestic burns accidents regularly referred to an array of household objects which posed potential fire hazards, claiming hundreds of lives annually and causing thousands of non-fatal, yet life-changing, injuries. In contrast to the potential dangers posed by household objects like lamps, candles and kettles, the fireguard was mentioned repeatedly in inquest reports, most notably in its absence, for it was recognised as a cheap item which would greatly improve the safety of the home and its youngest inhabitants.

Given the centrality of metal manufacture to British industry at this time, cheap versions of this useful object were sold for as little as a shilling in provincial towns, but newspapers often advertised the more elegant and expensive guards destined for middle- and upper-class homes. The comparative shortage of cheap fireguards, however, did not go unnoticed. H. S. Stokes of Truro wrote to his local newspaper in the 1840s stating that manufacturers prepared to supply an efficient fireguard, even at a low price, would 'realise a fair pecuniary remuneration', as the demand for this object 'outstripped supply'. Stokes further suggested manufacturers would 'earn a richer reward in the blessings of the poor'.[3]

In contrast to ornate guards advertised in newspapers, cheaper guards recommended for poorer houses were made of wire. Following a death in Hull in 1838, a wealthy landlord provided his tenants with wire fireguards.[4] Such fireguards were also described as the cheapest form of protection a year later in a London newspaper.[5] In one case, following the death of a child, the jury provided a family near Gray's Inn-lane with funds to purchase a fireguard; the father pawned the item the next day, and another child in the house lost its life after its clothes caught fire.[6] Recognising the value of newspapers as a medium for communicating preventive messages, coroners became increasingly vocal in their criticism of unguarded fires leading to child fatalities. In 1841, for example, the *Morning Post* used the occasion of an inquest held at Charing Cross Hospital on a four-year-old boy burnt to death to comment on 'The Great Sacrifice of Infant Life by Fire'. Left alone at home with another child while his parents were at work, the boy was 'frightfully burned all over' after his clothes caught fire while lighting a piece of paper at the unguarded fireplace. Noting that this was his fifth inquest within the past eleven days involving burned children, the coroner urged 'every person having children' to install fireguards, available at a 'trifling' cost, to prevent such 'a sacrifice of human life'. Noises were also being made regarding introducing legislation at this early point.[7]

Within years, coroners throughout the country publicised similar messages. *Lloyd's Weekly Newspaper* published an article on 13 April 1845 describing another fiery death, prompting *Lancet* founder and coroner Thomas Wakely to call for the wider distribution of these objects:

> for some time past he had been making efforts to impress upon the minds of the poor ... the necessity of procuring fire-guards for every poor family. The other day a similar case was investigated, when he made some remarks upon that important subject ... to impress upon the clergy and dissenting ministers ... the necessity of seeing that the poor ... should be furnished with them gratuitously.[8]

Earlier, Wakely had encouraged members of the Tract Society to distribute fireguards.[9] A year on, Wakely hoped other metropolitan wards would follow the example of Queenhithe, the parishioners of which provided the poor with guards 'and made them fixtures, so that they could not part with them without committing a felony'.[10]

Vicky Holmes has argued that coroners not only reported burns accidents in the 1860s, but they attributed these incidents to 'maternal ignorance and carelessness'.[11] Authorities deemed mothers to be responsible for accident prevention within the home, and fireguards became a 'recurring angst' at inquests from the 1860s onwards.[12] The London and Southwark Coroners' inquest depositions from 1860 certainly support Holmes's contention, with neighbours frequently reporting that the mother was absent from the home when fatal accidents occurred.[13] Fathers, by comparison, were usually reported as being out at work from an early hour, reinforcing the prevailing gender ideology at the time, with men as breadwinner and women as homemaker. Inquests also reveal how common it was for neighbours to watch over other people's children while mothers ran errands, as well as the disastrous consequences of not asking for help, fearful perhaps of not keeping up 'a good "front" in the eyes of neighbours'.[14]

Based on press advertisements, the purchase of a fireguard was not a 'trifling' cost. Those identified by Holmes in the *Ipswich Journal* ranged from 11s 6d to 26s 6d in the mid-1870s.[15] Some local authorities recognised the financial challenges of burns prevention. At an inquest into the death of a three-year-old child in Leamington in 1860, coroner W. S. Poole noted that a friend of his was an advocate for 'all kinds of good Societies' then being established throughout the country. What he wanted to see, however, was 'a Society for the purpose of extending the use of fire-guards'.[16] In

Objects of Poverty

the charitable and humane desire to prevent burning accidents, tradesmen in certain regions were reputedly willing to provide the poor with fireguards at a nominal price.[17] In Dundee, the Society for the Prevention of Cruelty to Children distributed fireguards for 'a trifling sum'.[18] Others encouraged greater use of 'the old nursery fireguard in working men's houses'.[19] As the tendency to distribute fireguards increased in the late nineteenth century, so too did cynical claims that the poor would merely pawn these objects.[20]

Many coroners voiced concerns that poor families continued to sell fireguards to purchase other necessities. In Lambeth Coroner's Court in December 1897, an inquest was held into the death of a three-and-a-half-year-old girl who had been fatally burned in her home at Hersham, Walton-on-Thames. To make ends meet, her mother gradually sold their furniture. When asked by the deputy coroner whether she had a fireguard, the mother replied that she had owned one, but sold it 'to get bread for my children'.[21] A similar case was heard in 1910, shortly after new legislation had been introduced, of another child burned after the mother sold the fireguard for food, as it 'was the only article upon which the woman could raise money'. On investigating the condition of the home, a police sergeant 'found the home absolutely clean, and the woman had since bought another fireguard out of the insurance money for the child'.[22] While one contemporary coroner expressed concern that the widespread availability of child life insurance for poor families was 'incentive to cruel neglect', there is no evidence to suggest that cases such as these constituted anything less than tragic accidents.[23]

The 1908 Children Act

Reports from approximately 200 coroners revealed that between 1899 and 1900, 1,425 of 1,684 (85 per cent) inquests involving children who died of burns were deemed the result of an absent fireguard, with the overwhelming majority of cases occurring in poor homes.[24] With the support of increasingly vocal coroners, the Liberal government elected in 1906 consolidated various pieces of legislation in the Children Act (1908), which covered the whole of Britain. Marking a new legal relationship between child, parent and the state, and described by one contemporary as heralding 'a great and fundamental step in child protection', the act dealt specifically with culpability regarding two particular types of fatal household accidents involving young children, overlaid infants and burnt children.[25] Section 15 of the act clearly outlines the putative regime that led to periodic lapses in the enforcement of the law. In cases where a child under the age of seven years was fatally injured at an unguarded fireplace, the adult in charge was liable to a fine of up to £10 (Children Act 1908: Section 15). Not every authority enforced the legislation to its full extent, most coroners choosing to mention the value of a fireguard during inquests;[26] it was also made clear that no offence was committed in cases where children were being supervised.[27] Yet despite legislation, fireguards were not always an effective preventative measure from playing with fire. Young children were still regularly burned after pushing paper or other combustible material through the gaps in the fireguard's wire meshing in efforts to play with flames. The risk was addressed in a 1930s poster campaign organised by the National 'Safety First' Association (later renamed the Royal Society for the Prevention of Accidents), showing a young child attempting to push a toy through the gaps in a wire guard.[28] The vivid orange and red colours of the fire and surrounding room provide a visually striking warning for the vulnerable child risking his safety in the absence of adult supervision. The central message – that fireguards alone provide insufficient protection for young children – must have resonated with audiences up and down the country who were well-versed in being lectured on the importance of installing guards but perhaps less so in the need for continued supervision of young children.[29]

Those who could not afford fireguards improvised makeshift guards. In one case in Portsmouth, a metal tray had been placed before a fire, but – perhaps unsurprisingly – this did not prevent a spark from igniting the cot of a ten-month-old infant sleeping nearby. During the inquest, the coroner suggested that an ordinary mesh fireguard would not have protected the child.[30] Others recognised that a cheap 1s-fireguard would not last long in a house full of children, and several MPs called for Section 15 to be amended to cover 'exposing the child to risk' rather than death or serious injury. However, government files reveal little interest in either strengthening the law or enforcing its compliance during the 1920s, mirroring a general apathy towards fire service reform at this time.[31]

Given the ineffectualness of the legislation, it is unsurprising that the fireguard remained absent in many poorer homes, years after the act's passage. For example, a Polish miner living in Linlithgow had been warned by the police in August 1911 of the necessity of guarding his fire according to the act but did not heed their advice. Over three years later, in November 1914, his wife briefly left their three children unattended to visit a milk cart in the street. In the few minutes she was absent, one of the children lit a piece of paper and ignited the clothing of another child. The Procurator Fiscal, upon questioning by the Sheriff who brought the case to trial, stated that the incident would have been impossible had a guard been in place. To this, the accused responded that he had ordered a fireguard some time ago, but there did not seem to be any in the district, including in any other houses, and his order went unfulfilled. A fine of 10s was nevertheless imposed by the Sheriff.[32] A similar story in the *Northern Whig* drew attention to the number of burned children being reported in the pages of the Belfast newspaper. Recognising the cruelty of fining parents whose children died of burns, the author of one such letter reminded readers of a local fund that had been set up by the late Sir William Ewart to provide the poor with fireguards. Besides drawing greater attention to the hazard in the press, the author suggested that social workers, given their access to the homes of the poor, assist inspectors in enforcing the legislation.[33]

Fireguard campaigns

In 1942, at the instigation of staff at the Glasgow Royal Infirmary, social worker Marion Wright investigated the social circumstances of fifty burns cases admitted to the

Infirmary. Following home visits and interviews, forty-five of these cases were found to have occurred in domestic circumstances, and 80 per cent of patients were under the age of fourteen. Lack of fire protection equipment and cramped living conditions were major factors in these accidents. Despite the terms of the Children Act, none of these homes, including the thirty-nine where children under seven years of age resided, had a fireguard. Wright believed that nineteen of the fifty accidents investigated would have been impossible or improbable had there been adequate fire protection, leading her to advocate that 'better housing conditions' and 'more rigorous enforcement of the Children Act' was required.[34] In an article in the *Lancet*, published in 1945, Wright stressed that parents remained unaware of their legal obligations; one housewife had even donated her fireguard to a 'salvage drive'.[35]

Despite governmental concerns over burns, Leonard Colebrook, head of the Burns Unit at Birmingham Accident Hospital, claimed legislation had achieved little. The Children Act had passed into law when Colebrook was still a medical student, during years when deaths from burns and scalds totalled 2,000 a year.[36] Although deaths from burns and scalds had decreased to 700 annually by 1950, 15,000–20,000 people were admitted to hospital annually, and another 50,000 outpatients were treated for non-fatal burns. Colebrook calculated that 120 deaths and 900 further severe injuries resulted from contact with gas or electric fires alone, many of which could have been prevented by fixing guards to fireplaces. Although successive home secretaries had failed to act on this knowledge since at least 1919,[37] Colebrook, joined by his wife Vera, pushed for new legislation using Private Members bills.[38] The safety message would now be communicated in the scientific, technical and lay press by the recently retired burns specialist to build a groundswell of professional and public support before approaching the government.

The Colebrooks went on a national tour of branches of the Women's Institute and persuaded them to pass resolutions about fireguards. At the same time, Leonard rallied his medical colleagues to produce a pamphlet emphasising the economic and physical toll of burns based on their hospital work.[39] The mere publication of the facts appeared to have no effect on reducing these numbers. Few people appeared willing to take up the cause of fireguards because the simple act of fixing a wire guard on a gas or electric fire was bound to make it more expensive, and no manufacturer wished to incur the financial penalty of making safer heaters. The Colebrooks, however, managed to get an appointment with the Labour Minister of Health, Sir Hilary Marquand, to explain their campaign. Having brought some guards for the purpose of demonstration, they attached one to the minister's electric fire, which, to their surprise, was unguarded at the time of the visit.[40] Pamphlets were subsequently sent to each Member of Parliament before Conservative backbencher Denys Bullard presented the Colebrooks' Bill 'to prohibit the sale of certain heating appliances without an effective fireguard'. It received cross-party support from the House and was read on 5 December 1951, receiving Royal Assent on 1 August 1952. The act introduced a fine of £50 on any person who, in the course of business, sold or offered for sale a gas fire, electric fire or oil heater which was either not fitted with a guard or contained an inadequate guard, subject to local inspection and testing.[41]

Nonetheless, the Act was not retrospective and, therefore, did not apply to the nation's 12 million open fires.[42] While it would take time to retire old appliances from household use, the open coal fire remained 'the outstanding hazard of the English home'.[43] As a result, in 1964, after attending a series of fatal fires, Walsall firefighter Raymond Dyke campaigned for the mandatory fitting of fire guards in all homes, especially council houses. Besides receiving early support from multiple organisations – including the Fire Brigades Union, Royal Society for the Prevention of Accidents (RoSPA), Consumer Council, local Chambers of Trade and Birmingham's Burns Unit – progress stalled, primarily because Walsall Housing Committee baulked at the expense of providing every council home with a guard, estimated at around £20,000.[44]

Dyke, nevertheless, advanced his campaign, turning to the media for support, having already successfully communicated his message about the compulsory installation of fireguards in council houses on *Midlands Today*, broadcast in May 1966. Unable to find a single shop that stocked guards locally, he started selling discounted fireguards at his local fire station,[45] before announcing his national campaign in January 1968 with an article in the *Times* encouraging 1,000 local authorities nationally to fit guards in council houses.[46] The National Archives include examples of fireguards suitable for installation, with one popular model being the 'Ajax', which could be fastened directly into the fireplace and fitted with a brass spark-proof front to provide additional protection, but no resolution could be agreed.[47] By July 1968, Dyke had provided all homes on a list drawn up by welfare services with an inexpensive guard, claiming that 'people know a good bargain when they see one'.[48] He was not wrong: the following year, ironmongers complained that Dyke was 'too good at selling fireguards' and was 'unfair competition' to their businesses.[49]

Conclusion

For approximately a century, the fireguard was the most highly politicised object in poorer homes, beginning in the mid-Victorian period when its absence frequently contributed to the deaths of working-class children. With the passage of the Children Act (1908), its absence from homes could lead to the imposition of fines on families too poor to buy even the standard household furnishings. The burden of providing fireguards, however, shifted dramatically in the middle of the twentieth century with the introduction of a campaign led by burns specialist Leonard Colebrook. Throughout Colebrook's campaign, issues like poverty retained their place in reports of children burned as a result of absent or faulty fireguards, but this household object was now frequently discussed in the pages of medical publications. The limits of the Fireguard Act (1952), which required only new gas and electric fires to be guarded, resulted in a final campaign led by Walsall firefighter Ray Dyke, who drew on modern media, as well as earlier Victorian charitable campaigns, to finally put fireguards in the homes of the poor, and keep them there.

Notes

1. There is no mention of fireguards in Mark Jackson, *Health and the Modern Home* (London: Routledge, 2007). Notable exceptions are Ellen Ross, *Love and Toil: Motherhood in Outcast London, 1890–1918* (Oxford: Oxford University Press, 1993), p. 181; Vicky Holmes, 'Dangerous Spaces: Working-Class Homes and Fatal Household Accidents in Suffolk, 1840–1900', PhD thesis (University of Essex, 2012). Also see Vicky Holmes, 'Absent Fireguards and Burnt Children: Coroners and The Development Of Clause 15 Of The Children Act 1908', *Law, Crime and History*, 2 (2012), pp. 21–58
2. Ryan Vieira, 'Rethinking the History of the Risk Society: Accident Reporting, the Social Order and the *London Daily Press*, 1800–30', in Tom Crook and Mike Esbester (eds), *Governing Risks in Modern Britain: Danger, Safety and Accidents, c. 1800–2000* (London: Palgrave Macmillan, 2016), pp. 55–76.
3. *Royal Cornwall Gazette*, 18 December 1846.
4. *Hull Advertiser and Exchange Gazette*, 2 November 1838.
5. *Morning Advertiser*, 29 March 1839.
6. *Morning Post*, 29 November 1841.
7. *Morning Post*, 26 November 1841.
8. *Lloyd's Weekly Newspaper*, 13 April 1845.
9. *Bell's Weekly Messenger*, 14 September 1844.
10. *Lloyd's Weekly Newspaper*, 13 April 1845.
11. Holmes, 'Dangerous Spaces', p. 311.
12. Ibid., p. 323-6.
13. London Metropolitan Archives (hereafter LMA) CLA/041/IQ/03/27, City of London Inquests, 1860.
14. Joanna Bourke, *Working-Class Cultures in Britain, 1890–1960* (London: Routledge, 1994), p. 180. For examples, see LMA CLA/041/IQ/03/27.
15. Holmes, 'Dangerous Spaces', p. 319.
16. *Leamington Spa Courier*, 25 February 1860.
17. *Walsall Free Press and General Advertiser*, 13 January 1866.
18. *Dundee Courier*, 'Dundee Society for the Prevention of Cruelty to Children', 6 February 1892.
19. *Edinburgh Evening News*, 'Fire-guards wanted for work men's houses', 2 March 1893.
20. Holmes, 'Dangerous Spaces', p. 303.
21. *Eastern Daily Press*, 30 December 1897.
22. *Dundee Evening Telegraph*, 10 March 1910.
23. Paul Johnson, 'Class Law in Victorian England', *Past & Present*, 141 (1993): p. 157; Daniel J. R. Grey, '"Liable to Very Gross Abuse": Murder, Moral Panic and Cultural Fears over Infant Life Insurance, 1875–1914', *Journal of Victorian Culture*, 18:1 (2013): pp. 54–71.
24. Holmes, 'Dangerous Spaces', p. 338.
25. John Stewart, 'Children, Parents and the State: The Children Act, 1908', *Children & Society*, 9:1 (1995): pp. 90–9; Harry Hendrick, *Child Welfare: Historical Dimensions, Contemporary Debate* (Bristol: Policy Press, 2003), pp. 82–6; Kate Bradley, 'The Children Act 1908: Centennial Reflections, Contemporary Perspectives, University of Kent, 30 June–1 July 2008', *History Workshop Journal*, 68:1 (2009): pp. 303–5.
26. *Birmingham Post*, 10 August 1921.
27. *Birmingham Mail*, 12 January 1920.
28. Wellcome Collection, 385381, A log fire with a guard in front, which a little boy touches with his rattle. Colour lithograph, 1937. https://wellcomecollection.org/works/m5rmqrf8 (accessed 3 May 2024).

29 Wellcome Collection 38538i, National 'Safety First' Association. Colour lithograph, 'Guard That Fire' (London and Sheffield: Loxley Brothers, 1937).
30 *Shields Daily News*, 16 March 1921.
31 See correspondence and minutes in the National Archives (hereafter TNA) HO 45/11053, File 174397/44, Amendments to 1908 Children Act, s.15; Shane Ewen, *Fighting Fires: Creating the British Fire Service, c. 1800–1978* (Basingstoke: Palgrave, 2009), pp. 117–24.
32 *Linlithgowshire Gazette*, 11 December 1914.
33 *Northern Whig*, 7 January 1921.
34 Marion T. Wright, 'Social Factors in Aetiology of Burns', *British Medical Journal*, 1:4336 (12 February 1944): p. 230.
35 Marion T. Wright, 'Relations of Burning Injuries to Social Circumstances', *Lancet* 245:6336 (3 February 1945): p. 155.
36 William Charles Noble, *Coli, Great Healer of Men: The Biography of Dr Leonard Colebrook* (London: Heinemann, 1974), p. 104.
37 TNA HO 45/11053, File 174,397/46, Commissioner of Metropolitan Police to Under Secretary of State on 'Gas Fires', 28 April 1919. A minute, dated 22 May 1919, recommended amending Section 15 of the 1908 Act to include gas fires, but was not acted upon.
38 This was a process by which public bills could be introduced by backbench MPs and Lords and which did not appear on the sitting government's legislative agenda.
39 L. Colebrook, *The Case for Legislation Which Aims at Reducing the Suffering and the Deaths Due to Burning Accidents in the Home* (Privately produced, 1952).
40 Noble, *Coli, Great Healer of Men*, pp. 107–8.
41 House of Commons Debates, 14 March 1952, vol. 497, cc. 1795–883.
42 Noble, *Coli: Great Healer of Men*, p. 110.
43 *The Times*, 7 January 1952.
44 *Birmingham Daily Post*, 4 July 1966.
45 *Walsall Observer*, 4 March 1966.
46 *The Times*, 9 January 1968.
47 TNA HLG 117/200, Ministry of Housing and Local Government, Provision of Fire Guard Fittings, c. 1963–1967
48 *Walsall Observer*, 26 July 1968.
49 *Daily Mirror*, 12 September 1969.

Further reading

Bourke, Joanna. *Working-Class Cultures in Britain, 1890–1960* (London: Routledge, 1994).
Bradley, Kate. 'The Children Act 1908: Centennial Reflections, Contemporary Perspectives, University of Kent, 30 June–1 July 2008'. *History Workshop Journal*, 68:1 (2009): pp. 303–5.
Ewen, Shane. *Fighting Fires: Creating the British Fire Service, c. 1800–1978* (Basingstoke: Palgrave, 2009).
Hendrick, Harry. *Child Welfare: Historical Dimensions, Contemporary Debate* (Bristol: Policy Press, 2003).
Holmes, Vicky. 'Dangerous Spaces: Working-Class Homes and Fatal Household Accidents in Suffolk, 1840–1900', PhD thesis (University of Essex, 2012).
Jackson, Mark. *Health and the Modern Home* (London: Routledge, 2007).
Noble, William Charles. *Coli, Great Healer of Men: The Biography of Dr Leonard Colebrook* (London: Heinemann, 1974).
Stewart, John. 'Children, Parents and the State: The Children Act, 1908'. *Children & Society*, 9:1 (1995): pp. 90–9.

CHAPTER 6
COAL IN THE BATH: POVERTY, MODERNITY AND THE WELFARE STATE IN POST-WAR BRITAIN
Michael Lambert

Introduction

In British history, coal is typically associated with wealth rather than poverty. Coal was mined, transported and burned to fuel the fires of industrialisation, urbanisation and modernisation, transforming Britain and the world throughout the nineteenth and twentieth centuries.[1] 'Our civilisation', wrote George Orwell in 1937, 'is founded on coal more completely than one realises'.[2] Workers and owners alike recognised its significance as 'King Coal'.[3] Yet, at the time Orwell was writing, coal was already declining. As a fuel, it was slowly being replaced by gas and electricity, a trend which continued after 1945.[4] The 1952 Great Smog of London accelerated coal's demise, imposing restrictions on the use of coal as a domestic fuel and new regulations over its quality as part of clean air public health policies.[5] The importance of coal and coal mining remained marked in post-war British politics, society and the economy despite decline and deindustrialisation.[6] However, it was no longer the basis upon which British affluence and civilisation were built.

Decline and deindustrialisation meant coal increasingly came to symbolise what was backwards, dirty and old in contrast with new, modern and clean Britain. It is here that it became associated with poverty rather than wealth, represented through the ubiquitous 'coal in the bath' myth. Emerging in the aftermath of the First World War, implicit in this fiction was the political argument that the state should not provide modern living conditions for ordinary working-class citizens to improve their welfare because *they*, like coal, are backwards, dirty and outdated. Little account was taken of the slum conditions which they were forced to endure. But it was with the creation of the welfare state following the Second World War that this myth took hold in both official and national consciousness. Despite extensive redistribution of wealth and the provision of social, health and other welfare services from 1945, poverty remained a behavioural rather than social problem in the eyes of the state. It is here that coal's symbolic power shifted from national wealth to household poverty.

This chapter uses coal as a lens to explore tensions between modernity and poverty in the post-war British welfare state. Such tensions were common to Western industrialised nations over the same period pursuing similar social policies.[7] Here, the materiality of coal is central. Politicians and officials saw it as a dirty pollutant associated with disease and squalor, where blackened places and unwashed people were synonymous. It became a justification for limiting state responsibility if people simply turned new homes into slums due to their backwardness. Yet slums were cleared slowly, and new homes were planned without considering the needs of their inhabitants. For working-class families, coal remained an important fuel in domestic life, especially for those unable to afford or access modern alternatives.

The chapter is divided into two parts. The first considers the origins of the 'coal in the bath' myth and its continued traction in the official understanding of working-class life and poverty after 1945. The second part uses reports from social workers – as everyday welfare state officials – encountering coal during decision-making in the lives of working-class families to consider its more complex and contradictory meanings as an object of poverty given the gap between the promises of the welfare state and its capacity to deliver. The chapter concludes by reflecting upon this gap, the persistence of poverty and the limits of modernity in post-war Britain.

Coal in the bath

The moral panic about 'coal in the bath' began with the rehousing of families from slums to new council properties in large numbers after the First World War. Public rhetoric by politicians focused on building 'homes fit for heroes', offering modern amenities and raising living standards.[8] Having piped water and a fixed bath became a 'barometer of modernity' as planners sought to replace shared toilets, often in alleyways behind or between houses, with more private, hygienic sanitation in individual homes.[9] Yet support was not universal and many grumbled at the public purse shouldering the cost for what they saw as a private problem. They saw working-class families and slums as synonymous, with rehousing only perpetuating squalor and dirt as tenants were transferred. 'If you give council houses to working people they will only use them to keep coal in the bath' was how the Labour Member of Parliament for Salford Frank Allaun characterised this dismissive but prevalent attitude among those who paid for but did not live in council housing.[10] Playing on political and class prejudices, 'coal in the bath' tropes became part of the mythology of 'middle class' respectability, the 'Tory stegosaurus' in central and local government, and welfare officials alike.[11]

By 1939, coal, as a source of dirt and ignorance, became a powerful symbol for middle-class observers, politicians and officials to view crude working-class habits. The coal-in-the-bath mythology supplied a simple explanatory framework which saw behaviour, not the environment, as the problem. This was an essentialist stereotype which cast working-class behaviour as aberrant, as the other, and bore little relationship to the realities of working-class lives.

This view intensified during and after the Second World War as state responsibility for welfare expanded. It had become widespread among officials rather than simply confined to reactionary politicians. Indeed, one social worker married to a midwife claimed to have experienced, second-hand, the practice for themselves while working in Langley, an overspill council housing estate for Manchester's slums:

> When [my wife and I] first went to Langley we'd heard the old stories about coal in the bath on council estates and lavatory seats used for picture frames … We expected to disprove all those slurs – as far as we regard them. In fact, *my wife has seen coal in the bath* when she went into a house to deliver a child.[12]

Similarly, a journalist reporting on social work practice found that she 'sometimes came across that despairing coals-in-the-bath view among welfare officials – and found it almost justified'.[13] Elizabeth Irvine, a psychiatric social worker, included in her typology of the 'problem family' – those living in poverty disproportionately consuming the time of social workers and resources of the welfare state – that there was often 'coals or worse in the bath'.[14] This played into the scatological qualities of the coal-in-the-bath mythology. The Deputy Medical Officer of Health (MOH) for Rotherham complained that when encountering 'problem families' 'tin baths containing several days' accumulation of faeces and urine are not unknown'.[15] The Deputy MOH for Liverpool summarised the dilemma as one of certain families having 'stone-age standards of conduct in the cities of an age of steel'.[16] The idea that working-class families stored coal – or worse – in the bath epitomised backwards, dirty habits and justified limiting the modern, material benefits of the welfare state in the eyes of politicians, officials and 'respectable' society.

The hoary mythology of coal in the bath contained several threads. Firstly, at a symbolic level it equated working-class families with slums. Secondly, it changed the focus of debates on poverty from the environment and society – the slum – to those which made it: working-class families both individually and collectively. Thirdly, the limits and failures of modernity were explained away as personal failings rather than those of the state or society. Fourthly, for officials in the welfare state working at the proverbial 'coal face' with families in poverty, it provided a means to separate the deserving from the undeserving and restrict state support when resources were limited.[17] The mythology was deeply stigmatising. The academic Diane Reay experienced this as a university student in the 1960s, when one of her sociology lecturers repeated the coal-in-the-bath myth as fact, much to her dismay as a working-class girl from a coal-mining community already out of place.[18] In short, coal in the bath came to represent class, social and professional judgements of poverty against expectations of modernity and the welfare state in post-war Britain.

Coal and poverty

Moving beyond 'coal in the bath' as a symbolic frame of reference about poverty, I now examine its place as a material object of working-class life in the post-war period. Using social work case files on working-class families labelled as a 'problem', I explore its more complex and contradictory meanings.[19] By reading such case files against the grain, coal can be used to explore the everyday lives and attitudes of those living in poverty, the gap between the rhetoric and reality of modernity, and how it shaped family routines and domesticity.

Although gas and electricity gradually replaced coal, many working-class families continued to live in properties which required solid fuel throughout the post-war period. Modernity spread only slowly and unevenly despite political promises.[20] According to Frank Trentmann and Anna Carlsson-Hyslop, 'Housing estates were planned with categories of imagined users in mind' and anticipated fuel use reflected certain expectations of comfort and convenience.[21]

For new properties, this meant central heating, but poorer working-class families often occupied older terraced or council housing. Indeed, authorities operated rigid housing hierarchies which excluded many and marginalised others to undesirable or unpopular properties.[22] For example, during the interwar period, houses on the Norley Hall Estate in Wigan were planned with three solid fuel fires because miners – the bulk of tenants – were entitled to free or concessionary coal. After the war, as the industry declined and restrictions on its use changed, tenants were left without alternatives.[23] Keeping families warm, fed with hot food and with clean dry clothes proved a constant struggle in such conditions as social workers reported,[24] although interventions were focused on educating mothers rather than modernising homes.

The presence or absence of coal was frequently an indicator of whether families could afford to heat their homes, have warm food and ensure that their limited resources were being used appropriately and with – in the eyes of the middle-class social workers – the right priorities in mind. The K family in the small mill town of Bury typified these judgements. The health visitor, part of the public health service, reported to the local 'problem family' committee in 1957 that the K family 'can maintain a constant heat with a coal fire' during the winter, allowing the family to have at least one warm meal a day.[25] Two years later, a different health visitor stressed that there was '*no coal fire in the house*' because the mother 'hadn't been able to pay for last months coal'.[26] Poor budgeting was seen as the difficulty, and there was discussion among officials about what this meant for the children, if it constituted neglect, and whether or not further intervention was required.

Sufficiency of coal was not considered in isolation but in relation to other sources of energy. A social worker working on Kirkby, a Liverpool overspill estate, in 1960 reported on one family that 'so far they still only have a coal fire to cook on' because the gas was disconnected due to debts. The family was 'not completely hopeless' in their eyes as the father had saved some of his pay towards clearing the debt allowing a return to a modern, cleaner fuel in place of coal as a reluctant but necessary substitute.[27] Such discretionary and judgemental decisions also underpinned decisions around disconnection by nationalised utility companies.[28] The 'problem family' committee for Halifax felt that Mrs M was 'clean and reasonable but is always up against the lack of money': in 1956 she was reported to have been without coal for eighteen months and did not clear gas and electricity debts for a further two years.[29] Again, discussion was held about the health of the children and questions of neglect, but action was deferred as she was otherwise considered a capable mother.

Coal afforded flexibility as a fuel because it could be bought and used when other, more modern and convenient means were unavailable. Gas and electricity were directly piped into houses but required payment meters which were collected periodically and, for families in poverty or its individual members, provided a ready and tempting financial resource in times of need. Ethnographic studies of inner-city Liverpool slums during the 1950s found this practice to be widespread and perceived as legitimate when necessary.[30] This was the case for Mrs AJ in Litherland, a Liverpool suburb, in 1963, who was found to be cooking on the coal fire following the disconnection of her gas after she was found to be using halfpennies instead of shillings for her meter.[31] While on probation for child neglect in 1966, Mrs GB from New Mills, Derbyshire, stole from her electricity meter to provide food and clothes for her three children. Using coal as an alternative fuel allowed her to continue to cook and heat the home despite extensive gas and electricity debts and rent arrears eventually leading to her prosecution.[32]

However, the flexibility afforded by coal was not always preferred to the convenience of other fuels, nor was it a reliable and secure alternative. Like the AJ and GB families, Mrs DBW, a 26-year-old mother of five from Ashton-under-Lyne near Manchester, also used coal through necessity owing to gas debts and disconnection. 'After cooking on a coal fire for the past two years she thinks it is a luxury to cook by gas', according to the health visitor's 1962 report on the family.[33] Electricity *and* coal debts left the MB family in Penwortham, near Preston, with 'no means of cooking … except on a paraffin stove which is not very satisfactory'. The health visitor recognised that this impacted other routine aspects of domestic life, leaving Mrs MB with no means of washing and drying clothes during the winter.[34] A 1975 report on fuel poverty in Manchester recognised the pitfalls of metered central heating systems with disconnection leaving families literally freezing rather than using fires as occurred in terraced housing.[35] Although there is some truth in sociologist Hilary Land's assessment that poorer families limited spending 'not by using cheaper substitutes … but by buying less coal altogether', the social work case files point to coal being used as a flexible rather than necessarily cheaper alternative.[36]

In other cases, the absence of coal signified that, like Mrs M in Halifax, no alternative source of fuel or energy was available. However, essential family needs dictated that *something* needed to be consumed for heating and cooking. For one family in Bury, officials reported 'the fire being kept going with wood only as there was no coal' in 1968.[37] In rural Warwickshire, the WML family resorted to burning furniture and household fixtures in the winter of 1956, as the property lacked gas and the electricity was disconnected due to debts. This left them with few alternatives to support their three children, much to the dismay of officials that led to warnings from the National Society for the Prevention of Cruelty to Children (NSPCC) about prosecution.[38] These instances led the MOH for rural Chesterfield to propose 'the erection of a special type of austerity house' made of indestructible concrete fittings to prevent damage and misuse.[39] Although 'unsatisfactory tenants' were subject to special consideration by the Ministry of Health,[40] even they rejected the proposal as a poor use of resources and stigmatising.

Objects of Poverty

The absence of coal should not be seen as an indicator of absolute poverty alone. It also showed how families in poverty relative to others made decisions about when to buy coal, heat their homes and cook given limited budgets. In 1955, one family in Halifax was without coal, gas and electricity owing to debts. The 'problem family' committee looked unfavourably upon this case, and the father was prosecuted for child neglect by the NSPCC. The debt should be seen in context, as it mounted in the run-up to Christmas with the family looking to celebrate the festivities and buy presents for the children.[41] A similar situation existed for Mrs MFB, who was also prosecuted in 1960 along with her husband. The MOH reported: 'No meals are cooked and hardly any means for cooking. No coal or other means of heating'.[42] Coal and warmth were sacrificed for other needs judged essential by officials. In another case, a mother wrote in 1952 that she was 'very sorry to have to tell you that as I am gradually getting into debt and having to refuse such necessities as coal'.[43] This was also seasonal, with families often using less coal and eating fewer hot meals during the warmer summer months. Views were divided over what constituted a necessity for families in poverty but making the 'wrong' choice in the eyes of officials could lead to severe judgement and intervention.

Conversely, the presence of too much coal was also deemed to be a hallmark of poverty. It showed a lack of proper budgeting in the eyes of officials. Social investigators complained that many families used coal 'lavishly' in Manchester as low costs encouraged consumption.[44] A public health study of housing and families found that the consumption of coal was excessive and wholly disproportionate given the small size of homes and the amount of heat that fires produced.[45] Complicating the distinction between absence and presence was an official judgement on the JW family in Liverpool in 1954. 'The gas was cut off, and the only means of lighting was by candle and all cooking had to be done on the fire', yet according to the health visitor this 'necessitated using more coal than the family could afford'.[46] Such distinctions also occurred within families. In 1962 Mr MEH bemoaned his wife's profligate use of fuel – especially when he was absent at work – along with other unnecessary spending. However, because Mr MEH handed his entire wage packet to his wife rather than retaining some, as husbands often did,[47] the NSPCC and health visitor found him equally complicit in the poor state of the children.[48]

Coal and its consumption existed within a larger narrative of poverty that alluded to a lack of judgement and poor behaviour. A study of the activities of a voluntary social work organisation in the 1970s included this vignette of encounters common to practice:

> The Barlows' house is run down even by the standards of the estate, the garden trampled into mud, the woodwork scarred, the window covered by a filthy piece of cloth supplemented by newspaper. Inside, a coal fire burns on a summer day in a front room which is crammed with indescribable junk, old clothes, clapped-out chairs, bits of wood, boxes, an ancient radio cabinet.[49]

Similarly, the practice of wrapping coal in disused newspapers from fish and chips to aid burning was considered one of the most 'gross sanitary habits' by middle-class women reformers.[50]

It was not just the presence or absence of coal, or when families did or did not burn it that pointed towards poverty. The ability to buy and store coal was significant. Coal debts normally mounted when families could not pay for deliveries or were excluded from clubs due to poor credit. Buying in bulk from the coal man made it cheaper, convenient and accessible, given the weight and dirt involved in transportation. Yet many older terraced properties lacked a coal bunker to store coal.[51] Even those with an external store, there was the issue of theft forcing some families to store coal inside their houses, an impractical solution in the eyes of officials.[52] Although, notably, none of the nearly 2,000 social work case files consulted mentioned coal being kept in the bath. A practical recourse was to buy coal only when they needed, but buying in smaller quantities meant coal was more expensive and availability was not always guaranteed. During the winter of 1966, a health visitor reported on the conditions of the F family in Bury: 'Very cold today – no room heating because the local shops have sold out of small bags of pre-packed coal and an electric fire is too expensive for this family'.[53]

If coal was not delivered in bulk, then transporting it home presented another practical problem. In 1960, a girl reported as persistently absent from school was seen out 'frequently, on one occasion fetching coal'.[54] This was due to her mother being ill, leading to her children fulfilling expected domestic responsibilities. Another girl remembers using an old pram to collect coal, or buying marked-up small bags from the corner shop when her family's debts meant deliveries were suspended.[55] This was relatively common. Similarly, as part of a lengthy review into her tragic death in 1973, officials noted that seven-year-old Maria Colwell was once seen struggling to carry a bag of coal home two-thirds of her own body weight.[56] Such practical issues were frequent, with mothers and their young children having to carry coal and other household goods over long distances as bus services were infrequent and expensive to outer council estates, and then struggling upstairs as lifts were often vandalised or broken.[57]

Dangerous housing was linked to the presence of coal, with the W household in Bury typifying some of the physical dangers posed. In 1965, the health visitor reported: 'All cooking is done on an unguarded coal fire – danger frequently stressed'.[58] This was echoed by a public health doctor in Blackburn who profiled a 'problem family' in his annual report: 'House and family always filthy, children often show minor burns though a fireguard (never in its place unless the fire is out!) has been provided'.[59] Of course, mothers were deemed responsible for ensuring the safety of their children rather than the material conditions of the home environment.[60] In Shoeburyness, Essex, Mrs MB had her three children taken into care and was prosecuted for neglect in 1963 because of a damaging house fire which began as washing dried on the fireguard during poor winter weather.[61] As Vicky Holmes has shown elsewhere, this prosecution reflected the culmination of changing professional and public attitudes towards risk and responsibility in the home, with household necessity being recast as neglect in the presence or absence of fireguards.[62]

On the other hand, the absence of coal and warmth stoked damp and other household hazards. In 1966, a health visitor in Bury complained that 'Milk for the children was being heated on the coal fire' in an unsanitary manner owing to gas and electric disconnection due to debt.[63] In 1956, one Halifax family complained that 'the house is very damp'. The 'problem family' committee reported that the 'Children have been ill since the move into the house. Chief Public Health Inspector is said to have reported the house to be unfit. Mrs C has never had a fire since she moved in'.[64] The family were denied rehousing, although it was common practice for such families to be allocated substandard property or houses condemned for demolition instead of new ones.[65] Mrs GL nearly suffered the same fate as Mrs MB in 1966 when authorities in Liverpool threatened to take her five children into care due to neglect unless she prioritised keeping the house warm.[66] Yet poverty placed both Mrs GL and Mrs C in situations where the ideals of social workers could not be realised. Rather than individual failure, as with coal across social workers' reports and accounts, this primarily reflects the limits of modernity and the welfare state in post-war Britain.

Conclusion

Despite its continued importance to political, social and economic life, coal became a signifier of poverty and backwardness rather than affluence and modernity in post-war Britain. The idea that working-class people kept coal in the bath continued to exert a hold on political and professional circles that ran the welfare state. It underpinned a behavioural explanation of poverty which saw people creating slums, rather than poor environmental and living conditions determining what they did and how they lived. It allowed officials to cling to the imagined ideals of modernity enabled by the welfare state, which, in turn, were used to restrict and ration its material benefits. This optimism about the state and society overcoming poverty proved overly ambitious and unrealistic, and the gap with reality can be seen when social workers encountered families during their duties.

However, coal was more than a symbolic association between people and places as old, dirty, backwards and primitive. Coal continued to shape domestic life, routines and lived experiences of working-class life beyond 1945. While there are clear limitations in using official case files to understand working-class attitudes, experiences and uses of coal in everyday home and family life given the middle-class viewpoint, they show how, as a material object, it exposed everyday struggles by families to survive in conditions of poverty. The physical remnants of coal on the grime that covers buildings and in domestic architecture, such as chimneys and coal bunkers, only scratch the surface of the more complex and contradictory set of shared meanings on what coal meant, how it was used, and its place in meeting a range of needs. For both families and officials, coal represents judgements on how to prioritise running a home, raising children and participating in society when a lack of money presents impossible choices between heating and eating. In short, coal as a material object tells us much about post-war Britain's perceptions and experiences of poverty.

Notes

1. Jeremy Paxman, *Black Gold: The History of How Coal Made Britain* (London: William Collins, 2022).
2. George Orwell, *The Road to Wigan Pier* (London: Secker and Warburg, [1937] 1959), p. 23.
3. Tony Hall, *King Coal: Miners, Coal and Britain's Industrial Future* (Harmondsworth: Penguin, 1981).
4. Frank Trentmann and Anna Carlsson-Hyslop, 'The Evolution of Energy Demand in Britain: Politics, Daily Life, and Public Housing, 1920s–1970s', *Historical Journal*, 61:3 (2018): pp. 807–39.
5. Peter Thorsheim, *Inventing Pollution: Coal, Smoke, and Culture in Britain since 1800* (Athens: Ohio University Press, 2006), pp. 159–92; Tony Fitpatrick, *A Green History of the Welfare State* (London: Routledge, 2014), pp. 10–59.
6. See contributions to 'Britain and the End of Coal', special issue of *Contemporary British History*, 32:1 (2018): pp. 1–141; Ewan Gibbs, *Coal Country: The Meaning and Memory of Deindustrialisation in Postwar Scotland* (London: University of London Press, 2021); Huw Beynon and Ray Hudson, *The Shadow of the Mine: Coal and the End of Industrial Britain* (London: Verso, 2021).
7. Philip Mendes, 'From Welfarist Support for Vulnerable Groups to a Social Justice Perspective: The Australian Council of Social Service and the Construction of Poverty, 1956–75', *Australian Journal of Politics and History*, 70:1 (2024): pp. 40–60; Christiane Reinecke, 'Localising the Social: The Rediscovery of Urban Poverty in Western European "Affluent Societies"', *Contemporary European History*, 24:4 (2015): pp. 555–76; Alice O'Connor, *Poverty Knowledge: Social Science, Social Policy and the Poor in Twentieth Century US History* (Princeton: Princeton University Press, 2001), pp. 139–65.
8. Alison Ravetz and Richard Turkington, *The Place of Home: English Domestic Environments, 1914–2000* (London: E&FN Spon, 1995); Alison Ravetz, *Council Housing and Culture: The History of a Social Experiment* (London: Routledge, 2001), p. 90.
9. Vanessa Taylor and Frank Trentmann, 'Liquid Politics: Water and the Politics of Everyday Life in the Modern City', *Past and Present*, 211 (2011): p. 238.
10. Frank Allaun, *Heartbreak Housing* (London: Hodder and Stoughton, 1968), p. 92.
11. *Tribune*, 25 May 1945; John Parris, 'Case Law 1: Housing Act 1974', *Built Environment Quarterly*, 1:1 (1975): p. 59; Ben Jones, *The Working-Class in Mid-Twentieth-Century England: Community, Identity and Social Memory* (Manchester: Manchester University Press, 2012), p. 199.
12. James Tucker, *Honourable Estates* (London: Gollancz, 1966), p. 38. Emphasis added.
13. W. Merrick, 'The Question Is: How Unmoved Can You Be', *Daily Express*, 31 January 1955.
14. Elizabeth E. Irvine, 'Research into Problem Families: Theoretical Questions Arising from Dr Blacker's Investigations', *British Journal of Psychiatric Social Work*, 2:9 (1954): p. 24.
15. Robert C. Wofinden, 'Problem Families', *Public Health*, 57:2 (1944): p. 136.
16. Clare O. Stallybrass, 'Problem Families', *Social Work*, 4:2 (1947): p. 30.
17. This is a common trope in recollections of officials from the period. See Jane Sparrow, *Diary of a Student Social Worker* (London: Routledge and Kegan Paul, 1978), p. xvi; Raymond J. Donaldson, *Off the Cuff: Reminiscences of My Half Century Career in Public Health* (Richmond: Murray, 2000), p. 42.
18. Diane Reay, 'A Life Lived in Class: The Legacy of Resistance and the Enduring Power of Reproduction', *PRISM: Casting New Light on Learning, Theory and Practice*, 2:1 (2018): p. 18.
19. The closure periods of social work files means that when mothers are included, their names are compressed to initials and identifying details kept to a minimum for research purposes only. Officials are identified where appropriate as their professional perspective is important

to understanding attitudes. For a full discussion, see Michael Lambert, '"Problem Families" and the Welfare State in North West England, 1943-74', PhD thesis (Lancaster University, 2017), pp. xxi-xxii.
20 Anna Carlsson-Hyslop, 'Past Management of Energy Demand: Promotion and Adoption of Electric Heating in Britain, 1945-1964', *Environment and History*, 22:1 (2016): pp. 75-102; Charlotte Johnson, 'District Heating as Heterotopia: Tracing the Social Contract through Domestic Energy Infrastructure in Pimlico, London', *Economic Anthropology*, 3:1 (2016): pp. 94-105.
21 Trentmann and Carlsson-Hyslop, 'Energy Demand in Britain', p. 822.
22 Michael Lambert, '"Dumping Grounds for … Human Waste": Containing Problem Populations in Post-War British Public Health Policy, 1945-74', in Alex Mold, Peder Clark and Hannah J. Elizabeth (eds), *Publics and Their Health: Historical Problems and Perspectives* (Manchester: Manchester University Press, 2023), pp. 40-74.
23 J. Haworth Hilditch and W. Steels, *Operation Phoenix: An Exercise in Domestic and Social Engineering* (Wigan: Wigan County Borough, 1970), p. 5.
24 Lancashire Archives, Preston (hereafter LA) DDX 2302/acc. 9037/box 6/ case number 2796, Assistant Medical Officer of Health report on Mrs EC, 3 July 1959.
25 Bury Archives (hereafter BA) Unlisted Health visitor report on K family, 27 February 1957.
26 BA Unlisted Health visitor report on K family, 3 March 1959.
27 Liverpool University Special Collections and Archives D495(LI)C1/1 D, Family Report, August 1960.
28 Joe L. Hesketh, *Inside the System: How an Electricity Board Deals with Fuel Debtors* (Manchester: Manchester and Salford Family Welfare Association, 1978), p. 32.
29 Calderdale Archive Service (hereafter CAS) 13645/1, Halifax Children's, Housing and Welfare Services Joint Subcommittee Minutes, 16 October 1956 and 5 June 1958.
30 Madeline Kerr, *The People of Ship Street* (London: Routledge & Kegan Paul, 1958), p. 119; John Barron Mays, *Growing Up in the City: A Study of Juvenile Delinquency in an Urban Neighbourhood* (Liverpool: Liverpool University Press, 1964), pp. 116-17.
31 LA DDX 2302/acc. 9037/box 11/case number 3151, HV report on Mrs AJ, 6 March 1963.
32 LA DDX 2302/acc. 9037/box 19/case number 3269, Probation Officer to Deputy Warden, 24 May 1956.
33 LA DDX 2302/acc. 9037/box 18/case number 2904, HV report on Mrs DBW, 11 April 1962.
34 LA DDX 2302/acc. 9037/box 4/case number 3199, County Medical Officer to Warden, 5 November 1963.
35 Joe L. Hesketh, *Fuel Debts: Social Problems in Centrally Heated Council Housing* (Manchester: Manchester and Salford Family Welfare Association, 1975), p. 80.
36 Hilary Land, *Large Families in London: A Study of 86 Families* (London: Bell, 1969), p. 52.
37 BA Unlisted Bury Coordinating Committee Minutes, 13 February 1968.
38 LA DDX 2302/acc. 9037/box 12/case number 2187, Area County Medical Officer to Warden, 28 February 1956.
39 *Annual Report of the Medical Officer of Health for Chesterfield Rural District Council, 1955*, p. 8.
40 Ministry of Health Central Housing Advisory Committee, *Unsatisfactory Tenants* (London: HMSO, 1955).
41 LA DDX 2302/acc. 9037/box 4/case number 2234, Assistant Medical Officer of Health to Warden, 5 October 1956.
42 LA DDX 2302/acc. 9037/box 16/case number 2969, County Medical Officer of Health to Warden, 29 November 1960.
43 LA DDX 2302/acc. 9037/box 17/ case number 1827, Mrs AW to Warden, 9 November 1952.
44 Manchester University Settlement, *Ancoats: A Study of a Clearance Area: Report of a Survey Made in 1937-1938* (Manchester: Manchester University Settlement, 1945), p. 39.

45 Mackintosh, *Housing and Family Life*, pp. 5–6.
46 LA DDX 2302/acc. 9037/box 17/case number 1981, HV report on Mrs JW, 10 March 1954.
47 Andrew Davies, *Leisure, Gender and Poverty: Working-Class Culture in Salford and Manchester, 1900–1939* (Buckingham: Open University Press, 1992), pp. 52, 56.
48 LA DDX 2302/acc. 9037/box 10/[no case number], HV report on Mrs MEH, 20 September 1958.
49 Patrick Goldring, *Friend of the Family: The Work of Family Service Units* (Newton Abbott: David and Charles, 1973), p. 123.
50 Women's Group on Public Welfare, *Our Towns: A Close-Up* (London: Oxford University Press, 1943), p. 89.
51 Ravetz and Turkington, *The Place of Home*, p. 196.
52 Stephen Humphries, *Hooligans or Rebels: An Oral History of Working-Class Childhood and Youth 1889–1939* (Oxford: Blackwell, 1995), p. 151.
53 BA Unlisted Health visitor report on F family, 12 December 1966.
54 Lichfield Record Office BD26/5/3 School Headmistress to Burton-on-Trent Director of Education, 3 March 1960.
55 Patsy Cuffe, '"The Coalman" and "Shopping"', in Sharon Lambert and Nigel Ingham (eds), *Fumigating the Cat and Other Stories from the Marsh History Group* (Lancaster: Marsh History Group, 2004), n.p.
56 Department of Health and Social Security, *Report of the Committee of Inquiry into the Care and Supervision Provided in Relation to Maria Colwell* (London: HMSO, 1974), p. 45.
57 Barbara N. Rodgers and June Stevenson, *A New Portrait of Social Work: A Study of the Social Services in a Northern Town from Younghusband to Seebohm* (London: Heinemann, 1973), pp. 213–14; Helen Jones, *Health and Society in Twentieth-Century Britain* (London: Longman, 1994), p. 61.
58 BA Unlisted Health visitor report on W family, 1 June 1965.
59 LA BRBl/2/1/57, *Annual Report of the Medical Officer of Health for Blackburn, 1956*, xxiii.
60 Joel A. Tarr and Mark Tebau, 'Managing Danger in the Home Environment, 1900–1940', *Journal of Social History*, 29:4 (1996): pp. 797–816; Joel A. Tarr and Mark Tebau, 'Housewives as Home Safety Managers: The Changing Perception of the Home as a Place of Hazard and Risk', in Roger Cooter and Bill Luckin (eds), *Accidents in History: Injuries, Fatalities and Social Relations* (Amsterdam: Rodopi, 1997), pp. 196–233.
61 LA DDX 2302/acc. 9037/box 10/case number 3156, Medical Officer of Health to Warden, 26 March 1963.
62 Vicky Holmes, 'Absent Fireguards and Burnt Children: Coroners and the Development of Clause 15 of the Children Act 1908', *Law, Crime and Society*, 2:1 (2012): pp. 21–58.
63 BA Unlisted Health visitor report on M family, 15 April 1966.
64 CAS 13645/1, Problem Families Meeting, 7 November 1956.
65 Lambert, 'Dumping Grounds for … Human Waste'.
66 Liverpool Record Office 352 MIN/CHI/1/6, Liverpool Children's Committee Minutes, 13 July 1966.

Select bibliography

Beynon, Huw and Ray Hudson. *The Shadow of the Mine: Coal and the End of Industrial Britain* (London: Verso, 2021).
Fitpatrick, Tony. *A Green History of the Welfare State* (London: Routledge, 2014).
Gibbs, Ewan. *Coal Country: The Meaning and Memory of Deindustrialisation in Postwar Scotland* (London: University of London Press, 2021).

Holmes, Vicky. 'Absent Fireguards and Burnt Children: Coroners and the Development of Clause 15 of the Children Act 1908'. *Law, Crime and Society*, 2:1 (2012): pp. 21–58.

Lambert, Michael. '"Dumping Grounds for … Human Waste": Containing Problem Populations in Post-War British Public Health Policy, 1945-74', in Alex Mold, Peder Clark and Hannah J. Elizabeth (eds), *Publics and Their Health: Historical Problems and Perspectives* (Manchester: Manchester University Press, 2023), pp. 40–74.

Ravetz, Alison. *Council Housing and Culture: The History of a Social Experiment* (London: Routledge, 2001).

Thorsheim, Peter. *Inventing Pollution: Coal, Smoke, and Culture in Britain since 1800* (Athens: Ohio University Press, 2006).

Trentmann, Frank, and Anna Carlsson-Hyslop. 'The Evolution of Energy Demand in Britain: Politics, Daily Life, and Public Housing, 1920s–1970s'. *Historical Journal*, 61:3 (2018): pp. 807–39.

PART III
CRAFTED OBJECTS

CHAPTER 7
CREATIVITY IN POVERTY: BRITISH SAILORS' CRAFT IN THE LONG NINETEENTH CENTURY
Maya Wassell-Smith

Introduction

Throughout the nineteenth century, the British sailor's connection to national defence and imperial expansion earned them respect, affection and pride. Songs and ballads were written for and about them, and glorified images of sailors populated the material environment in the form of household goods and popular prints. However, the reality of being a sailor did not reflect this cultural celebration. Men who worked at sea were subject to negative stereotypes, depicted as violent, feckless drunkards or promiscuous womanisers, lacking the domestic civilising entanglements of families, female relatives or partners.[1] They experienced bouts of unemployment and, on leaving the merchant or military maritime industries due to old age or injury, had to rely on meagre pensions that were difficult or impossible to obtain. Working away at sea for long periods of time made it difficult to build and maintain relationships with family and friends. This left them without the kinship and community support upon which surviving periods of poverty depended. Instead, men experienced homelessness or leaned on the panoply of charitable homes, missions and funds set up to assist injured or aged seamen.[2] Of course, sailors were often drawn from poverty themselves.[3] Many were sent to sea via philanthropic organisations that clothed and trained destitute boys, or as a more attractive sentence following a criminal conviction.[4] Alternatively, going to sea was a means to escape large, starving families and low, precarious wages; swapping the trap of poverty for a vocation with a strong sense of pride and identity and a life of adventure.[5]

This chapter considers the creative output of seafaring men, thinking about poverty not just as economic status governing the acquisition of goods, but as a cultural filter through which the material world took shape, was experienced and used. First, I introduce the sailor as a maker, negotiating material and monetary poverty at sea through his use of non-traditional craft materials.[6] Second, I will look at the changing image of the crafting sailor in relation to his position as a member of the working or non-working poor, a figure of concern for the national community and, in particular, the temperance and self-help movements. Finally, I will highlight examples of sailors who engaged with these improving forces through craft, using it for self-expression and to make ends meet. Sailors' craftwork was part of an 'economy of makeshifts', mobilised in the 'patchy, desperate and sometimes failing strategies of the poor for material survival'.[7]

Objects of Poverty

Their craftwork was a means of making money, but also materialised the 'makeshift' outlook where available materials and images, whether scavenged by sailors or directed at them by evangelical forces, were gathered and mixed together.

Materials and making at sea

For sailors at sea on long voyages of whaling, trade and war, craft materials and equipment were scarce. Opportunities to buy materials in port were fleeting and – because of irregular pay schedules and money storage limitations – the cash to pay for them was also in short supply. This meant that sailors' creativity needed to extend beyond making to include gathering materials, tools and skills wherever they could. Many sailors, therefore, developed an eye for finding and using non-traditional craft materials and adapting craft techniques to work them. Craft skill also became a shipboard currency in the absence of money, wherein men would barter creative ability, labour or products for food or rum.[8]

Food and food waste were fertile ground for creative expression. Sailors carved peach stones to gift to passengers; they dried and varnished their rations of salt beef to carve into ship-models and boxes; and painted on ship's biscuits (Figure 7.1). A hexagonal biscuit from the 1890s is painted with a sea scene in a frilly collar, surrounded by a line from the Lord's Prayer, 'Give us this day our daily bread'. The biscuit is impressed with the three-pronged broad arrow, cleverly incorporated into the painted ribbon bow, indicating that it is the legal property of the government or the Crown, as represented by the Royal Navy supply board. Ship's biscuits, or 'hard tack', were produced in industrial dockyard bakeries by baking wholemeal flour and water until it was so hard it could only be eaten after soaking. They were packed onto ships and stored for months or even years before being consumed, by which point they were often stale, mouldy or infested with weevils.[9] The unwavering unpopularity of the ship's biscuit suggests that this painted message is ironic rather than worshipful. The subversion of institutional food provision to creative canvas turns the act of painting into an act of protest. An act made significantly more dangerous given the presence of the broad arrow, as defacing or concealing marked goods was a criminal offence.[10]

Shipboard waste was plentiful and easily appropriated for craft endeavours, although limited in variety. One description of a British merchant ship in the 1890s, for example, said that the 'decks were littered with odd bits of rope, tattered hemp sails, and old pairs of dungaree trousers'.[11] Men used waste rope to knot mats or handles for their jackknives. They remade clothing into new garments or, like other poor homemakers, tore them up to make rag rugs.[12] Discarded sail canvas was used to make sea bags and wall pockets for men to protect their things. With few personal possessions, men used their craft skills to decorate their clothing and belongings and the spaces where they were stored.[13] Handkerchiefs were embroidered with floral patterns, while ditty boxes and sea chests were painted, adorned with knotted rope handles, decorated with photographs and collected ephemera.

Creativity in Poverty

Figure 7.1 Ship's biscuit painted by an unknown sailor, *c*. 1890s. © National Maritime Museum, Greenwich, London, AAB0005.

Sailors used the marine environment to source craft materials. The most well-known is scrimshaw, in which men used cast-off materials from whaling, such as teeth, bone and baleen, to make work tools and gifts.[14] Seafarers shot albatross, making coat hooks with their beaks, tobacco pouches from their feet, pipestems with their leg bones and stuffing pillows with their feathers. They also fished for sharks to make walking canes out of their vertebrae and sandpaper out of their skin. While walking on beaches, men collected seashells and, when stuck on becalmed ships, they gathered seaweed. Merchant-seaman Charles Protheroe, who worked across the Pacific and Southern Oceans from the 1870s, described men preserving bright yellow 'Gulf-weed' in discarded 'white glass fruit [juice] bottles'. Then, 'filled with sea-water and good samples of the weed, these were corked, sealed tightly, and stowed away as a small offering to their friends at home'.[15] Their creative endeavours became love tokens to ease their re-entry into the household.

However, economic circumstances often clouded their reception and sailors' gifts were snubbed in favour of cash.[16]

Images of ideal crafty sailors

When men returned from a voyage, they presented a challenging figure to the national community. Although they were celebrated for the role they played at sea in manning Britain's ships of war, trade and exploration, sailors on land were seen as bringing the chaos and violence of war and the homosocial shipboard environment home with them. The disconnect between the maritime hero and the maritime yob in the national consciousness led to the construction of idealised sailor characters, which evolved over the eighteenth and nineteenth centuries. 'Jack Tar' was a caricature of the merchant or Royal Naval seaman that appeared in print, pottery and performance and peaked during the Napoleonic wars, a time when the survival of the nation relied on its sailors. According to Margarette Lincoln, 'the ordinary seaman, so often a problematic, potentially disruptive figure, was made safe and acceptable as "Jack Tar," a caricature which glossed over his moral laxity and capacity for violence'.[17] Jack Tar's craft skills were connected to the adventure of a seafaring life and showed him to be adaptable and industrious. In his Napoleonic memoir, Robert Hay describes the craft skills of his friend, Jack Gilles, who teaches him a variety of craft practices, including 'the cutting out and making of jackets, shirts and trousers' and the 'making of straw hats and canvas pumps'. He continued:

> Jack excelled in all … from the making of a minor three-decker, with all her sails and rigging complete, to the pricking of a mermaid on the arm of his messmate, or carving a dolphin on the handle of his knife, nothing came amiss to him.[18]

Jack's skills were distinctly maritime. From the shipboard clothing that he made, including a woven sou'wester hat to protect his neck from the sun and canvas shoes for climbing rigging, to his ship-models, tattooing and dolphin carving. His skills were presented as evidence of a sailor's 'genius' in his own sphere. Like the sailor himself, his skills were agreeable, even commendable, when at sea but anathema to the demands of living and working on land.

As the century progressed, the Navy became less visible during long periods of peacetime and became patrollers rather than defenders of the empire.[19] Naval service became a career and the cultural image of the sailor changed. Mary Conley traces this shift and argues that 'by the late nineteenth century … Popular imagery cast naval men as symbols of respectable British manhood celebrating their duty to nation and empire and their devotion to the family'.[20] This shifting image echoed the seafarers' changing relationship with money, particularly in the Royal Navy. In the earlier period, pay was disregulated and seamen lived their lives boom and bust. Men were paid off with large amounts of money and either spent it hastily or were conned out of it quickly before returning to poverty.[21] As naval pay became more ordered with the 1853 introduction of Continuous Service, men earned regular higher wages, which they could send via allotment to their families, and earned pensions after twenty years.[22] As men became more reliable earners, their morality and behaviour were understood to become more regulated too.

Craft continued to be associated with this new idealised sailor, now recast as 'The Handyman' after a verse written by Harold Begbie printed in *The Army and Navy Illustrated*.[23] In another naval memoir, Sam Noble honours one of his shipmates as an 'all-round handy man', who could 'make a signal, fire a gun, write a rhyme, paint a picture, sing a song, clap a sole on a boot, or make or patch a pair of trousers – anything that came his way'. As Noble reflects on his service in the 1870s, he writes that during training, he became 'grounded in all the arts (and graces) that go to the make-up of that wonderful soul, The Handyman … You were tailor, laundry-maid, kitchen-wench, carpenter or cook, just as occasion needed'.[24] Such descriptions offered not just a demonstration of sailors' natural and learned handiness but also highlighted the domestic and transferable nature of many of their skills. Unlike the skills of Jack Gilles, these skills are not specific to a seafaring life; while Gilles made clothing suitable to the particulars of living and working on a sailing ship, the Handyman can make, fix or launder anyone's clothes on sea or land.

The Handyman was also self-sufficient, a model and vehicle for notions of self-reliance and thrift expounded by the nineteenth-century 'self-help' movement. Within the self-help ideology, poverty was understood as a symptom of a lazy and iniquitous working-class population and an overly generous welfare system. As Alan Kidd explains, it was the 'moral responsibility of the individual to avoid welfare dependency'. These beliefs empowered people to discriminate between the poor who were 'worthy' of help and those who were not.[25] Joanne Begiato argues that the self-help movement 'raised self-control to a cult, harnessing piety, morals, character, and bodies in a mythology of self-improvement … independence and self-discipline'.[26] The ability to care for, clothe and provide for themselves through craft suggests that sailors had independence, an improving desire to learn more skills and the economic discipline not to buy new or rely on welfare. Descriptions of sailors which highlight the construction, repair and cleaning of clothes and surroundings linked their skills to hygiene, ordered outward appearance and moral cleanliness, but also suggest impure urges could be redirected into morally acceptable, constructive activities. Not only this, craft delivered men from the indulgence of idleness.

Despite the shift from Jack Tar to The Handyman, the seafarer continued to be a figure of anxiety, particularly among the temperance and missionary movements, concerned with his predilection for drink, promiscuity and divergence from organised religion and its doctrine. The popular temperance newspaper *The British Workman* often featured seamen, either drunk and destitute or, having given up alcohol and found God, reformed. A lot of effort went into getting copies of *The British Workman* into the hands of seafarers so that they may embark on similar campaigns of spiritual, moral and sober self-improvement. Missionaries visited British ships and gave them out. Sponsorship

Objects of Poverty

schemes were set up whereby readers could pay for parcels sent to ships. Sailors' relatives even waved their kin off with copies to share with their shipmates.[27] The newspaper's signature was its artwork, particularly the characteristic frontispiece, by leading artists of the day. The editor's determination to 'give the people good pictures' contributed to the respectful tone that the paper used in communicating with the poor and their soft-footed approach to evangelism.[28]

In the newspaper's depictions of mariners, craft was regularly connected to their salvation, with his making practice demonstrating evidence of his good character. For example, portrayals show demobilised sober seamen making cabbage nets for sale, fishermen fixing nets and young naval recruits pasting the illustrated pages of *The British Workman* into the lids of their sea chests.[29] *Jack's Christmas Present* (Figure 7.2), one of the large frontispieces, shows a Royal Naval seaman on the gundeck of a ship, embroidering a Berlin woolwork picture surrounded by bundles of coloured wool. The title positions craft as a connector between a sailor and his friends and family, materialising a link between the disparate spheres of the seafarer's amphibious existence. Such illustrations were both moralising and multi-modal.[30] The images were not just supposed to influence working and military men to do better but were designed to be used as wallpaper to decorate the homes, barracks, schools and belongings of the poor. While the frontispiece was no doubt published to encourage seamen and other members of the poor to take up the needle, it actually depicts a Royal Naval seaman already in dialogue with the moralising message of *The British Workman* through stitch.

Gaining respectability and connecting with communities

Engraved by Robert Barnes, *Jack's Christmas Present* illustrates an anecdote recorded in a letter to the editors from missionaries touring Naval ships during a fleet review in Liverpool in September 1863. They describe seeing many men 'busily engaged with their needles, working some of the most beautiful samplers that he ever saw', containing 'the most beautiful embroidery work imaginable'.[31] The design being embroidered in the engraving reproduces another frontispiece from *The British Workman* released three months earlier in June 1863, Harrison Weir's *The Feathered Builders and Their Homes* (Figure 7.3). Another letter written to the editors names the seaman Andrew Andrews, a former crew member of HMS *Black Prince* now serving in the coastguard in Clovelly, North Devon. It invites interested parties to visit him at his posting if they wish to see the woolwork depicted or others by his hand.

The woolworks of Andrew Andrews survive and demonstrate his ability to gather images and text from multiple sources and bring them together in his embroidery practice.[32] On the embroidery of the nest-building birds (Figure 7.4), Andrews has added a floral surround and scripture from another moralising publication, the bible. A woolwork of a farmyard (Figure 7.5) remakes another *British Workman* frontispiece after Harrison Weir (Figure 7.6), this time paired with a reproduction of a plate depicting a young man grooming his donkey. The stitched inscription reads 'The Ass Which Jesus

Creativity in Poverty

Figure 7.2 *Jack's Christmas Present* frontispiece, Robert Barnes, *The British Workman*, December 1867. Photo credit: The author.

Figure 7.3 *The Feathered Builders and Their Homes* frontispiece, engraved by J. Knight after Harrison Weir, *The British Workman*, June 1863. Photo credit: The author.

Chose To Use, I'll Learn To Love And Not Abuse'. Both the plate and the poem from which the inscription is taken were printed in the annual edition of the *British Workman's* sister newspaper in 1857.³³ A third woolwork picture, a portrait of HMS *Black Prince*, underlined 'Go Into All The World And Preach The Gospel To Every Creature' (Mk

Figure 7.4 Woolwork picture embroidered by Andrew Andrews, 1863. Private collection. Photo credit: Robert Seymour.

16.15), situates his craft practice spatially, as well as in the global activities of the mid-Victorian Imperial Navy. These woolworks exhibit the creative dexterity of sailors in two ways. First, they show a makeshift reflexive creativity and distinctive taste in recognising and collaging appropriate written and pictorial material. Second, they show sailors' skills in reproducing that material, both in the technicalities of transferring the printed image and text to canvas and in the introduction and application of colour.

Andrews's attention to animals echoes a similar preoccupation in the *British Workman*. The regular features of animal interest and condemnations of cruelty to animals reflect the links between temperance and the burgeoning RSPCA, but, as Ann M. Hale has suggested, they also 'help make the hierarchies of labour in Victorian Britain visible'.[34] The donkey – a *British Workman* favourite – knows his place; he is loyal and hardworking. The birds are industrious, making a home with what they have and crafting with the materials to hand, like Andrews and his embroidering shipmates. In making the woolwork as a gift for his mother, Andrews honours another pillar of the *British Workman* ideology – the family. As adherents to the Victorian cult of domesticity, the newspaper positioned the family as a stabilising moral structure and the home as a refuge from the corrupting influences of the pub and the street. In both the farmyard image and

Objects of Poverty

Figure 7.5 Woolwork picture embroidered by Andrew Andrews, *c.* 1860. Private collection. Photo credit: Robert Seymour.

Andrews's embroidered gift, we see young men bearing their domestic responsibilities as sons and carers. Andrews's woolworks are suggestive of the internalisation of the medium and message of *The British Workman* and other forces focused on rehabilitating the working classes in the mid-nineteenth century. Here, respectable use of leisure time was key, with needlework related to patriotism, piety, industriousness and sobriety.

Exhibiting and selling their work

Another way sailors engaged with these ideas through craft was by showing their work in improvement and temperance-inflected exhibitions, such as the working-classes' industrial exhibitions of the 1860s. One commentator articulated that the exhibitions' objective was so that 'the working man might be induced to spend his leisure time more sensibly, profitably and innocently than amid the contaminated atmosphere and questionable enjoyments of the public house'.[35] These exhibitions, where the poor had the chance to prove their worth, were held against the backdrop of a series of

Figure 7.6 Farmyard frontispiece, engraved by J. Knight after Harrison Weir, *The British Workman*, July 1858. Photo credit: The author.

poor relief crises as unemployment grew during downturns in trade caused, in part, by the American Civil War.[36] This led to destitution and disorder among the poor and handwringing among the welfare commentators.

The South London Working Classes Industrial Exhibition was the first, organised in part by the Surrey Chapel Southwark Mission for the Education of the Working Classes. Held in Lambeth Baths, a description of the 1864 event recalls: 'In the artistic and literary classes ... two seamen contributed Berlin-wool-work representations, neatly worked by themselves, of ships, and other nautical objects'.[37] The catalogues of the North, South Eastern, West and City of London exhibitions also record sailors presenting woolwork embroideries of ships and flags, as well as beadwork cushions, drawings, patchwork quilts, ship models and models of maritime architecture.[38]

The motivations of men exhibiting work at such events were mixed. In the exhibitions, there were modest cash prizes and medals in silver and bronze, but this needed to be offset by the costs incurred. Craft materials, framing and labour, along with the costs of transporting, showing and removing their work all added up. Such costs were potentially significant, given that the men were often retired or residing in institutions such as Greenwich Hospital or having to travel across London or even from other cities to exhibit. Most men whose work was commended at the exhibition received a certificate of honourable mention, presented to them at the South London Exhibition by Prime Minister Lord Palmerston.[39] Entrants also enjoyed the possibility of meeting and having their work seen by royalty, as Queen Victoria and the Prince of Wales both made visits. Exhibiting, then, was a point of entry into an elevated social existence, a way of gaining respectability, demonstrating virtue, intelligence and sobriety, at a time when the poor were under attack.[40]

In other spaces, the display of sailors and their crafts had a definitive financial motivation. Seafaring men were often scarred by a life at sea, bearing injuries or disabilities from battle or shipboard accident, as described by Caroline Louise Nielson in this volume (Chapter 21). They had long used their craft skills to attempt to make money after retiring.[41] However, as Kidd distinguishes, 'selling homemade goods' should be thought of as 'defensive strategies against poverty rather than money-making ventures'.[42] Henry Mayhew's *London Labour and the London Poor* advises that selling craftwork conferred authenticity and protected retired seafarers from accusations of vagrancy or begging.[43] Sailors' craft set them apart from the 'wandering mendicants, who, in the tattered garbs of sailors, are constantly imposing on the credulity of the public'.[44] An article about pavement artists in the *English Illustrated Magazine* shows a retired seaman at his craft (Figure 7.7). The article describes 'an old sailor', who sells Berlin woolwork pictures, 'performing the work as he sits in the sum view of the passers-by'.[45] The accompanying photograph shows how the sailor is presenting himself to the customer. Although retired, he wears his peacoat and the name of his last ship on the ribbon on his cap. The woolworks at his feet are mostly ship portraits. These not

Figure 7.7 Retired sailor selling woolwork pictures, *The English Illustrated Magazine*, 20, 1899.

only indicate his proximity to the Royal Navy and its work but also offer an external, uncomplicated view of seafaring experience to his customers. He continues stitching as he sells his needlework, invoking the image of the industrious needleworker and demonstrating his profitable and productive use of time. As the caption intimates, he 'performs' a show, co-opting the image of the Handyman sailor to sell his work. This transaction of woolwork for spare change echoes a transaction of military service, social responsibility and veteran care. Men were not able to make these connections explicitly, as those who complained about the treatment of sailors in service or retirement risked being labelled disloyal, unmanly or unpatriotic malcontents.[46] Despite years of service to the national community, this man still finds himself poor. Purchasing a picture from him may go some way to settling the debt between him and his national community. While it is unlikely that selling these works was lucrative, the seller used his sailor credentials and craft skill to make ends meet.

Conclusion

Over the course of the nineteenth century, there was a shift in sailors' craftwork from an introspective crafted output of tattooing, ship models and carvings on work tools to mediums which presented seafaring to a landed community. As members of the poor, sailors took a makeshift approach by assembling a patchwork of materials, skills and iconography in an attempt to make money, love tokens and local connections. The crafting sailor – encountered on the street, at an exhibition, within the community or in print – contributed to the rehabilitation of the reputation of seamen. The ideological evolution of Jack Tar to The Handyman made the ambivalent figure of the amphibious sailor more palatable to the general public. However, within this is a complex interplay between the crafting sailor and the creation and distribution of the cultural image of the crafting sailor. The Victorian valorisation of sailor's craft was based on an existing craft culture at sea but went on to influence how seafarers viewed and made their work and how they exhibited and sold it. Sailors engaged with these moralising forces through craft, making use of the pacifying image of the crafting sailor as a means of gaining respectability, connecting with their communities and making money.

Notes

1 Valerie Burton, '"Whoring, Drinking Sailors": Reflections on Masculinity from the Labour History of Nineteenth-Century British Shipping', in Margaret Walsh (ed.), *Working Out Gender* (Aldershot: Ashgate 1999), pp. 84–101; Graeme Milne, *People, Place and Power on the Nineteenth-Century Waterfront* (Basingstoke: Palgrave Macmillan, 2016); Isaac Land, *War, Nationalism, and the British Sailor, 1750–1850* (New York: Palgrave Macmillan, 2009).

2 Roald Kverndal, *Seamen's Missions: Their Origin and Early Growth* (Pasadena, CA: William Carey Library, 1986), pp. 322–40; Alan Kidd, *State, Society and the Poor in Nineteenth-Century England* (Basingstoke: Macmillan, 1999), p. 2.

3   Ralph Davis, *The Rise of the English Shipping Industry in the Seventeenth and Eighteenth Centuries* (Liverpool: Liverpool University Press, [1962] 2017), p. 107.
4   Caroline Withall, '"And since that time has never been heard of …" The Forgotten Boys of the Sea: Marine Society Merchant Sea Apprentices, 1772–1873', *Journal for Maritime Research*, 22:1–2 (2022): pp. 115–37.
5   Quintin Colville, 'Life Afloat', in Quintin Colville and James Davey (eds), *Nelson, Navy & Nation: The Royal Navy and the British People, 1688–1815* (London: Bloomsbury, 2013), pp. 76–93; Robert Hay, *Landsman Hay – The Memoirs of Robert Hay 1789–1847*, ed. M. D. Hay (London: Rupert Hart-Davis, 1958); Alfred Spencer, *The Wanderer: Being the Story of a Life and the Reminiscences of a Man-o'-War's Man* (Leicester: Self-published, 1983).
6   The objects and practices described in this section are largely drawn from the Sailor's Craftwork collection at the National Maritime Museum, Greenwich.
7   This term was originally used by historian Olwen Hufton but is here summarised by Alannah Tomkins and Steven King, 'Introduction', in Steven King and Alannah Tomkins (eds), *The Poor in England 1700–1850: An Economy of Makeshifts* (Manchester: Manchester University Press, 2003), p. 1.
8   Christopher Thompson, *The Autobiography of an Artisan* (London: J. Chapman, 1847), p. 152.
9   Janet Macdonald, *Feeding Nelson's Navy: The True Story of Food at Sea in the Georgian Era* (London: Chatham, 2006), pp. 17–18, 98.
10 Albert Venn Dicey and John Leybourn Goddard, *The Admiralty Statutes* (London: Eyre and Spottiswoode, 1886), p. 585.
11 Paul Eve Stevenson, *A Deep-Water Voyage* (Philadelphia: J. B. Lippincott, 1897), p. 244.
12 Emma Tennant, *Rag Rugs of England and America* (London: Walker Books, 1992), p. 52.
13 For discussion of sailors' use of chests or bags in the Finnish context, see Laika Nevalainen 'Flexible, Portable and Communal Domesticity: Everyday Domestic Practices of Finnish Sailors and Logging Workers, *c.* 1880s to 1930s', in Joseph Harley, Vicky Holmes and Laika Nevalainen (eds), *The Working Class at Home, 1790–1940* (Cham: Palgrave Macmillan, 2022), pp. 213–35.
14 Janet West and Arthur G. Credland, *Scrimshaw: Art of the Whaler* (Hull: Hull City Museums & Art Galleries in assoc. Hutton Press, 1995).
15 Charles Protheroe, *Life in the Mercantile Marine* (London: John Lane, 1903), p. 49.
16 Caird Library, National Maritime Museum, London, BGR/38, 'Autobiography of Anthony Enright, Master of the Clippers *Reindeer* and *Chrysolite* and the Royal Mail Ship *Lightning*', p. 59.
17 Margarette Lincoln, *Representing the Royal Navy: British Sea Power, 1750–1815* (Aldershot: Ashgate, 2002), p. 3.
18 Hay, *Landsman Hay*, pp. 71–2.
19 Michael Lewis, *The Navy in Transition, 1814–1864: A Social History* (London: Hodder and Stoughton, 1965), p. 10.
20 Mary Conley, *From Jack Tar to Union Jack: Representing Naval Manhood in the British Empire, 1870–1918* (Manchester: Manchester University Press, 2009), p. 3.
21 Margarette Lincoln, 'The Impact of Warfare on Naval Wives and Women', in Cheryl A. Fury (ed.), *The Social History of English Seamen, 1650–1815* (Woodbridge: Boydell & Brewer, 2017), p. 78; Richard Woodman, *Masters under God, Makers of Empire* (Cheltenham: Boydell & Brewer, 2009), pp. 132, 290, 352.
22 Similar intentions for the merchant service were discussed and although the pay and pension situation improved, it was never on the same scale as the Navy. Brian Lavery, *Able Seaman: The Lower Deck, 1850–1939* (London: Conway, 2011); Lewis, *The Navy in Transition*, pp. 227–8; David Williams, 'Mid-Victorian Attitudes to Seamen and Maritime Reform: The

23 'The Handy Man', *The Navy and Army Illustrated*, 2 December 1899.
24 Sam Noble, *Sam Noble, Able Seaman: 'Tween Decks in the 'Seventies* (New York: Frederick A. Stokes, 1900), pp. 85, 205.
25 Kidd, *State, Society and the Poor in Nineteenth-Century England*, pp. 4, 21–2, 74.
26 Joanne Begiato, *Manliness in Britain 1760–1900: Bodies, Emotions, and Material Culture* (Manchester: Manchester University Press, 2020) p. 8.
27 'Among the Troopships', *The British Messenger*, November 1881; 'Notice to Correspondents', *The British Workman*, November 1863.
28 Francis Allen Murray, 'Thomas Bywater Smithies and the *British Workman*: Temperance Education and Mass-Circulation Graphic Imagery for the Working Classes, 1855–1883', PhD Thesis (University of Salford, 2007), p. 7.
29 'The Press Gang', *The British Workman*, June, 1859; 'Our Sailor Boys', *The British Workman*, May 1867; ''The Fisherman Mending his Net', *The British Workman*, May 1872.
30 Begiato, *Manliness in Britain: Bodies, Emotion and Material Culture*, p. 116; Holly Furneaux, *Military Men of Feeling: Emotion, Touch, and Masculinity in the Crimean War* (Oxford: Oxford University Press, 2016), pp. 147, 178.
31 'Jack's Christmas Present', *The British Workman*, December 1867.
32 I am grateful to the descendants of Andrew Andrews for allowing me to study his woolworks and reproduce them here.
33 'The Ass', *Band of Hope Review*, September 1857.
34 Ann M. Hale, 'Animals', Nineteenth Century Business, Labour, Temperance, & Trade Periodicals, [n.d]. https://www.blt19.co.uk/secondary-materials/topics/animals/ (accessed 13 May 2023).
35 John Plummer, 'Working Men's Industrial Exhibitions', *The British Almanac* (1866), p. 115.
36 George R. Boyer, 'The Evolution of Unemployment Relief in Great Britain', *Journal of Interdisciplinary History*, 34:3 (2004): pp. 393–433.
37 Plummer, 'Working Men's Industrial Exhibitions', p. 116.
38 J. F. Wilson (ed.), *A Memorial of the North London Working Classes' Industrial Exhibition of 1864* (London: Petter and Galpin, 1864); *South Eastern Industrial Exhibition, Held at the Royal Hospital, Greenwich…Official Catalogue* (London: Riley & Couchman, 1865); *West London Working Classes' Industrial Exhibition, Held at the Floral Hall, Covent Garden. Official catalogue* (London: Cassell, Petter and Galpin, 1865); *Catalogue of the City of London Working Classes' Industrial Exhibition, held in the Guildhall…* (London: J. & I. Tirebuck, 1866).
39 *Illustrated London News*, 8 April 1865.
40 Clare Rose, 'A Patchwork Panel Shown at the Great Exhibition', *V&A Online Journal*, 3:1 (2011). http://www.vam.ac.uk/content/journals/research-journal/issue-03/a-patchwork-panel-shown-at-the-great-exhibition/ (accessed 13 May 2023); Sue Prichard, 'Precision Patchwork: Nineteenth-Century Military Quilts', *Textile History*, 41:1 (2010): pp. 214–26.
41 For example, one of the street sellers portrayed by Paul Sandby in the preparatory drawings for his *Twelve Cries of London* is a demobilised sailor, selling hand-knitted socks in the 1760s. John Bonehill and Stephen Daniels, *Paul Sandby: Picturing Britain* (London: Royal Academy of the Arts, 2009), pp. 136–9.
42 Kidd, *State, Society and the Poor in Nineteenth-Century England*, p. 148.
43 Henry Mayhew, *London Labour and the London Poor, Vol. 4: Those That Will Not Work* (London: Griffin, Bohn, 1862), p. 417.
44 *Morning Chronicle*, 20 June 1832.
45 C. L. McCluer Stevens, 'Pavement-Artists and Their Work', *English Illustrated Magazine*, 20 (1899): pp. 186–7.

46 Land, *War, Nationalism, and the British Sailor,* pp. 107, 113, 115; Alexa Margaret Price, '"Our Proudest Heritage": Masculinity, Nostalgia, and the Sailing Navy on Display, 1820–1920', PhD Thesis (George Washington University, 2019), pp. 59–67.

Further reading

Banks, Steven. *The Handicrafts of the Sailor* (Newton Abbott: David & Charles, 1974).
Begiato, Joanne. *Manliness in Britain 1760–1900: Bodies, Emotions, and Material Culture* (Manchester: Manchester University Press, 2020).
Cuming, Emily. 'At Home in the World?: The Ornamental Life of Sailors in Victorian Sailortown'. *Victorian Literature and Culture*, 47:3 (2019): pp. 463–85.
Furneaux, Holly. *Military Men of Feeling: Emotion, Touch, and Masculinity in the Crimean War* (Oxford: Oxford University Press, 2016).
Hansen, Hans Jürgen (ed.). *Art and the Seafarer: A Historical Survey of the Arts and Crafts of Sailors and Shipwrights* (London: Faber and Faber, 1968).
Lodder, Matt. '"Things of the Sea": Iconographic Continuities between Tattooing and Handicrafts in Georgian-Era Maritime Culture'. *Sculpture Journal*, 24:2 (2015): pp. 195–210.
Millmore, Bridget. '"Success to the seventeen united bright stars": The Spithead Mutiny of 1797 Recorded on a Sailor's Love Token', in Antonino Crisa, Mairi Gkikaki and Clare Rowan (eds), *Tokens: Culture, Connections, Communities* (London: Royal Numismatic Society Special Publication No. 57, 2019), pp. 203–14.
West, Janet, and Arthur G. Credland. *Scrimshaw: Art of the Whaler* (Hull: Hull City Museums & Art Galleries in assoc. Hutton Press, 1995).

CHAPTER 8
BUTTONS FOR WHISTLES IN THE LATE VICTORIAN, EARLY EDWARDIAN ERA: UNBRANDED CALLS
Emily Cockayne

Introduction

The whistle in Figure 8.1 is an ingenious bit of recycling. Made, somewhat crudely, from two used buttons plus bits of metal remnants, sometime around the end of the nineteenth century or the start of the twentieth century, it is unbranded, lacking any maker's mark. Objects made, often at home, from bits and bobs, would have been found commonly in homes of the poor at this time. Recycling was a routine way for poor people to make the most of materials at hand, with cast-off items commonly repurposed to make new objects. Material reinvention was a common practice of makeshift. Such was the desire to eke out the utility of things and materials – that people lined up all kinds of items for reuse.[1]

There are many other Victorian and Edwardian utilitarian objects made from reused bits and bobs, including a barometer, made from old parts salvaged together (Figure 8.2). Objects like this are sometimes described as 'trench art', but 'art' makes them seem non-utilitarian and 'trench' takes objects from their more common domestic settings.

This material reuse by the poor undermines arguments put forward in the literature about the development of 'throwaway habits' in the Victorian era.[2] Rich people might have engaged in wasteful practices, but the Victorian poor were careful and habitual recyclers, and these habits continued into the early twentieth century. To label an entire nation as wasteful due to the practices of the richest few is to completely ignore the actual lived experiences of the poorest members of the community.

Making

To make a whistle from buttons, small offcuts of tinplate metal were required to connect the buttons and a circular object to serve as the 'pea'. Whistles could be fashioned from offcuts of wood and other cheap materials. Rudimentary ones had long been used in the countryside to call animals and birds. We can only guess at how the unbranded whistle was crafted – either at home using salvaged objects or in a small workshop using up

Objects of Poverty

Figure 8.1 An 'unbranded' whistle made from two plain brass uniform buttons alongside a similar button. Author's own item.

remnants. For example, David Black & Co of Glasgow, a packing case manufacturer, made whistles at this time, probably using waste materials from their main business.[3] Similarly, William Dowler & Sons, who made whistles for various institutions in the 1880s, also made buttons, so whistles were an obvious sideline for the company, perhaps reusing buttons that did not make the grade.[4]

In addition to a lack of a maker's stamp, the buttons have no insignia on their front, and there is also no owner's inscription: we can neither tell who made it nor who owned it. A home-made appearance and lack of a maker's stamp suggest that the 'unbranded' whistle could have been made by the erstwhile wearer of the buttoned garment. The person making the whistle needed the tools and the ability to solder metal. Itinerant tinkers soldered just using fire pots, and basic soldering irons would have been commonly available in industrial workshops. In fancier whistles, the pea was sometimes made from a dice of wood, the corners chamfered off to make it more ball-like. Some peas were corkwood; the one in the whistle in Figure 8.1 – although it cannot be seen in

Figure 8.2 Barometer made around the late Victorian period from reused wooden and brass objects. Author's own item.

the images – appears to be a fruit stone (possibly a cherry), demonstrating the range of discarded items that could go into the creation of a crudely fashioned whistle.

In contrast to good quality whistles that do not impart a taste of metal into the user's mouth, our unbranded whistle tastes tinny. There is no tooth-grip, so it would have been difficult for the user to keep it in place in the mouth without using their hands (this lacking feature probably rules it out as use for a cyclist to warn of their approach). The mouthpiece is wonky, and the triangular attachment (in lieu of a 'knop') is weak, as is the shrillness of the sound – although through time the sound might have, indeed, become somewhat muffled due to corrosion and an accumulation of dirt. Inserting an endoscope camera into the interior of the whistle reveals back-stamps to the buttons; their maker was James Platt & Co of St Martin's, London. Their plain domed fronts suggest they could have come from a mess waiter's uniform.

Whistling a tune by mouth was regarded as vulgar; something that labourers would do. Social expectations meant that women were unable to whistle freely: according to one satirical magazine, whistling had 'always been regarded as an essentially masculine accomplishment'.[5] A person wanting to issue a shriller whistle needed to use *a whistle*, sometimes known as a 'call'.

Whistle-making was not big business. De Courcy, from a family of immigrants from Cork in Ireland, trained in the Hudson Company until 1888 before setting up in competition. When de Courcy died in 1931, he had a net worth of only £484 (approximately £22,000 today). The census returns of 1881 include de Courcy as a 'brass stamper' in Birmingham, living with sisters working as 'button makers', and another sister worked as a 'button carder', one of the sweated trades commonly undertaken at home, whereby the worker would sew buttons onto a card ready for sale. In 1891 de Courcy was listed as a 'whistle manufacturer'.[6] De Courcy's whistles were not stamped

Figure 8.3 The button back-stamp. Author's own object.

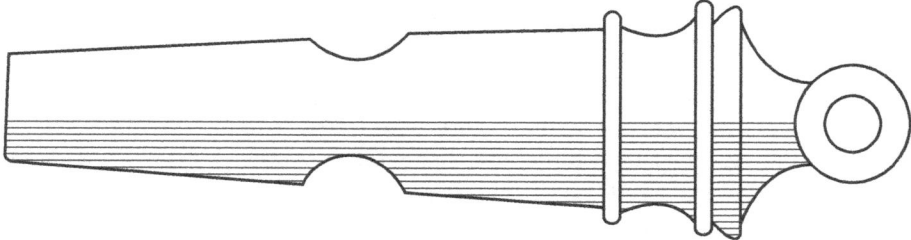

Figure 8.4 A type of police whistle illustrated in *The Boy's Own Paper* (1887).

with the company name until after 1906, and the company fulfilled orders to railways, fire brigades and similar institutions.

Our cobbled-together whistle looks like a crude version of the 'escargot' design of whistles sold by de Courcy and J. Hudson & Co. This snail-shaped design became known as the 'Thunderer'.[7] Whistles used by the police were of a different type, similar to Figure 8.4.

People in positions of authority used whistles to quieten or summon people and animals. Conductors of trams and omnibuses used whistles with finger holes to create more than one note to be 'heard for some distance even in a busy street'.[8] Dog-handlers, firefighters and factory overseers who needed to make loud shrill sounds easily heard over machinery or public spaces with low visibility often used whistles. This helped them communicate effectively in challenging environments like smoke, darkness or fog. As industrialisation took pace and many workers had experience of the military or navy, many would have become accustomed following signals and reacting to warnings issued by sound. Correct deployment and quick comprehension were essential for such signals to retain their utility.[9] Policemen, officials in public services and railway service workers were provided whistles as part of their work tools. Most surviving button whistles carry the insignia of organisations, companies and institutions, including the military, city

Buttons for Whistles

Figure 8.5 Whistle made from two King's Royal Rifles Corps uniform buttons. Author's own item.

fire brigades and the General Post Office. Whistles made from buttons carrying insignia were generally of a better finish than our surviving unbranded whistle, however, two hardly ever matched in construction.[10] The whistle shown in Figure 8.5, made using uniform buttons of the King's Royal Rifle Corps, has a more fashioned mouthpiece and sturdier triangular chain fix than the unbranded whistle.

Domestic whistling

Not all whistles were tools of work provided by employers. Domestic consumers with sufficient funds could buy whistles in various metals and several styles. A well-to-do Victorian parent might buy their child a 'Marine Suit' for role play, complete with a toy boatswain's whistle sold separately for 2 shillings.[11] Adults with a shilling or more to spare might buy a patented design whistle from the various Birmingham manufacturers who supplied companies and institutions for a range of practical purposes, including as warning paraphernalia for cyclists. Increasing bicycle use at the end of the nineteenth century led to fears that more pedestrians would be injured by colliding with a bike.[12] Cyclists needed to make audible warnings of their approach to other road users, so whistles became part of the cyclist's kit, along with 'cyclorns' and bells.[13] Hill Bros of Sheffield marketed horn and ivory whistles to cyclists wanting the benefit of a ring to fix it to a finger. The company promised their whistles would be audible to 'deaf old ladies'.[14] Nonetheless, some viewed the whistle as ineffective. In one article on public safety published in the *Pontypool Free Press* in 1896, it was argued that there was a need

Objects of Poverty

for a 'continuous noise' when cycling and that 'the whistles that they were supposed to carry were practically useless'.[15] That same year, the *Manchester Guardian* noted that, if correctly issued by all cyclists, signals would proliferate in very busy places until 'the foot passenger is perpetually surrounded by a bewildering and meaningless din'.[16]

Whistles issued other alerts. An advert for de Courcy from 1908 called attention to the utility of whistles 'for private houses in case of Fire or Burglars', and that his whistles were 'the cheapest'. The style of the whistle pictured was not the escargot shape but a long cylindrical style commonly used by the police (see Figure 8.4).[17] Whistles could also be carried for personal protection on the streets, akin to the personal alarms today.[18] A single woman, Eleanor Candey, approached by a knife-wielding attacker in Portsmouth in late September 1888, 'blew a whistle, which she said she had always carried since the Whitechapel tragedies'. A policeman heard the sound and came to assist. The *St James's Gazette* described Candey's foresight 'in arming herself with a whistle' at night as 'entirely admirable'.[19] Candey, on her way home at midnight, was the daughter of a cooper, who lived with her large family in a small house in Portsea. These facts, and a report of Candey accepting 5s to 'square' the affair, suggest such an amount would have been a significant sum to a clearly struggling household.[20]

Whistling nuisances

We have already seen how people in positions of authority could use whistles to control the behaviour of others and to call others for reinforcement of that authority. Poor people were generally expected to react to sounds made by whistles; they were not expected to be the issuers of whistled sound signals. Mill workers were summoned and dismissed by steam whistles heard across their neighbourhood.[21] An article in the *Milom Gazette* drew attention to the whistled drudgery of factory work in 1897:

> In every factory, the workers are slaves, toiling for the advantage of others; men and women who, at the blowing of a whistle, must begin their work, who only at the blowing of a whistle may eat, who at the blowing of a whistle must cease their meal, and only at the blowing of a whistle may give over the toil of the day.[22]

In 1881, a satirical magazine reported on 'The Plague of Whistling', bunching together all whistle sounds: ones made by mouth, by handheld whistles and by mechanical steam whistles. Making no distinction between musical sounds and sound signals, the article identified specific annoying whistles such as the sounds of the 'hatless butcher' on his cart; the 'Hansom cabman, after he has run over you'; tradesmen; postmen; 'policemen on their beats'; 'those dreadful B.W.s [British workmen] while they pretend to be plastering your walls or soldering your pipes'; the man on the omnibus; and 'countless thousands of trumpery little boys who infest the streets of London'. The author, declaring that no man, woman or child 'has a right to whistle about him', identified whistling as an urban nuisance.[23] Whistles to call cabs were, seemingly, a particular menace in London.[24]

There were many complaints about steam whistles, including those made by mills and factories to organise the workday steamships, and especially railways.[25]

Civic by-laws focused on disturbances which affected the workers' sleep had the power to gather an unruly crowd, or to interrupt corporation business.[26] The *Manchester Municipal Code*, published in 1894, gathered together various city by-laws. One forbade the use of 'any horn, bell, gong, steam whistle, or other noisy machine or instrument', on pain of a £5 fine. Another forbade anyone from blowing horns, ringing bells or using 'any other noisy instrument' excluding guards, postmen and the town crier.[27] Victorian service and provision vendors used whistles to attract attention to their trade – adding to the use of clappers, rattles and handbells. These sounds, useful for the customers of these tradespeople, were sometimes interpreted as nuisances to people who were not customers and wealthy people who did not manage household purchases. In 1890 'RAB' wrote to the editor of the *Glasgow Evening Post* complaining about a whistle used by a 'well-known provision dealer' who whistled his wares at 6.00 am, 6.30 am, 9.00 am, 10.00 am, 1.00 pm, 2.00 pm and 6.00 pm.[28] These may have been useful signals to customers but not to those able to be more selective in their purchasing choices. A milkman serving the Scottish border town of Hawick found himself in the Police Court in 1898 charged with 'disturbing the worshippers' of a church by 'blowing a whistle while vending milk'.[29]

Criminals used whistles to signal accomplices, while the police also routinely carried whistles to summon assistance. Some of the forces in northern England and Wales carried escargot-style whistles, including the police in Dewsbury, Sunderland, Durham, Carmarthen and Newcastle.[30] False alarms became problematic. In June 1890, on a 'drunken spree' early one morning in Cardiff, Henry Power blew a whistle that sounded like a police whistle. Power argued that he thought he was entitled to blow his own whistle but was cautioned for 'blowing a whistle at that time of the morning, as it might alarm the neighbourhood'.[31] The raising of a false alarm by blowing a whistle caused Edmond Ryan, a railway porter from Deptford to be bound over to keep the peace for three months in 1892. In court, Ryan was told that 'the police had quite enough to do with true alarms, without running after false ones'.[32] In a similar case three years later, Alfred King of Walthamstow was fined for distracting the police while on duty with 'violent blowing of a police whistle' on Fenchurch Street in London. A sense of weariness in the account of this case suggests this was becoming a common inconvenience. The sound 'caused two plain clothes officers to leave the duty on which they were engaged'. The Lord Mayor, after examining the whistle, was quoted as suggesting there ought to be regulations preventing 'people using these whistles except by the permission of the police ... A drunken man certainly had no right to use one'. King claimed to have paid 1s 3d for his whistle, but his intoxicated blowing of it cost him 10s.[33]

Conclusion

If we address the creation, ownership and use of our unbranded whistle we might situate it on the fringes of poverty. Its creation does not suggest the maker was in dire straits;

they had the space, materials, energy and ability to refashion a tool from waste materials. The whistle does, however, tap into everyday habits of repair and repurposing common among the poor, as it is evidence of an abhorrence of waste. James Platt, the maker of the buttons that form the whistle's sides, was one for frugality himself and would have approved of the practical reuse. In *Economy* (1882), Platt wrote: 'Every thrifty person is a public benefactor; every thriftless person a public enemy. "Waste not, want not" is a law of nature'.[34]

Making an unbranded whistle could have been a rebellious act, turning an old uniform button into something new. A person who was once signalled by sound now had the ability to make noise and take charge. It is more likely that the whistle was created for a humdrum practical use, by someone short of a couple of shillings to spare for a new whistle, but with the spare parts and time to craft one. Other chimeras crafted from old parts of abandoned items include livery buttons repurposed as sweetheart brooches, suggesting an emotional motivation for reuse. The reuse of buttons, possibly buttons from a uniform, also gives us clues about sentimental reuse.

Ownership of whistles suggests the possession of other stuff, property which might be stolen, bicycles needing attention alerted to them, animals, equipment and space for playing games. The poor had limited opportunities to engage in the leisure activities facilitated by whistle-use, again, teasing the edges of the label 'objects of poverty'. The ownership of things is only one part of material wealth; sometimes the freedom to *use* an object was limited by the social status of the owner. Not everyone could blow their own whistle; exclusive restrictions for sound-making were applied more readily to some people than to others.[35] Whistling presumed a certain level of authority to summon or warn others, an authority that impoverished individuals usually lacked. Specific rules and by-laws about the use of whistles were in place in certain circumstances, and the poorest members of society were most likely to be questioned about their transgressions. Whistles were more often used to control or summon the poor than used by them as part

Figure 8.6 A sweetheart brooch made from a British Royal Navy tunic button, the button was made by Firmin & Sons, London. Author's own item.

of their everyday lives. When poorer people were thought to be misusing their whistles – mimicking police calls or being disorderly – they could be fined for misusing a sound. The official argument centred on fears that signalling efficiency reduced with overuse or misuse, but the prosecutions more likely reflected a clash of lifestyles – what were useful signals to some were annoying noises to others. As an object of poverty, the *sound* issued by this whistle – its whistle – was more obviously the 'object' of poverty.

Notes

1. See Emily Cockayne, *Rummage: A History of the Things We Have Reused, Recycled and Refused to Let Go* (London: Profile Books, 2020).
2. Tom Licence, *What the Victorians Threw Away* (Oxford: Oxbow Books, 2015), p. 1.
3. Avner Strauss, 'Black & Co a Nineteenth Century Whistle Maker'. www.whistlemuseum.com (accessed 18 December 2017).
4. Avner Strauss, 'Button whistles I'. www.whistlemuseum.com (accessed 10 February 2018); 'William Dowler & Sons' (accessed 13 December 2020). For similar whistles, see Martyn Gilchrist, *Whistles* (Princes Risborough: Shire Publications, 2000), pp. 20–2.
5. 'Whistling in England', *Fishing Gazette*, 13 December 1879, p. 607; 'Our Lady Whistlers', *Judy*, 1 June 1887, p. 257.
6. Census of England, Wales & Scotland, 1881, Birmingham, Warwickshire, TNA RG 11/2997, folio 58, p. 12, schedule number 487; Census of England, Wales & Scotland, 1891, Birmingham, Warwickshire, TNA RG 12/2390, folio 99, p. 30, schedule number 175; De Courcy, Alfred Edward, 'Wills and Administration 1931', 82, Probate Registry 1858-2019. Calendar of the Grants of Probate and Letters of Administration made in the Probate Registries of the High Court of Justice in England; Avner Strauss, 'Acme Whistles Registered 1911'. www.whistlemuseum.com (accessed 26 March 2019).
7. 'A Loud Whistle', *Gatherer,* 19 (1892): p. 758. For an unsuccessful application for a trademark by Joseph Hudson in 1907, see John Cutler (ed.), *Reports of Patent, Design & Trade Mark and Other Case. Digest of Cases Reported in 1907* (London: Darling & Son, 1907), pp. 582–4; 'Registration of a Title', *Birmingham Daily Gazette*, 1 June 1907, p. 5.
8. 'Whistles of the World, Part II', *Boy's Own Paper*, 19 November 1887, pp. 126–7; 'Whistles of the World, Part III', *Boy's Own Paper*, 26 November 1887, pp. 141–2.
9. For more on sound signaling. see Flora Dennis, 'Material Culture and Sound: A Sixteenth Century Handbell', in Anne Gerritsen and Giorgio Riello (eds), *Writing Material Culture History* (London: Bloomsbury, 2015), pp. 151–5.
10. Gilchrist, *Whistles*, p. 23; Avner Strauss, 'Button Whistles I'. www.whistlemuseum.com (accessed 10 February 2018).
11. For example, see advert for John Redfern & Sons, Cowes, Isle of Wight, 1881, John Johnson Collection, Women's Clothes and Millinery 1 (9a).
12. 'Deservedly Punished', *Barnsley Independent*, 12 June 1897, p. 6.
13. 'Business', *Cycling*, 16 July 1892, p. 413; 'Business', *Cycling*, 23 July 1892, p. 14.
14. 'Business', *Cycling*, 18 November 1893, p. 296.
15. 'The Silent Bicycle and Public Safety', *Pontypool Free Press*, 11 September 1896, p. 3.
16. 'Cycling Notes', *Manchester Guardian*, 20 July 1896, p. 9.
17. Advert, *Walsall Observer*, 29 August 1908, p. 2. See also, Advert, *Kenilworth Advertiser*, 19 September 1908, p. 3.
18. For examples, 'A Burglar Baffled by a Lady', *Cardiff Times*, 3 February 1883, p. 8; 'Excitement at Hammersmith', *Echo*, 2 May 1894, p. 2.

Objects of Poverty

19 'Miscellanea', *St James's Gazette*, 28 September 1888, p. 12; 'Knife and Whistle', *Echo*, 28 September 1888, p. 3; 'Whistling for the Police', *Weekly Dispatch*, 30 September 1888, p. 5.
20 Census of England, Wales & Scotland, 1881, TNA, RG 11/1144, folio 69, p. 8, schedule number 584; 'Portsmouth Police Court', *Hampshire Post*, 28 September 1888, p. 7.
21 'The Buzzer Nuisance', *Huddersfield Daily Examiner*, 22 August 1872, p. 3.
22 'The Throb of the Machinery', *Milom Gazette*, 23 July 1897, p. 7.
23 'The Plague of Whistling', *Judy*, 23 November 1881, p. 240.
24 'Chance for New Magistrate', *Punch*, 26 July 1899, p. 37.
25 'The Whistling Nuisance', *Barnsley Chronicle*, 23 January 1875, p. 2; 'Whistling Nuisance at Jarrow', *Jarrow Express*, 29 June 1894, p. 5; 'The Mill Whistle Nuisance', *Dundee Courier*, 19 August 1884, p. 2; 'A County Court Judge on Railway Whistling', *Manchester Guardian*, 5 November 1886, p. 3.
26 For mayoral speeches drowned out by whistles and bells, see 'A Row at Rochester', *Greenock Advertiser*, 22 March 1859, p. 2.
27 Thomas Hudson (ed.), *The Manchester Municipal Code*, 6 vols. (London: Solicitors' Law Stationery Society, 1894), pp. i, 50, 63.
28 'The Whistle Nuisance', *Glasgow Evening Post*, 25 October 1890, p. 3.
29 'Milkman Disturbing a Congregation', *Edinburgh Evening News*, 7 June 1898, p. 2.
30 Avner Strauss, 'Police Button Whistles'. www.whistlemuseum.com (accessed 10 February 2018).
31 'On a Drunken Spree in Cardiff', *South Wales Echo*, 28 June 1890, p. 3.
32 'Greenwich', *London Evening Standard*, 26 September 1892, p. 1; 'False Alarms to the Police', *Sydenham, Forest Hill & Penge Gazette*, 1 October 1892, p. 2. Census of England, Wales & Scotland, 1891, St Paul's Deptford, Greenwich, TNA RG 12/495, folio 68, p. 2, schedule number 11.
33 'Blowing a Police Whistle', *Echo*, 9 October 1895, p. 3; 'Blowing a Police Whistle', *Globe*, 10 October 1895, p. 7; 'Blowing a Police Whistle', *Weekly Dispatch*, 13 October 1895.
34 James Platt, *Economy* (London: Simpkin, Marshall, 1882), p. 22.
35 For restrictions on the wearing of bequeathed clothing, see Madeleine Ginsburg, 'Rags to Riches: The Second-Hand Clothes Trade 1700-1978', *Costume*, 14:1 (1980): pp. 125-31; Margaret Spufford and Susan Mee, *The Clothing of the Common Sort 1570-1700* (Oxford: Oxford University Press, 2017), esp. p. 76; Sarah Bendall, *Shaping Femininity: Foundation Garments, the Body and Women in Early Modern England* (London: Bloomsbury, 2022), p. 98.

Further reading

Bendall, Sarah. *Shaping Femininity: Foundation Garments, the Body and Women in Early Modern England* (London: Bloomsbury, 2022).
Cockayne, Emily. *Rummage: A History of the Things We Have Reused, Recycled and Refused to Let Go* (London: Profile Books, 2020).
Dennis, Flora. 'Material Culture and Sound: A Sixteenth Century Handbell', in Anne Gerritsen and Giorgio Riello (eds), *Writing Material Culture History* (London: Bloomsbury, 2015), pp. 151-5.
Gilchrist, Martyn. *Whistles* (Princes Risborough: Shire Publications, 2000).
Ginsburg, Madeleine. 'Rags to Riches: The Second-Hand Clothes Trade 1700-1978'. *Costume*, 14:1 (1980): pp. 121-35.
Platt, James. *Economy* (London: Simpkin, Marshall, 1882).
Strauss, Avner. 'Button Whistles I'. www.whistlemuseum.com (accessed 10 February 2018).

CHAPTER 9
MAKESHIFT DOLLS AND WORKING-CLASS CHILDHOOD, c. 1880–1930
Emily Cuming

Introduction: Edward Lovett's doll collection

In 1914, the National Museum of Wales exhibited a collection of hundreds of dolls from across the world amassed by the folklorist Edward Lovett. Among these was a display of what Lovett labelled 'Emergency and Slum Dolls', belonging to 'the very poor children of the slums of London, and large provincial towns, as well as the small villages throughout the country' of the late Victorian and Edwardian period.[1] The term 'emergency' referred to their manner of construction, for these were makeshift dolls put together from household materials that families had to hand. One doll in the collection had been repurposed from a nine-pin skittle (Figure 9.1), while others were fabricated from household items including a blacklead brush, a wooden spoon, meat bones, a clog sole and an old shoe. Lovett noted in his guide to the exhibition of these dolls:

> It is remarkable how clever some poor children are, and how they contrive to make quite a decent little dolly 'out of nothing'. Some of these dolls are merely bundles of rag, crudely bunched up into human form; some are roughly cut from wood, probably by little one's father; others are simply a mutton bone dressed up; while others again are made from skittles or ninepins.[2]

A handmade mutton bone doll takes up her place today among her more lavish counterparts in the Young V&A museum collection, her scrawled facial features peeping out from underneath a handsewn ruffled bonnet (Figure 9.2). Purchased by Lovett from a young girl on the streets of Bethnal Green in the 1890s, the doll offers a rare piece of material evidence of the playthings belonging to the urban poor. Another of Lovett's 'emergency' or 'slum' toys is a shoe doll, which now occupies a place at the Museum of Childhood in Edinburgh (Figure 9.3). Contrived from the heel of a shoe, her stuffed arms and legs are fitted into what appears to be a brown stocking; on her head is a small bonnet with a glimpse of lace trim, a fabric also used to prettify the top of a roughly crafted patterned dress. Her face consists of scraps of material that form a plain collage of two eyes, a nose and a mouth. Propped up in a seated position, she is a forlorn yet humane figure, potentially inviting more interest among visitors than the classic porcelain collector's piece.[3]

Objects of Poverty

E 2. Doll made of a Ninepin by a Poor Child. London.

Figure 9.1 'Doll made of a ninepin by a poor child in London', in Edward Lovett, *Handbook to the Exhibition of the Lovett Collection of Dolls* (Cardiff: National Museum of Wales, 1914), Plate 4, E.2.

Lovett was a different kind of collector and curator. His exhibition was intended to illustrate 'the scientific history of the doll, from the standpoints of ethnography and folklore', rather than show off valuable and intricately manufactured objects that formed the basis of the museum collection's usual display of toys.[4] His collection had radical potential, for as one critic writes:

> Of necessity, the history of the doll is connected, especially in the nineteenth century and early twentieth centuries, with the lives of the middle class and wealthy children who would have owned them. Regrettably, few items remain from the rag and bone toy boxes of the very poor child. Where they do [survive], they are discussed and illustrated, but their appeal is to the more socially-minded collector. A pathetic bundle of rags wrapped in a filthy shawl would have little appeal to the cabinet collector, who is at pains to collect status-advancing investment pieces.[5]

Makeshift Dolls

Figure 9.2 Mutton bone doll, *c.* 1900. © Victoria and Albert Museum, London, Misc. 12 – 1924.

Part of Lovett's motivation was to contribute to a 'serious history' of the doll, a history that he described as hitherto 'fragmentary and trivial', treated 'merely from the childish point of view'.[6] The collection remains unique today because of his singular preservation of dolls representative of the childhoods of impoverished children. What Lovett's collection and catalogue cannot tell us in any depth, however, is the story of how these dolls were made and, more importantly, what they signified to the children who owned them. This chapter, therefore, attempts to delve more deeply into the meanings of the makeshift and cheap dolls of the poor in order to examine them as important historical objects of poverty, childhood and emotions.

Dolls and cultures of childhood

Dolls are unique and complex material objects, despite their apparent simplicity and ubiquity.[7] At their broadest level, they appear to be among the most typical representative objects of transglobal childhood – particularly girlhood – which explains their prominent visibility within museum toy displays.[8] Cherished by children, dolls, like toys more generally, retain an evocative fascination for adults as they revisit them physically in museums or virtually through forms of remembering.[9]

Figure 9.3 Shoe doll, c. 1905. Photo credit: The City of Edinburgh Council Museums and Galleries; Museum of Childhood and by permission of Amgueddfa Cymru – National Museum Wales.

The emotional pull of dolls may be attributable to their anthropomorphic form – the fact that they are designed, to an extent, to resemble small people. In the specific context of the dolls of the poor, this means that their rather forlorn and decrepit state can prompt feelings of intense sympathy or pity; these humanised objects may even appear as a stand-in for the little person in the past who played with them. As with the examples of the bone doll and the shoe doll, these objects, therefore, have the capacity to invoke strong feelings of pathos, not only for the object but, by association, for the poor or ragged child of the past, a part-historical, part-cultural figure cultivated through social reports, fiction, poetry, etchings and photography.[10] In this sense, there is, of course, a risk of sentimentalising the object of the ragged or makeshift doll to the point where it becomes a vessel for projections of our own emotional responses to the (partly imagined) figure of the poor child in the past. While sentimentality and empathy are complex emotions – and by no means necessarily politically redundant – it is worth noting that a sentimental reaction to objects, such as the shoe doll, can have the effect of obscuring a fuller picture of the meaning of these kinds of historical objects in the past, particularly as they relate to specific cultures of childhood.

As already indicated, one of the main things that prevent us from knowing what dolls signified to the children who owned them is the fact that so few of these objects have survived in material form. Other sources are, therefore, required to fill in the gaps. Visual

Makeshift Dolls

Figure 9.4 Emma Brownlow, *The Sick Room*, oil on canvas, 1864. Image credit: © The Foundling Museum, London.

images, such as paintings, illustrations and photography, might indicate that poor children had access to toys such as dolls, including within contexts where we might not expect to see evidence of play, such as in the sickroom of a charitable home for parentless children (Figure 9.4) or in a poor labourer's home (Figure 9.5). Yet this visual evidence needs to be treated with caution. Dolls could be deployed by artists as broad visual signifiers; simple markers, for example, of innocence, pathos or a shorthand symbol to denote girlhood and femininity. In nineteenth-century children's literature, for example, dolls were sometimes simplistically deployed to signify the gulf between the 'haves' and the 'have nots' in stories featuring poor children who long for dolls they cannot afford or in didactic tales in which middle-class children bestow expensive dolls upon the longing poor (Figure 9.6).[11]

Makeshift dolls and impoverished childhoods

An important source for developing a fuller understanding of the role of dolls in impoverished childhoods can be found through the testimony of autobiographies. Working-class autobiographies and memoirs have been used as a rich source of social

Figure 9.5 Illustration from Mrs H. M. Stanley (Dorothy Tennant), *London Street Arabs* (London: Cassell, 1890).

and historical evidence of lived experience through their vivid accounts of home, family, school and workplace. Childhood often forms a focus of the working-class memoir, in which writers reflect on the sensory and emotional memories bound up with the past. Autobiographies, therefore, offer an important form of historical evidence as sources that emphasise subjective experience, including writers' recollection of the sensory, emotional and tactile world of childhood. Indeed, memoirs of childhood often favour the small and the particular in terms of the objects of their focus and the provision of granular detail. Read collectively, autobiographies enable a vivid picture to emerge of everyday minor objects – such as the doll – that have hitherto occupied a marginal place in the historical record.

A number of things are striking about the descriptions of dolls that populate the pages of women's working-class autobiographies. The first is the sheer frequency with which dolls are mentioned.[12] This is important to note, since stock images of Victorian and early twentieth-century working-class childhood have often represented the child as having little access to forms of leisure or, indeed, other forms of pleasure. The poor child is commonly envisaged as inhabiting the street or the exploitative workplace or, in the case of girls in particular, figured as a domestic drudge performing housework and childrearing duties within the home.[13] Less attention has been paid to cultures of

Figure 9.6 Illustration from an advert for Louise Chandler Moulton's *Bedtime Stories* included in *Aunt Jo's Scrap-Bag* (Boston: Roberts Brothers, 1880), Volume 5. Wikimedia Commons CC BY-SA 4.0.

working-class play or, indeed, the imaginative life of children living in poverty. The second striking thing to note is the detail with which female autobiographers describe the dolls of their childhood. Despite the passage of time (and the likely disappearance of the childhood object itself), the autobiographers' recollections are often microscopically detailed, and include valuable information on how the dolls were acquired, their material characteristics, and the feelings and emotions they evoked.

This autobiographical evidence suggests that many working-class children had access to a variety of cheap dolls, such as celluloid, rag and wax dolls. Indeed, some

Objects of Poverty

of the memoirs refer precisely to the type of improvised and 'makeshift' dolls that Lovett recorded, including individual writers who reminisce on dolls made of clothes pegs, bones, stuffed rolls, potatoes, rags, socks and stockings. Yet it is striking that the memoirists do not refer to these possessions in the collector or folklorist's terms of 'slum' or 'emergency' dolls. Instead, their accounts often resonate with affection and pride as they recall both the ingenuity that went into the purchase or construction of their dolls and the awareness that these fabrications were evidence of care and gift-giving within family and kinship networks. May Jones, for example, the daughter of a carpenter and wood carver who grew up in a small village in Macclesfield in the 1890s, recalled the pleasure she took in what were simple 'home made' play items: 'a rag doll, a little wagon made out of an old wooden box, a piece of wallpaper to write on and a penny box of crayons was a great treat'.[14] Edith Hinson, the daughter of a soldier and factory worker born in Stockport in 1910, bought dolls cheaply from the Penny Bazaar in Stockport Market, 'made from wood and joined at the shoulder, elbow, hips and knees', while others were home-made from clothes pegs and – with perhaps the shortest of shelf-life of any doll – raw potatoes, 'using matchsticks for arms and legs, bits of coal for eyes'. Hinson's mother would also help her to create dolls: 'mam rolled some cloth, and put a white bit for a face with pencilled eyes, nose and mouth; it was like a baby in swaddling clothes'. Using bundles of cloth sold for a penny at the drapers, Hinson made clothes for her dolls and put them to bed in a shoebox covered by a home-made patchwork coverlet. One of her favourite games was to play shop on the back steps of her house using home-fabricated pieces: 'Everything was makeshift', she reflected.[15]

In this way, dolls were part of a broader strategy of 'makeshift' practices within working-class families and their extended social networks. In spite of limited financial resources, it is clear that parents and other relations found innovative ways of providing toys for their children, from buying cheap and affordable dolls, repurposing everyday items or by 'home-making' objects. The practice of makeshift extended to the clothing and accessorising of dolls. One historian notes, in reviewing evidence of cheaply made waxed plaster dolls, that 'the excellence of their costume' was often at odds with their cheap construction', adding that 'The Poor mother, who could not afford a fine doll for her child, seems to have compensated for this by dressing the doll to the best of her ability'.[16] In a memoir detailing her destitute 1920s childhood in Collyhurst, Manchester, Annie Ford recalled how 'kind neighbours' donated pieces of material with which to clothe her half-penny celluloid dolls.[17] Meanwhile, Edith Lowe, the daughter of a policeman and a tailoress, raised in a household of 'poor pay' and a principle of 'make do and mend', described how her rag dolls were 'lovingly dressed' by an aunt as a Christmas surprise, while her mother fashioned a little shade from cardboard for her wooden doll's pushchair.[18] Jean Court, the daughter of an itinerant actor and painter-decorator, also recalled with affection how the small baby doll of her 1920s childhood was 'lovingly dressed' by two godmothers: 'Each garment from vest to bonnet and bootees [were] all knitted with fine wool and using intricate patterns must have taken some days of busy knitting'.[19]

The word 'makeshift' suggests a compensatory function in a world where toys and other non-utilitarian items came at a premium. Yet the memoirists express little regret or embarrassment at the cheapness of the home-made nature of their dolls (in contrast to their consistently more marked embarrassment at having to wear second-hand or worn clothes and shoes). In fact, they were more likely to marvel at or recall with fondness, the alchemy of makeshift practice, by which ordinary items seemed transformed – fairytale-like – into personal and meaningful objects. Even the plainest doll could be accessorised using off-cuts of fabric, giving the doll a fashionable attire that might have been beyond the means of their owners in reality. Anne Tibble, for example, recalled how few toys she had in her rural childhood in a North Yorkshire village 'as a poor man's child', but the dolls she and her sisters did possess allowed for creative possibilities: 'we made trousseaux for these dolls with the help of Mother; and her sewing-machine we used from the age of about five. We begged shoe-boxes to trim with white muslin and blue ribbon from Mother's "bits-and-pieces bag" for dolls' beds'.[20] Likewise, in their joint memoir of sisterhood, Amy Gomm and her sister Laurie reflected on their possession of plain penny dolls made of thin crock (a type of clay) that was 'easily broken', filled with sawdust, with hair merely painted on. Despite the dolls' simple forms, Laurie would raid the household 'rag-bag' to create for her doll 'beautifully hand-sewn garments, from chemise right through to her pinafore, as well as knitware'.[21] One ball of wool could furnish supplies for many garments and potential transformations of identity, making their doll by turns, a 'woman of fashion, a 'cuddly baby in a shawl' or 'an invalid with a gay-coloured bedspread'.[22] Against the common assumption that dolls were primarily used to discipline girls into domestic ideology and motherhood, the evidence of the Gomms' memoir is hardly unique in suggesting that, for young girls, dolls in fact represented imaginative play and escapism from domestic drudgery. Thus, while the Gomm sisters were expected to perform domestic duties at home from a young age, including taking care of their youngest brother, playing with dolls was a way of enjoying a world of creativity and fashion. 'I can't say that mother-love came into it', Amy Gomm commented of her attachment to dolls; 'I will say, though, that ours could, with justice, claim to be the best-dressed dolls in our neck of the woods'.[23]

As noted, the material value of dolls was not proportional to the affection girls bestowed on these childhood objects. Indeed, a number of memoirists professed their love for their 'poorer' dolls rather than more expensively manufactured ones that came their way. This was the case in the memoir of Louise Jermy, for example, born in 1877 to a father who worked as a stonemason's foreman, and whose mother died while she was in infancy. Due to these circumstances, Jermy lived with her grandmother for some of her childhood, residing for a time in a charitable almshouse in Kent. There she remembered her father coming to visit her bearing a doll as a gift, 'a very smart lady in a red frock with a wax face and yellow hair like my own'. Yet the young girl did not take to this fancy doll. Whether by choice or persuasion (her grandmother pronounced it was 'too good' for her) Jermy recalled:

> I was quite content with my old one, which was a wooden one minus arms and legs, and with nearly all the paint licked off its head, but that didn't matter. I wrapped it up in grannie's red handkerchief and folded it in my pinafore as I sat in front of the

fire in a little wooden stool, and I divided my caresses and remarks pretty equally between that and Madame, the tortoiseshell cat.[24]

Born in 1912 to parents who worked as commercial travellers, memoirist Elisabeth Dale also expressed fondness for a plain doll over a more expensive one. Her father had managed to procure a luxury doll from a sale at a London hotel of items left behind by the 'children of the well-to-do patrons'. Dale recalled the doll as being 'very beautiful with real hair' and 'eyes that opened and closed with long lashes'. She was also accessorised in a fine green satin dress with matching hat and underclothes, and cords which prompted her to say 'Mama' and 'Papa'. Despite these accoutrements, the doll remained unnamed and unloved. It failed to rival the doll made for Dale by her grandmother, fabricated from the 'leg of a black woollen stocking stuffed with rags', with 'hair contrived [from] a piece of black astrakhan fur', pearl button eyes, and a mouth 'embroidered on with scarlet wool'. 'This doll I loved because I could take her to bed with me and if I rolled on her during the night she didn't stick in me', Dale recalled approvingly.[25] The working-class writer Joyce Storey recalled her own strong emotional attachment to a 'battered celluloid doll with a bashed nose and cracked face', that she had stumbled upon at the 'open-air' hospital to which she had been sent to recover from tuberculosis as a child. In the sanatorium, the plain doll offered the girl comfort and companionship: 'I adopted it and carted it everywhere. It resembled a boy doll and because it was warm to the touch and not cold like a china doll, I would cuddle it and kiss it and held it close to me. I talked to it for hours and together we would hide away in my secret place in the tree'.[26] On her return home to her parents, from whom she felt estranged after the period of separation, Storey was gifted a new china doll that her mother had dressed for her. Subsequently, she 'hardly looked at it', feeling it was no substitute for 'the warm celluloid boy doll that I had left at the home and once more I struggled with emotions that were made the harder by having to repress them'.[27] These examples seem to confirm the insight, noted by Sharon Brookshaw, that 'To a child, toys (and certain other objects of desire) can be something more than or different from the original adult design'.[28]

Cuddled and accessorised, bestowed as gifts and acting as companions, dolls offer a unique form of 'emotional object', suffused with sentiment and feeling.[29] In this way, the study of dolls is well-placed to contribute to the growing field of the history of emotions, as well as the more overlooked field of the material culture of children. Yet it should be noted that dolls do have the potential to be 'emotional objects' in the more literal sense mentioned earlier in the chapter, as items that can prompt acute feelings of pity and sentimentality, particularly in the context of childhoods lived in conditions of abject poverty. And there are plenty of examples of heart-rending and pathetic tales centring on the object of the doll within the autobiographical corpus. One example can be found in the recollections of Anita Hughes, born in 1892, the daughter of an irregularly paid gardener. Hughes and her six siblings were regularly dressed in donations of old coats and worn clogs bestowed on them by the local police 'clog fund'. Presents were a rarity, but in her memoir Hughes makes a point of noting how her mother had 'managed to buy Nellie [her sister] and me a wooden doll for 6d and [dressed] them in coloured crepe paper', a gift which appeared along with an apple, orange and carrot in their Christmas stockings.[30] The inclusion of such sparse details of a gift are affecting, particularly in light of the fact that Hughes's childhood, along with the possibilities of play it might have afforded, would turn out to be severely curtailed. By the age of twelve, like her sister before her, she was working as a weaver at the local mill. Another former mill girl, Lily Purvis, recalled how she saved up for 23 weeks in order to buy herself a coveted doll. The straw-stuffed, golden-haired 'dolly' was then placed by adults in her Christmas stocking, even though it was effectively a gift to herself, procured with the earnings of her own exploited labour.[31] Gladys Otterspoor, who provided an oral account of her impoverished childhood in a Cambridgeshire village at the end of the nineteenth century, recalled in detail a precious doll bought for sixpence by her sister who had entered domestic service. Her mother helped her to make the best of this plaything: 'I only had one doll, a wax doll, in those days. And my mother got a little shoe box and tied a piece of string on it and put some wheels on and I dragged it along. And we were ever so pleased with that'. Otterspoor's only doll, however, did not last very long. As she played one day near the fires that surrounded the local lime pits, she accidentally dropped the doll into the flames where it 'shrivelled all up'. Her acute sense of loss was still felt as she recounted her life story as an adult: 'I sat and cried. I always remember that. I was so upset about it'.[32] Like accounts given by other autobiographers of the grisly fate of childhood dolls – dolls sat on, left out in the rain, or wax dolls that came to a (literally) sticky end near fireplaces – the doll object emerges as a conduit for the intense emotions, sensitivities, attachments and indeed disappointments of the child. What Lovett perhaps too quickly dismissed as the limited 'childish point of view' in relation to the history of the doll, can, through sources such as autobiographies, be reclaimed as a significant point of enquiry.

Not all memories of dolls in working-class memoirs are heart-rending, sentimental or confirm the expectation that working-class girls were always attached to their dolls. A small but telling number of female autobiographers related their complete indifference or indeed animosity towards dolls that were foisted on them.[33] This is an important reminder of the complex subjectivity of people's relationship to things. For if material culture 'consists not merely of "things", but also of the meanings they hold for people', it is necessary to recall that those meanings can diverge, depending on the perspective of the child, or the individual looking at, holding, gifting or remembering the object.[34]

Conclusion: Recollecting dolls

As this chapter has shown, dolls emerge as revealing items in the material culture of childhood poverty. Their very invocation is potentially disruptive, unsettling stock images of the poor child in history, as it proved for the famous Victorian journalist and social investigator Henry Mayhew who was puzzled when a young, destitute seller of watercresses began talking to him about her toy possessions.[35] In contrast to the trope of the careworn child, old before its time, too fatigued to play or lacking the creative vision of the middle-class child, dolls – 'emergency' or otherwise – serve as a reminder that working-class children had access to toys, played and existed in rich sensory and imaginative worlds, and were acutely sensitive to family dynamics. As working-class autobiographies show, emotional objects have a lasting afterlife through words and memories, often surviving well beyond the duration of the object itself and thus enduring as recollections rather than as objects in material collections.

Dolls have the additional and paradoxical quality of being both personal and generic items. In this way, they have the capacity to resonate with readers or observers outside of the particular circumstances of childhood in which the doll was located. Plain, cobbled together, bashed about, propped up alone in the museum's display or thrown out with the rubbish, dolls as material or remembered objects of poverty can transcend the particularities of their environment in order to evoke general memories of childhood, including vivid feelings of attachment and vulnerability that are common to children across social divides. Indeed, given that, as Thomas J. Schlereth puts it, the 'child's world is also a world we have lost',[36] dolls, like other toys and lost possessions, can 'remind the collector of a childhood they themselves have grown out of'.[37] Far from signifying the divide between us and the poor Victorian or Edwardian child, or the gulf between adult and child, the doll remains a transitional object that can forge feelings of empathy and identification with historical and social 'others'.

Notes

1. Edward Lovett, *Handbook to the Exhibition of the Lovett Collection of Dolls* (Cardiff: National Museum of Wales, 1914), p. 16.
2. Ibid. Similarly Clara E. Grant, the educator and social reformer known for her 'farthing bundles' of recycled toys distributed to the poor, observed the creativity of the doll creations fabricated by the young children at an East End school: 'In a collection of "Our Dolls" which I have found our children cuddling are a bit of carpet rolled up, an old broom head, a carpet slipper, a jam tin in a rag "frock", a bit of firewood with a china head at one end, another bit of wood dressed in pink paper, and one, looking like a little doll with one eye, turned out to be a dolly's arm dressed up!', in Clara E. Grant, *Farthing Bundles* (London: C.E. Grant, 1931), p. 97.
3. Thanks to Vicky Holmes for bringing this special doll to my attention.
4. Lovett, 'Introduction', in Lovett, *Handbook*, n. p.
5. Constance Eileen King, *The Collector's History of Dolls* (London: Robert Hale, 1977), p. xxviii.
6. Lovett, 'Introduction', n. p.
7. Lovett's 1914 collection, for instance, featured a selection of dolls from across the globe stretching back to ancient Egyptian civilisation. For a broader history of dolls, see Manfred Bachmann and Claus Hansmann, *Dolls: The Wide World Over*, trans. Ruth Michaelis-Jena (New York: Crown, 1973). On the role of makeshift dolls as part of a hidden and radical history in the context of Black history and slavery, see Nora McGreevy, 'Black Dolls Tell a Story of Play – and Resistance – in America'. https://www.smithsonianmag.com/smart-news/african-american-history-black-dolls-toys-180979530/#:~:text=Many%20of%20the%20earliest%20dolls,'%E2%80%9D%20says%20Jean%2DLouis (accessed 1 October 2023).
8. Megan Brandow-Faller, 'Introduction: Materializing the History of Childhood and Children', in Megan Brandow-Faller (ed.), *Childhood by Design: Toys and the Material Culture of Childhood, 1700–Present* (London: Bloomsbury, 2018), p. 5; Sharon Roberts, 'Minor Concerns: Representations of Children and Childhood in British Museums', *Museum and Society*, 4:3 (2006): p. 157.

9   Thomas J. Schlereth states: 'Toys are, without doubt, adults' favourite form of childhood material culture', in Thomas J. Schlereth, 'The Material Culture of Childhood: Problems and Potential in Historical Explanation', *Material History Bulletin*, 21 (1985): p. 2. See also Sherry Turkle's work on material objects as 'companions to our emotional lives or as provocations to thought', in Sherry Turkle, 'Introduction: The Things That Matter', in Sherry Turkle (ed.), *Evocative Objects: Things We Think With* (Cambridge, MA: MIT Press, 2007), pp. 3–10. On dollhouses specifically as a form of emotional, 'feeling' or 'moving' object, see Joanne Begiato, 'Moving Objects: Emotional Transformation, Tangibility, and Time-Travel', in Stephanie Downes, Sally Holloway and Sarah Randles (eds), *Feeling Things: Objects and Emotions through History* (Oxford: Oxford University Press, 2018), pp. 229–42.
10 On the historian's emotions towards the figure of the impoverished child in history, see Carolyn Steedman, *Landscape for a Good Woman* (London: Virago, 1986), pp. 30, 51. For a sensitive and imaginative reflection on Lovett's shoe doll, see Imogen Duthie, 'No. 1 – Shoe Doll', *Portrait of a Plaything*, n. d. https://www.portraitofaplaything.com/work/portraitplaythingshoedoll (accessed 1 May 2023).
11 Sharon Marcus, *Between Women: Friendship, Desire, and Marriage in Victorian England* (Princeton: Princeton University Press, 2007), p. 159; Victoria Ford Smith, 'Dolls and Imaginative Agency in Bradford, Pardoe, and Dickens', *Dickens Studies Annual*, 40 (2009): pp. 171–97.
12 From my own database of over 200 memoirs by working-class female authors, at least one-third contain specific reference to dolls in childhood. All the following references in the chapter refer to this broad corpus of working-class autobiographies by women writers, many of which are gathered in the Burnett Archive of Working Class Autobiographies at Brunel University, London.
13 See, for example, the photographs of impoverished East End children engaged in forms of housework and handiwork captured by Horace Warner in the Spitalfields area in 1912, reproduced in Horace Warner, *Spitalfield Nippers* (London: Bedford Institute Association, 1975).
14 Burnett Archive of Working Class Autobiography (hereafter BAWCA) 1:401, May Jones, untitled autobiography (*c.* 1970s), p. 4.
15 Edith Hinson, *Mary Ann's Girl: Memories of Newbridge Lane* (Stockport: Stockport Metropolitan Borough, 1984), p. 18.
16 King, *Collector's History*, p. 265.
17 BAWCA 2:291, Annie Ford, Untitled autobiography (n.d.), p. 6.
18 BAWCA 2:487, Edith Gibson Lowe, 'Autobiography of Early Childhood, 1913–1920 and Before' (1978), pp. 1–2.
19 BAWCA 2:188, Jean Court, 'Living in the Lane' (n.d.), p. 3.
20 Anne Tibble, *Greenhorn: A Twentieth-Century Childhood* (London: Routledge & Kegan Paul, 1973), book jacket, p. 22. 'Trousseaux' refers to a bride's outfit of clothes, including other items such as house linen, gifted to a bride in preparation for the wedding and married life.
21 BAWCA 2:324, Amy Frances Gomm, 'Water under the Bridge', 2:324 (1975), p. 68.
22 Ibid., pp. 68–9.
23 Ibid., p. 68.
24 Louise Jermy, *The Memories of a Working Woman* (Norwich: Goose & Son, 1934), p. 5.
25 BAWCA 2:199, Elisabeth Dale, Untitled autobiography (n.d.), pp. 37–8.
26 Joyce Storey, *Our Joyce: 1917–1939* (London: Virago, 1993), p. 22.
27 Ibid., p. 24.
28 Sharon Brookshaw, 'The Material Culture of Children and Childhood: Understanding Childhood Objects in the Museum Context', *Journal of Material Culture*, 14:3 (2009): p. 380.

Objects of Poverty

29 John Styles, 'Objects of Emotion: The London Foundling Hospital Tokens, 1741–60', in Anne Gerritsen and Giorgio Riello (eds), *Writing Material Culture History* (London: Bloomsbury, 2015), pp. 165–72.
30 BAWCA 1:357, Anita Elizabeth Hughes, 'My Autobiography' (1977), pp. 1–2.
31 BAWCA 2:643, Lily Purvis, 'Reminiscences of My Childhood Days in Lancashire' (1975), p. 1.
32 Mary Chamberlain, *Fenwomen: A Portrait of Women in an English Village* (London: Virago, 1977), p. 33.
33 Barbara Bell, the daughter of a Lancashire cotton mill worker born in 1914, accidentally smashed her first gifted doll's head on a lamppost, beginning a life-long aversion to that particular play object: 'Life was far too interesting to play with dolls', she happily declared, in Barbara Bell, *Just Take Your Frock Off: A Lesbian Life* (Brighton: Ourstory Books, 1999), p. 19. Likewise, Angela Rodaway, who wrote a memoir of her working-class Islington childhood in the 1920s and 1930s, confessed that 'almost the only game I ever played with [dolls] was to hang them up round the room and hit them with a stick as I passed', in Angela Rodaway, *A London Childhood* (London: Virago, 1985), p. 26.
34 Styles, 'Objects of Emotion', pp. 165–72.
35 For a crucial exploration of the encounter between the social investigator and the little watercress girl, see Steedman, *Landscape*, pp. 136–7.
36 Schlereth, 'Material Culture of Childhood', p. 2.
37 Brookshaw, 'Material Culture of Children', p. 368.

Further reading

Begiato, Joanne. 'Moving Objects: Emotional Transformation, Tangibility, and Time-Travel', in Stephanie Downes, Sally Holloway and Sarah Randles (eds), *Feeling Things: Objects and Emotions Through History* (Oxford: Oxford University Press, 2018), pp. 229–42.
Brandow-Faller, Megan (ed.). *Childhood by Design: Toys and the Material Culture of Childhood, 1700–Present* (London: Bloomsbury, 2018).
Brookshaw, Sharon. 'The Material Culture of Children and Childhood: Understanding Childhood Objects in the Museum Context'. *Journal of Material Culture*, 14:3 (2009): pp. 365–83.
Davin, Anna. *Growing Up Poor: Home, School and Street in London, 1870–1914* (London: Rivers Oram, 1996).
King, Constance Eileen. *The Collector's History of Dolls* (London: Robert Hale, 1977).
Lovett, Edward. *Handbook to the Exhibition of the Lovett Collection of Dolls* (Cardiff: National Museum of Wales, 1914).
Schlereth, Thomas J. 'The Material Culture of Childhood: Problems and Potential in Historical Explanation'. *Material History Bulletin*, 21 (1985): pp. 1–14.
Turkle, Sherry (ed.). *Evocative Objects: Things We Think With* (Cambridge, MA: MIT Press, 2007).

PART IV
OBJECTS OF CHILDHOOD

CHAPTER 10
TOYS FOR THE POOR, c. 1700–1918
Ken Sneath

Introduction

This chapter explores the toys and playthings enjoyed by the poor across two centuries. Before commencing our analysis, we need to consider how toys and, indeed, children are defined. Modern definitions of toys emphasise the concept of children playing. For the Encyclopaedia Britannica, a toy is 'A plaything, usually for an infant or a child, and often an instrument used in a game'.[1] According to Collins Dictionary, 'A toy is an object that children play with, for example, a doll or a model car'.[2] Childhood is understood as the early phase of the life-course of all people in all societies. It is characterised by rapid physiological and psychological development and represents the beginning of the process of maturation to adulthood. In terms of age, preadolescence is frequently defined as ages nine to twelve, with childhood ending at puberty.[3] However, childhood is a constantly shifting concept and varies by place, class, religion and ethnicity.[4]

Interpretations of childhood are highly contested. Lawrence Stone contended that sentiment was intimately related to demography, arguing that affection and love were impossible before the eighteenth century because conditions of preindustrial life were so insecure that one would not dare to enter into a deep relationship for fear of it abruptly ending. Stone suggested that the value of children rises as their durability improves; in other words, when most children no longer die, it becomes worthwhile to lavish profound affection upon them. Steven Ozment profoundly disagrees with these ideas. Mining the records of families' private lives, from diaries and letters to fiction and woodcuts, Ozment showed that a preindustrial family was not significantly different from the later family of high industry that is generally viewed as the precursor to the sentimental nuclear family of today. Some have suggested that parents remained emotionally distant from their children.[5] For the poor, this was often the result of their economic status.

Children's play and the extent to which they enjoyed toys reflected economic conditions. In the latter eighteenth century, working-class budgets were under great pressure. For example, Sara Horrell's working-class expenditure patterns for 1787–96 showed that after rent, food, clothing and fuel were provided, little was left for anything else.[6] Although there were improvements in some workers' wages in the proceeding decades, considerable numbers of people were perpetually poor and continued to fall well below the poverty line.[7] Toys by the Victorian period and beyond were still costly compared to incomes and were primarily aimed at middle and upper social groups. Only wealthy families could afford the most desirable toys, such as a rocking horse for their

Objects of Poverty

children, and the cost of other toys, such as a doll's house, could exceed the average weekly pay of a working man.[8]

Of course, an essential factor in the enjoyment of toys was time for poorer children to play. Children as young as seven years were employed full-time in factory mills, which could mean thirteen-hour days for six days a week in textile mills. The 1833 Factory Act limited the lower employment age to nine years and stated that children could work a maximum of nine hours a day but had to attend school for a further two hours. Legislation further reduced children's hours of work in 1844.[9] Furthermore, children, particularly girls, were expected to perform housework and childcare alongside employment and schooling.[10] Nonetheless, their lives were not completely devoid of toys and play.

There is an immediate problem in studying the toys of poor children: few toys and playthings owned or encountered by the poor have survived. Therefore, this chapter examines toys that have survived in museum collections; in addition, it turns to Old Bailey Records, literature and works of art to piece together their place in the history of poverty. Naturally, these sources have their limitations. Museums tend to hold better quality examples, not those played with by poorer children. Works of art must be interpreted with caution for the artist's first concern is not always historical accuracy. The *Proceedings of the Old Bailey* is a valuable source for the production and distribution of toys in London, as toys were often mentioned as incidental details of trials and, therefore, overcome some of the problems of social bias in their evidence.[11]

Production of toys and makeshift

Tin plate toys handmade by tinsmiths produced from the 1830s were initially expensive. The industrial revolution allowed toys to be mass-produced and gradually become cheaper. From the latter nineteenth century, mass production of these toys enabled even poor parents to buy penny Christmas gifts for their children. Henry Turner, who lived in a poor part of East London, described Christmas morning at the beginning of the twentieth century:

> We used to hang our stockings up, wake up in the morning and there would be a bright new penny and a penny toy. That was it.[12]

However, many toys enjoyed by the poor continued to be made by impoverished outworkers at home, immortalised by Charles Dickens in his character Jenny Wren in his novel *Our Mutual Friend*. The disabled Jenny makes dolls' clothes, the only means of survival for her and her drunken father.[13] Evidence for outwork is also found in *Proceedings of the Old Bailey*.[14] For example, Joseph Saunders, a labourer from Bethnal Green, testified in 1866, 'I saw the deceased, William Webb, inside the passage of a house where toys are made'.[15]

Makeshift toys also remained at the centre of play for poorer children. The most accessible toys for poor families were handmade or created from everyday objects. Simple toys crafted from natural materials such as sticks, stones and even bones were common among poorer households. For example, all that is required to play five stones are five small stones; although originally, sheep knucklebones were used to play the game, as shown in Bruegel the Elder's *Children's Games* 1559.[16] Market Harborough Museum has a collection of more than 200 toys made by children from pig's knuckle bones, wood and fabric.[17] Further examples of the ingenuity of children in making their own toys from readily available materials include makeshift dolls dressed in rags. Dressing-up games typically included props such as old clothes or scarves to create slings to assist 'healing' of a broken arm. Toys and props for play made from these primitive materials were fashioned both by children and family members.

Distribution of toys

Toy shops started to appear in the eighteenth century. For example, *Chase's Norwich Directory* listed three toymen in 1783, and toy dealers were listed in the major centres of London, Manchester, Bristol and Norwich in *Pigots Directory* of 1822.[18] Evidence for toy stalls and shops – targeted at the poorer market – also appeared regularly in the *Proceedings of the Old Bailey*. William Covell bought and sold toys from a stall down by Tower Hill in 1845.[19] Others sold toys from what appeared to be small-scale shops that sold a range of items. Rachel Palmer, the wife of a coachman, kept 'a little bit of a shop; I sell tapes and penny toys, and such like'.[20] In 1882, Mary Child testified, 'I keep a toyshop in Grafton Street-on 6th January between 5 and 6 p.m., the prisoner came to my shop, and selected two penny toys'.[21] George Evans, a coachmaker's labourer, stated as a witness, 'My wife keeps a little shop, and sells children's clothes, and shoes, and toys'.[22] John Gummell, a defendant, sold 'children's toys, and various things, mops and brushes'.[23] Even higher-status shops, such as the 'fancy repository' of Fanny Cheeseman, sold penny dolls in 1856.[24] Those selling toys would have displayed them in shop windows as in one theft case in which the two defendants claimed that they were merely looking at the toys in the shop window.[25] Details of the toys were rarely given, but their valuation was recorded when they were stolen. These were sometimes very low in value and represent toys that might subsequently be enjoyed by poorer children. For example, William Hillman stole 144 toys, the property of his master, valued at just two shillings in 1829.[26]

Beyond the shops, itinerant chapmen, hawkers and pedlars continued to sell toys, as well as other small items, directly to households throughout the nineteenth century, as captured in the paintings of Mark Langlois, particularly *The Village Toy Seller*, in which we can see the little girl eagerly inspecting the contents of the seller's basket.[27]

Toys for poorer children

Many toys and playthings could be obtained relatively cheaply and, therefore, be available to poorer children.[28] As noted above, tin plate toys, like trains and boats, are a good example. As their cost reduced, street hawkers sold these toys at Ludgate Hill and outside Gamages in Holborn, London, in the weeks prior to Christmas.[29] Indeed, some of these hawkers were only children themselves.[30] The tin toys typically measured between three and four inches in length, such as the examples found in the Ernest King collection at the Museum of London.[31] King's collection covers a range of subjects, from politics and war to royal memorabilia and popular culture. The collection includes guns, animals, a sweet container and Father Christmas with a pair of clowns. Some of these tin toys had intricate features. A spring-action banjo-playing Pierrot clown with a performing dog on a turning circle was purchased for just one old penny from a street trader in 1907. As the spring lever beneath the base moves, the clown advances forwards, and the circle beneath the dog rotates.[32] A small collection of highly coloured penny tin toys produced by German manufacturers was held at the Chester Toy and Doll Museum, now closed, where some in the collection had simple movements, such as wheeled vehicles.[33]

The toys changed as modes of transport evolved. Wooden boats gave way to model railways and the first cars. Wooden model trains were popular in the nineteenth century. They sometimes included fine details of the livery of the railway companies, including the London, Brighton and South Coast Railway. While many wooden toys such as these were beyond the poorest, simple imitations could be made from discarded pieces of wood. Humble building blocks made from wood dating from the Victorian period can be found in many local museums, such as the Curtis Museum in Alton.[34] For those of little means, wooden bricks could be home-made.

Steps towards literacy among the poor were small and education, such as required by the Factory Act of 1833, was not welcomed by many poor families as it inhibited vital earning opportunities. Sunday schools proliferated in the Victorian period, and as well as teaching literacy, religious belief was promoted. Middle-class and more affluent working-class children experienced the Victorian Sunday. The only toys permitted in evangelical households on Sundays were wooden Noah's Arks with their pairs of exotic animals such as lions, tigers and giraffes which appealed to children's imaginations. Examples on display in many museums are usually of high quality, such as those at Dorset County Museum, Hollytrees Museum, Colchester, and Whitby Museum.[35] However, the story of Noah and his animals could be fashioned from the cheapest materials. During the First World War, for example, disabled soldiers in London made biblical animals from wood and paper for children as part of their rehabilitation.[36]

Animals proved to be popular toys for all social groups, particularly horses, teddy bears and farm animals. A simple soft toy animal made from wool, dated c. 1906, is held by the Young Victoria & Albert Museum in Bethnal Green.[37] The Portable Antiquities Scheme reported that the most common toys dated to the nineteenth century were low-value cast lead alloy animals including elephants, pigs, horses and dogs.[38] However, just as the poorest children played with elementary dolls made from rags, so too did they create animals from similar materials when lead alloy toys were out of reach of their parents' pockets. Nevertheless, as Emily Cuming suggests in Chapter 9, even with toys of such rudimentary design and materials, poor children developed a strong emotional attachment to their toys.[39]

Toys for the Poor

The poorest children played with marbles. They were usually made from glass, but cheaper ones were manufactured from clay.[40] A set of late nineteenth-century glass marbles are held by the Young Victoria & Albert Museum.[41] A second set of seventeen marbles, fifteen made from glass and two made from stone, are also held there. The two marbles made from stone are not perfectly spherical and are chipped and scratched, reflecting energetic use.[42] Both sets of marbles were found on the banks of the River Thames by a licensed 'Mudlark'. An example of clay marbles was also discovered under the wooden floor when a former building for the free education of sons of local fishermen in Lowestoft was excavated in 2000.[43] Various games could be played with marbles, the most common being knocking marbles out of a circle. Marbles could be won and lost, or children could retain the ones they started with. Enjoyment of the game during the nineteenth century was captured by *Children Playing Marbles* in a painting by Edward Thomson Davis.[44] The Davis painting depicted the game in a pastoral scene as an innocent boyhood pursuit reflecting the Romantic view of children in this period. There is little sense of children anxious not to lose precious marbles.

Emulation is an important element of playing with toys. By the mid-eighteenth century, tea drinking had spread far beyond the elite and middling sorts and, by the 1790s, poorer families in Middlesex and Surrey drank tea not only in the morning and evening but in large quantities even at dinner.[45] Children want to act like their parents and so the miniature toy tea set became popular. Victorian girls could gather their friends around a table and have a tea party like their mother. Children's tea sets made from porcelain or glazed ceramic ware resembled regular tableware, and the cups, saucers and teapots were fully functional but smaller to fit the hands of children. These tea sets were targeted at the wealthy, but *Children Playing with a Tea Set* by Thomas Webster in 1862 shows such a set in a relatively poor Victorian home.[46] As demand increased, tea sets became more affordable and companies who had initially focused on making adult-sized tableware began to mass-produce tea sets for the toy industry. Nevertheless, most poor children no doubt improvised this kind of role-play. Moreover, as tea items became cheaper and more widespread from the late eighteenth century, it is reasonable to think that old teacups, saucers and other paraphernalia used by their parents might have been given to children to play with, rather than thrown away when they upgraded their own sets.[47]

Play

Poorer children tended to play outdoors because of the cramped conditions of nineteenth-century working-class homes. Thus, the streets and waste ground became the playgrounds of the urban poor.[48] Outdoor games were frequently improvised by poor children with many paintings showing children playing without the need for toys. Most games depicted are familiar, and the paintings need little introduction. They include James Wood's *Mumble the Peg*, George Morland's *Blind Mans Buff* and *Children Playing at Soldiers*, John Morgan's *Snowballing*, William Gill's *Leapfrog* and Kate T. Hill's

Objects of Poverty

Children Playing Ring o' Roses. Mumble the Peg, which depicts the hazardous practice of throwing a knife close to your foot.[49] George Morland's *Children Playing at Soldiers* showed children participating in a military drill.[50] In winter, throwing snowballs and riding home-made sledges were popular pastimes. *Snowballing* by John Morgan in 1856 showed country children wearing traditional smocks, still used by working men and boys in country districts in the 1860s. Dorothy Tennant painted children from perhaps the lowest stratum of society. Her *Street Arabs at Play* (1890) depicted ragged urchins swinging on a railing along the Embankment in London.[51] The numbers of such children were significant, and Sarah Wise suggested that there were some 30,000 'street arabs' in Victorian London.[52]

Henry Turner described his childhood in *The Island*, five poor streets in the London Borough of Hackney, at the beginning of the twentieth century. Play in the street involved marbles and creating amusements from makeshift items:

> My childhood was pretty poor; there were ten of us kids together. We played in the street, cigarette cards, marbles, peg tops, hoops; we made grottos between Easter and Whitsun, using bits and pieces from the garden. We did it to make money, because all the pocket money we got was a farthing which we spent on sweets.[53]

Minnie Ferris moved to 'The Island' in 1907 when she was nine months old. Despite acute poverty, play was pleasurable, 'We did have fun as kids'. Like Henry Turner she recalled that play took place outdoors, 'We did a lot of skipping in the road'.[54]

Toys did not always have to be personally owned to be enjoyed. Toys and play were associated with community events, such as festivals or fairs, where poorer children might have the chance to participate. The first children's playground was built in a park in Manchester in 1859. In the late nineteenth century, town councils established public parks for recreation. Playgrounds featured play equipment, including swings, slides, roundabouts and climbing frames.[55] These parks and recreation grounds were accessible to all and no cost was involved. Sports, such as football, provided opportunities for sharing material goods. The experience of football was more challenging for children than today, as Victorian footballs were made from leather and had laces to keep the ball intact. The balls absorbed water and were painful to head in wet conditions.[56] An alternative for those who could not afford a manufactured football was to make one out of bundled sheets, rags or old tin cans.

Conclusion

This is but a brief survey of toys and children's play up to the end of the First World War. It demonstrates that there were obvious differences in the possession of toys by social class. Toys owned by affluent children were not available to many, especially the poorest. Working-class children were also restricted in the time available for play and poor housing conditions meant that they usually played outside. While there were budget constraints in many families, often severely so, the use of makeshift materials meant that much creative play was possible. Often, all that was needed was a stick of chalk, a few stones or old rags for dressing up. The ingenuity of children of all social groups frequently overcame barriers and created many opportunities to participate in play which was important to their social development. There was little evidence of a lack of affection by parents for their children. Even poor parents usually managed to provide cheap toys for their offspring, if only at Christmas. Children's devotion to their toys was unaffected by social class. Love for toys, particularly soft toys that occupied their bed, often stayed with children for the rest of their lives. This affection blurs the distinction in the enjoyment of toys by age group and stimulates interest in toy museums in various parts of the country.

Notes

1. Encyclopaedia Britannica. www.britannica.com/technology/toy (accessed 22 May 2023).
2. *Collins English Dictionary* (London: William Collins, 2023).
3. Jean Piaget's definition of four stages of childhood comprises of infancy (0–2 years), early childhood (2–7 years), middle childhood (7–11 years) and adolescence. Paul Musson, 'Piaget's Theory', in Paul Mussen and William Kessen (eds), *Handbook of Child Psychology. Vol. 1: History Theory and Methods* (New York: John Wiley, 1983), pp. 41–102.
4. Martin Woodhead, 'Early Childhood Development: A Question of Rights', *International Journal of Early Childhood*, 37:79 (2003): pp. 79–98.
5. Emma Griffin, 'The Emotions of Motherhood: Love, Culture and Poverty in Victorian Britain', *American Historical Review*, 123:1 (2018): pp. 60–85.
6. Sara Horrell, 'Consumption', in Roderick Floud, Jane Humphries and Paul Johnson (eds), *Cambridge Economic History of Modern Britain. Vol. 1: 1700–1870* (Cambridge: Cambridge University Press, 2014), p. 296.
7. Manual workers' real wages grew by more than 1 per cent between 1820 and 1850 and again towards the end of the nineteenth century as real earnings grew by 1 per cent per annum between 1873 and 1913. By the end of the nineteenth century, four out of five inhabitants in London were classified by Charles Booth as working class with well over a third of these families' incomes falling below the poverty line. Theodore Hoppen, *The Mid-Victorian Generation* (Oxford: Oxford University Press, 1998), pp. 61–2.
8. Gamages catalogue (1914) listed a rocking horse at 95 shillings. See: Clive Reynard, *Yesterday's Shopping: Gamages General Catalogue 1914* (London: Gamages LTD, 1994).
9. Eric Evans, *The Forging of the Modern State: Early Industrial Britain, 1783–1870*, 2nd edn (Harlow: Longman, 1996), pp. 129–31.
10. Anna Davin, *Growing Up Poor: Home, School, and Street in London, 1870–1914* (London: Rivers Oram Press, 1996), pp. 63–81.
11. There were 153 references to various kinds of toys in the *Old Bailey Papers* (hereafter *OBP*, all accessed 07 April 2024) (https://www.oldbaileyonline.org/) between 1700 and 1914. See also: Hans-Joachim Voth, *Time and Work in England 1750–1830* (Oxford: Clarendon Press, 2001).
12. Federation of Worker Writers, 'Henry Turner', in *The Island: The Life and Death of an East London Community, 1870–1970* (London: Centerprise Trust, 1979), p. 20.
13. I am indebted to Judith Kay for this reference.
14. *OBP*.

15 *OBP* t18660507-473, Trial of William Read, 7 May 1866.
16 Irina Diana Calu, 'Pieter Bruegel's Children's Games', 2022. www.dailyartmagazine.com (accessed 22 May 2023). Kunsthistorisches Museum, Vienna, Austria.
17 'Growing Up', Market Harborough Museum. https://www.harboroughmuseum.org.uk/displays/growing-up/ (accessed 09 April 2024).
18 For example, listed in *The Norwich Directory or Gentlemen and Tradesmens Assistant* (Norwich: William Chase, 1783) are John Lovick, 'Cutler, Toyman and Haberdasher', Isaac L. Marsh, 'Silversmith and Toyman' and William Yallop 'Haberdasher and Toyman'. The *OED* gives toyman (1707) as 'a man who sells toys or who keeps a toyshop'. C. Harrison, *Pigot's Directory*, 1922.
19 *OBP* t18450707-1538, Trial of Edward Fitzpatrick, 1845.
20 *OBP* t17930529-12, Trials of David Collyer, William Short and Samuel Steele, 29 May 1793.
21 *OBP* t18820130-231, Trial of George Berard, 30 January 1882.
22 *OBP* t18330905-51, Trial of Mary Jones, 5 September 1833.
23 *OBP* t17940430-46, Trial of John Napper and John Gummell, 30 April 1794.
24 *OBP* t18560915-868, Trial of Maria Allen, 15 September 1856.
25 *OBP* t18310106-11, Trial of George Flanner and John Dullage, 6 January 1831.
26 *OBP* t.18281204-140, Trial of Catherine Long, 28 November 1828; t18290409-280, Trial of William Hillman, 9 April 1829.
27 Lorelei Williams and Sally Thomson, *Marlborough Probate Inventories, 1591–1775* (Chippenham: Wiltshire Record Society, 2007), p. 281; Wiltshire and Swindon Archives P1/R/291, Inventory 428 Clement Raynolds, Brazier, 26 March 1724; Margaret Spufford, *Small Books and Pleasant Histories: Popular Fiction and Its Readership in Seventeenth-Century England* (Cambridge: Cambridge University Press, 1991), p. 120; Margaret Spufford, *The Great Reclothing of Rural England: Petty Chapmen and Their Wares* (London: Hambledon Press 1984), p. 57; Reading Museum and Town Hall REDMG: 1997.57.1, Mark William Langlois, *The Village Toy Seller*, 1876.
28 Harry Hendrick, *Children, Childhood and English Society* (Cambridge: Cambridge University Press, 1997), p. 88; Joseph Harley, *At Home with the Poor: Consumer Behaviour and Material Culture in England, c. 1650–1850* (Manchester: Manchester University Press, 2024), p. 196.
29 Deborah Jaffe, *The History of Toys: From Spinning Tops to Robots* (Stroud: Sutton Publishing, 2006), p. 163.
30 Ibid., pp. 49–50.
31 Beverley Cook, *Penny Toys and Poverty: An Edwardian Christmas*, 2016. www.museumoflondon.org.uk/discover/penny-toys-and-poverty-edwardian-christmas (accessed 20 June 2023).
32 Ernest King's collection contains some 1,650 items. Jaffe, *History of Toys*, p. 50. Museum of London, 80.525/934, Toy Clown and Dog, 1907.
33 Jack Tempest, *Collecting Tin Toys* (London: William Collins, 1987), p. 24.
34 The childhood gallery of the Curtis Museum, Alton, has a collection of toys and dolls dating from the eighteenth century to the present.
35 Dorset County Museum 1986.310.1; Hollytrees Museum COLEM 1989; Colchester and Ipswich Museums IPSMG:R 1968.84.A; Whitby Museum, Noah's Ark, early nineteenth century. https://whitbymuseum.org.uk/noahs-ark/ (accessed 09 April 2024).
36 Jaffe, *History of Toys*, p. 86.
37 Victoria & Albert Museum (hereafter V&A), MISC.73-1979, Soft Toy, *c*. 1906.
38 Portable Antiquities Scheme, https:/finds.org.uk/database (accessed 09 April 2024).
39 Ginger Frost, *Victorian Childhoods* (Santa Barbara: ABC-CLIO, 2008), p. 77.
40 Museum of Archaeology and Anthropology, Cambridge, 1974.291 A, Marbles, early twentieth century.
41 V&A B.333:1 – 24-2013, Marbles, nineteenth century.

42 V&A B.335-2013, Marbles, late nineteenth century.
43 Edward Martin, Colin Pendleton, Judith Plouviez, Gabor Thomas and Helen Geake, 'Archaeology in Suffolk 2000', *Proceedings of the Suffolk Institute of Archaeology and History*, 40 (2000): p. 105.
44 Courtauld Institute of Art, London, D.1952.RW.4571, Edward Thomson Davis, *Children Playing Marbles*, mid- nineteenth century.
45 Joanne Sear and Ken Sneath, *The Origins of the Consumer Revolution: From Brass Pots to Clocks* (Abingdon: Routledge, 2020), p. 86; Joseph Harley (ed.), *Norfolk Pauper Inventories, c. 1690–1834* (Oxford: Oxford University Press, 2020).
46 Harris Museum and Art Gallery, Preston, PRSMG: P672, Thomas Webster. *Children Playing with a Tea Set*, 1862.
47 Harley, *At Home with the Poor*, pp. 164–9.
48 Janet Sacks, *Victorian Childhood* (Oxford: Shire Books, 2011), p. 55; Beamish Museum, Stanley, Audio History Recording, AUD2007-111, Mrs Coates Peoples Collection.
49 Butler Institute of American Art, Ohio, IAP 81470180.I, James Wood, *Mumble the Peg*, 1829.
50 British Museum, London, 1940,1109.120, George Morland, *Children Playing at Soldiers*, 1788.
51 Edward Morris, *Victorian and Edwardian Paintings in the Lady Lever Art Gallery* (London: National Museums & Galleries on Merseyside, 1994), pp. 114–15.
52 Sarah Wise, *The Blackest Streets: The Life and Death of a Victorian Slum* (London: Bodley Head, 2008), p. 295.
53 Federation of Worker Writers, 'Henry Turner', in *The Island The Life and Death of an East London Community, 1870–1970* (London: Centerprise Trust, 1979), p. 18.
54 Federation of Worker Writers, 'Minnie Ferris', in *The Island*, p. 30.
55 Jon Winder, 'Revisiting the Playground: Charles Wicksteed, Play Equipment and Public Spaces for Children in Early Twentieth-Century Britain', *Urban History*, 50:1 (2023): pp. 134–51; Hazel Conway, *People's Parks: The Design and Development of Victorian Parks in Britain* (Cambridge: Cambridge University Press, 1991); Katy Layton-Jones, *National Review of Research Priorities for Urban Parks, Designed Landscapes and Open Spaces* (London: English Heritage, 2014), p. 28.
56 Vintage leather footballs dating from the period of the First World War can be seen at the York Castle Museum, the Regimental Museum in Camberwell and Dover Castle Museum. See, for example, https://pwrrqueensmuseum.co.uk/2022/08/26/the-somme-football/ (accessed 07 June 2024).

Further reading

Ariès, Philippe. *Centuries of Childhood: A Social History of Family Life* (London: Penguin, 1973).
Brown, Kenneth. *The British Toy Industry* (Oxford: Shire Books, 2011).
Jaffe, Deborah. *The History of Toys: From Spinning Tops to Robots* (Stroud: Sutton Publishing, 2006).
Pollock, Linda. *Forgotten Children: Parent-Child Relations from 1500 to 1900* (Cambridge: Cambridge University Press, 1983).
Sacks, Janet. *Victorian Childhood* (Oxford: Shire Books, 2011).
Tempest, Jack. *Collecting Tin Toys* (London: Collins, 1987).

CHAPTER 11
'MODELS OF NEEDLEWORK': A NEEDLEWORK SAMPLE BOOK FROM THE DUBLIN FEMALE ORPHAN HOUSE, c. 1860-90

Eliza McKee

Introduction

The National Museum of Ireland (NMI), Decorative Arts and History at Collins Barracks in Dublin, houses a rich collection of Irish needlework. On a research visit to consult the collection of needlework sample books created at Ireland's national schools for the education of Irish children, first established in the 1830s, the curator produced a sewing workbook that sat curiously among the other examples:[1] a needlework book produced not by a national school – as is most common in the collection – but by the children housed inside the Female Orphan House in Dublin – the only known example in existence.[2] The volume, dating from the 1860s to the 1890s, is unique material evidence of the needlework and clothing construction skills of destitute female orphans in nineteenth-century Ireland.

While some miniature samplers are included in this workbook, the volume shows a much broader range of the orphans' sewing and dressmaking skills than is typical of other orphan needlework.[3] Without other family or relatives with the financial capacity to care for them, girls in the orphanage came from impoverished backgrounds with minimal, if any, support networks, which sets them apart from working-class children who attended national schools and were not necessarily destitute. In contrast, examples of needlework produced by wealthier children survive in much larger numbers. This needlework sample book is also unique in its quality, its inclusion of multiple girls' work, and its compilation over a thirty-year period. Most national school needlework sample books were compiled by one pupil and were completed during their time at school, thus representing the evidence of one child's needlework education. In all, such sample books are valuable as they provide great insight into the lives of poor girls in the past, in this case, impoverished orphan girls whose lives left few traces in other historical records.

Until now, this particular orphan house needlework sample book has not drawn attention from historians. Orphan needlework, however, is not without a history. English orphan needlework has been the subject of much analysis in exhibition and auction house catalogues.[4] National school needlework sample books have appeared in some books on dress history written on other subjects. When they are, they are referenced in

Objects of Poverty

passing as evidence of sewing skills possessed by girls in the past, rather than examining in-depth the circumstances within which they were created in Ireland.[5] National school needlework sample books survive in museum collections in Europe and in north America, and I have examined these sample books in my forthcoming book.[6]

This chapter continues to address this gap in needlework history, beginning by outlining the context of the orphan house and its aims. The contents of the needlework sample book and the unique information the volume reveals on the needlework and dressmaking skills taught to female orphans is assessed. Finally, the samples are examined for what they reveal about the gendered education of poor female orphans and their training for future employment opportunities. Textile historians have started to utilise the history of emotions in their work, revealing the powerful role that objects can have eliciting affective states and emotions across temporal boundaries.[7] Sewing is very emotive and this article contends that needlework allowed the orphan girls to develop and display their domestic virtues and piety and provided them with an opportunity for emotional expression.[8] The needlework samples are an emotionally rich source that provides a rare glimpse into the emotional history of a neglected social group, orphan girls. The chapter will argue that the samples reveal the central importance of needlework and dressmaking to the education of female orphans to prepare the girls for their gendered roles in life beyond the institution. It will also argue that the samples reveal the strength of material knowledge and material literacy possessed by the orphans.[9] The samples connect us to the lives and experiences of Irish orphan girls in the Dublin Female Orphan House, constituting an unwritten legacy demonstrable of the needlework skill and industry of the largely unnamed orphan girls.

The Female Orphan House

The Female Orphan House – run by the Church of Ireland – is Ireland's oldest charity, established formally in 1791 by one of the last acts of the Irish Parliament before the Act of Union of 1800.[10] Orphans admitted to the institution were raised in the Anglican religion, regardless of the religion of their parents. Initially, the girls were lodged at a small property at 42 Prussia Street in Dublin. Money was later used to purchase a larger house at North Circular Road in Dublin – the location where this needlework sample book was produced – accommodating up to 160 orphans. Here the girls were lodged, clothed, taught to read and write, instructed in bookkeeping and numeracy, and trained in cleanliness and household work. Needlework and fibre skills – plain needlework, clothing construction, spinning and knitting – were core elements of the young girls' education and training.

The method of instruction, when it came to sewing skills on the curriculum, was centred around teacher-led demonstration and learning-by-doing. Teachers were recruited for the institution with a specific focus on their needlework ability that could be disseminated to the girls in the belief that the skill level of the teacher affected the ability of their charges. The needlework was created in a place of safety in a secure and clean environment at a time of vulnerability for the girls, and the skills learnt were intended to prevent them from future insecurity. Unfortunately, a needlework manual for the institution does not survive, so it is not possible to cross-reference with the written curriculum to verify the structure of the girls' education and the needlework tasks the girls had to complete. Instead, I have turned to the history of the institution to understand how needlework fitted into their daily routine. The girls would wake at 6.00 am and go to bed at 10.00 pm. Eight hours per day were spent on work and instruction, eight hours were expended on religious worship and leisure, and eight hours were reserved for sleep. Work in the morning typically consisted of plain needlework, and after lunch, the girls moved to knitting and spinning.[11]

The needlework sample book

The needlework sample book is a black-cloth-bound volume with a printed paper label on the front page stating: 'The Female Orphan House, North Circular Road, Dublin'. The volume contains seventy-five pages of hand sewn needlework samples and miniature-to-scale garments produced by the orphan girls. On these pages, 159 samples are mounted onto coloured pages of blue, green and pink paper. The inside page of the volume contains a small handwritten contents page stating:

> In Book.
> Models of Needlework ---
> In Box.
> 1 Honey Comb Overall
> 6 Diaper Pinafores
> 2 Bead Stands
> 1 Orphan Doll
> Female Orphan House
> North Circular Road, Dublin
> 24th August 1861.

The box of miniature garments and the orphan doll mentioned on the inside of the volume have not survived.[12] While the volume is dated August 1861 on the inside cover, a couple of samplers in the volume reveal that there are needlework samples dating from the 1860s to the 1890s, indicating that the volume was compiled across thirty years. Given the large number of girls housed within the orphanage at any time, the samples are just a cross-section of those produced between 1860 and 1890 and are likely to be the highest-quality samples of needlework made by the girls.

The volume was compiled for multiple reasons. Firstly, the samples were pasted into a volume to document and demonstrate the high-quality needlework produced by the orphan girls to show to governors, subscribers and visitors to the institution. The sewing samples were also used to demonstrate the girls' skills to prospective employers interested in hiring or apprenticing them when they reached sixteen. One of the intentions of teaching plain work skills was to enable the institution to take in sewing work as the charity advanced, with the profits applied to the costs of running the orphanage.[13] The orphan house was known for its high level of needlework teaching and outputs from the girls, even making linen shirts for King George IV in 1821, which helped generate sales among Dublin women.[14] One of these shirts survives in the NMI collection and shows that the orphan girls could scale up their clothing construction skills to make high-quality clothing for adult bodies.[15] In fact, the orphan house had such a high reputation for its needlework among the public in Dublin that it secured consistent sales for plain sewing work for much of the nineteenth century. Not forgetting the school commercial aspect, the volume could also be used to demonstrate the girls' sewing quality to potential customers.[16]

While there were many reasons the needlework sample book was compiled by the workmistress, the most important was for educational examination so that inspectors could assess the quality of instruction inside the institution. In contrast, needlework sample books produced in national schools were typically made by one girl, and they kept the book beyond their education as a convenient way to show potential employers their needlework skills. Minute books for the orphan house demonstrate that the girls were examined on their needlework proficiency using the samples on an annual basis. Women members of the board for the orphanage were involved in the examination. On 28 May 1889, for example, a Mrs Brooke, Mrs La Touche and Miss Hern completed the annual assessment of needlework. They judged that the samples were 'models of needlework':

> [The] work was generally so good that it was difficult to decide on the relative merits of the pupils, and extra rewards were given in some of the classes – Each of the ladies present promised special rewards next year for marking, damask darning and smocking all of which had been admirably done by the pupils formerly, and it is hoped that they will now be revised. The book containing specimens of the work done formerly was ordered to be laid on the table in the board room on board days.[17]

Indeed, the women inspectors frequently remarked in their annual assessments that the standard was so high as to make awarding prizes incredibly difficult. They also regularly commented on the high quality of teaching.[18] Clearly, it was a primary concern of female members of the board to ensure that needlework was strong and an educational priority, while other subjects such as religion, arithmetic, reading and writing were assessed by the male diocesan inspectors in a gendered division of examination.

The samples and the needlework skills taught

The needlework specimens and miniature-to-scale garments demonstrate that the skills taught to the orphan girls mirrored those taught to female primary school pupils under the national school system of education. As in national schools, surviving minute books show that instruction was divided into six classes determined by age and proficiency and needlework prizes were given in each class to the most proficient children.[19] The samples document the stitches taught, the patterns and fashions of the time and other skills deemed appropriate to teach the girls. The fine quality of the stitching, intricacy and finishing on the specimens illustrates the care, technical skill, dedication, concentration and steady industry of the girls, alongside the attention of the needlework teacher to their instruction. The orphan girls invested a lot of time into creating the samples, and while making them, they undoubtedly experienced a mix of pride and pleasure. The lengthy process of making the samples encouraged thoughtful meditation on the task.

Given the wide period that the samples cover, it is clear that they were not all produced by only one talented girl. Unfortunately, the names of only two girls are included next to two darning samples in the book. The first darning sampler worked by Mary Wilson in 1890 in green and purple thread contains six darns including plain, twill, single diamond, tartan plaid, stocking and wave darns. Darning was an important skill as it would enable the girls to mend and repair garments and textiles for their future families or in employment. The second contains eight darning samples, including single diamond, double diamond, tartan plaid, wave, plain, twill, bird's eye and stocking darns, alongside the name Annie Marshall and the date 8 May 1890. It has two crowns sewn on it in yellow and green thread (Figure 11.1). It is not possible to reconstruct who these girls were, their backgrounds and their lives beyond the institution. They are not named individually in records for the institution and the census for Ireland only survives for 1901 and 1911. The 1901 census for Ireland lists 1,079 people with the name Mary Wilson and 79 people with the name Annie Marshall.[20] None of these people were living in the orphan house on the night the census was taken. Therefore, Mary Wilson and Annie Marshall were either working outside the institution when the census return was completed, or they may have married and taken a new surname. The remaining 157 specimens constitute the material legacies of entirely unknown orphans.

Some of the small samplers contain religious quotes and are worked with devotional texts, through which we can unpick the faith of the orphan girls. The words stitched in these samplers were specifically chosen by the girls after years of bible study. They are likely to be lines that struck a chord with the girls during religious instruction, though no doubt their words would have had to have been approved or overseen by their workmistress. The biblical references and quotes evidence the performing of religious expectations and reveal the religious contexts within which the orphans lived. The religious quotes worked into canvas by the girls included a quote that emphasises the importance of the bible and the word of God, 'The sword [sewn bible] of the spirit … the spirit breathes upon the word, and brings the truth to sight. Precepts and promises afford, a sanctifying light' (Figure 11.2). The 'sword of the spirit' was used by Paul in Eph. 6.17 to describe the word of God and its role in spiritual warfare.

Other religious quotes worked in the samplers are biblical verses that relate to orphans, and that suggest God shows orphans mercy, care and protection among oppressed groups. For example, one sampler reads, 'Believer! Thou'rt not alone, let this assurance

Objects of Poverty

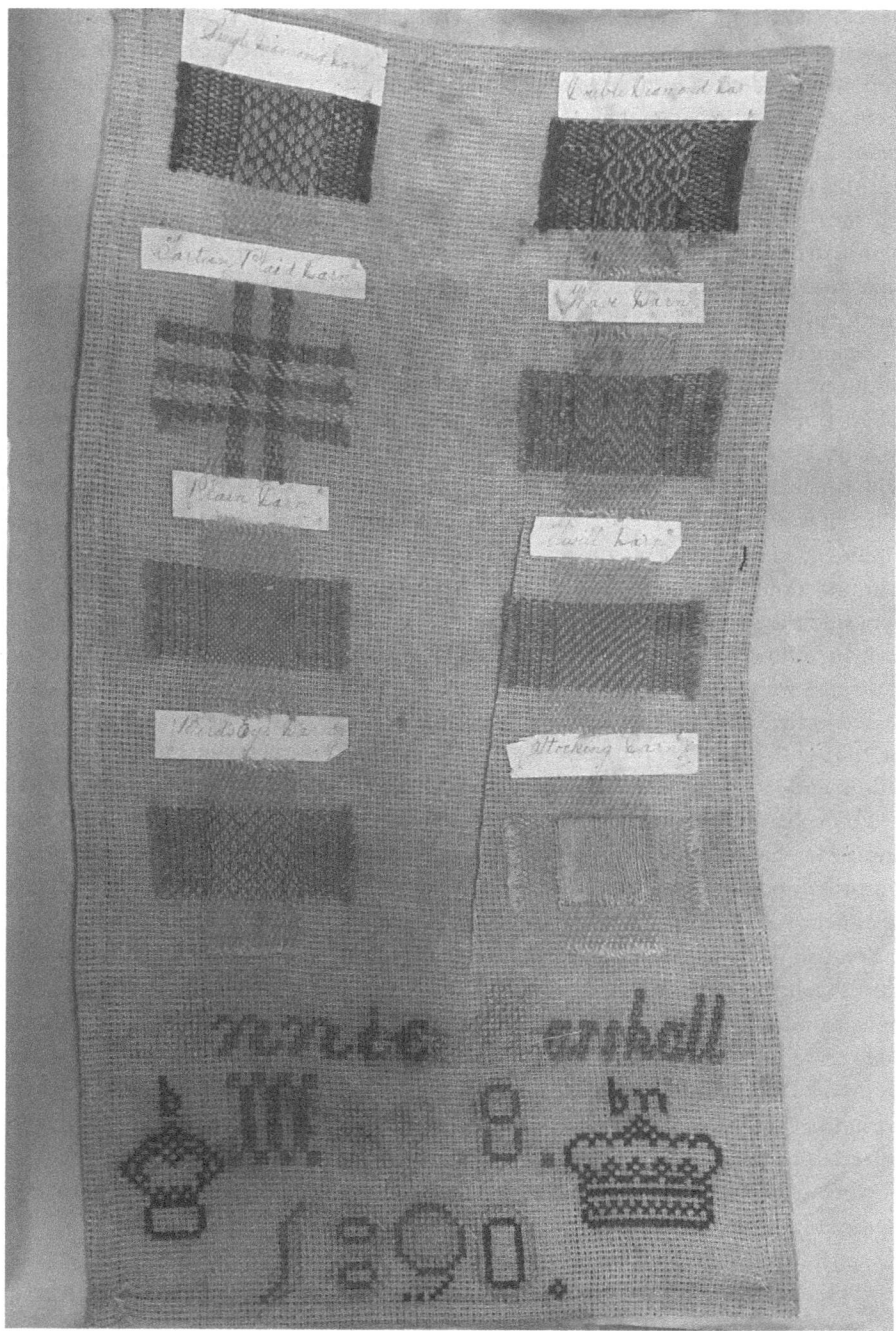

Figure 11.1 A darning sampler worked on canvas with yellow and green thread produced by Annie Marshall and dated 1890. Research image by Eliza McKee © National Museum of Ireland.

'Models of Needlework'

Figure 11.2 A miniature dress with smocking detail around the neckline, lace trimming around the neckline and cuffs of the sleeves, and three rows of four horizontal pleats on the skirt. Red silk band tied at the waist. A religious sampler worked in red thread. Research image by Eliza McKee © National Museum of Ireland.

there thee – To one thine inmost soul is known, and he is ever near thee' and 'Alone thou are not when care, and grief they soul opposes, he doth they every burden bear, and feels in thy distresses' (Figure 11.3). The most direct of the orphan quotes worked onto a sampler is a verse from Jer. 49.11 that reads, 'Leave thy fatherless children, I will preserve them alive; – 49th chap Jeremiah vssth'. These quotes must have been chosen for the comfort they provided the girls, encouraging them to believe that they were not alone. The quotes evidence their love, commitment and religious devotion. It was an emotional practice to work the sampler and communicate the orphan's faith, emotions over orphanhood and parental loss in stitch.

Most of the samples are made from white or undyed wool, cotton and linen. Sewing in the nineteenth century generally fell into two broad categories: plain work and fancy work. Plain work included making and mending simple articles of clothing. Fancy work encompassed decorative work including crochet work and embroidery.[21] The majority of the samples in the workbook are of plain sewing including patchwork, darning and miniature garments including shirts, underwear and baby clothes, as well as samples of knitting. There are also some examples of fancy needlework including trimming, drawn thread work, embroidery, crochet and lacework such as strips of lace work, crochet edging samples, fringed borders, whitework embroidery and embroidered motifs. For example, Figure 11.4 depicts a crochet edging sampler with five rows of crochet trimming that could be used to adorn clothing or homeware. The inclusion of fancy work samples in the volume shows that the girls of the Female Orphan House were taught decorative needlework skills; a skill that would make them more employable when they left the institution.

All of the sewing samples were produced by hand. Included are examples of bedding and homewares such as crocheted bed covers, crocheted place mats (Figure 11.4), pillowcases and cushion covers. Other items of decorative homeware include alphabet and number samplers, darning samplers and drawn thread work samplers. There are embroidered tokens or souvenirs such as small butterflies. Core sewing skills, stitches and techniques are demonstrated in the making and attaching of buttons and buttonholes, seaming, gathering and fastening-in gathers, and smocking. The clothing items largely constitute baby clothing, including bonnets made of linen and lace (Figure 11.5), slips, aprons and tabards, alongside undergarments and night clothing for adults, correlating with the garments that women were expected to be able to produce for their families. The emphasis on practical instruction for girls was indicative of the powerful ideology of domesticity, that working-class women's work should revolve around domestic work and the upkeep of the home.[22] Sewing was perceived as a woman's duty and girls needed to develop needlework skills to fulfil these future roles. As adults they would be expected to make and repair clothing for their families and charges.[23] In the creation of the samples, the orphans practiced their future wifely, motherly and domestic duties. Through the creation of the baby clothing, they emulated the love, care and dedication to create clothing for their own babies and the children they would care for in future.

Other clothing items included in the samples are miniature dresses, chemises, blouses, blouse inserts or panels, socks, stockings, day shirts, night shirts and night dresses,

'Models of Needlework'

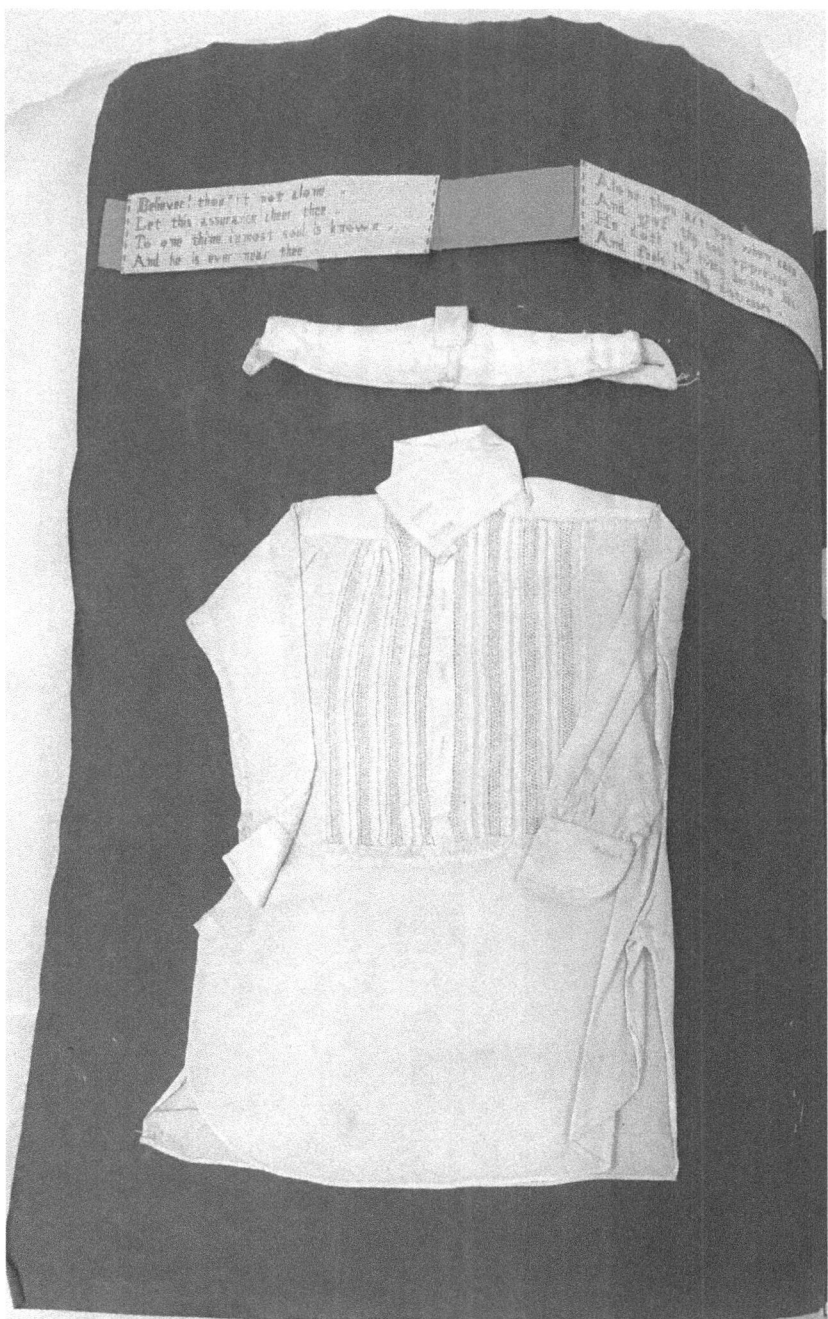

Figure 11.3 A miniature white shirt with four panels of vertical lacework on either side of the centre front. A miniature white shirt collar. A religious sampler worked in red thread. Research image by Eliza McKee © National Museum of Ireland.

Figure 11.4 Crochet edging sampler with five rows of crochet trimming. Two crocheted place mats with frayed trim. Research image by Eliza McKee © National Museum of Ireland.

'Models of Needlework'

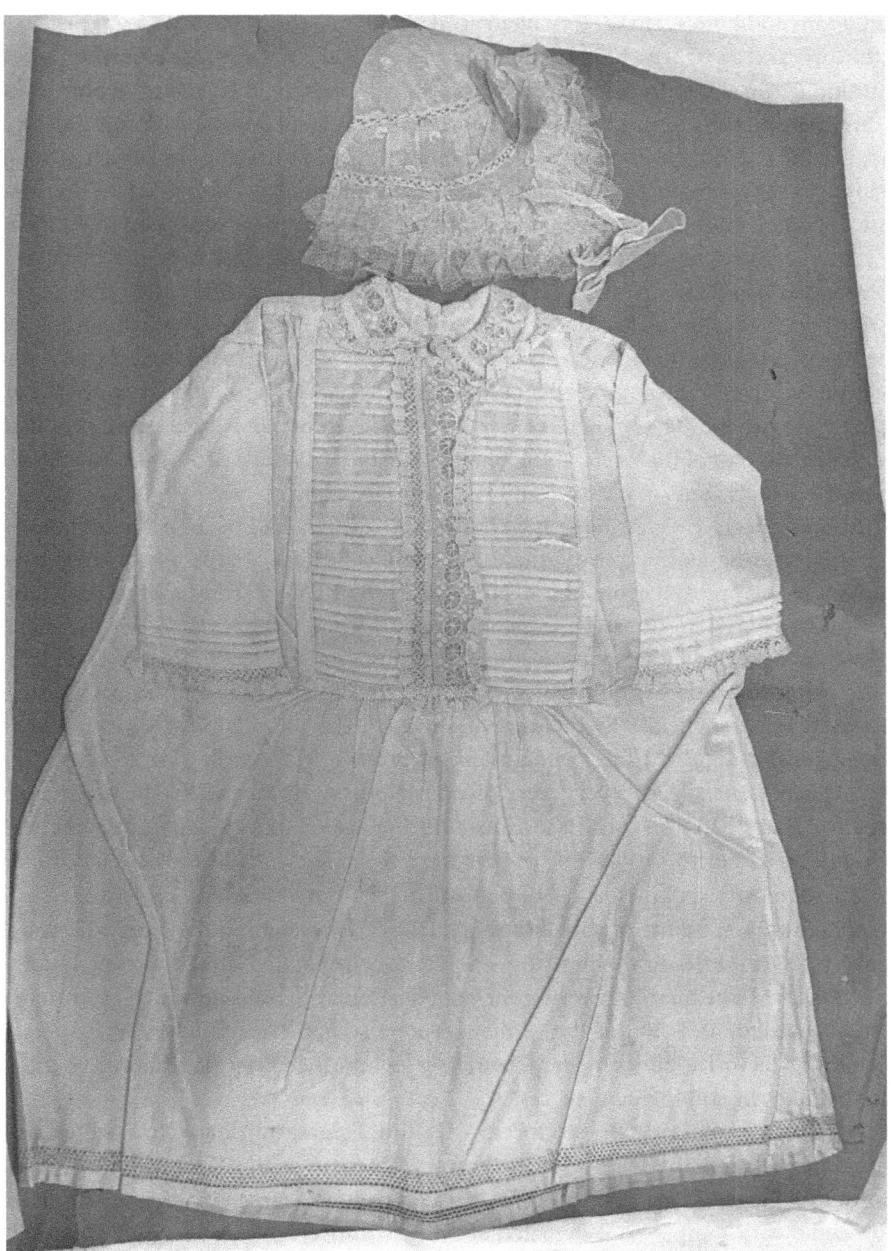

Figure 11.5 A miniature lace bonnet with two strings for fastening. A night shirt with drawn thread work at the hemline, three rows of pleats above the sleeve cuffs, broderie anglaise trimming at the centre front of the shirt placket at the collar and at the sleeve cuffs. Nine rows of three pleats on either side of the centre front placket. Research image by Eliza McKee © National Museum of Ireland.

pantaloons and tunics. These clothing items demonstrate the wide variety of skills taught to the girls and those which had most utility for the girls in the future after they left the institution. The ability to construct adult clothing items would be useful to both clothe themselves and their future husbands as part of their unpaid domestic labour. Indeed, in post-famine Ireland, lower-class women commonly made baby clothing, undergarments and nightwear for the men of the household, as well as constructing much of their own clothing, whereas outer clothing and tailored garments for men were often purchased.[24]

While the volume reveals information on institutional life inside the orphanage, the samples also demonstrate what the girls were being trained for when they left the institution. It speaks to class and gendered ideals regarding needlework training and teaching practices in the nineteenth century. Needlework crosses the boundaries within the everyday lives of these girls – it could be associated with domestic life, work life and leisure time depending on when the needle was picked up. These girls were producing needlework as part of their education, but it would be later utilised for work. Sewing was, of course, also a means of pleasure and relaxation for many.

The orphanage, as a charitable and religious institution, had the objective of housing, educating, raising and preparing the orphans for adult life. At the age of sixteen, the orphans were removed from the orphanage. Initially, they were apprenticed under an indentured system of seven years and later they were apprenticed out for shorter periods of a year when a review of their placement would occur. Thus, a central aim of the institution was to train the orphan girls for employment and keep them from poverty that parental loss had thrown them into. The foundation documents of the orphan society highlight one of the main purposes of the needlework lessons: 'They [the orphans] shall learn every part of household work to qualify them for useful servants. They shall be kept in the House till the age of sixteen, when they are to be apprenticed or put to service'.[25] The girls were typically sent out of the institution to work as domestic servants, such as parlour maids, nursery maids or governesses in the homes chosen by the orphan house governors. Protestant individuals who sought a governess or domestic servant from the orphanage applied directly to the board of governors, with the board reviewing each application and deciding which girl to assign for each placement. Some of the orphans were also apprenticed to trades, especially to clothing factories and drapery businesses, where needlework training would be essential to their employment success.

The surviving minute books for the Dublin Female Orphan House document that some girls left the institution to become teachers at the Kildare Place Teacher Training College.[26] This institution was a centre of teaching excellence in Ireland, and needlework sample books created at this institution have survived in remarkable numbers in museum, library and archive collections around the world. The fact that girls went from the orphan house to train at the teacher training college is evidence of their high levels of needlework skill. At this college, the attending women had to possess needlework prowess. After attending Kildare Place, the women would become teachers in Ireland's national schools, where needlework skills were a central part of the curriculum for girls.

Conclusion

The needlework sample book connects us to the everyday lives of poor orphan girls living inside the Dublin Female Orphan House between *c.* 1860 and 1890. The uniqueness of this source lies in the quality of the samples and in the fact that it is the only known orphan needlework sample book to survive in Ireland. It also shows the whole range of needlework and dressmaking skills possessed by multiple orphans. Making the needlework samples was about labour, both mundane (darning and plain sewing) and emotionally charged (baby clothes and religious samplers). Some of the samples offer a way of exploring how the orphan girls represented their own emotions. The needlework samples are an achievement of the care, dedication and investment of the girls.

The samples are a lens through which we can build an understanding of the training the orphans received, the work they produced and their routine labour inside the institution. The book is also evidence of the gendered history of needlework education and it is indicative of a highly feminised form of educational training and labour. The material literacy of the girls, the time, care and skill devoted to the production of needlework inside the institution is demonstrated. Immense importance was put on the teaching of needlework to prepare the girls for appropriate gendered careers once they left the institution. It thus speaks not only to life inside the institution but also to the lives the girls were trained for outside the orphanage. The skills taught to the orphan girls could be used to stitch their way out of poverty if faced with destitution again in their lives in the absence of a social welfare system. These needlework skills could be relied on in future to prevent admittance to the workhouse and provide a means by which to financially support and materially care for their own future families.

The needlework sample book constitutes an unwritten legacy of the lives of these largely unknown and unnamed orphan girls and demonstrates their steady industry. While these samples were produced by girls aged under sixteen, with such a high level of ability displayed in childhood, the skill level and the quality of their needlework finishing would only increase in adulthood with time, experience and practice. This source is a material record made and left behind by the orphan girls themselves, when the majority of sources about the poor, including destitute orphans, were written or compiled 'from above' by people higher up the social hierarchy. The book allows you to look at the lives of the poor in minute detail, on something that they cared about, needlework skills that would be utilised throughout their lives.

Notes

1. National Museum of Ireland (hereafter NMI) DT:1987, 33, Female Orphan House Needlework Sample Book, 1860–90.
2. The orphanage was variously called The Female Orphan House, The Female Orphanage House and Kirwan House.

3 English examples of orphan needlework survive in museum and private collections, particularly samplers containing moral verses or biblical extracts. See Joy Jarrett, *Stitched in Adversity: Samplers of the Poor* (Oxford: Witney Antiques, 2006), pp. 36–7, 41, 45–54; Rebecca Scott, *The Educated Stitch: Historic Samplers, 1700–1900* (Oxford: Witney Antiques, 2019), pp. 33–53.
4 Ibid.
5 Barbara Burman and Ariane Fennetaux, *The Pocket: A Hidden History of Women's Lives, 1660–1900* (London: Yale University Press, 2019), p. 97.
6 Eliza McKee, *Clothing the Irish Poor* (Liverpool: Liverpool University Press, 2025).
7 See, for example, Alice Dolan and Sally Holloway, 'Emotional Textiles: An Introduction', *Textile: Cloth and Culture*, 14:2 (2016): pp. 153–9; Stephanie Downes, Sally Holloway and Sarah Randles, 'A Feeling for Things, Past and Present', in Stephanie Downes, Sally Holloway and Sarah Randles (eds), *Feeling Things: Objects and Emotions through History* (Oxford: Oxford University Press, 2018), pp. 8–23; John Styles, *Threads of Feeling: The London Foundling's Hospitals Textile Tokens, 1740–1770* (London: Foundling Museum, 2010).
8 Sasha Handley 'Objects, Emotions and an Early Modern Bed-Sheet', *History Workshop Journal*, 85 (2018): p. 171.
9 On the concept of material literacy, see Serena Dyer and Chloe Wigston Smith (eds), *Material Literacy in Eighteenth-Century Britain: A Nation of Makers* (London: Bloomsbury, 2022).
10 'An Act of Incorporating Governors and Governesses on the Circular Road Near Dublin', 5 August 1800, Chap. LXV.
11 Anonymous, *A Brief Record of the Female Orphan House, North Circular Road, Dublin. For Over One Hundred Years, from 1790 to 1892* (Dublin: Sealy, Bryers and Walker, 1893), p. 16.
12 Email from Alex Ward, curator and Acting Keeper Art and Industrial Division, NMI, 25 April 2023.
13 Anonymous, *A Brief Record of the Female Orphan House*.
14 Ibid., p. 34.
15 NMI DT: 1987, 32, Large man's linen shirt, one of two dozen made at the Female Orphan House, Dublin, for King George IV, 1821.
16 The Reverend Canon C.T.A. Carter M. A., *Kirwan House: 'The Foremost Irish Charity', 1790–1990* (Dublin: Colour Books, 1996), p. 4.
17 Representative Church Body Library (hereafter RCBL) MS 517, 1.1 7, Minute book of Female Orphan House Dublin, 3 June 1889.
18 Ibid., 2 June 1890; 4 June 1888.
19 Ibid., 7 May 1889.
20 1901 and 1911 Census of Ireland. https://www.census.nationalarchives.ie/ (accessed 28 January 2024).
21 For the difference between plain sewing and fancy work, see Susan Burrows Swan, *Plain & Fancy: American Women and Their Needlework, 1700–1850* (New York: Holt, Rinehart and Winston, 1977).
22 Annemarie Turnbull, 'Learning Her Womanly Work: The Elementary School Curriculum, 1870–1914', in Felicity Hunt (ed.), *Lessons for Life: The Schooling of Girls and Women 1850–1950* (Oxford: Blackwell, 1987), p. 87; Jane McDermid, *The Schooling of Girls in Britain and Ireland, 1800–1900* (New York: Routledge, 2012), pp. 9–11.
23 McDermid, *The Schooling of Girls*, p. 46.
24 Eliza McKee, 'Non-Elite Clothing Acquisition in Post-Famine Ulster, c. 1850–1914', PhD thesis (Queen's University Belfast, 2022), p. 161.
25 Anonymous, *A Brief Record of the Female Orphan House*, p. 4.
26 RCBL MS 517, 1.1 7, Minute book of Female Orphan House Dublin, 7 March 1893.

Further reading

Carter, M. A., The Reverend Canon C.T.A. *Kirwan House: 'The Foremost Irish charity', 1790–1990* (Dublin: Colour Books, 1996).

Dolan, Alice, and Sally Holloway. 'Emotional Textiles: An Introduction'. *Textile: Cloth and Culture*, 14:2 (2016): pp. 153–9.

Downes, Stephanie, Sally Holloway and Sarah Randles. 'A Feeling for Things, Past and Present', in Stephanie Downes, Sally Holloway and Sarah Randles (eds), *Feeling Things: Objects and Emotions through History* (Oxford: Oxford University Press, 2018), pp. 8–23.

Dyer, Serena, and Chloe Wigston Smith (eds). *Material Literacy in Eighteenth-Century Britain: A Nation of Makers* (London: Bloomsbury, 2022).

Jarrett, Joy. *Stitched in Adversity: Samplers of the Poor* (Oxford: Witney Antiques, 2006).

McDermid, Jane. *The Schooling of Girls in Britain and Ireland, 1800–1900* (New York: Routledge, 2012).

Scott, Rebecca. *The Educated Stitch: Historic Samplers, 1700–1900* (Oxford: Witney Antiques, 2019).

Styles, John. *Threads of Feeling: The London Foundling's Hospitals Textile Tokens, 1740–1770* (London: Foundling Museum, 2010).

Turnbull, Annemarie. 'Learning Her Womanly Work: The Elementary School Curriculum, 1870–1914', in Felicity Hunt (ed.), *Lessons for Life: The Schooling of Girls and Women, 1850–1950* (Oxford: Blackwell, 1987), pp. 83–100.

CHAPTER 12
FRAGMENTARY FINDINGS: A VICTORIAN SCHOOL NEEDLEWORK SAMPLE
Vivienne Richmond

Introduction

Strange as it may sound, it is nevertheless true, that, although we fasten most of our garments either by means of buttons or strings, as a rule they are not well sewn on. Therefore, teachers would be wise to give lessons on these matters, because it is important that their pupils should learn to finish off their work as perfectly as possible.[1]

Kate Stanley, Head Governess and Teacher of Needlework, Whitelands College, London, 1883.

On my wall, framed between two pieces of glass, is a postcard-size piece of calico – a cheap cotton fabric – folded to make a double thickness, the raw edges tacked together. On it are a small hand-stitched buttonhole, a linen button and a label stating: 'Annie Sawden Standard V January 20th 1896' (Figures 12.1a and 12.1b). This combination of text and textile is a sample of needlework made for assessment by a British schoolgirl in the late nineteenth century, and similar samples, demonstrating a range of sewing techniques, would have been made by virtually every girl who attended elementary school in the 1800s. It is both despite and because of this ubiquity that few survive: as utilitarian exercises in the plain sewing taught to working-class girls, they were considered of no value or significance beyond their immediate demonstration of the maker's proficiency.

Nor has their perceived worth increased with time. This sample was given to me by a student who had taken my undergraduate module 'Dress, Poverty and Identity in Nineteenth-Century England', which included a study of school needlework instruction.[2] She chanced upon it in the bargain bin of an antiques' store and, realising what it was, kindly bought it for me. Without this serendipitous encounter, it would likely have languished indefinitely in the bargain bin.

As a small example of the work of a named individual it provides a glimpse of one particular child's life. But because every girl who attended a nineteenth-century elementary school would have made a number of such samples, it is a window onto the everyday lived experience of millions of working-class girls. It is also an example of the chance way in which the material culture of the poor survives and is, or is not, valued in

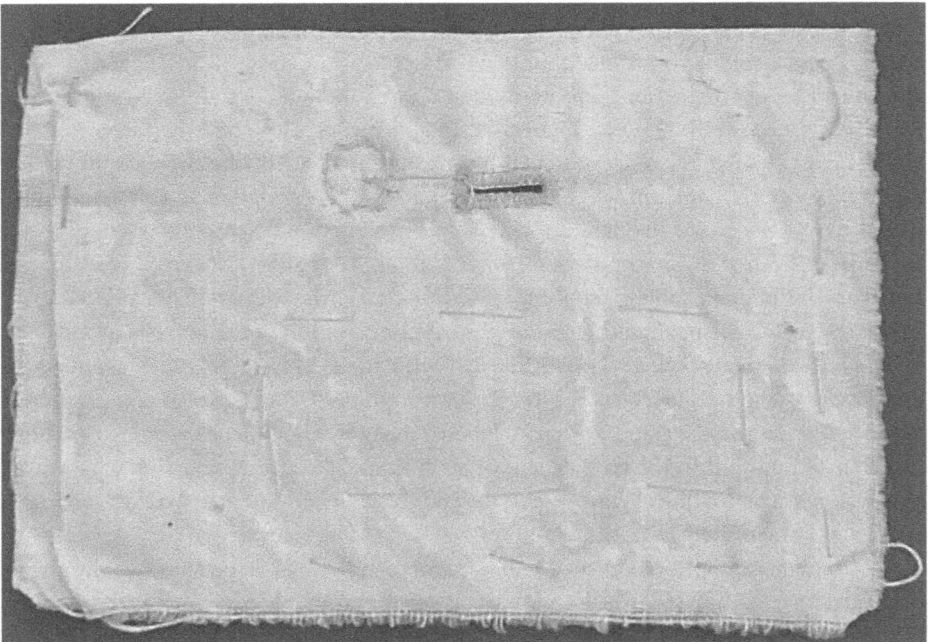

Figure 12.1 (a) Annie Sawden's sample, front side; (b) Annie Sawden's sample, reverse side. Source: Author's collection.

the present; Annie Sawden – and her teachers – would, I am sure, be astonished to know that I consider her button and buttonhole worthy of framing and display.

In contrast, some ninety years after the sample was made, anthropologist Claude Levi-Strauss recalled a conversation with the influential French historian Lucien Febvre who 'wished historians would address problems such as the origin and spread of the button'. His focus was the different effects of draped and fitted clothing, the latter achieved through the use of buttons:

> He was absolutely clear ... that the presence or absence of this modest item demarcated important ways of human behaviour: it divided the draped and the sewn, two styles of clothing, one of which posing greater demands on the body, the other posing greater demands on the material – but also reflecting on bodily posture, the art of life, ways of integrating in the world, which distinguish different civilisations.[3]

Annie Sawden's sample evidences one step in the spreading use of buttons. In late-Victorian England, common present-day fastenings such as the zipper and hook-and-loop were yet to be invented, but cheap mass-produced buttons were becoming increasingly common. In comparison with alternative fastenings then available, such as pins, ties and laces, buttons were less liable to come undone and did not tangle or knot. By easing the process of getting and staying dressed they made a small but significant impact on the daily lives of the majority.

This chapter will first consider the educational context in which the sample was produced, highlighting the perceived moral and practical value of needlework instruction for working-class girls. It will then examine the different elements of the sample to see what it reveals about its maker and to show that this humble specimen of school needlework sheds light on multiple facets of late-nineteenth-century proletarian life in Britain and beyond.

Poverty, education and needlework

Formal education for working-class children in England and Wales expanded throughout the nineteenth century. Originally in the hands of religious bodies, 1870 marked the move from state assistance to direct state provision of elementary education. By 1896, when Annie Sawden made her buttonhole, school was free and compulsory for children between the ages of five and eleven.[4] Importantly, these state-funded elementary schools were established specifically for, and attended by, working-class children. While the term 'working-class' embraces a range of incomes, fin-de-siecle surveys concluded that some 30 per cent of the population lived in poverty and identified childhood as one of the life stages when it was most likely to be experienced.[5] And even for working-class families not actually in poverty, factors such as job insecurity and potential illness made it an ever-present possibility.[6] Even if Annie Sawden's family was not poor, those of many girls in the same class and sewing the same samples, would have been.

Objects of Poverty

The schools aimed to prepare pupils for their expected role in adult life. For girls, this was domestic work, either as a paid servant or as an unpaid dutiful daughter, wife and mother. As such, the curriculum, set out in the Codes of Regulations issued by the government's Education Department, was different for boys and girls – with several hours of needlework each week mandatory for the latter from 1862.[7]

Needlework instruction and examination were arranged into levels from Infants through Standards I–VII, the girls moving from one standard to the next on the basis of attainment, not age. The Codes of Regulations stipulated the work to be done at each standard, and this was reproduced in the many textbooks published to guide schoolteachers.[8] Pupils 'Below Standard I' (infants) were required to perform needle and knitting pin drills, 'simple hemming' and a strip of knitting 15" × 3" (38 × 7.5 cm). Making a buttonhole and attaching a button were introduced at Standard IV, but Annie Sawden did this also at Standard V because as girls moved to the next Standard they were to learn not only new skills but also to do 'The work of previous Standards with greater skill'. Finally, at Standard VII, the girls were to make a garment such as 'a night dress with frill', to demonstrate different types of darning and patching, to knit 'a long stocking with heel thickened' and to cut out 'any under-garment for making up in Standard IV'.[9] A girl who completed Standard VII – and would be a maximum of twelve years old – would, therefore, be in command of a wide range of plain sewing skills and able to make and mend a variety of functional garments and household textiles. These skills were not merely a technical exercise, but of real practical use. Despite the rapid growth of cheaper, mass-produced, ready-made clothing in the second half of the nineteenth century, it remained too expensive for many working-class families to purchase. They relied exclusively or partially on home-made and second-hand clothing, the latter often requiring alteration. Additionally, damaged textiles would be repaired or repurposed rather than simply discarded and replaced.[10]

Furthermore, needlework was taught not only for its practical utility but also because it was thought to instil modesty, obedience and self-discipline, generally considered as desirable female traits.[11] This is evident in the militarily inspired needlework drills used to teach infants how to thread a needle or put on a thimble. These simple processes were broken down into a series of movements to be performed by the children in response to the teacher's commands. Drill was also considered an effective way to manage large classes at a time when pupil numbers were rapidly increasing. According to Louisa Floyer (1830–1909), principle of the London Institute for the Advancement of Plain Needlework and a school needlework examiner, in order to educate pupils it was necessary to instil in them obedience and discipline:

> and both can only be attained, when large numbers have to be dealt with, by 'Drill'. This fact has already been acknowledged in the Army and Navy, and among those who have had to deal with boys, and though it may be comparatively a new idea among Infants and Girls Schools, experience is giving daily proof of its utility.[12]

While the perceived link between femininity and needlework meant it was taught to girls of all classes, the type of needlework they learned was divided along class lines. The mention of Victorian samplers generally conjures an image of a decorative piece, framed for display, on which are worked the alphabet, numbers, a religious quotation, the maker's details and ornamental motifs. But these are mostly the samplers of elite girls. In 1876, the Education Department's New Code of Regulations stipulated that in state-funded elementary schools 'no fancy work of any kind may be done in school hours'.[13] Decorative 'fancy work' or embroidery was deemed inappropriate for working-class girls as it served no practical purpose.[14] They were to be taught only 'plain sewing' – the techniques and processes needed to make and mend simple utilitarian garments and household linen. As Floyer explained, the items made were 'supposed to be "elementary garments," suited to the wants of the girls attending "elementary" schools'.[15] As such, the samplers of working-class girls comprised a collection of the plain sewing exercises they worked on in the various standards, such as Annie Sawden's buttonhole (Figure 12.2).[16]

Learning from Annie

Little of the poor's own clothing from this period still exists. Therefore, the needlework of poor females most often survives anonymously in the seams and darns they sewed in the garments and household linen of their social superiors. As such, Annie Sawden's calico sample is also rare because it bears her name. We do not know who she was or where she went to school, but having reached needlework Standard V, Annie would probably have been aged around ten when she worked the sample in 1896. She would, therefore, have been born in the mid-1880s. According to an Ancestry search, the few girls born then and named Annie Sawden were all in the county of Yorkshire.[17] But, as the London schoolgirl's sampler in Figure 12.2 shows, the same needlework curriculum was taught to girls across England.

While we know little about Annie from written records, we can learn a great deal from her needlework. It is often difficult to know to what extent the idealised prescriptions of instructional literature were observed in reality. Annie Sawden's sample provides a bridge between the regimented directions of school curricula and needlework manuals and the girls' classroom experience. The Education Department's needlework examination required the pupil to 'cut and work a button-hole, one end round, the other braced, and to sew on a linen button', which is exactly what Annie Sawden did. For this, she was to be supplied with 'A piece of calico 3 inches [approximately 7.5 cm] square, and a linen button not pierced' – Annie's folded piece of calico is slightly larger, measuring approximately 4.5 × 3 inches (11.5 × 7.5 cm). To improve their strength, buttonholes were to be worked through a double thickness of fabric. This increased the challenge of making them since the hole was cut before stitching (the precise method of cutting being also described in some detail), so it was necessary to keep in line the raw edges

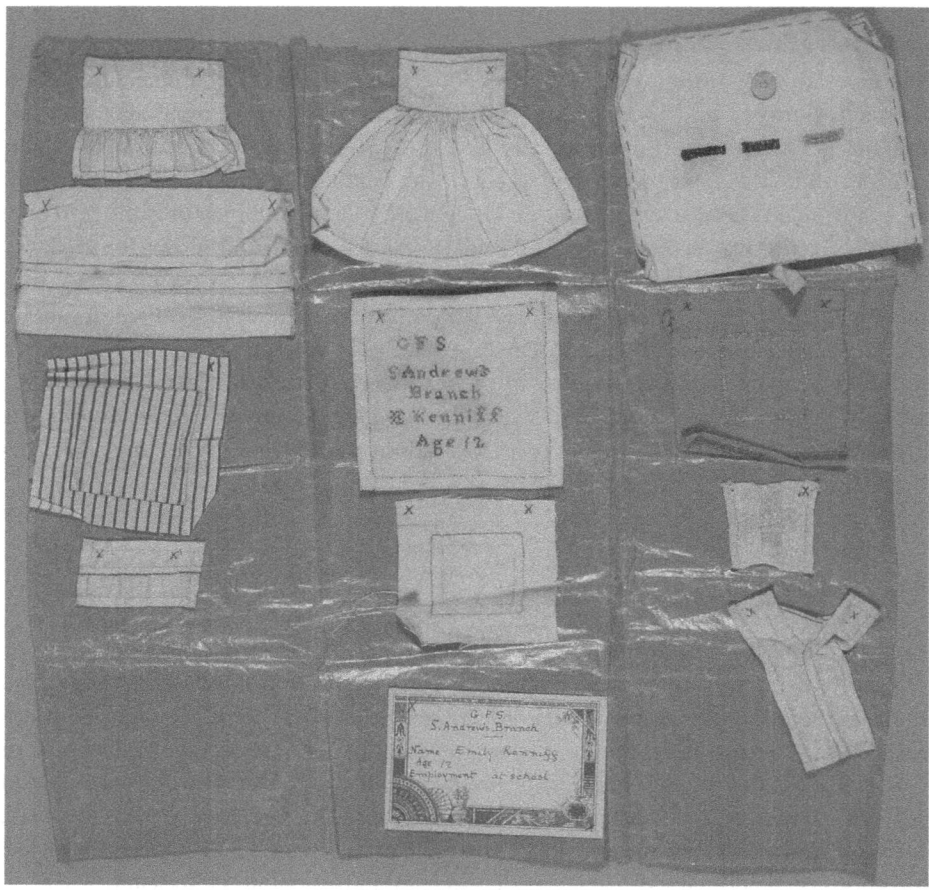

Figure 12.2 A plain-sewing sampler, incorporating a button and buttonholes, worked by a London schoolgirl in 1888. Source: The Women's Library at LSE Library, 5GFS/12/1/11.

of the buttonhole on both layers to achieve a neat and serviceable finish.[18] Again, Annie was successful.

The stitching attaching the label to Annie Sawden's sample and holding the two layers of fabric together around the edges is large and rather irregular. But on the right side, at least, the buttonhole is neatly sewn. On completion of the buttonhole the girl was to 'fasten the cotton off securely on the wrong side ... which must be as neat and as free from ends as the right'. Annie Sawden would have lost some marks here as the reverse side of her buttonhole is a tangle of loops and irregular stitches. Also, rather than fastening off the thread and starting afresh to sew on the button, she carried the thread across between the buttonhole and the button. Likewise, the buttonhole 'ought to be long enough to admit the button easily'.[19] However, Annie's button has a 17-mm diameter while the buttonhole opening measures only 10 mm and is therefore too small for the button to pass through. Nevertheless, worked at the correct size a buttonhole of this quality would have been serviceable and long-lasting. And while the stitching on the button does not form a perfect circle and is rather too near the edge which, in use, would distort a buttonhole, the stitches are again neat and even and the button is securely attached to the fabric.[20] Annie Sawden was clearly a proficient, if not expert, needleworker and the sample is an indicator of achievement, since to have progressed to Standard V Annie must already have passed Standards I–IV.

Literacy was another compulsory elementary school subject and Floyer was keen that its teaching be linked to needlework by, for example, including words such as 'stitching' in spelling lessons.[21] The writing on the label of Annie Sawden's sample is very neat. We do not know if she wrote it – although the slight error on the 'n' of Sawden hints at a pupil rather than a teacher – but if so, it is of a piece with the neat stitching of the button and buttonhole, both indicating a person who took care with her work.

Annie Sawden's sample provides a small window into the material culture of the elementary school classroom, the fabric, thread, button and paper implying the presence of other objects such as pins and scissors. But also, the cotton calico on which the buttonhole is worked is class-specific. Traditionally, underclothes, which included shirts, shifts and men's drawers, were made of hard-wearing linen. In the nineteenth century, the rapid growth of the cotton industry in Britain meant that in working-class households linen was replaced by cotton calico, which, though cheaper, was much less durable.[22]

The button on Annie Sawden's sampler is also historically specific and of the type used to fasten underclothes. These buttons were made by covering linen with a circle of pasteboard on the outer edge of which is a metal ring. They have no buttonholes or shank but are held in place by sewing through the button itself. Early-nineteenth-century school sewing manuals include instructions on how to make such buttons by hand.[23] But the button on Annie Sawden's sample is mass-produced because by the mid-nineteenth century, their manufacture had been industrialised.[24] Instruction manuals now dealt only with the process of sewing-on a button supplied by the teacher, on the assumption buttons would be purchased.[25] These mass-produced buttons were indeed cheap. In 1907 the Army and Navy stores offered a card of twelve dozen (144) 'superior' linen buttons of the size on Annie Sawden's sampler for 9½d – less than a penny for twelve.[26] And doubtless they were available elsewhere more cheaply and in smaller quantities. But even this might have been beyond the budgets of the poorest. In a 1913 survey of the weekly budgets of impoverished London housewives, a few allocated 3d to the purchase of 'Cotton and tapes', but no other haberdashery is noted.[27] At a time when the use of these buttons had been normalised, missing buttons or the use of tapes where buttons had become customary would have been visible symbols of poverty. As Febvre noted, the presence or absence of buttons may well have affected integration.[28]

The use of mass-produced buttons is an example of new technologies infiltrating superficially insignificant corners of quotidian life. In contrast, some half-century after the introduction of the domestic sewing machine, Annie Sawden's sample shows that schoolgirls were still sewing by hand. Sewing machines were expensive and, in the

1890s, the majority were bought for professional use by homeworkers.[29] Furthermore, a domestic sewing machine that could stitch a buttonhole or attach a button was yet to be invented.

Annie Sawden's sample is a material manifestation of the prevailing regimented scheme of needlework education set out in numerous teachers' instruction manuals. It directly links the idealised goals portrayed in text and illustrations with the classroom experience of poor girls. It underscores the perceived connection between needlework and femininity and, decades after the invention of the domestic sewing machine, the continued importance of hand sewing. Some of Annie Sawden's peers would have been more skilled needlewomen, some less, but part of the sample's representative value lies in its lack of exceptionalism. It is probable that by the time she produced it, Annie would already have been making and mending some of her own clothing and that of her family. The sample evidences her ability to do so and offers an insight into the quality of clothing they may have worn.

Conclusion

Annie Sawden's sample is unique, but her experience was almost universal among poor girls in Britain. It was also shared by large numbers in the British Empire, to where the same needlework education and ideology of utility were exported.[30] Embedded in this scrap of calico, found in the bargain bin of an antique store, is evidence of the co-existence of ancient craft skills and new technology, the spread and limitations of that technology, the history of industrialisation and education, and the politics of class and gender in nineteenth-century Britain and the territories it colonised. Annie Sawden would have held this fabric for an extended period, pressing it between her fingers as she manipulated needle and thread and unwittingly embedding traces of the skin cells, oil and sweat from her hands – her DNA. My analysis is based on what can be seen with the naked eye, but modern scientific examination now or in the future could perhaps tell us more about the maker of this ostensibly unremarkable fragment.

I do not know why Annie Sawden's sample has survived when literally millions of others have not, but like so much historical evidence, it was probably chance rather than deliberate preservation. The antiques dealer from whom my student bought the sample likely acquired it as part of a job lot and indicated its perceived lack of worth by putting it in the bargain bin. Annie Sawden would have produced many samples in her numerous needlework classes as she progressed through elementary school. It is proficient, but there is nothing to suggest she took exceptional pride in its production. Similarly, her teacher and examiner would have seen thousands of schoolgirl needlework samples, and there is no obvious reason for them to have placed a particular value on this one. But for my student, it held a meaning she would not have realised several months earlier. For me, it is invaluable. Annie Sawden's sample is a rare extant example of the commonplace, a direct, tangible link to the daily life of one working-class schoolgirl who stands as an unwitting representative of the shared experience of millions.

Notes

1. Kate Stanley, *Needlework and Cutting-Out: Being Hints, Suggestions, and Notes, for the Use of Teachers in Dealing with the Difficulties in the Needlework Schedule* (London: Edward Stanford, 1883), p. 14. Whitelands was a female teacher training college.
2. To my regret, I cannot remember the student's name. I would be delighted if any reader can enlighten me.
3. Ulinka Rublack, *Dressing Up: Cultural Identity in Renaissance Europe* (Oxford: Oxford University Press, 2010), p. 17.
4. Keith Evans, *The Development and Structure of the English School System* (Sevenoaks: Hodder and Stoughton, 1985), pp. 37, 44–6.
5. Charles Booth, *Life and Labour*, 17 vols (London: Macmillan, 1902–3); Seebohm Rowntree, *Poverty: A Study of Town Life* (Bristol: Policy Press, [1901] 2000).
6. Eric Hobsbawm, *The Age of Capital 1848–1875* (London: Weidenfeld & Nicolson, 1995), pp. 219–20; François Bédarida, *A Social History of England 1851–1990*, trans. A. S. Forster and Jeffrey Hodgkinson (London: Routledge, 1991), pp. 150–1.
7. Annmarie Turnbull, 'Learning Her Womanly Work: The Elementary School Curriculum, 1870–1914', in Felicity Hunt (ed.), *Lessons for Life: The Schooling of Girls and Women 1850–1950* (Oxford: Basil Blackwell, 1985), pp. 84–5.
8. See, for example, Stanley, *Needlework and Cutting Out*, pp. 131–44.
9. Ibid., pp. 131–3.
10. See Vivienne Richmond, *Clothing the Poor in Nineteenth-Century England* (Cambridge: Cambridge University Press, 2013).
11. Turnbull, 'Learning Her Womanly Work', pp. 88–9.
12. Mrs. L. S. Floyer, *Needle Drill, Position Drill, Knitting Pin Drill, to Which Is Added 'Thimble Drill' as Required by Mundella's Code, Educational Department. Needlework Drill, 1881 'Girls' and Infants' Departments, Boys and Girls below Standard I'* (London: Griffith and Farran, 1881), p. 3.
13. *Education Department. 1876. New Code of Regulations with an Appendix of New Articles and of All Articles Modified, by the Right Honourable the Lords of the Committee of the Privy Council on Education*. Parliamentary Papers 1876 LIX, p. 6.
14. Rozsika Parker, *The Subversive Stitch. Embroidery and the Making of the Feminine* (London: Women's Press, 1984), p. 154.
15. Anon. [Mrs. L. S. Floyer], *Plain Cutting Out for Standards V., VI., and VII., as Now Required by the Government Education Department, 1885, Adapted to the Principles of Elementary Geometry, Containing Also a Copy of What Is Required in Other Subjects (Schedules I, II, III) and a Copy of the Instructions to Her Majesty's Inspectors* (London: Griffith, Farran, Okeden & Welsh, 1885), p. 13.
16. For an analysis of the sampler shown in Figure 12.2, see Vivienne Richmond, 'Stitching the Self: Eliza Kenniff's Drawers and the Materialization of Identity in Late-Nineteenth-Century London', in Maureen Daly Goggin and Beth Fowkes Tobin (eds), *Women and Things 1750–1950: Gendered Material Strategies* (Farnham: Ashgate, 2009), pp. 43–54; Vivienne Richmond, 'Stitching Women: Unpicking Histories of Victorian Clothes', in Hannah Greig, Jane Hamlett and Leonie Hanna (eds), *Gender and Material Culture in Britain Since 1600* (London: Palgrave, 2016), pp. 90–103. For examples of more decorative samplers stitched by non-elite girls, as well as examples of exceptional plain sewing, see Anon. [Joy and Stephen Jarrett, Rebecca Stott], *Stitched in Adversity: Samplers of the Poor* (Witney: Witney Antiques, 2006); Carol Humphrey, *Quaker School Girl Samplers from Ackworth* (Great Britain: Needleprint, 2006).
17. www.ancestry.co.uk (accessed 15 February 2023).
18. Stanley, *Needlework and Cutting Out*, pp. 28, 31–5, 139.

19 Ibid., pp. 34–5.
20 Compare the much smaller circle of stitching on the Figure 12.2 sampler button which also will fit through any of the three adjacent buttonholes.
21 Turnbull, 'Learning Her Womanly Work', p. 89.
22 Richmond, *Clothing the Poor*, pp. 67–8.
23 See, for example, Anon., *A Manual of the System of Teaching Needlework in the Elementary Schools of the British and Foreign School Society*, 2nd edn (London: British and Foreign School Society, 1821), pp. 21, 28–9 and Specimens of Needlework No. 8.
24 Nina Edwards, *On the Button: The Significance of an Ordinary Item* (London: I.B. Tauris, 2012), p. 5.
25 See, for example, Stanley, *Needlework and Cutting-Out*, pp. 14, 16–17. Stanley instructs that the button should be attached with the stitches making a star formation, radiating from the centre, rather than in a circle.
26 Anon., *Yesterday's Shopping: The Army & Navy Stores Catalogue 1907. A Facsimile of the Army & Navy Co-operative Society's 1907 Issue of Rules of the Society and Price List of Articles Sold at the Stores* (Newton Abbot: David & Charles Reprints, 1980), p. 840.
27 Maud Pember Reeves, *Round about a Pound a Week* (London: Virago, [1913] 1979), pp. 81, 86.
28 Rublack, *Dressing Up*, p. 17.
29 Andrew Godley, 'Homeworking and the Sewing Machine in the British Clothing Industry 1850–1905', in Barbara Burman (ed.), *The Culture of Sewing: Gender, Consumption and Home Dressmaking* (Oxford: Berg, 1999), pp. 258–9.
30 Vivienne Richmond, *A Remedy for Rents: Darning Samplers and Other Needlework from the Whitelands College Collection*, a booklet accompanying the 2016 exhibition of the same name. https://viviennerichmond.com/a-remedy-for-rents (accessed 22 March 2024).

Further reading

Burman, Barbara (ed.). *The Culture of Sewing: Gender, Consumption and Home Dressmaking* (Oxford: Berg, 1999).

Daly Goggin, Maureen, and Beth Fowkes Tobin (eds). *Women and Things 1750–1950: Gendered Material Strategies* (Farnham: Ashgate, 2009).

Hunt, Felicity (ed.). *Lessons for Life: The Schooling of Girls and Women 1850–1950* (Oxford: Basil Blackwell, 1985).

Parker, Rozsika. *The Subversive Stitch. Embroidery and the Making of the Feminine* (London: Women's Press, 1984).

Richmond, Vivienne. *Clothing the Poor in Nineteenth-Century England* (Cambridge: Cambridge University Press, 2013).

PART V
LIVING OBJECTS

CHAPTER 13
THE POOR'S BEST FRIEND? DOG OWNERSHIP AND COMPANIONSHIP IN ENGLAND, c. 1780-1880

Joseph Harley[1]

Introduction

Dogs are not 'objects' per se. They are living and breathing creatures with their own thoughts, emotions and characteristics.[2] Nevertheless, dogs are usually viewed as possessions of humans in the legal sense – as owners can be prosecuted for their dog's transgressions – and in the informal sense – for they reside in our homes, eating the food we give them. Throughout the eighteenth and nineteenth centuries, dogs were a vital part of people's lives and a frequent encounter of millions of people. Dogs were crucial in food production, being utilised to herd sheep and protect livestock, while thousands more retrievers, pointers and foxhounds were used for hunting. Many more pet and working dogs acted as watchdogs, with their barks alerting owners to trouble afoot, while the smallest of dogs hunted vermin or could power spits by walking inside a wheel. Dogs were even used for entertainment, such as acting as dancing performers at fairs and were made to take part in various forms of fighting.

From the eighteenth century, there was a rise in 'pets', especially pet dogs and birds, whereby people named their animals, kept them for pleasure and not as a source of food, and felt an emotional connection to the creature.[3] The most famous of these is the lapdog. Favoured by wealthy women, lapdogs were worth considerable money and were often fed and looked after better than the majority of society. For the poor and working classes, dogs assumed a similar importance as possessions. Indeed, they were widespread among the group, as evidenced in countless pictorial materials and written accounts, but exactly how they were important is difficult to say. A handful of publications have been written in recent years which look at companionship and emotions among the working class and their dogs. This work has found that dogs (and pets more widely) were important to the group and that they shared deep emotional bonds.[4] However, we still know little about the wider population's ownership of dogs prior to the late Victorian period. Except for work by Jane Hamlett, Julie-Marie Strange and Claudia Soares, most research on the poor and working classes is also based on the words of middling and upper-class commentators and not the group's own feelings and views.[5]

Objects of Poverty

This chapter, therefore, uses working-class autobiographies and other first-hand accounts to uncover the extent to which the Georgian and early- to mid-Victorian poor and working class saw their dogs as companions. It is argued that, similar to today, there are ample examples of dog abuse, people who did not like dogs and individuals who were very heavy-handed, but many people (especially owners) saw dogs as allies and friends by the late eighteenth century.[6] Life was hard. People would not have gone to the trouble and expense of keeping a dog with no use if they were not fond of them. The dogs might have been primarily kept by people for the services that they provided their owners, but weaved into this was affection and companionship. Indeed, even those dogs labelled as 'useless' by contemporaries and had no discernible function were likely cherished by their masters.

This chapter covers a broad range of poor and working-class groups, such as paupers, labourers, beggars, poachers and gamekeepers. While this scope is, to some extent, the consequence of the difficulties in finding sources, looking at a range of actors is beneficial as it highlights how disparate working people could share the same feelings towards their dogs but also how they could be set in opposition to one another. Examples of this include the gamekeeper who protected and maintained his master's lands versus the poacher who used his dog to catch a rabbit or two, or the bully who tried to steal his neighbour's canine companion. As these tensions played out, the dog often suffered most, whether the dog was loved and cared for or not. With this, there was a limit to the poor and working class's affection for dogs, especially if the dog was in the way of somebody doing their job or had become too troublesome to keep.

Views 'from above'

Middling and elite people commonly contended that the poor and their dogs were of equal disrepute. Both were labelled as objects of distrust and fear, as well as immoral, illogical and disease-ridden creatures. Animal welfare organisations such as The Society for the Prevention of Cruelty to Animals largely ignored animal cruelty among the middle and upper classes and instead focused on the 'real' problem of the masses and their pets.[7] During perceived and actual rises in cases of rabies and plague infections, the dogs of the poor were culled in the largest numbers as they were seen as most culpable of being infected and passing it on.[8] Roaming dogs were a frequent sight in cities around the world. Owned or ownerless, the poor were blamed for all the public safety worries and wrongdoings that materialised from these dogs.[9] In the home, the dogs of paupers were seen to directly take food out of the mouths of families and were yet another way in which people wasted their poor relief payments alongside drink, gambling and other immoral activities.[10] In contrast, the dogs of the middle and upper classes, especially the dogs which lived in the home, were seen like their owners, to be of a better character and composition. Their dogs were generally pedigrees and seen to be of a better quality compared to the motley assortment of mongrels that the poor owned, since the breeding and ancestry of the dogs were carefully managed. Rather than being trained in illicit

The Poor's Best Friend?

Figure 13.1 William Hogarth, *The Four Stages of Cruelty*, 1751. Wellcome Collection, 38379i, 38380i, 38381i, 907i, Public Domain Mark.

activities which played on the dogs' natural instincts such as fighting, their dogs were raised to be less 'wild' and be compliant, docile domestic companions.[11]

From the second half of the eighteenth century, people were much more aware and vocal about animal cruelty.[12] Accordingly, some writers emphasised how it was cruel on dogs to be owned by the poor. Dr Edward Barry, in one pamphlet, remarked that the poor could starve their dogs with little chance of punishment.[13] To combat this abuse, one anonymous writer paradoxically suggested that hanging dogs was the best option, as 'I believe it frequently relieves the poor man's dog from many lingering years of torture and of ultimate starvation'.[14] One of the main claims made by social

Objects of Poverty

Figure 13.1 (*Continued*)

reformers was that animal cruelty led to brutality among humans. It was regarded as only a short step from the poor starving and hurting their dogs to harming people in unimaginable ways. This idea is most famously portrayed in William Hogarth's *Four Stages of Cruelty* (Figure 13.1). In the first plate, the protagonist Tom Nero and other boys are seen torturing dogs and other animals for their amusement, while in the second and third pictures, Nero has moved on to professional cruelty as a coachman, and later theft and the brutal murder of a pregnant woman. Nero's life has gone full circle by the final plate, *The Reward of Cruelty*. After being executed for his crimes,

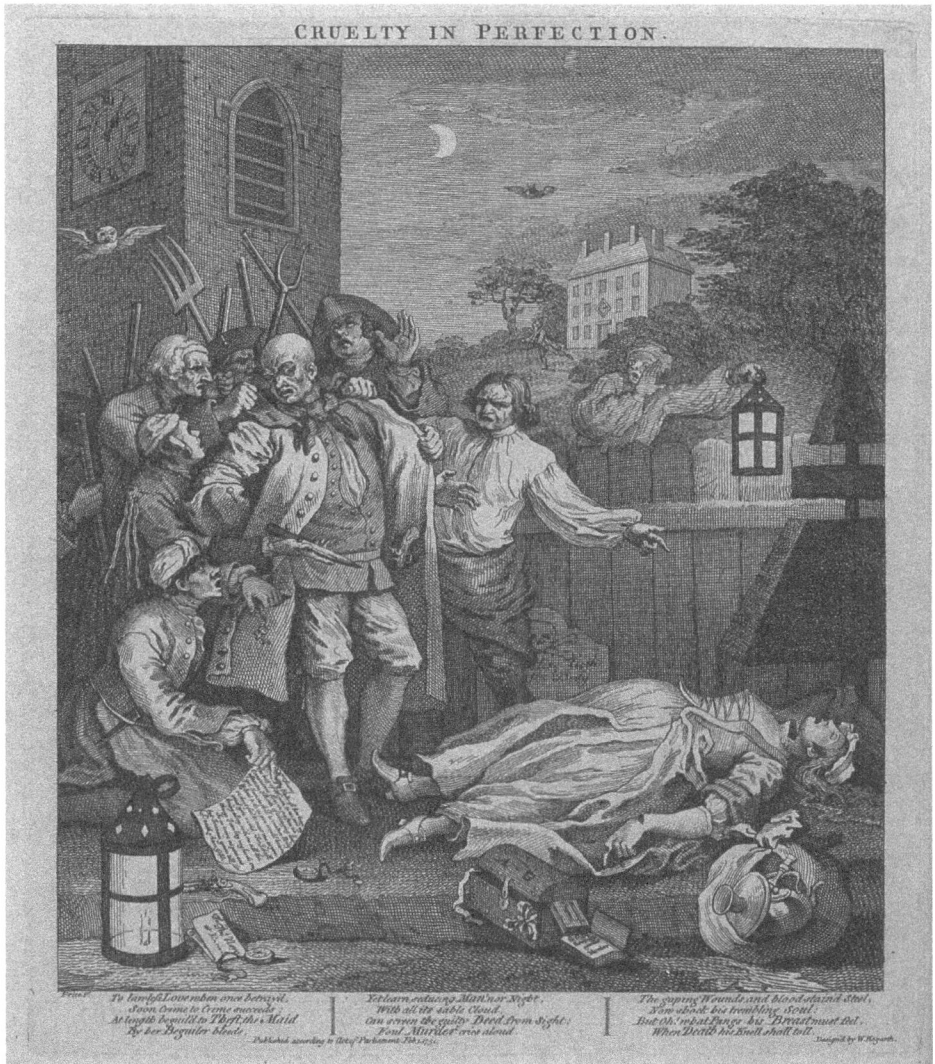

Figure 13.1 (*Continued*)

a dog is depicted eating his entrails after his body has been given over for grotesque public dissection – a fate that could terrify even the most hardened of criminals.[15] These accounts portray the poor as ruthless human beings who cared about little other than their own gratification.

While most people with wealth and power were critical of the poor's ownership of dogs, it is important to acknowledge that a small number of individuals saw beyond this. For example, in 1796, during parliamentary debates on whether to introduce a dog tax, the MP William Windham argued:

Objects of Poverty

Figure 13.1 (*Continued*)

With the poor the affection for a dog was so natural, that in poetry and painting it had been constantly recorded, and in any sort of domestic representation, we scarcely see a picture without a memorial of this attachment. If the rich man feels a partiality for a dog, what must a poor man do, who has so few amusements? He would be destitute without one. A dog was the companion of his laborious hours, and when he was bereft of his wife and children it filled up the dreary vacuity.[16]

Windham was also reported to have said that because a pauper shares what 'pittance' he has with his dog, 'it was an additional proof of the affection which the people of this country in the most indigent situation felt for that animal'.[17]

Views 'from below'

Most contemporaries disagreed with Windham and were unequivocal in their views: being poor meant that people were inherently cruel and abused their dogs. Indeed, the words of people 'from below' show how many mistreated dogs, such as by engaging them in fighting or killing them when it was thought necessary.[18] Some people were not particularly cruel to dogs but simply disliked or were indifferent to them. For example, the autobiographical writings of the mechanic/turner Benjamin Shaw (1772–1841) reveals that he was not fond of dogs. Benjamin described how his brother, George, 'spent all he had' playing with animals as a 'Hobby' during his childhood years, while Benjamin 'did not like' this and 'did all in our Power to hinder' this.[19] Perhaps this was sibling rivalry, immaturity or jealousy at play, but it is an important reminder that, like today, not all people liked dogs and were not ashamed to say so. Using first-hand sources, I argue that, despite this important caveat, people (especially owners) were generally fond of their own dogs and shared deep emotional bonds with them. This contradicts much of the assumptions which underpinned middling and elite ways of thinking about the masses and demonstrates that emotional bonds with dogs were present in labouring homes before the Victorian period.

Antony Errington, a colliery waggon and wagonway wright, wrote in some detail about his dog. Walking down a street in North Shields, Tyneside, late at night sometime during the 1810s, Errington met a 'Strange Dog' when it 'came to me and walked Close to mee'. He named the dog Tom, asking the canine 'Poor fellow, has thee lost thie Master?' and gave the dog a 'peace [of] Spice'. Suddenly, two men appeared from a bush and tried to rob Errington. Tom, the dog, 'downed' the thief, while Errington struck the other man and they both ran off. Errington took the dog home, 'gave him super and he Lay down'. The next day, his son became very fond of the dog and played with him, yet he was soon 'in tears' after somebody stole the animal. Despite Errington saying that he 'feared' the man who took the dog, he went to 'get the Dog again'. What followed was a heated argument with the thief and Errington asking a constable to take the man to the magistrate. However, the two men ultimately ended up having drinks together, parting as 'friends' with Errington having retrieved his dog Tom back. Errington later gifted the dog to his father and sister where it acted as 'a gardien' to them.[20] Here is a clear example of a man and his family bonding with a dog. It started when the dog kept him company on a lonely street and protected him from thieves, developing into a friendship and trusted partnership when he saw his son playing with the dog and acting as a protector to his father and sister. Had Errington felt little attachment to the dog, he could have easily not brought the stray home or refused to retrieve the dog when it was stolen.

Objects of Poverty

Dogs were increasingly present in portraits of middling and elite families from the early modern period. Such depictions demonstrate how many people saw their pets as part of the family and close companions.[21] For obvious reasons, there are fewer paintings of poorer abodes and those which do survive were mostly made to satisfy middle-class ideas of humble rural life. However, there exist more representative pictures of the homes of poor and working-class people from the 1830s to the 1860s. The clergyman Richard Cobbold (1797–1877) left behind a unique archive of paintings which depict the people and buildings in his village of Wortham, Suffolk. His paintings closely match the descriptions of the individuals and their abodes in his writings, and there is no reason to think that he falsified the portraits since he did not paint to satisfy a paying client.[22] The pursuit was simply a hobby of the parson. Cobbold contended that the pictures 'are genuine specimens of the features they record' as he 'intimately' knew everyone in his village.[23]

Dogs and cats were common in Cobbold's portraits, featuring numerous paupers, widows, ex-soldiers and various labourers, as well as a barber, butcher, bricklayer/mason, dairywoman, gamekeeper, housekeeper, miller, molecatcher, nurse, servant, thatcher and yardman.[24] The animals were usually shown following their master around outside, sitting on the subject's lap or adjacent to their chair. This suggests that the two were close, with the dogs following their owners wherever they went and being most comfortable in the company of their masters. Figure 13.2, for example, shows June Mark and his 'spotted dog'. A former farmer and in receipt of poor relief by the 1830s, Mark and his dog went everywhere together. Even when he went to church, the dog would come along and 'always sat in his lap'.[25] The home of the pauper widow Bet Mattock was described by Cobbold as containing 'two paper portraits of but little worth'. One picture depicted the 'celebrated highwaymans portrait' of '[Dick] Turpin flying o'er a ditch', while the other was of 'her husband and his terrier bitch' (Figure 13.3).[26] The fact that her deceased husband is depicted with his dog is a clear sign of companionship and affection. In another portrait, John, her husband, was also painted by Cobbold with his terrier next to him (Figure 13.4). Cobbold said that he and 'his favourite terrier' were 'well known features in the parish'.[27]

Attachment could come from the loyalty and valuable service that the dogs had given their owners. The dogs might have been used for poaching, protection, stealing and a host of other licit and illicit activities, but threaded through or sprouting from this service was affection and an emotional connection. One blind vagabond was said to have looked after his dog for so long as it 'once guarded his house when he had one, and preserved the family from being robbed and murthered'.[28] It is common to find accounts of dogs who faithfully followed their owners wherever they went. In London, one writer said: 'If we meet with a vagabond on the road, he is sure to be accompanied with his dog; if you see a pauper or mechanic of any sort in the streets, he cannot go from house to house without his dog dangling after him'.[29] Dogs were also vital in helping the blind and disabled maintain their independence.[30] The bond between the two was deeply entrenched as a result of this company and service. One blind man said, 'I feels more for my little dog than I do for myself as she sits there a-shiverin', while another recounted

The Poor's Best Friend?

Figure 13.2 Portrait of June Mark, pauper/seasonal farm worker, eighty-four years old, c. 1833. Suffolk Archives HA 11/A13/10. Reproduced by kind permission of the owner.

how he ate only two meals a day but 'my dog though has plenty. I feeds him well, poor fellow'.[31]

Dogs and poachers were likely to have had strong bonds to have worked together and for the dog to faithfully bring back the catch to its master intact. So close was their bond that such dogs were said to be distrustful of everybody except their masters.[32] One anonymous elderly poacher, recounting his life in 1892, said that his dogs were

Objects of Poverty

Figure 13.3 Portrait of Bet Mattock, widowed pauper, eighty-two years old, c. 1862. Suffolk Archives HA11/A13/10. Reproduced by kind permission of the owner.

his 'fastest friends'. He marvelled at how 'invaluable' they were when trained and that it is 'wonderful how soon the dog takes on the habits of its master'.[33] He even said that many poachers 'would as soon have been shot himself as seen his dog destroyed' by authorities.[34] Among some, however, there could be a limit to this affection, especially when it came to saving their own skin. Unlike others in his poaching gang, the poacher George Jones allegedly avoided gaol by begging to be let off and promising never to

The Poor's Best Friend?

Figure 13.4 Portrait of John Mattock, pauper/colt breaker, seventy-one to seventy-two years old, c. 1851–2. Suffolk Archives HA11/A13/10. Reproduced by kind permission of the owner.

poach again, as well as 'blew[ing] out his [dog's] brains' to further strengthen his assurances. The dog, Bob, was said to be one of the 'cleverest' and most 'celebrated' poachers around, but Jones does not appear to have hesitated in choosing to kill his dog rather than go to gaol.[35] This serves as an important reminder that there were always limits to people's affections. Here is a dog that became a symbol and a substitute for the treachery and crimes of its human owner.

179

Objects of Poverty

Born around 1815, John Wilkins's autobiography details his experience of living with working and non-working dogs. His writings reveal that although working people could be strict, they were highly affectionate and very fond of dogs. John saw his dogs as loving friends as well as obedient companions, and he often went into minute detail about the many dogs he owned over his life. John spent his childhood helping his father, Luke, a gamekeeper. One of their dogs kept John 'company' while he kept watch on pheasants during the breeding season. The dog was described as 'a poor, worn-out retriever dog',[36] showing that even dogs who were at the end of their working lives continued to be looked after out of loyalty and companionship. John also went above and beyond to attend to the needs of dogs. 'Many a time, after a hard day's hunting', the dogs were exhausted, so John would:

> lay my coat on the ground and put two dogs on it, whilst I took two more up in my arms and carried them forward for half a mile; then I would come back for the first two, and so keep on repeating the operation until I got them safely home. When dogs are thoroughly tired out, you should warm their food, give them a good meal, and dry them well before the fire.[37]

John may have been especially attentive to these dogs as they were valuable hunting dogs owned by his master or because he genuinely cared about them, but he certainly seems to have gone the extra mile by letting them lie on his coat and carrying them back.

During John's teenage and early adult years, he worked in various industries, such as carpentry and charcoal burning, before eventually becoming a gamekeeper himself sometime during the 1830s. He continued to show empathy and care for dogs throughout his life. John was very knowledgeable on how to feed and look after his dogs. This was in part due to his job, as well as a necessity as specialised dog food and veterinary care was out of the reach of most working people until well into the twentieth century.[38] However, this attentiveness also stemmed from John's desire to keep his dogs happy and healthy. John said that many ladies' dogs 'go wrong, or get out of sorts through eating too much meat', so for dog food, he would 'Cut up some boiled greens very small, mash some potatoes, make some bread crumbs, and cut up some meat very fine and small' and then mixed it together with some 'rich gravy'.[39] To 'make your dog's coat like a looking glass', John gave his dogs 'some bread and butter and treacle'.[40] From his many years of looking after dogs, John learnt how to manage various skin diseases such as mange and eczema, and treat dogs for worms and re-set bones. Neighbours, he claimed, also turned to him to treat their dogs as he 'always returned such dogs to their owners, cured'.[41] While John was certainly overstating his medical competence, especially since he contended that he knew how to stop dogs from catching rabies,[42] there is no doubt from his account that he cared a lot and assisted both his and his neighbours' dogs to the best of his ability.

A common complaint of elite and middling people was that the poor and working classes allowed their dogs to roam freely and fight, to breed and cause general chaos with impunity.[43] John's dogs were afforded the freedom to roam as they pleased, but they generally behaved well and only pushed their luck in minor ways. Two of his dogs, 'Help, the retriever pup, and Topsy, the poodle', would routinely 'slide off down the park, and lay up under a tree near by the footpath to Stanstead'.[44] John and his wife would take their dogs for walks. Even when they struggled to because they were going to places where dogs were not allowed, John and his wife would often bend to the will of the dogs. On numerous occasions, when John's wife went to town to shop, Help and Topsy would follow her, beg and crawl 'sheepishly towards her', until there was 'no resisting this so she says: "'Come along then"'. The dogs would then be thrilled, showing 'exuberant joy ... barking and yelping like fury'.[45] Topsy followed John to the chapel one day. After telling the dog to go home numerous times, he said "'Well if you'll be a good dog, you can come"'. He then 'took him up under my coat skirt, marched in, and sat down in my pew, sitting him up on the seat by my side'. The dog kept quiet during the service and 'kept touching me on the arm with his paw, looking up into my face the while'.[46]

John and his wife's dogs came into the domestic sphere and were often affectionate helpers. As soon as John started taking his boots off, one puppy he owned would 'go across the room for my slippers, and they were by my side before I had time to draw off my boots'. The dog would then 'drag my boots off to where I was accustomed to place them, and the gaiters as well, and then he would come up to me, wagging his tail, and lick my hand as if well pleased with his job'.[47] At night, John's 'house dogs' slept indoors while his 'hunting and sporting dogs' slept in a kennel. John made sure that the dogs who slept outside were happy in their accommodation, as he warned against putting dogs in their kennel in a 'bad temper' and said that one should 'cheer them up into a good one, play with them, or give them something nice to eat out of your pocket'.[48]

When discussing how he trained his dogs, John could be strict. For example, the dogs who tried to eat the meat of their fellow canines would receive 'a rap over the head with the handle of a knife'.[49] However, John again showed empathy and affection. He tried to see the world from the dogs' perspectives and create bonds with them. He noted how it is important to 'Put yourself in the dog's place' when it came to getting them used to gunfire, as 'you could not stand four or five guns banging off unexpectedly over your head, when your attention was firmly fixed elsewhere'.[50] He disliked beating or whipping dogs and used it only as a last resort. He said, 'No retriever puppy ought to be beaten under any circumstances, if you want him to become a good, loving, and obedient companion, and to defend and guard you night and day; by rash treatment you will probably entirely take away his love and respect for you'.[51] Instead, he would 'talk to him quietly, cautioning him before you use the whip' if the dog was behaving incorrectly.[52] Once broken in, John would make the dog 'come and humble himself, lick my hands and so forth, so that we may part good friends'.[53] John even used to play with his dogs by throwing balls and other objects for them to fetch.[54]

While caring and, in many ways, a soft touch to his dogs, John had to be practical in his line of work and could be harsh when necessary. For the dogs John was unable to break in, he 'used either to destroy them or return them to their owners'.[55] John also noted the killing of countless dogs of navvies and poachers, even those he found 'beautiful' and of which he liked their colourations.[56] This indicates that while John was affectionate and took good care of the dogs he owned and helped, he had to put these feelings aside

Figure 13.5 John Wilkins, gamekeeper, *c.* 1892. Source: Wilkins, *Autobiography*, front plate.

under the parameters of his role as gamekeeper. He justified these actions to the reader, surmising that the killing of dogs 'may appear cruel and unnecessary, but it is the only thing to be done; a dog trained for poaching is incurable, and will always be a poacher'.[57] He also reasoned that it was a means to an end, as killing the dogs would break up the poaching gangs.[58] This is one among many of the reasons why gamekeepers could be viewed as enemies of the poor, despite the fact that they, too, were working people and might face similar economic precarities throughout their lifetimes. Nevertheless, love, affection and companionship were John's overriding feelings towards his dogs, so much so that in his portrait for his autobiography, he chose to be photographed next to one of his beloved pets (Figure 13.5).

Conclusion

Contemporaries usually condemned the poor and working classes and their dogs, seeing them both as equally reprehensible, violent and immoral. Indeed, it is true enough that some were dishonest, cared for little other than themselves and treated dogs in unimaginable ways. Likewise, by looking at the gamekeeper Wilkes and other examples, we learn that dogs were often the casualty of tensions between various working-class actors. However, on the whole, most people (especially owners) treated their dogs well and developed strong bonds with them. These findings show that 'pets' were not just owned by the middling sort and the elite in Georgian and early- to mid-Victorian England but a much wider socio-economic group. Because most research on dogs and companionship focuses on the well-to-do and contemporaries were scathing of the dogs of the poor and working class, one might be forgiven for thinking that these affectionate and loving characteristics were absent among the wider population. This was simply not true. Dogs were not just owned by people for their function and utility; they were objects of affection and companionship. Indeed, for many, they were the poor man's best friend.

Notes

1 I'd like to thank Vicky Holmes and Julie-Marie Strange for their kind and constructive feedback on earlier drafts of this chapter.
2 Ingrid H. Tague, 'The History of Emotional Attachment to Animals', in Hilda Kean and Philip Howell (eds), *The Routledge Companion to Animal-Human History* (Abington: Routledge, 2019), pp. 345–66.
3 Keith Thomas, *Man and the Natural World: Changing Attitudes in England 1500–1800* (London: Penguin, 1983), esp. pp. 92–142; Kathryn Shevelow, *For the Love of Animals: The Rise of the Animal Protection Movement* (New York: Henry Holt, 2008), pp. 55–75; Ingrid H. Tague, *Animal Companions: Pets and Social Change in Eighteenth-Century Britain* (University Park: Pennsylvania State University Press, 2015); Philip Howell, *At Home and Astray: The Domestic Dog in Victorian Britain* (London: University of Virginia Press, 2015); Jane Hamlett and Julie-Marie Strange, *Pet Revolution: Animals and the Making of Modern British Life*

(London: Reaktion Books, 2023). Note that the term 'pet' is contested among scholars and was not widely used in the eighteenth century.
4   Julie-Marie Strange, 'When John Met Benny: Class, Pets and Family Life in Late Victorian and Edwardian Britain', *History of the Family*, 26:2 (2021): pp. 214–35; Claudia Soares, '"The many lessons which the care of some gentle, loveable animal would give": Animals, Pets, and Emotions in Children's Welfare Institutions, 1870–1920', *History of the Family*, 26:2 (2021): pp. 236–65; Hamlett and Strange, *Pet Revolution*.
5   Such as Sarah Amato, *Beastly Possessions: Animals in Victorian Consumer Culture* (Toronto: University of Toronto Press, 2015), pp. 21–55; Harriet Ritvo, *The Animal Estate: The English and Other Creatures in the Victorian Age* (Cambridge, MA: Harvard University Press, 1987), pp. 125–66; Ingrid H. Tague, 'Eighteenth-Century English Debates on a Dog Tax', *Historical Journal*, 51:4 (2008): pp. 901–20.
6   It is possible that people felt this affection prior to this date, but all the evidence I quote below is dated between c. 1780 and 1880.
7   Amato, *Beastly Possessions*, p. 47.
8   Joseph Harley, 'Poverty, Mad Dogs and Culling: Dogs and Entitlement to Poor Relief in England, c. 1750–1834', *Family & Community History*, 27:3 (2024), pp. 210–13; Neil Pemberton and Michael Worboys, *Mad Dogs and Englishmen: Rabies in Britain, 1830–2000* (Basingstoke: Palgrave, 2007), pp. 26–33; Mark S. R. Jenner, 'The Great Dog Massacre', in William G. Naphy and Penny Roberts (eds), *Fear in Early Modern Society* (Manchester: Manchester University Press, 1997), pp. 54–6.
9   Chris Pearson, *Dogopolis: How Dogs and Humans Made Modern New York, London, and Paris* (London: University of Chicago Press, 2021), pp. 13–46.
10 Harley, "Poverty, Mad Dogs and Culling', pp. 215–16.
11 On pedigree and the dogs of the wealthy, see Michael Worboys, Julie-Marie Strange and Neil Pemberton, *The Invention of the Modern Dog: Breed and Blood in Victorian Britain* (Baltimore: Johns Hopkins University Press, 2018); Ritvo, *Animal Estate*, pp. 45–121; Amato, *Beastly Possessions*, pp. 39–54; Pearson, *Dogopolis*, pp. 31–5.
12 Ritvo, *Animal Estate*, pp. 125–66; Thomas, *Man and the Natural World*, pp. 143–91; Shevelow, *For the Love*; Emma Griffin, *Blood Sport: Hunting in Britain since 1066* (New Haven: Yale University Press, 2007), pp. 141–51, 163–82; Keith Tester, *Animals and Society: The Humanity of Human Rights* (London: Routledge, 1991); David Perkins, *Romanticism and Animal Rights, 1790–1830* (Cambridge: Cambridge University Press, 2003); Pearson, *Dogopolis*, pp. 83–114.
13 Edward Barry, *On the Necessity of Adopting Some Measures to Reduce the Present Number of Dogs...* (Reading: Smart and Cowslade, 1796), p. 8.
14 Anonymous, *Some Considerations on the Game Laws...* (London: T. Egerton, 1796), p. 68.
15 Sarah Tarlow and Emma Battell Lowman, *Harnessing the Power of the Criminal Corpse* (Cham: Palgrave, 2018).
16 Quoted from: Tague, *Animal Companions*, p. 167.
17 *Gazetteer and New Daily Advertiser*, 26 April 1796.
18 Such as: John Brown, *Sixty Years' Gleanings from Life's Harvests: A Genuine Autobiography* (Cambridge: J. Palmer, 1858), pp. 315–17.
19 Benjamin Shaw, *The Family Records of Benjamin Shaw Mechanic of Dent, Dolphinholme and Preston, 1772–1841*, ed. Alan G. Crosby (Stroud: Alan Sutton, 1991), p. 80.
20 P. E. H. Hair (ed.), *Coals on Rails or the Reason of My Wrighting: The Autobiography of Anthony Errington* (Liverpool: Liverpool University Press, 1988), pp. 90–2.
21 Hamlett and Strange, *Pet Revolution*, pp. 116–23; Diana Donald, *Picturing Animals in Britain: 1750–1850* (New Haven: Yale University Press, 2007); James H. Rubin, *Impressionist Cats & Dogs* (New Haven: Yale University Press, 2003); Tague, *Animal Companions*, pp. 181–200.

22 Suffolk Archives (hereafter SA) HD 1025/1-2; SA HA 42/1-2; SA HD 1888/1; SA HD 368/1; SA HA 11/A13/10; David Dymond (ed.), *Parson and People in a Suffolk Village: Richard Cobbold's Wortham, 1824–77* (Ipswich: Wortham Research Group/Suffolk Family History Society, 2007); Ronald Fletcher (ed.), *The Biography of a Victorian Village: Richard Cobbold's Account of Wortham, Suffolk* (London: B.T. Batsford, 1977).
23 SA HD 368/1; SA HA 11/A13/10; SA HA 42/2.
24 SA HD 1025/1-2; SA HA 42/1-2; SA HD 1888/1; SA HD 368/1; SA HA 11/A13/10. It is not possible to reproduce all of these prints here, but a number of them can be found in Dymond, *Parson*; Fletcher, *Biography*.
25 SA HD 1025/1; Dymond, *Parson*, pp. 166–7.
26 SA HA 11/A13/10; SA HD 1025/1; Dymond, *Parson*, pp. 167–9.
27 SA HD 1025/1.
28 *Public Advertiser*, 11 June 1792.
29 *Public Advertiser*, 2 June 1792.
30 Jennifer Esmail, '"The Little Dog Is Only a Stage Property": The Blind Man's Dog in Victorian Culture', *Victorian Review*, 40:1 (2014): pp. 18–23.
31 Quoted from ibid., p. 21.
32 John Wilkins, *The Autobiography of an English Gamekeeper*, ed. Arthur H. Byng and Stephen M. Stephens (London: T. Fisher Unwin, 1892), pp. 65–6.
33 Anonymous, *The Confessions of a Poacher*, ed. John Watson (London: Leadenhall Press, 1890), pp. 59–60.
34 Ibid., pp. 63–4.
35 Wilkins, *Autobiography*, pp. 82–3.
36 Ibid., p. 13.
37 Ibid., pp. 36–7.
38 Hamlett and Strange, *Pet Revolution*, pp. 179–208.
39 Wilkins, *Autobiography*, p. 372.
40 Ibid., pp. 372–3.
41 Ibid., pp. 373–6.
42 Ibid., pp. 376–7.
43 Such as: *The Times*, 18 June 1830.
44 Wilkins, *Autobiography*, p. 176.
45 Ibid., pp. 175–6.
46 Ibid., pp. 176–7.
47 Ibid., p. 174.
48 Ibid., pp. 168–9, 371–2.
49 Ibid., p. 175.
50 Ibid., p. 164.
51 Ibid., p. 171.
52 Ibid., pp. 167–8.
53 Ibid., p. 168.
54 Ibid., p. 174.
55 Ibid., p. 192.
56 Such as ibid., pp. 60, 64–6, 74, 78–9, 222–8, 232–4, 354, 366.
57 Ibid., p. 354.
58 Ibid., p. 66.

Further reading

Hamlett, Jane, and Julie-Marie Strange. *Pet Revolution: Animals and the Making of Modern British Life* (London: Reaktion Books, 2023).
Harley, Joseph. 'Poverty, Mad Dogs and Culling: Dogs and Entitlement to Poor Relief in England, c. 1750–1834'. *Family & Community History*, 27:3 (2024): pp. 207–21.
Howell, Philip. *At Home and Astray: The Domestic Dog in Victorian Britain* (London: University of Virginia Press, 2015).
Pearson, Chris. *Dogopolis: How Dogs and Humans Made Modern New York, London, and Paris* (London: University of Chicago Press, 2021).
Soares, Claudia. '"The many lessons which the care of some gentle, loveable animal would give": Animals, Pets, and Emotions in Children's Welfare Institutions, 1870–1920'. *History of the Family*, 26:2 (2021): pp. 236–65.
Strange, Julie-Marie. 'When John Met Benny: Class, Pets and Family Life in Late Victorian and Edwardian Britain'. *History of the Family*, 26:2 (2021): pp. 214–35.
Tague, Ingrid H. *Animal Companions: Pets and Social Change in Eighteenth-Century Britain* (University Park: Pennsylvania State University Press, 2015).
Tague, Ingrid H. 'Eighteenth-Century English Debates on a Dog Tax'. *Historical Journal*, 51:4 (2008): pp. 901–20.
Thomas, Keith. *Man and the Natural World: Changing Attitudes in England 1500–1800* (London: Penguin, 1983).

CHAPTER 14
'UP WITH THE HEN HOUSE': CHICKENS, COOPS AND CLASS IDENTITY IN BRITISH MUNICIPAL COTTAGE ESTATES, 1920-50

Lesley Hoskins and Rebecca Preston

Introduction

This chapter considers the chicken coop and its feathered occupants as a focus of contested class identity in the back gardens of interwar municipal 'cottage' estates.[1] It might be thought that keeping hens would conform with local authorities' ideas of the cottage, in a pretty and productive garden, as the ideal working-class home, but many councils prohibited poultry on their estates, while others restricted the number of hens allowed. These restrictions remained in place even when there was a national imperative to produce more food. Councils that did allow chicken-keeping nonetheless remained concerned about the appearance of coops and hutches because, for the authorities, the wrong kind of henhouse was redolent of urban 'slums'. Many of the tenants of the new outlying estates had been rehoused from 'slum' areas and, as we will show, the henhouse was an object the authorities believed needed reform in exactly the same way that the tenants needed to be reformed or re-educated. In the authorities' view, unreformed tenants were in danger of bringing chickens and the 'wrong' kind of coops from the slums to the improved and improving environments of the new municipal cottage estates. Tenants, though, fought back, sometimes quietly ignoring the rules or sometimes publicly objecting to them – they were evidently either content with, or pragmatic about, the need for what the authorities saw as slum practices.

The battle over chickens and unreformed coops was prolonged and resulted in the design and promotion of a model henhouse – by an 'outsider', a champion of domestic chicken-keeping, Mr A. P. Thompson – to mediate between tenants and their landlords. The need for a model poultry house was prompted partly by depressed economic conditions, and then the worsening political situation in the late 1930s and the accompanying drive to increase domestic egg and meat production. Yet it was also the product of decades of wrangling between the tenants and landlords of municipal housing. On the one hand, tenants wished to keep small livestock animals at home; on the other, the authorities were determined that the new council estate gardens did not become the slum backyards of the past – overrun with animals, and chock-full of makeshift coops and ramshackle sheds to house them.

Objects of Poverty

Our chapter explores this conflict, focusing on municipal 'cottage' estates, which were built in large numbers around English towns and cities from the early twentieth century. We find that, although public health played an important part in the authorities' objections to the keeping of poultry and other small animals, there were also deeper culturally and socially rooted prejudices at play concerning the way that working people chose or felt obliged to live.

We are treating the coop and its chickens as a single object, for, of course, it was not feasible to keep chickens without shelter, but also because the coop seems to have exercised the authorities as much, if not more, than the sight, smell and sound of the birds themselves. We are interested, too, in the ways in which the contested class identity of tenants coalesced around this object and its associated practices. In uncovering our object's story we use tenants' first-hand testimony about chickens, chicken-keeping and chicken housing. Their voices, choices and motivations, as well as the negotiations and accommodations with councils, appear in a small number of later interviews with tenants and, more indirectly, in newspaper reports, written by the tenants themselves and by others, discussing campaigns (formal and informal) for tenants to be allowed to keep chickens. We also read the words and images produced by local authorities on the topic as strong evidence for the existing practices of the tenants.

Reforming the tenants

By the early twentieth century, local authorities were attempting to provide decent homes for the working classes and, in addition to urban tenements, had begun building 'cottage estates' of small houses with gardens on the outskirts of English towns and cities. After the First World War, when the housing situation was recognised as desperate and politically charged, the programme fully took off. Initially, the costs of building were so high that councils had to charge rents that were only affordable to better-off working people. Even when costs fell in the mid-1920s, there was still such a shortfall in provision that councils could pick and choose their tenants. The Housing Acts of 1930 and 1936 took a new approach, focusing on demolishing inadequate, insanitary, unhealthy and overcrowded housing, and (ideally) rehousing occupants in new, good-quality homes. Over a million new council houses were built between the wars, most of them on suburban estates.[2]

The tenants' new homes were intended to foster a happier and healthier way of life. As the Ministry of Health's 1939 *Management of Municipal Housing Estates* – a publication as much concerned with managing the tenants as the properties – put it, the new houses would 'by a process of filtering up, ease the problem of the slums'.[3] It also emphasised that simply providing improved accommodation was not enough to change people's existing behaviours and attitudes: some tenants 'without continuous supervision will produce a slum atmosphere wherever they are sent'.[4] As an earlier Ministry of Health manual summed up, 'The slum problem is one of persons as well as of accommodation'.[5] The new tenancies were, therefore, accompanied by many rules and exhortations designed to prevent tenants from continuing with material practices associated with the poverty of their old homes. But they were also formed in response to how tenants behaved in the new 'improved' surroundings. The regulations, along with housing management techniques, were 'in effect a form of social education'.[6]

The 1930 Housing Act itself did not use the word 'slum' for clearance areas although it was in wide use in contemporary housing reform discourse, which often blamed the poor for their defective, inadequate housing.[7] But, as Alan Mayne wrote in 2007, 'slum' is, and was, a bourgeois imaginary, 'part of the complicated control and reform agendas pursued to comprehend and regulate an urbanizing world'.[8] We are mindful of this when we use the term here.

Chickens and social identity

Front gardens were often at least partly maintained by the local authority, but the back gardens were looked after by tenants themselves. What the tenants did – or, rather, wanted to do – with their back gardens was the outcome of their own choices and circumstances. These choices can be seen – and certainly were so seen by the authorities – as being expressive of an individual tenant's social identity or culture. We focus here on one back-garden practice that was particularly contentious as far as local authorities were concerned: the keeping of fowl, rabbits and pigeons, and the erection of coops, hutches and other structures to house them. The authorities put forward arguments about public health and community cohesion: the smells, dirt and noise of the animals and the shabby appearance of the gardens could affect the amenity and value of the neighbourhood. But the authorities' opposition also demonstrated a fear that these new working-class dwellings would deteriorate into the kinds of conditions which the occupants were supposed to have left behind. The rules, regulations and publications of the Ministry of Health and local authorities were an attempt to tame what they saw as an unsatisfactory working-class culture.

Working people had always kept animals for food. During the First World War and afterwards, there was a drive to boost domestic food production and, by the 1920s, the number of town dwellers keeping small animals was said to have greatly increased. However, bye-laws and leases across all types of housing tenure and status often stipulated the number and type of animals allowed, especially in urban districts. Such regulations were strictly policed in the new council estates, although the rules varied between areas and over time. In 1921, the London County Council (LCC) Housing Committee noted that it had always permitted chickens in back gardens 'subject to certain restrictions'.[9] But by 1933, the handbook for the LCC's Becontree estate ruled that no pigs, rabbits, fowls or pigeons were to be kept without prior consent.[10] Mrs Winifred Vincent, who had lived on a borough council estate in Southgate, Middlesex, since the late 1920s, remembered that her family kept chickens and rabbits in the long back garden, where they also grew vegetables.[11] Perhaps they had asked permission to keep the animals because, in 1941, even at the start of the Second World War, when home food production was urgently encouraged, Southgate Council stipulated that no animals, fowls or pigeons were to be kept on the premises without the permission of the controlling committee.[12] There were, though, differences between authorities. The National Utility Poultry Society – set up in the First World War and of which A. P. Thompson was by 1938 Organising Secretary – in 1939 praised one Lancashire urban district council for its 'patriotic' decision to permit poultry-keeping but reported elsewhere that only 60 per cent of councils now did so.[13] Towards the end of that year, the Minister of Agriculture joined in, stating that 'Backyarders can help – help more than they realise – to feed themselves and others by keeping poultry. Poultry kept in city and suburban gardens or on allotments can be fed almost entirely on all forms of household waste'.[14] In a national correspondence campaign with newspapers, Thompson highlighted the large municipal authorities, such as Liverpool, Manchester, Birmingham, Northampton and Coventry, which had already responded to the appeal by the minister, and repeated the assertion that the LCC had always permitted poultry-keeping on its estates, while naming those, like Burnley Council, which did not.[15] There were, apparently, still nearly 500 councils which refused to reconsider the bans.[16] Even though the Ministers of Health and Agriculture had approved poultry-keeping on council estates and 750 authorities now permitted it, many of those councils placed a limit of six to eight hens per household, under certain conditions, and only then until hostilities ceased.[17] There appears to have been agreement from the early days of the cottage estates that keeping cockerels was antisocial. In 1921, the chairman of the LCC Housing Committee, in banning cockerels, answered those opposed to over-regulation by saying the idea was to make tenants comfortable and that he believed the majority was against the keeping of cockerels.[18]

There were public health concerns about bird disease and rats linked to fowl houses. District Medical Officers for the greater London and other areas reported regularly on the rats encouraged by domestic henhouses. Local authorities continued to have concerns about a return to slum conditions in the new municipal back gardens. One Southall councillor, in a debate in 1939 about chicken-keeping in the Middlesex borough, recalled the 'deplorable' conditions in back gardens before the ban on poultry.[19] A Socialist councillor in Edmonton, Middlesex, in the late 1920s, claimed that some tenants were said 'to keep chickens in their bathrooms and rabbits in the parlour', adding, 'We hoped that their new surroundings would reform the bad tenants, and that in their new environment they would learn to keep their houses decently'. 'We used to be proud of our estate', he went on, 'but now I would not live there'.[20] Indeed, some council tenants themselves complained that such regulations were necessary and not strictly enough enforced. A resident of Greenford, Middlesex, claimed that the restrictions on fowl and dogs were flagrantly flouted 'and one has got to live in this estate to realise the din that goes on from daybreak until late at night … disturbing people's rest'.[21] In Southall, only twenty of the council's 997 tenants had made an application to keep chickens by late November 1939, indicating that this was either far from a universal practice or that they defied the rules.[22]

However, the very existence of these regulations implies that at least some tenants wanted to keep fowl in their back gardens. More directly, correspondence and reports in newspapers are evidence that wider public opinion and tenants' views and activities sometimes ran counter to the restrictions. Defence of poultry-keeping could be couched in terms of promoting British produce while 'a few backyard hens' on a council estate would benefit an unemployed man and his family a great deal, according to one Nottingham correspondent in 1931.[23] A long fight by Stanmore Ratepayers' Association and the National Poultry Council, presumably assisted by Thompson, was begun by Mr G. F. Brown, a Mount Pleasant postal worker, who wanted to help feed his large family. In 1939, this resulted in Harrow Council allowing tenants at its estates in Middlesex to keep a limited number of hens.[24]

Some councils were obviously ambivalent. Andrzej Olechnowicz found that in Becontree, the LCC used its discretion to encourage hobbies and that both housewives and husbands took part in 'new activities such as poultry-keeping'. In Manchester, at around the same time, a municipal tenants' association representative reported that 'there are prohibitions galore, but people are evading them every day. The Corporation ignore some of their own rulings too. Plenty of rabbits, dogs, cats, and other pets are to be found on the estates'.[25] Poultry-keeping circles were encouraged on the new cottage estates, with classes and shows held in social centres at the LCC's Becontree and Bellingham, for example. A BBC wireless series from 1932 – *New Ways for Hard Times* – created by the chairman of the National Allotment Committee, included programmes on making use of backyards and gardens and keeping chickens in a small way.[26] Such mixed messages must have played in tenants' favour and made it harder for councils to keep control. By 1933, the proposed ban on fowl-keeping on council estates in Coulsdon and Purley on south London's Surrey fringes had failed, and the Housing Committee's order to remove roosts and chickens within one year was overturned.[27]

The reasons for wanting to keep birds were manifold. There was a long-standing working-class tradition of keeping pigeons for food, sport, competition, human sociability or inter-species companionship. The significance of chickens or rabbits is harder to gauge. For some, they were hobby creatures, or pets, but they could at the same time be a source of income and food. In 1928, a tenant of the LCC's Watling Estate, at Burnt Oak, Middlesex, was advertising his last year's Rhode Island Reds for sale 'cheap' and 'laying'.[28] Defence of poultry-keeping could be couched in terms of promoting British produce: a Nottingham correspondent in 1931 argued that it would 'keep the foreign eggs out'.[29] During wartime, it could be seen as a patriotic duty and part of the war effort. Harold Smith, who moved to the new Becontree estate as a child, recalled that before and after he was called up in 1942, the family grew vegetables and 'we used to … keep chickens; livestock … tame rabbits', and cooked them at Christmas. He remarked: 'we thought it was marvellous to have a tame rabbit for Christmas dinner'.[30] But another early Becontree resident recalled that her friend came over to her house for dinner on the day she heard her father killing her pet rabbit.[31]

A mass of rusty corrugated iron passing under the name of chicken sheds

The birds and rabbits had to be kept somewhere – in fowl houses, hutches, runs, lofts or coops. The District Medical Officer for Barking Town (in which part of Becontree estate then fell) reported in 1930 that, while most of the cottages in the borough had the 'essential amenities' of open space and air at the rear, it was unfortunate that householders had erected 'the shed structures which are to be seen in the back gardens', breaking 'the laws introduced to provide a sanitary environment'. He estimated that 70 per cent of the houses (in both council and private ownership) in his district had temporary buildings erected in their back gardens, most of which were 'ugly and misshapen, and almost all are open to objection'. The officer contended that poultry houses, fowl runs, tool sheds and motorcycle sheds were 'among the types of structures which *should never* be allowed in the small gardens of cottage dwellings', and he pressed the council to deal with them.[32] His objections, apparently on sanitary grounds, were also partly aesthetic, cultural and class-based judgements. By 1933, the handbook for the LCC's Becontree estate ruled that no structures should be erected without prior permission.[33] This attitude was often found in local authorities. Bath Corporation tenants were allowed to keep a few birds or rabbits, the only proviso being 'that they shall be kept in decent houses, and not any old shack such as many people think is a suitable place to house poultry'.[34] In Southall Council's 1939 discussion, some councillors objected to the 'mass of rusty corrugated iron, old sacks, etc, that sometimes passed under the name of chicken sheds'.[35] The *Southgate Tenants' Handbook* of 1950 noted the 'Injury to the amenities of Estates by the erection of some of the monstrosities called sheds – bits of corrugated iron, old bedsteads, advertisement signs, and suchlike'. Here and elsewhere, the phrase 'injury to the amenities of estates' is used to summon up a dystopian vision of slum spaces that would devalue the council's investment.

However, authorities recognised that their tenants needed and wanted sheds and coops, and, in order to counter the 'monstrosities' that would turn their estates into slums, many developed restrictions on the size, number, siting and design of outside structures from the 1920s. The Second World War changed the use and appearance of back gardens, which then accommodated air-raid shelters and vegetable patches but, even in 1940, Southgate tenants still needed prior consent for the erection of 'any Toolhouse, Shed, Greenhouse, Fowlhouse or other building'.[36] After the war, Southgate's Housing Management Committee devoted a part of its meetings to applications – not always successful – for 'Garden Sheds'.

A 'neat, cheap and simple to manage' henhouse

It was in this context – disputes over chicken-keeping and inappropriate coops – that the aforementioned advocate for chicken-keeping, Alan Prescott Thompson, stepped into the debate. Thompson wrote the *Daily Herald*'s regular Saturday poultry advice column from the mid-1930s to about 1950, and was also one of the editors of the longstanding weekly paper, *The Feathered World*, for those who made a hobby or a living from pigeons, song birds and poultry. He offered to help tenants whose council landlords did not allow poultry-keeping in the late 1930s, promoting a 'neat, cheap and simple to manage' henhouse that was 'specially designed for people with little space and conform[ed] with County Council regulations'.³⁷ In this way Thompson's model henhouse came to wider notice beyond the specialist bird press. From early 1938, his increasingly insistent letters, addressed from the *Feathered World* offices, appeared in many local and national newspapers, naming the local authorities which banned poultry-keeping on their estates, and stating that 'tenants should be ashamed to submit to tyranny in this matter'.³⁸ 'Where the facts are pointed out', he wrote in the *Daily Mirror*, 'reasonable Councils realise that back garden poultry-keeping is an asset to the national food supply, and remove the ban'.³⁹

The caption to the photograph in Thompson's 'Poultry Notes' column in the *Daily Herald* in February 1939 makes his position as an intermediary between tenants and authorities clear: 'She is pleased with her new "Feathered World" Poultry House. It's on a Council Estate, too'. This photograph was also reproduced in *The Ideal Home* magazine (Figure 14.1).

Thompson did not come from a working-class background, but he was committed to the right of everyone, including council tenants, to keep chickens. He argued that where this was forbidden in the lease, it should be made permissive, as 'simple prohibition is tyrannous and lazy and an unnecessary interference with the liberty of the householder to use what he pays for'.⁴⁰ To satisfy the authorities' demands, he also recommended that a standard pattern of poultry house, as well as cleanliness, could be insisted upon.⁴¹ Prior to beginning his regular column (as a named author) for the *Daily Herald*, he also took up the matter in a letter to the editor of that paper, complaining of the 'unreasonable

Figure 14.1 The *Feathered World* Poultry House from *The Ideal Home*, November 1939, p. 368. Authors' collection.

Objects of Poverty

ban' by many local councils on poultry-keeping in their housing estates; he also asked 'any poultry keepers who are being interfered with' in this way to write to him for help.[42] Thompson was already very well-known in poultry-fancying circles, and from 1938 became a familiar voice on the wireless through his 'Profits for the Small Poultry-Keeper' and similar broadcasts for the BBC: 'Up with the Hen House' was the title of one of the talks in 1939, which was published with a diagram illustrating how to construct the model henhouse in *The Listener*.[43]

Ideals and realities in the municipal back garden

The contrast between what councils wished their tenants to do in relation to their gardens and what some tenants were actually doing was sometimes presented visually, giving us an immediate impression of the practices that were under contention. Figure 14.2, from Southgate Borough Council's *Municipal Tenants' Handbook* of 1950, is an example.[44] Pairs of images like this had long been employed by reformers to contrast 'good' (modern/reformed) and 'bad' (old/slum) environments and practices. The top photograph depicts an immaculate front garden, the archetype of Southgate Council's vision for maintaining the amenities of its estates. Outside spaces were particularly important to local authorities because of their visibility. The Ministry of Health's 1939 report pointed out that 'The appearance of a row of houses, however attractive and well built, can easily be spoilt by one badly kept garden' and that restrictions on the exterior 'are clearly necessary for the good of the community as a whole'. Visibility was stressed as a means of education: 'The bad tenant will learn more readily by eye than by ear; example is better than precept'.[45]

The back garden in the lower image is the epitome of what Southgate Council did *not* want. This and the neighbouring gardens are dominated by patched-up sheds, apparently for birds, animals and other storage, with a ramshackle water butt and wireless aerials, which also caused friction between tenants and landlords. The image depicts outside space and storage on a cottage estate in a way that bears comparison with the photographs of backyards of 'slum' housing that were taken as part of clearance programmes. Figure 14.3 shows 'slum' backyards, with bird coops and other sheds for animals ranged behind the back extensions and in triple-decker stacks at the ends. Photographed just prior to being swept away for a model social housing block, the view is a classic example of this kind of visual propaganda.

A. P. Thompson used the same good/bad visual comparison to promote his model henhouse in a wartime publication devoted to increasing domestic food production (Figure 14.4). Unlike much 'slum' photography, however, there is no implication in his text or images that class and poverty lay behind the 'faulty' shack. Thompson's section of the book – 'Produce the Victory Egg' – was aimed at 'anyone with a piece of ground ten foot by six' – a 'backyard corner' – up to those with acres in the country for flocks of free-range birds.[46]

Figure 14.2 *The Borough of Southgate Municipal Tenants Handbook*, 1950. Enfield Local Studies and Archives.

Objects of Poverty

Figure 14.3 Backyards photographed by the London County Council in Southwark before clearance in 1913 for the Tabard Gardens Estate. The London Archives/Heritage Images/Alarmy Stock Photo.

Figure 14.4 A. P. Thompson, 'Poultry', in C. H. Middleton (ed.), *War Time Allotments*, *Daily Express*, 1940, p. 99. Authors' collection.

Control, autonomy and livestock

Alongside district medical officers who monitored the outside spaces of tenants' homes, rent officers, who lived on the estates, made weekly rounds. Becontree-born Stan Buzer remembered that there were 'very strict' rules about keeping the front gardens 'clean' and that their officer was known as Hitler.[47] There were, however, wider concerns about council over-regulation. 'Is Your Landlord a Dictator?' asked a headline in the patriotic newspaper *John Bull* in 1938 before listing Tynemouth Council's prohibition on dogs, hens and rabbits and Ebbe Vale's ban on pigeon-keeping despite pigeon-racing being the area's most popular sport.[48] Some councils were well aware of criticisms of over-regulation. Southgate's 1941 *Municipal Tenants' Handbook* protested that the corporation had

> no desire or intention to interfere with the freedom of the tenants to live their own lives unsubjected to petty restrictions, and it is hoped that the conditions of tenancy are regarded, not as unreasonable restrictions of personal liberty, but as having been conceived in the best interests of everyone concerned.

The aim was instead to

> help to secure the *co-operation* of all tenants in preserving the amenities of the estates, large or small, a matter of vital importance if these estates are not to deteriorate into little better than the unsuitable housing conditions which they were designed to eliminate.[49]

It would be interesting to discover whether this was an acceptable or effective form of persuasion. Either way, the council's intervention betrayed an underlying class prejudice that was as much a view of how working people should live as it was a matter of public health or of protecting the authority's investment. More to our point, it was also a view of how tenants should *not* live. The amount of time, energy and money expended by councils on attempting to reform outside spaces on their estates suggests that the tenants who pursued these 'slum' practices were not just a tiny minority.

Mr Thompson, as the most vehement single protestor against council landlords' over-regulation of keeping chickens and henhouses on local authority estates, was a staunch supporter of tenants' rights – and their patriotic duty – to keep poultry, provided they were housed in appropriate sheds. But, rather than being simply a top-down directive to increase hen-keeping for economic reasons among the poor, his intervention demonstrated that working people were already keeping chickens – or wished to do so – and were housing them as they saw fit, regardless of the authorities' rules.

Conclusion

Prompted by the title of this volume – *Objects of Poverty* – we were interested in the existence and regulation of sheds, coops, hutches and their occupants in thousands of local-authority back gardens. Many tenants evidently considered poultry- and small livestock-keeping as a right and wanted to put up coops and runs in their gardens, while the need for sheds, for general use as well as for animal housing, appears to have been

Objects of Poverty

near universal. Tenants certainly resisted the restrictions, although some did support the councils in policing animal-keeping on their estates. Council regulations were a way to control undesirable working-class domestic practices that were seen as a hangover from the 'slums'. But the fact that the rules appear to have been so widely ignored, deliberately or otherwise, may be seen as a form of resistance, while newspaper and other campaigns were a more defiant, public assertion of tenants' rights. In each case, the henhouses, coops and hutches, and the chickens and other livestock inside, offer material evidence of a continued and widespread aspect of working-class culture and identity.

Notes

1 We would like to thank John Clark at Enfield Local Studies and Archives and Karen Rushton of Barking and Dagenham Archive Service for their help while researching for this chapter.
2 Mark Swenarton, *Homes Fit for Heroes: The Politics and Architecture of Early State Housing in Britain* (London: Heinemann, 1981).
3 Ministry of Health, *The Management of Municipal Housing Estates: Report of the House Management and Housing Associations Sub-Committee of the Central Housing Advisory Committee* (London: HMSO, 1939), p. 7.
4 Ibid.
5 Ministry of Health, *Manual of Unfit Houses and Unhealthy Areas* (London: HMSO, 1919), p. 23.
6 *Management of Municipal Housing Estates*, p. 9.
7 See, for example, John J. Clarke, 'Slums and the Housing Act, 1930', *Town Planning Review*, 14:3 (1931): pp. 163–93, which includes other contemporary references.
8 Alan Mayne, 'Review Essay: Tall Tales but True?: New York's "Five Points" Slum', *Journal of Urban History*, 33:2 (2007): p. 321.
9 *Norwood News*, 10 June 1921, p. 5.
10 LCC, *Becontree Tenants' Handbook*, 1933, p. 14, LMA LCC/HSG/GEN/03/011. https://www.becontreeforever.uk/historical-archive/tenants-handbooks (accessed 24 November 2024).
11 Interviewed by Lesley Hoskins, for 'In Search of Suburbia' exhibition, 2005, Museum of Domestic Design and Architecture.
12 *The Tenants' Handbook. A Reference Book for Municipal Tenants in Southgate* (Cheltenham: Ed. J. Burrow, 1941), p. 8.
13 *Lancaster Guardian*, 27 October 1939, p. 4; Andrzej Olechnowicz, *Working-Class Housing in England between the Wars: The Becontree Estate* (Oxford: Oxford University Press, 1999), p. 106.
14 Reported in the *Burnley Express*, 1 November 1939, p. 4.
15 Ibid.
16 *Daily Herald*, 19 June 1939, p. 7.
17 *West Middlesex Gazette*, 2 December 1939, p. 1.
18 *Norwood News*, 10 June 1921, p. 5.
19 *West Middlesex Gazette*, 2 December 1939, p. 1.
20 *Weekly Dispatch*, 23 September 1928, p. 5. The claim that working people kept livestock in the house is similar to the unsubstantiated stereotype of their keeping coal in the bath, as discussed in chapter 6.
21 *West Middlesex Gazette*, 20 August 1938, p. 9.
22 *West Middlesex Gazette*, Southall edition, 2 December 1939, p. 1.

23 *Nottingham Evening Post*, 14 March 1931, p. 6.
24 *Daily Herald*, 19 June 1939, p. 7.
25 Olechnowicz, *Working-Class Housing in England between the Wars*, pp. 55, 106.
26 *Radio Times*, 1 January 1932, p. 24.
27 *West Sussex Gazette*, 6 July 1933, p. 4.
28 *Hendon & Finchley Times*, 18 May 1928, p. 5.
29 *Nottingham Evening Post*, 14 March 1931, p. 6.
30 Barking and Dagenham Archive and Local Studies Centre (hereafter BDA) BD356/2, Interview with Harold Smith.
31 BDA BD356/5, Interview with Stan and Brenda Buzer.
32 *Report of the Medical Officer of Health for Barking*, 1930, pp. 57–8, and 1931, p. 47. Emphasis ours.
33 LCC, *Becontree Tenants' Handbook*, 1933, p. 14.
34 *Somerset Guardian*, 15 September 1939, p. 16.
35 *West Middlesex Gazette*, 2 December 1939, p. 1.
36 *A Reference Book for Municipal Tenants in Southgate*, 1941, p. 8.
37 *Daily Herald*, 18 March 1938, p. 13.
38 *Halifax Evening Courier*, 10 February 1938, p. 6, *Faversham News*, 19 February 1938, p. 5, and many others.
39 *Daily Mirror*, 7 March 1938, p. 13.
40 *Halifax Evening Courier*, 10 February 1938, p. 6.
41 *Tonbridge Free Press*, 18 February 1938, p. 5.
42 *Daily Herald*, 11 March 1938, p. 10.
43 *The Listener*, 9 November 1939, p. 924.
44 Other councils produced very similar handbooks. Some of the London County Council's can be seen at https://www.becontreeforever.uk/historical-archive/tenants-handbooks (accessed 24 November 2024).
45 *Management of Municipal Housing Estates*, p. 20.
46 C. H. Middleton (ed.), *War Time Allotments*, *Daily Express*, 1940.
47 BDA BD356/5.
48 *John Bull*, 26 November 1938, p. 10.
49 *Reference Book for Municipal Tenants in Southgate*, 1941, pp. 5, 7.

Further reading

Burnett, John. *A Social History of Housing, 1815–1985*, 2nd edn (London: Methuen, 1986).
Hoskins, Lesley, and Rebecca Preston. 'Chickens, Ducks, Rabbits, and Me Dad's Geraniums: The Use and Meanings of Yards, Gardens and Other Outside Spaces of Urban Working-Class Homes, 1890–1930', in Joseph Harley, Vicky Holmes and Laika Nevalainen (eds), *The Working Class at Home, 1790–1940* (Cham: Palgrave, 2022), pp. 145–69.
Olechnowicz, Andrzej. *Working-Class Housing in England between the Wars: The Becontree Estate* (Oxford: Oxford University Press, 1999).
Ravetz, Alison, with Richard Turkington. *The Place of Home: English Domestic Environments, 1914–2000* (London: Routledge, 1995).
Scott, Peter. *The Making of the Modern British Home: The Suburban Semi and Family Life between the Wars* (Oxford: Oxford University Press, 2013).
Swenarton, Mark. *Homes Fit for Heroes: The Politics and Architecture of Early State Housing in Britain* (London: Heinemann, 1981).

PART VI
MONETARY OBJECTS

CHAPTER 15
'WAS MUCH REDUCED AND HAD BEEN UNDER THE NECESITY TO PAWN HIS CLOATHS': PARISH PAYMENTS TO REDEEM PAWNED GOODS IN LONDON IN THE LONG EIGHTEENTH CENTURY

Samantha Williams

Introduction

For the urban poor, pawning was an excellent method by which material goods could be turned into ready cash. With pawn shops being ubiquitous in urban centres, particularly in London, pledging moveable items was a common day-to-day response to the vagaries of living on the breadline.[1] Pawn shops even issued trade cards, such as that seen in Figure 15.1. Such was the frequency of use of pawn shops that, for poor families, 'things were continually in pawn'.[2] John Styles has demonstrated that 'so familiar a part of everyday life was pawning for plebeian Londoners that they were expected to have a regular pawnbroker'.[3] When the London street seller Ann Icorn was asked, 'What is the name of the pawnbroker you deal with?', she replied, 'Davis, in London Wall'.[4] Historians have long recognised pawning as one of the many means by which the poor put together a living in the 'economy of makeshifts'. Pawning was one, usually short-term, means by which a household might use when at risk of destitution.[5] A further strategy was to ask the parochial authorities for poor relief, and another was to combine the two: asking the overseer to pay to redeem items pledged in pawn shops. This aspect of pledging, poor relief and the parish redeeming pauper goods has been little explored by historians.[6] This chapter explores this practice in London in the long eighteenth century.

Pawning goods was a feature of many urban centres.[7] In London, the business of pawning was on an immense scale, partly due to its size: London's population was enormous in the eighteenth century, growing from 575,000 at its start to 900,000 at its end.[8] It has been estimated that there were about 250 larger pawn shops in the metropolis in the second half of the eighteenth century, as well as numerous smaller shops, unlicensed 'dolly shops', casual pawnbrokers and money lenders.[9] Pawnbroking also grew over the eighteenth century in larger towns, including the northern urban centres of Beverley, Halifax, Hull, Richmond, Sheffield, York and Whitby.[10] Many pawnbrokers in London combined pawnbroking and lending money with haberdashery; selling

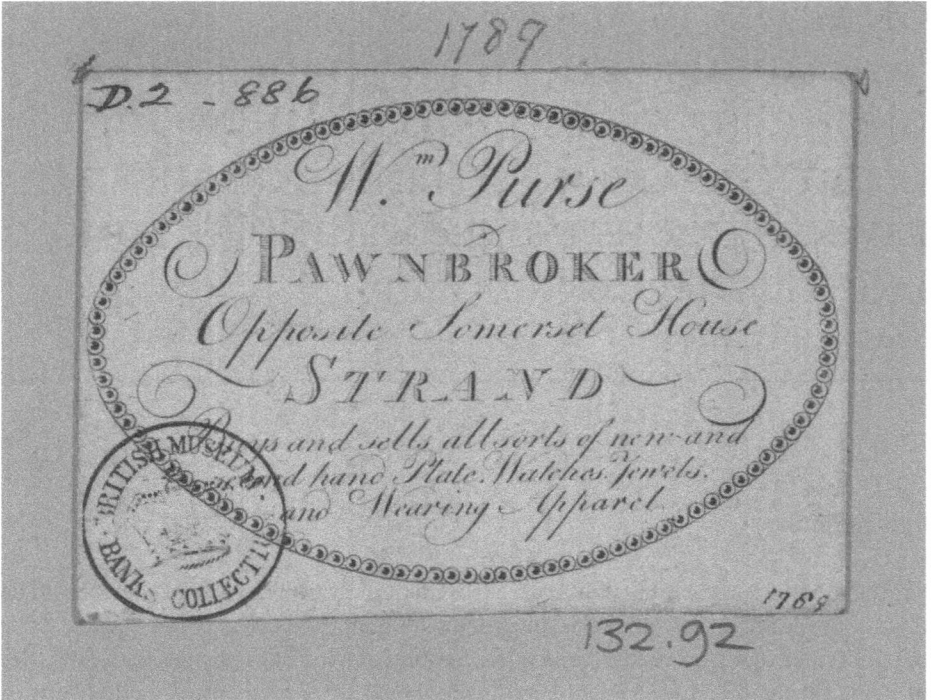

Figure 15.1 Draft trade card of William Purse, pawnbroker, © The Trustees of the British Museum.

second-hand clothing; silversmithing; the selling of gold, silver and jewellery; and the retailing of ale, gin and other spirits.[11] Running a pawn shop was also a business activity open to women, including those who were married (despite legal restrictions).[12] While the more reputable pawn shops would have turned away the very poor, many casual brokers – especially in London – were more willing to risk such pledges.[13]

Urban dwellers were particularly vulnerable to fluctuations in income as cash transactions increased over the century.[14] For those using the pawn shop for short-term credit – pawning their 'Sunday best' clothes – many pledged these items on a Monday. Then they redeemed them the following Saturday, allowing the owner to continue to wear the clothes on Sunday but leveraging credit on them during the working week. A quarter of pledges were redeemed within a week and a further quarter within a month. However, the pawn shop met temporary needs in terms of not only daily or weekly credit but also during seasonal poverty, the unexpected costs of illness and to cover periods of under- or unemployment.[15] The radical Francis Place recalled various ways of using the pawn shop to get by. He commented: 'As long as we had any thing which could be pawned we did not suffer much from actual hunger', but also that there were times when everything had been pawned except 'what we stood up in' and at that point he and his wife 'suffered much from actual hunger'. He described his wife as in a 'comfortless, forlorn and all but ragged condition'.¹⁶ In another case, William King, who was in distress in London, wrote back to the overseer of Braintree, Essex, for poor relief, complaining that 'Every thing of My Wearing apparel and Even My wifes Ring is Put of [pawned] to Procure food'.¹⁷

Ledgers survive for two pawnbrokers in this period: John Pope in Southwark, London, 1666–71, and George Fettes in York, 1777–8.¹⁸ Their ledgers reveal that customers were overwhelmingly female: 84 per cent in Southwark and three-quarters in York, and in the latter they made more frequent visits.¹⁹ Plebeian women played a crucial role in balancing resources in the makeshift economy, being thrifty and utilising household credit, which extended to responsibility for pawning items.²⁰ As household managers, women had more recourse to moveable goods in the home and rather fewer options in terms of employment.²¹ They might even lend each other items to pawn.²² For the very poor, precarity characterised their day-to-day experience.

The pledging of adult clothing was the most popular in Fettes's York business – more than two-thirds of pledges – followed by watches and jewellery, equipment and tools, household metalware such as irons and cutlery, books and soft furnishings.²³ Styles argues that Fettes's pledge book reveals 'just how extensive the clothes side of a specialist pawnbroker's legitimate business could be'.²⁴ The satirist George Cruikshank drew two male pawnbrokers standing behind their counter in a metropolitan pawnbrokers' shop, examining items of clothing brought in to pawn (see Figure 15.2). Women pawned, in particular, their aprons and gowns.²⁵ Fettes's books also demonstrate that women tended to pawn more costly and decorative gowns and retained their everyday gowns to wear.²⁶ Clothing was a significant expense for the poor – and for the poor law when providing it for them – and clothes retained value as they could be pawned so easily or sold in the extensive second-hand clothing market.²⁷ To that point, Margot Finn argues that clothes 'were instruments of credit as much as they were objects of a fashion-driven wave of consumption'.²⁸

Historians of crime, as well as of poverty, have highlighted that the poor would criminally pawn items. These might have been stolen or pledged without the knowledge of their owners, who might then bring a prosecution at the Old Bailey, while pawnbrokers might be prosecuted for accepting stolen property.²⁹ For example, Lynn MacKay and Lisa Huggins have demonstrated the link between poverty and stolen or misappropriated goods which were pawned.³⁰ Analysis for this chapter of the St Botolph Aldgate parish vestry minutes reveals that this might even extend to parish goods. At a meeting held at the Bell Tavern, Church Row, on Tuesday 10 March 1759, an account was made of all the sheets in the St Botolph Aldgate parish workhouse, and it was found that thirty-nine were missing, 'severall of which besides many other Things have been found pawned at Different Places'. The vestry blamed the workhouse master and mistress for allowing inmates to go in and out of the workhouse, presumably taking with them and pledging workhouse property. The master and mistress were promptly dismissed and new applications accepted for the posts.³¹ As with St Botolph Aldgate parish workhouse, parish authorities across London and further afield also marked their goods and prosecuted pawnbrokers who accepted parish property. In January 1781 the St Clement Danes minute books recorded that:

Objects of Poverty

Figure 15.2 Two men are standing behind the counter of a pawnbroker's shop in London, examining some articles of clothing which have been brought in to pawn, etching by George Cruikshank, 1836. Wellcome Collection, 29537i, Public Domain Mark.

Mr. Davidson the Pawn broker having Attended this Board with regards to taking in Cloaths into Pawn having the Parish mark thereon which he was liable to be prosecuted for but he making a Concession and beging Pardon for the Trouble he put them thereto The Churchwardens and Overseers on his making such

Parish Payments to Redeem Pawned Goods

Concession and Asking Pardon They Agreed to Stop all further Proceeding agt. Him as also the Expences they were put unto on Account thereof.[32]

Although pawning is acknowledged as a common strategy employed by the poor, the depth of poverty faced and the level of material wealth by those pledging items are important considerations. Alannah Tomkins has analysed Fettes's pawnbroking pledge books to estimate the extent to which eighteenth-century paupers were involved in pawning their goods in York. She found that 'pawning by paupers was the exception rather than the rule' and that Fettes's pawn shop was 'rarely used by paupers'. She estimates that paupers accounted for 4–12 per cent of customers. These individuals redeemed their goods more quickly than other customers at twenty-five days rather than the average of fifty-six days. Although there were a couple of cases of items redeemed with parish money, no paupers who routinely made pledges were in receipt of regular relief and instead received ad-hoc casual relief.[33] While Tomkins accounts for the low number of the very poor engaging in pawning by their low material wealth, recent work by Joseph Harley has argued that 'with regular or casual relief rarely being enough to live off, most people would have gone through periods of selling and pawning their goods before and during the time that they received poor relief'.[34]

It might indeed have been the case that the very poor only accounted for a minority of the wider pool of poor customers pledging items in respectable pawnshops in provincial urban centres. However, in London, there were far more pawnshops than in other towns and a large number of informal pawnbrokers who were willing to allow paupers to pledge goods. The evidence of metropolitan parish authorities being prepared to redeem the goods of paupers from local pawn shops demonstrates that the poor had access to goods that could be pawned, that pawn shops were willing to lend to them, and that parochial officers recognised the utility of redeeming their items.

Parish payments for pawned goods

There were at least 170 entries for items to be redeemed from pawn shops by the parish authorities recorded in account books of the churchwardens and overseers of the poor, parish minutes and clothing books in the three metropolitan parishes of St Botolph Aldgate, St Clement Danes and St Dionis Backchurch in the long eighteenth century.[35] St Botolph Aldgate was a large parish (13,000–15,000 population), densely populated, and divided between the City and the poorer part of eastern Middlesex, with a large proportion of poorer households. St Clement Danes was in the West End and inhabited by a more mixed socio-economic population (11,500), while St Dionis Backchurch was a wealthy and small parish (less than 1,000) located in the heart of the City, with ample poor relief and charitable funds.[36]

The poor in London were not only pawning their goods but also having their goods redeemed by the parish. Churchwardens and overseers of the poor recognised that the poor had pledged their goods in an attempt to makeshift and that they required parish

Objects of Poverty

assistance to reclaim them. Moreover, paying for the poor to redeem their goods restored some measure of independence to them. This was spelt out on occasion: in January 1726 Mary Sadler's goods were redeemed at a cost of £1 11s to 'Enable her to provide for her Family', while £1 6s was paid out for William Underwood's goods to enable him to provide for his 'Verry Large Family'.[37] This might also work at a distance, as in the case of Thomas Broadways in 1723, when St Botolph Aldgate's parochial officers paid £1 6s for his goods to be redeemed, 'he his wife & two Children being Past On us From Bethnall Green hamblet himself Sick'.[38] In another case, the same parish even paid 17s to redeem Ann Cook's clothes before she was carried 'to her Settlement at Stanes'.[39]

Of course, with interest being charged, the sums paid to redeem items would be larger than the amounts paid to pledge them.[40] Fettes's book recorded the sums that were pledged; these payments were for the costs of redeeming the goods. In August 1765, for instance, St Dionis Backchurch paid for Mary May 'To Redeem her Cloaths in Pawn', with the clothes valued at 12s but the total amount coming to 16s 4d, presumably with the added interest.[41] The amounts paid by the three parishes varied from as little as 1s to redeem Elizabeth Stevenson's shoes in March 1790, to as much as £11 16s – a huge sum – given to Mary Read in October 1764 'for fetching her Cloaths out of Pawn & Interest', due to the number of items and their value, plus the interest accrued (see Figure 15.3).[42] The most common sum paid was between 2s and 3s, but there was still a large range of sums, with 81 per cent of sums being more than 3s, 43 per cent for more than 10s and 13 per cent of payments for over £1. Such large payments would have been beyond the means of most of the poor to redeem without the assistance of the parish. These sums

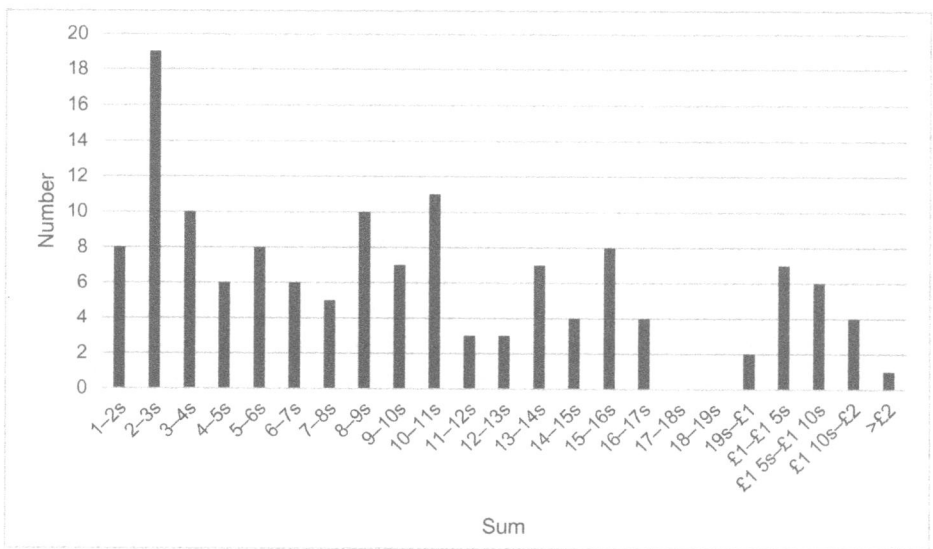

Figure 15.3 Sums paid by the parish to redeem pledges in three London parishes, 1695–1808. Source: See endnote 35.

were far in excess of weekly parish pensions, which would have been around 2s 6d.[43] It also suggests that higher value and/or multiple items were pawned together for the redeemable value to have been so high in so many cases.

Frustratingly, the items to be redeemed were at times described in unhelpful ways, such as 'goods', 'things' or 'sundries' (24 per cent). When goods were itemised, clothing and shoes were the most common items pawned (71 per cent), like Beverly Lemire, Tomkins and Styles found in Fettes's pawnbroker's book for York.[44] Most of the remaining items were bedding, such as sheets, blankets and quilts. Similar to Fettes's and Pope's pawnshop, the majority of those whose goods were redeemed were women (73 per cent).

The poor's clothing

Simply, the term 'clothes' was used in half of the entries. In the other half of instances, individual items of clothing were recorded. The most common pieces of clothing that were pawned and redeemed were women's clothes: gowns and shifts (14 per cent and 13 per cent, respectively), followed by cloaks (10 per cent) and stays (9 per cent) (Table 15.1).[45] This reflects not only the predominance of women pawning goods, but that more women were on poor relief and, therefore, eligible to have their pawned goods redeemed. It might also have meant that they were more willing or able to pawn their own clothes rather than those of husbands and children, although women who turned to the poor law were more likely to have been widowed, deserted or unmarried.[46] Moreover, the redemption of goods from the pawn shop was not necessarily a one-off: one-third of paupers in St Dionis Backchurch had their goods redeemed at parish expense more than once. Twelve paupers had items redeemed twice, seven thrice, one four times, and two – Elizabeth Steventon and Ann Wright – on no less than five occasions.

As Styles has demonstrated, the most expensive women's clothing to buy were cloaks and better-quality gowns. The average pledge value of silk, cotton and linen gowns in Fettes's pawn book was between 4s and 4s 5d, while that for a worsted stuff gown was 2s 5d.[47] Thus, poor women might have been pledging their most valuable pieces of clothing – acquired in better times and provided by the parish – in order to raise the most in ready cash. The redeemable value of gowns in the London parish sample was between 2s 6d (at Fettes's lower end) and as high as 8s 6d, perhaps due to a large amount of interest that might have accrued on the pledge. Cloaks must have varied in quality, age, and wear and tear since their redeemable value ranged from just 1s 6d to 10s 6d.

Given the range of material wealth of the poor, some of those pledging their underclothes would have had more than a change of clothes and could pawn their spares. On the other hand, that so many women were willing to pledge their shifts also reveals that they might have reached the point of destitution. Women's shifts and men's shirts were essential to contemporary understandings of both decency – as Adam Smith claimed – and cleanliness since they were changed and washed regularly.[48] Pawning such goods could have significant implications as their absence would indicate poverty and even provoke shame in those pledging and disgust at their absence in others.[49] Even the

Objects of Poverty

Table 15.1 Types of Clothing Redeemed and Sums Paid by the Parish Authorities in Three London Parishes, 1695–1808. Source: See endnote 35.

Item	Total n	Per cent	Range of sums redeemed
Gown	13	14	2s 6d–8s 6d
Shift	12	13	1s 6d–2s 0d
Cloak	9	10	1s 6d–10s 6d
Stays	8	9	2s 0d–4s 0d
Coat	7	8	2s 1d–3s 6d
Apron	7	8	
Petticoat	7	8	2s 0d–6s 0d
Shirt	6	6	1s 10d–10s 6d
Breeches	5	5	1s 3d–2s 6d
Handkerchief	5	5	
Shoes	5	5	1s 0d–2s 0d
Waistcoat	3	3	2s 2d
Stockings	2	2	
Bedgown	2	2	
Bodice	1	1	
Frock	1	1	

poor would need to own two such pieces so that the other could be worn when one shirt or shift was being washed.[50] If a pauper only owned two of these garments then pawning them would be an act of desperation.[51] Their desperation is also exemplified in the fact that these items did not raise much ready money (Table 15.1).

Pawning one's clothes could result in destitution and admittance to the workhouse: Elizabeth Bury, Alexander Lowery and Mary Collins were all admitted to the workhouse in St Luke's Chelsea because they had pawned their clothes.[52] These individuals were frequently in and out of the workhouse: Collins nine times, Bury nineteen times and Lowery on twenty-two occasions. Elizabeth Bury, in her sixties, was recorded as pawning her clothes twice, while at other times she was described as 'almost naked' and 'without a shift' as the reason for admittance. For example, Mary Collins, when in her late thirties and early forties, entered the workhouse because she had 'pawn'd all her Cloths' and on another occasion because 'everything maid away with'. When in his fifties, Alexander Lowery, often described in the register as 'lazy' and 'infirm', was once

Parish Payments to Redeem Pawned Goods

admitted 'to be cleand' and on another 'to get Some cloths'. He was provided with a coat, a pair of britches and some new shoes when he was discharged.

Other items of clothing pawned in lesser proportions (and in descending order) were coats, aprons and petticoats; shirts; breeches and shoes; waistcoats; stockings and bedgowns; a bodice and a child's frock (Table 15.1).[53] Men's coats and waistcoats were expensive items of clothing to buy and would raise a higher level of cash when pledged; 14 per cent of payments were for shirts, breeches and waistcoats.[54] Breeches and waistcoats were redeemed at between 1s 3d and 2s 6d, while shirts for as little as 1s 10d and as high as 10s 6d, possibly due to its quality or, again, due to the interest. Nevertheless, it was women's clothing that predominated in these redeemed pledges.

Clothing was a particular concern to the parish officials. St Dionis Backchurch contracted workhouse provision with Richard Birch between 1761 and 1767 in Rose Lane, detailing payments per week per head for paupers' board and lodging.[55] The agreement was particularly concerned with clothing: if the churchwardens agreed that inmates could go out of the House and then they pawned or sold their clothes, then they were responsible for re-clothing them; if Richard Birch let them leave, then he was responsible.[56] Yet there was also a payment recorded for Birch to redeem items for one Joseph Chambers, who was in the workhouse, in July 1762.[57] In the 1790s there were also payments for paupers in the workhouse run by Messrs Hughes and Philip at Hoxton to have their goods redeemed.[58]

Clothing was considered essential for domestic service, such as for Jane Gough (at 10s 6d), Ann Stevens (at 7s 2d) and Susanna Keel (at 10s), who all had their clothes redeemed by the parish so that they could go back out to service.[59] The parish authorities placed a high priority on assisting the poor to work and independence from the parish. Items used to produce clothing, and, thus, income, would also be redeemed: in late October 1737, Elizabeth Shaw, an occasional recipient, was allowed 2s by the parish vestry to 'redeem her [spinning] Wheel'.[60]

There were various levels of poverty with which the poor law authorities might assist. The first might be just for the parish to pay for the return of goods. In other circumstances, the poor might also require casual relief or a regular parish pension. What is evident, however, is that the vast majority of those whose goods were redeemed with parish money were currently in receipt of some form of poor relief, although it is not always clear when recipients were considered casual recipients or regular pensioners. In St Dionis Backchurch, for instance, there were many payments to or on behalf of Christian Purton between 1711 and 1728, including a trip to the hospital from which he returned again 'incureable in a Miserable helpless condicon', pension payments, nursing care, lodging and 9s 6d in 1727 for his things to be redeemed from pawn.[61] Many paupers whose clothes were redeemed were also bought clothing by the parish.[62] In the metropolitan parish of St Martin-in-the-Fields, the most common items the parish gave out were shoes, shifts and aprons.[63]

In the three parishes analysed here, there is no evidence that the parish marked the clothing given to paupers to prevent them from pledging them. Instead, sources suggest that the parish accepted that the poor would pawn these goods to alleviate poverty for short periods, in the hope that they would not request further poor relief. This means that paupers might have been pawning the very items the parish had paid for, raising credit on them, and then having the parish pay to redeem those same items.[64] In this way, clothing was an instrument of credit twice over – it was provided free of charge by the parish and then could also be used to raise a cash loan, which the pauper did not have to pay back. The parish had, in effect, provided poor relief twofold for the pauper.[65] The fact that they did so on many occasions suggests that clothing held value in both its material form and as credit and that the pledge sums were another form of occasional cash-poor relief.

There is lively debate between historians as to the quality of the clothing worn by the labouring poor and of the clothing provided by the parochial authorities to those on poor relief. Lemire has argued that 'The worthy poor were never provided with more than the minimum of clothing', while Steven King has countered that paupers were 'well clothed' and might be better clothed than many of the rest of the labouring poor or even some tenant farmers.[66] More recently, however, Peter Jones and Styles have disagreed. Jones believes that parishes operated a 'compassionate pragmatism' in terms of clothing policy: although 'good quality, hard-wearing clothes' were provided fairly frequently, they were not fashionable or better than those of the non-poor.[67] Styles disagrees and argues that parishes provided only clothes that were narrow 'in terms of price, range and quality' and that there was a 'minimum of sartorial sufficiency' over the course of the eighteenth century. He also highlights that the admission registers of St Marylebone workhouse in 1770 recorded the condition of the clothing worn by the poor entering the house: while just over half were fairly well clothed, the other half were in 'ragged' or 'old' clothes.[68]

There are various reasons why parishes might have been motivated to redeem paupers' goods. One was to get the poor back to work, as was shown above. Another was that it was probably cheaper to redeem the goods than to buy new clothes. A final explanation is that vestries sought to ensure the respectability of the dress of their parish poor. As King and Jones have demonstrated, parishes might be seeking to avoid the perception of 'nakedness' and raggedness. Indeed, their motivation might have been pride in the appearance of the poor and the reputation of the parish.[69] In a crowded location such as London, this was one way in which to express civic pride and differentiate the parish. The actions of St Dionis, in particular, suggest this was an important reason for their willingness to provide clothing and to redeem the clothes of the parish poor; this parish accounted for two-thirds of the cases explored in this chapter and was a wealthy City parish who could well afford to show such generosity.

Conclusion

Pawning goods was a common expedient exploited by the poor in the metropolis. Parish officials not only recognised the utility of redeeming these goods but that, without assistance, these goods would go unclaimed, with the possibility that the parish would have to provide more costly replacements. Moreover, many payments to redeem goods were beyond the means of the poor without assistance. In this makeshift economy of short-term credit, women feature heavily and they were also most likely to require poor relief. They pawned their own clothing – notably gowns, shifts, cloaks and stays. Some of these women – who pledged dresses and cloaks – would have been like the 'better clothed' poor arriving at St Marylebone workhouse, while others – who pawned shifts and stays – would have been like the other 'raggedly' clothed half. The fact that many women pledged their undergarments suggests a level of desperation and destitution, and also from those men who pawned their shirts. Some of the parish poor benefitted from parish generosity more than once: not only did the parish pay for clothes for them, and paupers received cash when they pledged them, but the parish then paid for them to be redeemed so that the clothes benefitted the poor twice. Others had goods repeatedly redeemed.

These payments allow us to reflect upon much wider themes that have preoccupied historians, such as the bespoke nature of poor relief, the agency of the poor and local social relations under the old poor law. Poor relief was tailored very specifically to the needs of individual paupers; indeed, the system was a versatile tool that assisted in a wide variety of circumstances. That the poor could persuade overseers to redeem their goods, and even those provided by the parish in the first place – and repeatedly – suggests real creativity on the part of the poor, particularly in the face of their lack of control over the clothing provided by the parish in the first place.[70] It also indicates that parishes were more understanding than might be expected of the need to pawn items in the search to make ends meet. Overseers recognised how pawning items, including parish clothing, was a pragmatic response to economic distress to the extent that they were prepared to redeem paupers' goods. The clothing of the poor was symbolically important to the poor and to the parish in terms of their reputation. Examining such payments reveals the breadth of assistance available under the old poor law, the material lives of the poor and the involvement of the parish in the household economies of the poor.

Notes

1   Peter Earle, *The Making of the English Middle Classes: Business, Society and Family Life in London 1660–1730* (Berkeley: University of California Press, 1989), pp. 49–50; Beverly Lemire, 'Petty Pawns and Informal Lending', in Kristine Bruland and Patrick O'Brien (eds), *From Family Firms to Corporate Capitalism: Essays in Business and Industrial History in Honour of Peter Mathias* (Oxford: Clarendon Press, 1998), pp. 112–13; Garthine Walker, 'Women, Theft and the World of Stolen Goods', in Jennifer Kermode and Garthine Walker (eds), *Women, Crime and the Courts in Early Modern England* (London: Routledge, 1994), pp. 98–9; Janice Turner, 'An Anatomy of a "Disorderly" Neighbourhood: Rosemary Lane and Rag Fair, c. 1690–1765', PhD thesis (University of Hertfordshire, 2014), pp. 164–80.
2   Old Bailey Proceedings, *London Lives, 1690–1800*, t17961130-40 (www.londonlives.org, version 2.0 March 2018) (hereafter *LL*), November 1796, trial of Mary Murray, cited by Lucy Huggins, '"I'll Vamp it and Tip you the Cole": Poverty, Pawning and Prosecutions in London: Evidence from the Old Bailey, 1750–1799', *London Journal*, 46:3 (2021): p. 288.

3 John Styles, *The Dress of the People: Everyday Fashion in Eighteenth-Century England* (New Haven: Yale University Press 2007), p. 176.
4 Proceedings, *LL*, t17850629-99, June 1785, trial of Ann Icorn, cited in Styles, *Dress of the people*, p. 176.
5 Steven King and Alannah Tomkins, 'Introduction', in Steven King and Alannah Tomkins (eds), *The Poor in England 1700-1850: An Economy of Makeshifts* (Manchester: Manchester University Press, 2003), p. 13. See also Alannah Tomkins, *The Experience of Urban Poverty, 1723-1782: Parish, Charity and Credit* (Manchester: Manchester University Press, 2006), ch. 6; Joseph Harley, 'Consumption and Poverty in the Homes of the English Poor, *c.* 1670-1834', *Social History*, 43:1 (2018): pp. 84, 100; Joseph Harley, *At Home with the Poor: Consumer Behaviour and Material Culture in England, c. 1650-1850* (Manchester: Manchester University Press, 2024), pp. 55-83.
6 Alannah Tomkins finds only a couple of payments in the overseers' accounts for York for redeeming paupers' goods: 'Pawnbroking and the Survival Strategies of the Urban Poor in 1770s York', in King and Tomkins, *The Poor in England*, p. 185. Steven King cites two examples in Garstang, Lancashire: Steven King, 'Reclothing the English Poor, 1750-1840', *Textile History*, 33:1 (2002): pp. 41-2.
7 Turner, 'Rosemany Lane', pp. 169-70.
8 Leonard D. Schwarz, *London in the Age of Industrialisation: Entrepreneurs, Labour Force and Living Conditions, 1700-1850* (Cambridge: Cambridge University Press, 1992), table 5.1, p. 126.
9 Kenneth Hudson, *Pawnbroking: An Aspect of British Social History* (London: Bodley Head, 1982), pp. 33-5; Schwarz, *London in the Age of Industrialisation*, table 1.2, p. 21. And see Turner, 'Rosemany Lane', pp. 169-70, and wider discussion pp. 164-80; Tomkins, 'Pawnbroking', p. 183.
10 Styles, *Dress of the People*, p. 164.
11 Lemire, 'Petty Pawns', pp. 114; Turner, 'Rosemary Lane', p. 169; Earle, *English Middle Classes*, p. 55.
12 Earle, *English Middle Classes*, table 6.2, p. 170; Walker, 'Women, Theft and the World of Stolen Goods', pp. 99-100; Alexandra Shepard, 'Minding Their Own Business: Married Women and Credit in Early Eighteenth-Century London', *Transactions of the Royal Historical Society*, 25 (2015): pp. 53-74.
13 Tomkins, 'Pawnbroking', p. 183; Turner, 'Rosemary Lane', pp. 169-70.
14 Lemire, 'Petty Pawns', p. 112.
15 Tomkins, 'Pawnbroking', pp. 178, 180, 183; Lynn MacKay 'Why They Stole: Women in the Old Bailey, 1779-1789', *Journal of Social History*, 32:3 (1993): pp. 630-1. And see Alison Backhouse, *The Worm Eaten Waistcoat* (York: Self-published, 2003).
16 Mary Thale (ed.), *The Autobiography of Francis Place (1771-1854)* (Cambridge: Cambridge University Press, 1972), pp. 124, 128, 158, cited by Styles, *Dress of the People*, p. 59. On Place, see Ruth Mather, 'Politicising the English Working-Class Home, *c.* 1790-1820', in Joseph Harley, Vicky Holmes and Laika Nevalainen (eds), *The Working Class at Home, 1790-1940* (Cham: Palgrave Macmillan, 2022), pp. 47-72.
17 Thomas Sokoll (ed.), *Essex Pauper Letters, 1731-1837* (Oxford: Oxford University Press, 2001), pp. 121-2, cited by Harley, 'Consumption and Poverty', p. 100.
18 On Pope, see Lemire, 'Petty Pawns', pp. 112-38. On Fettes, see Tomkins, 'Pawnbroking'; Styles, *Dress of the People*, p. 101; Alice Dolan, 'Touching Linen: Textiles, Emotion and Bodily Intimacy in England, *c.* 1708-1818', *Cultural and Social History*, 16:2 (2019): pp. 148-50; Backhouse, *Worm Eaten Waistcoat*; Harley, 'Consumption and Poverty', pp. 93, 100.
19 Lemire, 'Petty Pawns', table 4.2, p. 118, table 4.6, p. 131; Styles, *Dress of the People*, p. 101; Tomkins, 'Pawnbroking', pp. 180-1; Dolan, 'Touching Linen', p. 149.

20 Lemire, 'Petty Pawns', pp. 124–5.
21 Ibid., pp. 124–5; Huggins, 'I'll Vamp it', p. 294.
22 MacKay, 'Why They Stole', p. 630.
23 Lemire, 'Petty Pawns', tables 4.7–4.8, p. 132; Tomkins, 'Pawnbroking', pp. 180–1; Styles, *Dress of the People*, p. 163; Dolan, 'Touching Linen', pp. 148–50; Harley, 'Consumption and Poverty', p. 100. And see Margot Finn, 'Debt and Credit in Bath's Court of Requests, 1829–39', *Urban History*, 21:2 (1994): p. 230.
24 Styles, *Dress of the People*, p. 163.
25 Tomkins, 'Pawnbroking', p. 181; Styles, *Dress of the People*, p. 163; Dolan, 'Touching Linen', table 1, p. 149.
26 Styles, *Dress of the People*, p. 163. And see Dolan, 'Touching Linen', table 2, p. 149.
27 Styles, *Dress of the People*, p. 176; Beverly Lemire, *The Business of Everyday Life: Gender, Practice and Social Politics in England, c. 1600–1900* (Manchester: Manchester University Press, 2005), pp. 92–6. Lemire shows that clothing dominated pledges in London from the late sixteenth century to the early nineteenth century. And see King, 'Reclothing the English Poor'; Peter D. Jones, '"I cannot keep my place without being deascent": Pauper Letters, Parish Clothing and Pragmatism in the South of England, 1750–1830', *Rural History* 20:1 (2009): pp. 31–49.
28 Finn, 'Debt and Credit', p. 230.
29 Tomkins, *Urban Poverty*, pp. 211–13.
30 MacKay, 'Why They Stole'; Huggins, 'I'll Vamp it'. And see Tomkins, 'Pawnbroking'.
31 St Botolph Aldgate, Minutes of Parish Vestries, 21st May 1739–13th May 1762, 1759, *London Lives, 1690–1800*, GLBAMV114010144 (www.londonlives.org, version 2.0 March 2018) (accessed 17 April 2024), London Metropolitan Archives (hereafter LMA), Ms. 2642/2.
32 St Clement Danes, Minute Books of Parish Vestry Sub-Committees, 5th January 1779–5th October 1790, 1781, *LL*, WCCDMO361030033, Westminster Archives Centre (hereafter WAC), Ms. B1147. On marking goods, see also Louise Falcini, 'Cleanliness and the Poor in Eighteenth-Century London', PhD thesis (University of Reading, 2018), p. 132.
33 Tomkins, 'Pawnbroking', pp. 183–91.
34 Ibid., p. 192; Harley, 'Consumption and Poverty', p. 102.
35 There were at least 170 identifiable cases from a keyword search, 1695–1808 (some were not identifiable because of the way they had been transcribed) across all these sources: St Botolph Aldgate, Churchwardens and Overseers of the Poor Account Books, 1689–1802 (*LL* GLBAAC10002-GLBAAC10006, GLBAAC10009-GLBAAC10010, GLBAAC10102-GLBAAC10103) (LMA Mss. 9235/2-2, 9235/3, 9235/3-5, 2625/1A-1B, 2625/1C-5, 2625/6-12), Miscellaneous Parish Account Books, 1746–1748 and 1770–1800 (*LL* GLBAAO10100-GLBAAO10101) (LMA Mss. 2627/1-3), Regular Parish Payments to Paupers, 1755–1788 (*LL* GLBAAP10200-GLBAAP10204) (LMA Mss. 9953, 2628/1, /1A-1B), Minute Books of Parish Vestry Sub-Committees, 1734–1738 and 1768–1795 (*LL* GLBAMO10008, GLBAMO11302-GLBAMO11303) (LMA Mss. 2680/1, 2680/20-103, 2690), Minutes of Parish Vestries, 1690–1804 (*LL* GLBAMV11300-GLBAMV11301, GLBAMV11400-GLBAMV11402) (LMA Mss. 2644/1, 2642/1-3, 2644A/1); St Clement Danes, Miscellaneous Parish Account Books, 1719–1730 and 1794–1796 (*LL* WCCDAO35200-WCCDAO35201, WCCDAO35300-WCCDAO35304) (WAC Mss. B1222-8), Books of Clothing Provided by the Parish, 1785–1796 (*LL* WCCDBC35500-WCCDBC35504) (WAC Mss. B1250-3), Minutes of Parish Vestries, 1686–1800 (*LL* WCCDMV36200-WCCDMV36217) (WAC Ms. B1060-B1074), Minutes Books of Parish Vestry Sub-Committees, 1771–1808 (*LL* WCCDMO36100-WCCDMO36105) (WAC Ms. B1272-3, Ms. B1275, Ms. B1147-B1148); St Dionis Backchurch, Churchwardens and Overseers of the Poor Account Books, 1689–1798 (*LL* GLDBAC30000-GLDBAC30010) (LMA Mss. 4215/1-2, 4222/5-8, 4215/1-2, 4222/1-4), Churchwardens'

Objects of Poverty

Vouchers/Receipts, 1683–1782 (*LL* GLDBPP30700-GLDBPP30703) (LMA Mss. 11280/Box1-Box2, 4220/1-2, 4224/1), Books of Clothing Provided by the Parish, 1788–1793 (*LL* GLDBBC30600) (LMA Mss. 11269/1-2), Minute Books of Parish Vestry Sub-Committees, 1772–1795 (*LL* GLDBMO30300) (LMA Ms. 4217/1–2), Miscellaneous Parish and Bridewell Papers, 1669–1797 (*LL* GLDBPM30603-GLDBPM306014) (LMA Mss. 11280A, 11280A/2-3, 11280A/5, 11281-2, 20213/1, 18483A, 4226, 4235/1-3, B1206), Workhouse Inquest (Visitation) Minute Books, 1761–1788 (*LL* GLDBIW30200-GLDBIW30203) (LMA Mss. 11275/1, 4219/1-3). For the lists of parish sources and their *LL* codes and manuscript call numbers, see https://www.londonlives.org/static/Documents.jsp#docaz. Thanks to Tim Hitchcock, Robert Shoemaker, Sharon Howard and Jamie McLaughlinfor permission to use the transcriptions for *London Lives, 1690–1800* (www.londonlives.org, version 2.0 March 2018) (accessed 17 April 2024).

36 Tim Hitchcock and Robert Shoemaker, *London Lives: Poverty, Crime and the Making of a Modern City, 1690–1800* (Cambridge: Cambridge University Press, 2015), p. 24; www.londonlives.org/static/StBotolphAldgate.jsp, www.londonlives.org/static/StClementDanes.jsp, www.londonlives.org/static/StDionisBackchurch.jsp (accessed 17 April 2024).
37 St Botolph Aldgate, Churchwardens and Overseers of the Poor Account Books, 1723–1731, 1726, *LL*, GLBAAC100030346.
38 Ibid., 1723, GLBAAC100030174.
39 Ibid., 1728, GLBAAC100030388.
40 See Lemire, 'Petty Pawns', p. 121; Lemire, *Business of Everyday Life*, p. 49, n.1.
41 St Dionis Backchurch, Churchwardens and Overseers of the Poor Account Books, 1764–1770, 1766 [1765], *LL*, GLDBAC300080083.
42 St Dionis Backchurch, Minute Books of Parish Vestry Sub-Committees, 1772–1795, 1790, *LL*, GLDBMO303000305; St Dionis Backchurch, Churchwardens and Overseers of the Poor Account Books, 1764–1770, 1764, *LL*, GLDBAC300080059.
43 Hitchcock and Shoemaker, *London Lives*, pp. 50, 142.
44 Lemire, 'Petty Pawns', p. 132; Tomkins, 'Pawnbroking', pp. 180–1; Styles, *Dress of the People*, p. 163.
45 See Styles on the clothes worn by those admitted to St Marylebone workhouse in *Dress of the People*, tables 8–9, pp. 340–1 and discussion on pp. 64–7.
46 For urban centres, see Jeremy Boulton and John Black, 'Paupers and Their Experience of a London Workhouse: St Martin-in-the-Fields, 1725–1824', in Jane Hamlett, Lesley Hoskins and Rebecca Preston (eds), *Residential institutions in Britain, 1725–1970: Inmates and Environments* (London: Pickering & Chatto, 2013), pp. 79–91; Alannah Tomkins, *The Experience of Urban Poverty, 1723–1782* (Manchester: Manchester University Press, 2006), pp. 45–50; Alysa Levene, 'Children, Childhood and the Workhouse: St Marylebone, 1769–1781', *London Journal*, 33:1 (2008): pp. 41–59.
47 Styles, *Dress of the People*, pp. 100–1, and table 19, p. 346. And see Dolan, 'Touching Linen', table 2, p. 149.
48 Adam Smith, *An Inquiry into the Nature and Causes of the Wealth of Nations* (London: Electric Book, [1776] *c.* 2001), Book 5, p. 1168; Styles, *Dress of the People*, p. 265; Susan North, *Sweet and Clean? Bodies and Clothes in Early Modern England* (Oxford: Oxford University Press, 2020), chps 3, 4, 6, 9.
49 Dolan, 'Touching Linen', pp. 147–50.
50 Elizabeth Spencer, 'Clothing the Poor', in Peter Collinge and Louise Falcini (eds), *Providing for the Poor: The Old Poor Law, 1750–1834* (London: University of London Press, 2022), pp. 70–1. And see Falcini, 'Cleanliness and the Poor'.
51 Dolan, 'Touching Linen', p. 148.

52 St Luke's Chelsea, Workhouse Admission and Discharge Registers, March 1743–July 1769, January 1782–December 1801 (*LL*) (LMA P74/LUK/110-111), . Thanks to Tim Hitchcock for permission to use this dataset.
53 On such items pledged with Fettes, see Dolan, 'Touching Linens', table 1, p. 149.
54 On money raised on such items with Fettes, see Styles, *Dress of the People*, pp. 100–1.
55 'St Dionis Backchurch' https//www.londonlives.org/static/StDionisBackchurch.jsp (accessed 3 February 2025)
56 St Dionis Backchurch, Miscellaneous Parish and Bridewell Papers, 1707–78, 1761, *LL*, GLDBPM306140009.
57 St Dionis Backchurch, Churchwardens and Overseers of the Poor Account Books, 1758–62, 1762, *LL*, GLDBAC300070326.
58 St Dionis Backchurch, Churchwardens and Overseers of the Poor Account Books, 25th April 1795–24th September 1798, 1797, *LL*, GLDBAC300040057, 1798, GLDBAC300040143, 1798, GLDBAC300040025.
59 St Botolph Aldgate, Minutes of Parish Vestries, 1724–37, 1734, *LL*, GLBAMV114000219, GLBAMV114000229; St Clement Danes, Minute Books of Parish Vestry Sub-Committees, 1798–1808, *LL*, WCCDMO361050357.
60 St Botolph Aldgate, Minute Books of Parish Vestry Sub-Committees, 1734–8, 1737, *LL*, GLBAMO100080206.
61 St Dionis Backchurch, Churchwardens and Overseers of the Poor Account Books, 1689–1720, 1721–8, quote from 1711, GLDBAC300000506.
62 This is very apparent in St Dionis Backchurch, where each pauper was allocated a page each with their payments specified, see the Churchwardens and Overseers of the Poor Account Books.
63 Jones, 'Clothing the Poor', table 2, p. 22. Outside of London, Styles found that shirts, shifts, shoes and clogs were most commonly given, in *Dress of the People*, table 29, p. 352.
64 For an example from Garstang, Lancashire, see King 'Reclothing the English Poor', p. 41.
65 Harley notes that the poor might sell items that the parish had given them: 'Consumption and Poverty', p. 100.
66 Lemire, 'A Good Stock of Cloaths', p. 317; King, 'Reclothing the English Poor', pp. 41, 45.
67 Jones, 'Clothing the Poor', pp. 27–9, 33–4.
68 Styles, *Dress of the People*, pp. 64–5, 266, 275.
69 King, 'Reclothing the English Poor'; Steven King, 'The Clothing of the Poor: A Matter of Pride or Shame?', in Andreas Gestrich, Steven King and Lutz Raphael (eds), *Being Poor in Modern Europe: Historical Perspectives 1800–1940* (Bern: Peter Land, 2006); Jones, 'I cannot keep my place without being deascent'.
70 On the involuntary consumption of the poor through parish clothing and how the poor 'exercised little or no control' over clothing provided by the parish, see Styles, *Dress of the People*, p. 257.

Further reading

Harley, Joseph. 'Consumption and Poverty in the Homes of the English Poor, *c*. 1670–1834'. *Social History*, 43:1 (2018): pp. 81–104.

Hitchcock, Tim, and Robert Shoemaker. *London Lives: Poverty, Crime and the Making of a Modern City, 1690–1800* (Cambridge: Cambridge University Press, 2015).

Jones, Peter D. 'Clothing the Poor in Early-Nineteenth-Century England'. *Textile History*, 37:1 (2006): pp. 17–37.

King, Steven. 'Reclothing the English Poor, 1750–1840'. *Textile History*, 33:1 (2002): pp. 37–47.

Lemire, Beverly. 'Petty Pawns and Informal Lending', in Kristine Bruland and Patrick O'Brien (eds), *From Family Firms to Corporate Capitalism: Essays in Business and Industrial History in Honour of Peter Mathias* (Oxford: Clarendon Press, 1998), pp. 112-38.

Styles, John. *The Dress of the People: Everyday Fashion in Eighteenth-Century England* (New Haven: Yale University Press 2007).

Tomkins, Alannah. 'Pawnbroking and the Survival Strategies of the Urban Poor in 1770s York', in Steven King and Alannah Tomkins (eds), *The Poor in England 1700-1850: An Economy of Makeshifts* (Manchester: Manchester University Press, 2003), pp. 166-98.

CHAPTER 16
'NO MONEY VALUE': THE SALVATION ARMY SOCIAL WORK TOKENS IN THE LATE NINETEENTH CENTURY

Flore Janssen[1]

Introduction

The object collection at the Salvation Army International Heritage Centre (IHC) contains a handful of metal discs (Figure 16.1), listed in the catalogue as 'miscellaneous Social Work tokens' dated 1890–1900. Of the eleven different designs, one is oval and one is square in shape, but the rest are round and resemble coins. Around the edge are the names of different elements of the Salvation Army's Social Work scheme at this time: 'Social Centre', 'Social Wing', 'Social Work', 'Elevator' and 'Farm Colony'. The majority, seven out of the eleven, are further marked with an 'F' and an 'S', suggesting they were in use in the so-called Food and Shelter Depots, the Salvation Army's affordable cafeterias and hostels for homeless people. In the centre, the tokens are stamped with a value, but there is little correlation between size or shape and value or purpose.

The design reflects precautions taken to prevent confusion with actual money. The beaten zinc from which the tokens are made is thin and very lightweight, which makes the discs feel flimsy as if they could easily bend or snap. The information has been stamped into the metal, so the reverse side only shows the indentation. The token marked 'Farm Colony', in the middle on the far left of Figure 16.1, only shows the number '1' instead of a monetary amount and, crucially, adds the phrase 'No Money Value'.

Information about the precise history and use of the tokens is limited. They seem to have emerged with the different institutions of the Salvation Army Social Work in the 1890s. Within these institutions the tokens functioned in lieu of cash, being given in remuneration for labour and redeemable for food and accommodation. The system was expanded internationally along with the Social Work itself. Indeed, the wider collection at the IHC also includes tokens used in Salvation Army institutions in Switzerland.[2] The tokens remained in use in some Salvation Army institutions as late as the mid-twentieth century.[3]

The tokens are transient objects. Intended to be repeatedly exchanged, they have now passed out of use completely. Their slight appearance and flimsy feel are deceptive: they were designed for frequent reuse and, therefore, had to be durable. Yet their single purpose as a unit of exchange within the organisation required that they should have no

Objects of Poverty

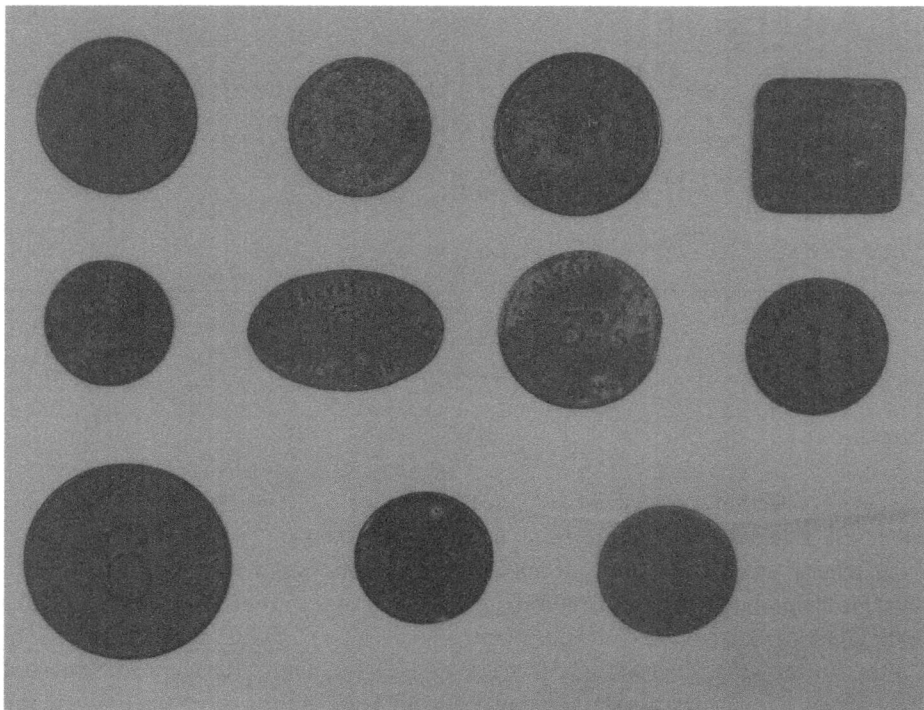

Figure 16.1 The collection of Salvation Army Social Work tokens (M54). Courtesy of the Salvation Army International Heritage Centre.

value in any alternative context – hence the use of cheap metal and the clear institutional markings. They were even manufactured within a Social Work institution on Spa Road in Bermondsey, southeast London.[4] Their lack of value and meaning outside Salvation Army institutions explains why relatively few of these widely used tokens have survived to enter the IHC collection and why they have only rarely been an object of study.[5]

The Social Work tokens are not objects of poverty in the sense of possession or ownership. Rather, they are signifiers of dispossession, extreme poverty and destitution on a significant scale. They belong to an institutional economy of moneyless exchange designed for those without alternative access to employment, food and accommodation. Beyond this indication of the economic status that unified all users of the Salvation Army's Social Work services, the tokens themselves can tell us nothing about the identities, experiences or emotions of the individuals who used them. No evidence survives of first-hand accounts from service users about the tokens. Available sources on the tokens come almost exclusively from within the Salvation Army itself. However, in this chapter, I consider the tokens as a valuable material reflection of a system that sought to provide a more humane response to poverty conditions than the contemporary alternative of the workhouse, but simultaneously imposed a one-size-fits-all structure of social, economic and moral control.

'No Money Value'

I begin this chapter with evidence of the practical use and significance of the tokens within the Salvation Army's Social Work institutions. I will then consider the tokens as a more general example of a moneyless economy. With reference to these contexts, I will explore their potential emotional associations as institutional objects used by individuals experiencing extreme poverty. The tokens represent a loss of personal identity and agency but also, as part of a system that offered the promise of redemption, a possible route towards a reinvention of the self. As signifiers of destitution, the tokens must be emotionally charged. As institutional items, they blur together individual stories and experiences into a generalised organisational response to poverty.

The tokens in Salvation Army Social Work institutions

The founders of the Salvation Army, 'General' William Booth and his wife Catherine (née Mumford), originally established the organisation as a nonconformist Christian mission in the deprived neighbourhoods of east London. They soon found that many of the people they encountered needed material assistance just as much as spiritual support. From the 1880s, the organisation established a range of institutions to support people in poverty.[6] The tokens under consideration here were used predominantly in the institutions for destitute men: the so-called City Colonies and the Farm Colony.

The use of the word 'colonies' derives from William Booth's 1890 publication *In Darkest England and the Way Out*, in which he appealed for funds to expand the Salvation Army's Social Work.[7] The 'City Colonies' were focused on urban poverty and became shorthand for the Elevator workshops that offered employment in relatively low-skilled industries which required no previous training or experience, such as woodcutting, paper sorting or mat-making. The 'Farm Colony', on the other hand, was established in Essex in 1891 with the intention of removing workers from what was perceived as the economic and moral deprivation of urban centres. Its aim was to train service users for agricultural labour to allow them to start new lives away from cities, including outside the UK in territories such as Canada and Australia.

In the provision of labour, board and lodging for destitute people, the Elevators, the Farm Colony and the Food and Shelter Depots functioned as alternatives to the workhouse system. The 1834 poor law established the workhouse as a centralised, institutional response to poverty, offering casual and longer-term accommodation in exchange for labour. Yet, the workhouse – by its very design – was a 'shameful and harrowing prospect' and was generally viewed as a final resort.[8] The work given to inmates, such as stone-breaking or oakum-picking, was generally hard, non-constructive and similar to that done by prisoners. The workhouse was also viewed as resembling a prison in other ways, including in its policies of depriving inmates of personal liberty.[9] Contemporary sources generally agreed that the Salvation Army's response constituted 'a more humanizing effort than that put forth by the Poor Law system'.[10] One press report, for example, described:

221

the unmistakeable good that is being done to the man completely 'stranded,' who knows not which way to look for food and shelter until he finds the doors wide open here, and a something better than workhouse fare and workhouse stone-breaking provided him till he can turn round and do better for himself.[11]

This emphasis on 'do[ing] better for [one]self' was key to the Salvation Army Social Work. Its institutions were strongly focused on the notion of 'salvation' or redemption in a material and a spiritual sense. The point, especially for users of the Elevators, was to support service users back towards living and working outside the institution.

In most Salvation Army institutions, it was common for men and women to 'work for food and lodging only, pay being the exception rather than the rule'.[12] In the Elevators, the tokens were given to service users as a money substitute in remuneration for completing the allocated work and spent again by the workers for their board and lodging. However, service users who did extra work were rewarded with additional cash payments. The tokens were, therefore, a part of this system in which service users were given support but were also asked to prove themselves able to function within and subsequently outside the organisational structure.

Labour, reward and economies in the institutions

Detailed instructions for the consistent and correct running of Social Work institutions are given in the *Orders and Regulations for Social Officers of the Salvation Army* (*O&R*) (Figure 16.2). Strict stipulations set out how the 'Commanding Officer' (CO) in charge of an Elevator should pay 'Colonists' in tokens described as 'zinc, paper, or other cheques or counters of various nominal values, exchangeable for Food and Lodging in the Home'.[13] On the first day, the service user was given enough tokens to pay for their initial board and accommodation. On subsequent days, they were paid based on the amount of work completed.[14]

There was a strong emphasis on fairness. Indeed, one CO stated: 'Opportunities for promotion are placed within the reach of all. Men are paid exactly according to the work done, so that the indolent do not fare as well as the industrious'.[15] Workers were organised into three 'classes' based on the recognition of their efforts, as follows:

> All those applying for assistance are placed in ... the first class. They must be willing to do any kind of work allotted to them ... they are entitled to three meals a day and shelter for the night, and are expected, in return, cheerfully to perform the work allotted to them.
>
> Promotions are made from this first class to the second class of all those considered eligible by the Labour Directors. They ... receive sums of money up to five shillings at the end of the week, for the purpose of assisting them to provide themselves with tools to get work outside.
>
> Third-class workers are arranged for, who receive such further sums as are mutually agreed upon from time to time.[16]

> **Section 7.—REMUNERATION.**
>
> **59.** The C.O. will be responsible for seeing that the Colonists are paid in harmony with the Regulations herein provided, in the following manner :— Regulations for payment of Colonists.
>
>   (a) Provide for their use zinc, paper, or other cheques or counters of various nominal values, exchangeable for Food and Lodging in the Home. (See previous Section.)
>
>   (b) Each Colonist is to be given, on the first day he is at work, sufficient of these counters to enable him to meet his necessities, irrespective of the amount or value of the work he does, although a careful record must be made of that.
>
>   (c) On the second day he is to be paid on the basis of his first day's work, and on the third day on the second day's work, and so on, always, of course, provided that the Regulations with regard to weak but willing men, and special circumstances, have been observed.
>
> *Deduct from each days' earnings for Sunday.*   (d) A proper allowance must be deducted from the amount of each day's earnings for the cost of food and lodging on Sundays, and the weekly half-holidays where granted.
>
> *Payments in presence of two persons.*   (e) All payments must be made in the presence of two persons, who will certify that they have been duly made, as it may be found inconvenient to obtain separate receipts when the sum is of less value than two shillings and sixpence, or its equivalent in counters.

Figure 16.2 Extract on remuneration in City Colonies, from *Orders and Regulations for Social Officers of the Salvation Army*, 1898, pp. 235–6. Courtesy of the Salvation Army International Heritage Centre.

In this way, service users were rewarded for proving themselves to be industrious and willing workers. This CO's explanation indicates that the motivation behind such hard work should be the desire for new employment opportunities, as second-class workers were expected to use their wages to buy tools for work outside the Elevator.

An 1898 article published in a Salvation Army Social Work periodical is the first to provide an extensive explanation of the token system. The article is focused on Battersea Wharf Elevator, a self-contained workshop opened in 1891 that was primarily focused on 'salvage' or waste recycling industries (Figure 16.3). Among the illustrations in the article are sketches of first-, second- and third-class tokens marked 'City Colony Works' (Figure 16.4). The article explains:

> First-class tokens have purchasing power to the value of fourpence; second-class will buy food to the value of threepence; and third-class are worth twopence. Men are
>
> Paid Four Times a Day

in these metal tickets, and they can buy what they like with them at the food-bar inside the Elevator.[17]

The fact that workers were paid four times a day – for which no further explanation is given – indicates a strict daily routine. The work must have been frequently checked, which would mean that workers were constantly undergoing evaluation to earn each meal. Moreover, contemporary accounts strongly suggest that it was not solely the quality of the work that was being assessed but also the workers' economic and moral motivation.

The IHC collection contains no tokens with the 'City Colony' design from Figure 16.4. However, the tokens in the illustration are similar to the 'Farm Colony' token from the

Figure 16.3 Illustration of Battersea Wharf Elevator, from the *Darkest England Gazette*, 31 March 1894, p. 2. Courtesy of the Salvation Army International Heritage Centre.

Figure 16.4 Illustrations of first-, second- and third-class tokens from Battersea Wharf City Colony, from the *Social Gazette*, 19 November 1898, p. 3. Courtesy of the Salvation Army International Heritage Centre.

collection. Like the 'City Colony' tokens, this token does not give a money-equivalent value but only displays the number '1'. This indicates an internal system of values, as in Battersea, where each class of token represented a specific small money value. Such a system made sense in 'colonies' that operated fully on-site, providing food and accommodation at the same location as the workplace. In contrast, the separate Food and Shelter Depots were open to anyone able to pay the low charges for a bed and a meal. As cash payments were generally taken, tokens with a more obviously money-equivalent value would be required. Nevertheless, a system of tokens was maintained. Users paid at a till, where they were issued tokens for the value of their payment, which they then redeemed at a separate refreshment counter.[18] A sense of an internal economy was thus still preserved, even for those who passed through the institution on the more casual basis of a single meal or one night's sleep.

Moneyless economies: Contexts and comparisons

Systems based on cheques, counters and tokens appear to have been common in nineteenth-century Britain. Writing in the *British Numismatic Journal*, R. H. Thompson and A. J. Wager identify token-based systems used in entertainment venues such as pubs and concert halls and by organisations such as friendly societies.[19] It is likely, therefore, that the use of tokens would not have been unfamiliar in principle to users of the Salvation Army Social Work services.

However, in contrast to other token-based systems, this internal currency system allowed the Salvation Army to impose social control within its institutions. The Salvation Army was – and remains – a strictly teetotal organisation. As the tokens could only be spent internally, service users were prevented from acquiring tobacco and alcohol. In this controlled system, service users thus had to demonstrate that they could cope with the temptations of the outside world before they were trusted with the means to procure them. In Salvation Army narratives, religious salvation is often linked to temperance and, consequently, to material advancement as more money could be saved.[20] Moral behaviour is thus directly connected with economic worth.

More broadly, internal systems of cashless exchange are open to criticism as infantilising and potentially exploitative. Notorious operations such as 'tommy shops' or 'company stores', for instance, forced workers to buy from shops run by their employing corporation. Labour historian Peter Gurney notes that these systems often worked by paying workers in tokens to be exchanged in the corporation's shops. As these stores held a monopoly, they were able to sell lower-quality goods for inflated prices, often causing workers to fall into debt.[21] Over the course of the nineteenth century, governments responded to such conditions with the Truck Acts. The first of these, passed in 1831, was explicitly entitled 'An Act to prohibit the Payment, in certain Trades, of Wages in Goods, or otherwise than in the current Coin of the Realm'.[22] In spite of legislation, however, forms of 'trucking' continued to occur throughout the century.

Objects of Poverty

In the present day, it has been a controversial practice to issue people seeking asylum – who are legally barred from working – with a living allowance in vouchers or prepaid cards that can only be redeemed at selected businesses. Such restrictions obviously curtail personal choice in spending with manifold potential financial, personal and emotional consequences for the individual. As part of its 'Refugee and asylum seeker patient health toolkit', the website of the British Medical Association explains that these restrictions 'can make it difficult to manage every-day demands such as food, prescriptions, sanitary products, transportation to appointments, fees for medical letters and phone credit'. These issues are a significant source of stress that may negatively impact mental health.[23]

Of course, the parallels between the Social Work tokens and these other examples are not exact. Nevertheless, the comparisons may provide insights into the possible experiences of the users of the Salvation Army tokens which are not available to us in other ways. For instance, users of the Salvation Army's institutions may have associated payment in tokens with the history of exploitative company stores, which may have been part of their own or family experience. On the other hand, the debt and deprivation associated with such structures will not have applied within the internal system of the Elevators as these provided affordable food and accommodation to all service users. Although the intentions behind these three examples differ widely, they nevertheless share aspects of social and economic control. It is important to recognise that the Social Work tokens at least hold the potential to spark the negative connotations of other cashless economic systems.

A key feature of each of these different moneyless economies is the way they signal dispossession. In analysing connections between objects and emotions, it is tempting to focus on possession, not least as a personal expression of identity and ideas of value. Sociologist Eva Illouz points out in her analysis of emotions as commodities under capitalism: 'Far from heralding a loss of emotionality, capitalist culture has … been accompanied with an unprecedented intensification of emotional life, with actors self-consciously pursuing and shaping emotional experiences for their own sake'.[24] The Salvation Army's alternative economies, through the application of social control and internal value systems, largely disconnected from the wider economy, disabled precisely this understanding of personal and individual agency. If, as historian Katie Barclay puts it, 'economies made emotions', depersonalised objects of poverty such as the tokens can be a starting point to explore emotions related to systematic economic exclusion.[25]

Token experiences: Some conclusions

It is, unfortunately, impossible to recover the individual experiences of service users with the token system. Nevertheless, in speculating on what these experiences may have been, it is possible to imagine both positive and negative reactions. Some service users are likely to have felt frustrated and patronised at not being trusted with money until they had earned it through extra effort. For others, the institutional system may instead have provided a break from the stress of seeking casual labour for low wages in the regular economy.

'No Money Value'

The Salvation Army's institutions may also have represented relief from the threat of the workhouse. Time spent in the Elevators would have been an interruption in everyday life, but the institutions also implemented their own routine, welcome or otherwise.

Entering an institution like an Elevator must have been an emotional decision. Seeking the kind of support the Elevators offered meant acknowledging destitution. Even if the Salvation Army's institutions provided a more humane system than the workhouse, they must have confronted service users with the knowledge that they were not able, at that moment at least, to earn the means to pay for food and accommodation in the regular economy. Given the strict centralised systems on which Salvation Army institutions were run, it is inevitable that individual identity became subordinate to institutional systems and individual agency was constrained by institutional rules. At the same time, however, helping service users return to economic independence was a fundamental aim for the Elevators. The tokens, then, are a physical representation of an interruption in normal life but also, perhaps, of a way or even a motivation to return to it.

Notes

1   I wish to acknowledge the help of Steven Spencer, Ruth Macdonald and Chloe Wilson of the Salvation Army International Heritage Centre in collecting the research material for this chapter.
2   The relevant catalogue entry reads: 'M5. A pair of brass tokens, one circular one square, with raised lettering "Die Heilsarmee" and "Wertmarke" issued by The Salvation Army in Switzerland for internal use in SA hostels. Early-mid 20thC'.
3   'Jeffrey Gardiner, who has spent some 30 years studying the tokens of Northumberland and Durham believes that the Social Wing tokens were in use up to c. 1960'. Denzil Webb, 'The Salvation Army and Its Tokens', *Coin News*, September 1997, p. 34.
4   Ibid.
5   Existing research on the tokens appears to be primarily internal to the Salvation Army. The IHC holds a pamphlet on a specific collection of tokens by American Salvation Army officer Paul Seiler (Pam.827 in the IHC catalogue). Besides this, there is Webb's article which also draws on research by Jeffrey Gardiner.
6   On the early history of the Salvation Army, see Pamela J. Walker, *Pulling the Devil's Kingdom Down: The Salvation Army in Victorian Britain* (London: University of California Press, 2001). On the history of the social work, see: Jenty Fairbank, *Booth's Boots: Social Service Beginnings in the Salvation Army* (London: United Kingdom Territorial Headquarters of the Salvation Army, 1983). On the development and historical context of the Social Work, see Victor Bailey, '"In Darkest England and the Way Out": The Salvation Army, Social Reform and the Labour Movement, 1885-1910', *International Review of Social History*, 29:2 (1984): pp. 133-71.
7   The term 'colonies' here is not directly indicative of imperialism but had some connection to it. The title *In Darkest England* deliberately echoed *In Darkest Africa* (1890) by Henry Morton Stanley. Booth sought to establish a Salvation Army 'Overseas Colony' and entered into negotiations with colonial administrators over colonised land to achieve this. The proposed farming colony overseas never came into being but the Salvation Army did run migration schemes into the twentieth century.
8   Charlotte Newman, 'To Punish or Protect: The New Poor Law and the English Workhouse', *International Journal of Historical Archaeology*, 18:1 (2014): p. 123.

9 Many examples of negative and fearful views of the workhouse can be found in the letters included in the Workhouse Voices collection of the National Archives. https://www.nationalarchives.gov.uk/education/resources/workhouse-voices/?show=all#more (accessed 8 August 2023).

10 Frank Smith, 'The Salvation Army Social Scheme', *Illustrated London News*, 17 January 1891, p. 75.

11 F. W. Robinson, 'A Salvation Army Shelter for Women in Whitechapel', *Graphic*, 27 February 1892, p. 278.

12 Ibid. The practice of non-payment periodically sparked conflict as, for instance, trade unions and employers questioned whether the Salvation Army institutions undersold regular businesses or exploited their workers. In general these conflicts were managed without far-reaching consequences for the Salvation Army's practices. For more on this topic, see Marjorie Gerhardt, 'Salvation Army Retail Activities in the Late-Nineteenth and Early-Twentieth Centuries', in George Campbell Gosling, Alix Green and Grace Millar (eds), *Retail and Community: Business, Charity and Global Britain in the Long 20th Century* (Bristol: Bristol University Press, 2024).

13 The clergy in the Salvation Army are known as 'officers'. The Commanding Officer in this context was the Salvation Army minister in charge of the institution.

14 William Booth ['The General'], *Orders and Regulations for the Social Officers of the Salvation Army* (London: International Headquarters, 1898), pp. 235–6.

15 Adjutant Oldenburg, 'A Hive without Drones', *Social Gazette*, 19 November 1898, p. 3.

16 Smith, 'The Salvation Army Social Scheme', p. 75.

17 Oldenburg, 'A Hive', p. 3. Original emphasis.

18 Booth, *Orders and Regulations*, p. 175.

19 R. J. Thompson and A. J. Wager, 'The Purpose and Use of Public-House Checks', *British Numismatic Journal*, 52 (1982): p. 215–33.

20 On these Salvation Army narratives of material self-help, see Jill Rappoport, *Giving Women: Alliance and Exchange in Victorian Culture* (New York: Oxford University Press, 2012) and Flore Janssen, '"Buy Cheap, Buy Dear!": Selling Consumer Activism in the Salvation Army c. 1885–1905', *Journal of Victorian Culture*, 27:4 (2022): pp. 670–85.

21 Peter Gurney, 'Exclusive Dealing in the Chartist Movement', *Labour History Review*, 74:1 (2009): pp. 90–110.

22 'An Act to prohibit the Payment, in certain Trades, of Wages in Goods, or otherwise than in the current Coin of the Realm', 1831. https://www.legislation.gov.uk/ukpga/Will4/1-2/37/contents/enacted (accessed 10 March 2023).

23 'Refugee and asylum seeker patient health toolkit', *British Medical Association*, 2023. https://www.bma.org.uk/advice-and-support/ethics/refugees-overseas-visitors-and-vulnerable-migrants/refugee-and-asylum-seeker-patient-health-toolkit/claiming-asylum-in-the-uk (accessed 10 March 2023).

24 Eva Illouz, 'Introduction: Emodities or the Making of Emotional Commodities', in Eva Illouz (ed.), *Emotions as Commodities: Capitalism, Consumption and Authenticity* (Abingdon: Routledge, 2018), p. 5.

25 Katie Barclay, 'The Emotions of Household Economics', in Susan Broomhall and Andrew Lynch (eds), *The Routledge History of Emotions in Europe 1100–1700* (London: Routledge, 2019), p. 186.

Further reading

Bailey, Victor. '"In Darkest England and the Way Out": The Salvation Army, Social Reform and the Labour Movement, 1885–1910'. *International Review of Social History*, 29:2 (1984): pp. 133–71.
Booth, William ['General']. *In Darkest England and the Way Out* (London: International Headquarters of the Salvation Army, 1890).
Fairbank, Jenty. *Booth's Boots: Social Service Beginnings in the Salvation Army* (London: United Kingdom Territorial Headquarters of the Salvation Army, 1983).
Janssen, Flore. '"Buy Cheap, Buy Dear!": Selling Consumer Activism in the Salvation Army c. 1885–1905'. *Journal of Victorian Culture*, 27:4 (2022): pp. 670–85.
Rappoport, Jill. *Giving Women: Alliance and Exchange in Victorian Culture* (Oxford: Oxford University Press, 2012).
Walker, Pamela J. *Pulling the Devil's Kingdom Down: The Salvation Army in Victorian Britain* (London: University of California Press, 2001).

CHAPTER 17
THE PURSES OF THE POOR: MONEY, AUTONOMY AND EVERYDAY LIFE IN VICTORIAN AND EDWARDIAN ENGLAND
Julie-Marie Strange

Introduction

In this chapter, I examine the purse as an everyday object implicated in the Victorian ideology of 'respectability'. As the tied-in-pocket declined in popularity during the nineteenth century, the purse became more common.[1] Purses came in a variety of shapes and sizes, and could be bought new or second-hand. Some were improvised or home-made. For people with limited means, the purse was a vital object for keeping account of ready cash and knowing where it was. It could be particularly important for people in lodging houses where the security of possessions could not be taken for granted. Conversely, a purse could be easier to pick from a pocket than loose coins. From the earliest nineteenth-century designs, purses enabled the separation, sorting and security of money. The purse represented thrift and independence, qualities that were the bedrock of the new poor law and philanthropic agencies' classification of poorer people into the 'deserving' and 'undeserving'. A purse could be a marker of citizenship, demarcating those with small amounts of change from those with nothing. Migrants to and from Britain often carried all their savings in a purse. The theft of a purse, especially if it contained the entire sum of one's capital, highlighted economic precarity but, also, the role of objects in practices and processes that discriminated between members of the working class and those in poverty, and between the supposedly 'rough' and 'respectable'.

Despite its crucial role in helping people navigate everyday economics, the purse is almost invisible in studies of working-class life. To a point, this reflects the curious absence of material money from an extensive scholarship on abstracted working-class economies – wages, living costs and welfare.[2] More perplexing, the absence of material money from studies of working-class economy risks perpetuating assertions by middle-class Victorian moralists that money was not the differential between poverty and stability but character (often referred to as 'respectability').[3] By turning attention to the purse, this essay looks anew at the everyday experiences of Victorian and Edwardian working-class people's relationship with money. It exposes how 'character' or 'respectability', with their implications for who deserved welfare assistance (and who did not), were arbitrary categories that misdirected responsibility for poverty away from those who benefited from capitalism onto those deemed 'rough' or 'undeserving'.

The purse as an object

Purses were made for carrying money. Sometimes a purse contained tokens or paper money, rolled or folded, but mostly, purses were made for coins. Pocketbooks, used for paper money (of higher values), were uncommon among the working classes who rarely carried paper money. When working-class people did access paper money (for example, sailors' pay at the end of a voyage or in the withdrawal of savings), they often used public houses for help in identifying values and changing it into coins. Victorian coinage was wide ranging: from higher-value coins like sovereigns (a pound), crowns (five shillings) and half crowns, to the mid-range value of florins (a two-shilling piece issued from 1849) and shillings to low-value monies like the sixpenny, fourpenny (groats), threepenny or penny bits, to halfpennies, and the farthing (a quarter of a penny, issued first in copper and from 1860 in bronze). Working-class wages were largely paid in shillings and pence, but everyday economies – food, drink, fuel, leisure – rested for much of this period on stretching pennies, so much so that the 'penny' became a key adjective for advertising affordable goods and services, from the penny press to the penny gaff to the penny bazaar.

As a consumer good, purses could be a luxury item depending on materials used (fine leather, silk, gold clasps) and quality of craftwork. Cheaper purses were available and sold to working-class men and women. According to Henry Mayhew, in his surveys of London labour in the mid-nineteenth century, purses and money bags could be purchased from street sellers, bazaars or haberdashers. Street vendors, whose primary market was selling to working-class consumers, sold the cheapest purses. Decorative, beaded purses were available from jewellery and haberdashery sellers where goods might range in price from 2d to 1s 6d but most items retailed at 3d. Beaded purses were not necessarily 'feminine' goods but could appeal to men and women; much depended on the design. Plain 'money bag' or 'pouch' purses were cheaper still and more likely to be sold by children or juveniles alongside matches, leather straps or belts, fly papers and garters.[4] The economical quality and sheer mundanity of an everyday purse means that, like many of the objects discussed in this collection, relatively few have survived. Beamish Museum in County Durham holds substantial collections relating to everyday life in the northeast of England from the end of the eighteenth century to the 1950s.[5] They currently have 198 catalogued nineteenth- and twentieth-century purses. Of these, just over half are what might be termed 'occasion' purses: decorative purses of high-quality materials (silk, silver and mother of pearl), purses brought to Britain as souvenirs from overseas travel or large 'evening' purses (small bags) reserved for 'best' or special use. The remainder are everyday purses, often knitted, crocheted or made from rough leather. Sometimes, catalogue descriptions note their 'grubby' state, indicating heavy use.[6] These are the kinds of purses that Mayhew identified being sold on the streets in the 1850s. The cheapest 'purse' is not in any museum collection because it was not a purse at all: coins could be tucked inside a stocking, in between the breasts, inside a bodice or carried loose in a pocket.[7] But the objective was the same – to sort, store and carry money safely.

At its most rudimentary, a handkerchief or piece of tied cloth could be utilised as a receptacle for cash. More secure were drawstring bags ('pouch' or 'money bag' purses) that pulled tight and could be knotted.[8] These were easy to sew and could have decorative features. Some 'pouch' purses were knitted or crocheted from materials ranging from fine yarn to rough brown twine. Others were made from plaited straw in natural and dyed colours.[9] Many were plain but one early-nineteenth-century example from Beamish is a pouch-shaped purse, gathered at the base, with a small tassel trim. The purse fastened with a double drawstring of twine at the top. Of simple construction, the purse had decorative detail with three stripes of double-knotted yarn. Pulled flat, it measures 240 mm long and is 195 mm wide when pulled open.[10] Another example replaced the drawstring with a metal clasp and chain.[11] Some purses eschewed the circular, three-dimensional pouch for a relatively flat rectangle. These were complex designs that typically demanded more advanced craft skill. A crochet purse often had 'chains' of crocheted cotton threaded through the flap of the purse (coins could pass through the chains when loosened). An example from Beamish dating to the end of the nineteenth century was worked in beige cotton crochet stitch with scalloping and pulled together with drawstring.[12] These purses could be made with additional decorative materials, notably glass or steel beads, while home-made examples could be fashioned from scrap textiles or repurposed pieces of leather.

The other core nineteenth-century design was the 'stocking' purse, sometimes known as the 'miser's purse', as it released one coin at a time. It mimicked the use of stockings as a repository for storing or saving money and, as the name suggests, was long and thin but with both ends stitched tight. Coins were inserted through an opening in the middle and two rings on either side ('sliders') could be pushed up and down to hold coins in place. Most stocking purses were intended to hold higher-value coins at one end and low values at the other. These purses could be highly decorative

Figure 17.1 Stocking purse, *c.* 1880. Author's collection.

Figure 17.2 Pouch purse, *c*. 1910. Author's collection.

with beading and colourful designs.[13] Some had beaded tassels on the ends. The slider rings could be made of brass, tin, steel, fabric-covered metal or more expensive materials like silver or gold. Stocking purses could also be rudimentary, crocheted from cotton or made from scraps of yarn or recycled twine.[14] The stocking purse featured in Figure 17.1 dates from the latter half of the nineteenth century, is made of contrasting crocheted yarn (blue and orange) and tiny steel beads and is 215 mm long and 40 mm wide. It has two tin sliders with decorative marks. Some purses combined the features of the stocking purse with the pouch. Figure 17.2 dates from around 1910 and shows two small, crocheted cotton pockets in cream (edged with red), each around 70 mm long, tied together by fastening chains of cotton with a bone hoop in the middle. Like the stocking purse, two pouches enabled owners to separate money into different values.

Towards the end of the nineteenth century, mass-produced leather (or fabric) clasp purses became more common. These ranged from very simple designs with a single pocket to purses with interior compartments, sometimes with a secondary clasped pouch, or a double opening, effectively creating the two compartments of the stocking purse for separating coins according to value or purpose. These purses were often small, ranging in width from 50 mm to 80 mm. The purse in Figure 17.3 measures 60 mm across and has a cardboard layer between thin pieces of machine-stitched leather to give the purse some rigidity. The clasp is steel. The purse weighs just 18 g. The diminutive size and shape of these purses meant they were not too bulky to show in a trouser or coat pocket. Some came with fabric- or leather-lined interiors. More elaborate purses might have multiple inside pockets; some were in coloured leathers with contrast piping around the edges; others had filigree designs engraved into the clasp, chain handles or

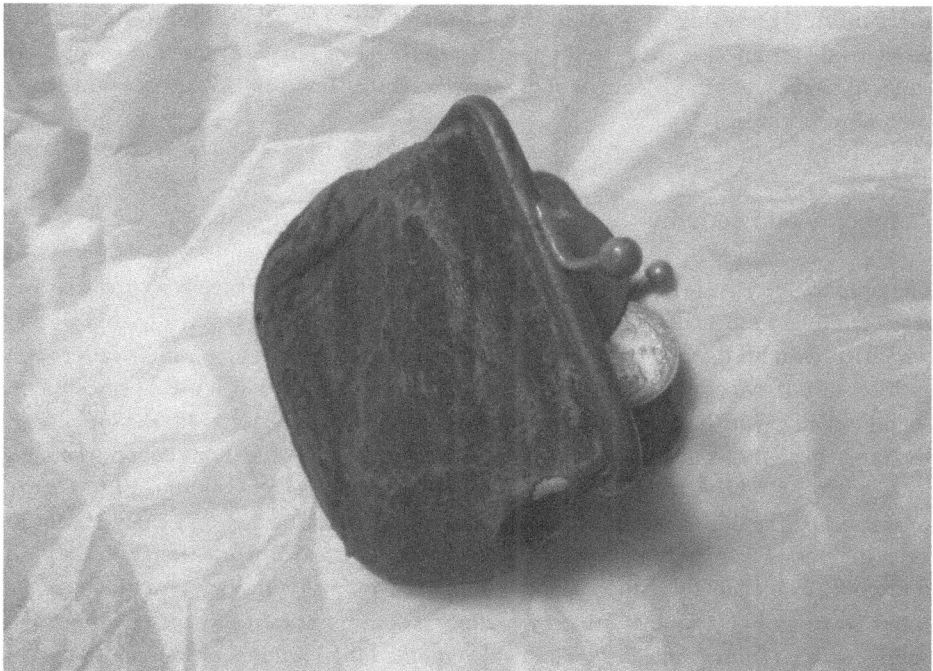

Figure 17.3 Clasp purse, *c.* 1900. Author's collection.

beading attached to the bottom seam.[15] The clasp purse could be home-made too, either from scraps of leather or pieces of fur with a repurposed clasp.[16]

Newspaper reports of pickpocket purse thefts indicate that both men and women carried all kinds of purses in plain, beaded and decorative designs. In the Beamish catalogue, gender-aligned purses tend to be plain for men and decorative for women. Beaded purses were popular across genders as was the leather clasp purse. The purse in Figure 17.3 belonged to my great uncle for most of his adult life. As a disabled, working-class bachelor, making leather goods was one of the few occupations that enabled him to be self-supporting (and therefore 'deserving'). He made purses, belts and bags for other working-class people at the turn of the twentieth century. Men tended to slip their purse into coat or trouser pockets. For men who were ageing or struggling with rheumatism, loose coins in trouser pockets could feel cold against the hip. A purse contained money and kept it warm. Women's textile or knitted purses were easy to tuck inside a bodice or stocking, although women's risk of being victim to purse theft often overlapped with risks of sexual violence in public spaces. Pockets in old and worn clothing were unreliable and loose coins were likely to fall out of seams that were coming apart. Purses might only be carried when spending was necessary or likely, suggesting that working-class people made decisions about when and where to take money. It is striking that the inventory of contents in night shift miners' pockets when their remains were recovered from the Wellington Pit mining disaster (Whitehaven, 1910) included coal tokens (a

Objects of Poverty

mechanism for tracking who was in and out of the mine), watches, a tobacco box and a woman's garter but no purses or money.[17] The absence of purses in the miners' pockets suggests a conscious management of money whereby cash was mostly left at home when men were working.

Autonomy and security

The primary purpose of a purse was to contain money, sort it and keep it secure. Keeping track of money, especially when mobile, was crucial. When John Dove, a retired weaver who lived with his daughter, removed his savings from the bank on a winter's afternoon in 1853, he put two notes and seven coins into a small leather purse. It was a princely sum for an 'old' man who had stopped working some years previous: 20l 5s 3d. Having shoved the purse deep into a trouser pocket, John put the extra 3d piece in his coat pocket and left the bank. On his way home, he called into the Nag's Head for a tot of rum and water to warm up. The 3d bit was easily accessible from his coat pocket and enabled him to keep his purse, and more particularly its contents, concealed from view. After all, no one would expect an old man in shabby clothes to have just withdrawn his life's savings. John's sorting of his money in this way reflected common desires to keep all but small change hidden from public view. Purses also muffled the 'clinking' or 'jinking' sound of heavier coins.[18] What people did not know you had, they could not covet and steal.

The flipside of this was that the very presence of a purse made individuals vulnerable to the pickpocket. John Dove had been observed putting the purse into his pocket on leaving the savings bank. He was followed to the Nag's Head by a group of five men who tried to get him drunk and, when he resisted, jostled him into an outdoor water closet to pick his pocket. John's purse with all his savings were gone. If purses gave a feeling of security on the one hand, they were an object of desire for the thief, and to a degree, facilitated the easy removal of the victim's money. The purse itself often had little value and thieves would typically abandon it, perhaps with a couple of coppers still inside, to make off with the higher value contents. This meant that, even if caught, they would not have the incriminating evidence of a purse on their person.

As an 'object of poverty', then, the purse could represent different kinds of money and opportunity depending on who handled it and how.[19] For John Dove, who had taken an empty purse to the bank, it represented a receptacle of safety and security for his savings, described in court as his 'pension', probably his contribution towards his daughter's household costs and the thing that gave him a degree of dignity and autonomy while living with her. That he had savings bolstered John's moral capital in a context where the state (via the poor law), capitalism (the employers of labour) and philanthropy (which propped up both the state and capitalism) pedalled an ideology of 'respectability' that divided working-class people who fell upon hard times into the 'deserving' and 'undeserving' poor. Thrift signified citizenship. When John Dove's assailants pointed to his presence in the public house as reason to doubt the veracity of his story and his character (alcohol was a signifier of thriftlessness), it was the evidence of John's commitment to 'self-help' in the form of his savings that operated as guarantor for his 'respectability'. For the five men who assaulted John, his purse represented easy money. The men were all in middle to older age, a period in working men's lives when employment became more precarious. From the age of forty, working-class men's labour was less competitive than that of younger men, they were more likely to be laid off, to fall ill and take longer to recover. Only two of the assailants appeared to have regular work: one as a furrier and one in the boot trade. The constable assigned to the savings bank thought the men made a habit of loitering around the bank. They appeared to have a practiced routine of preying on savers like John Dove, getting them drunk and trying to rob them, preferably without the victim putting up much resistance or remembering detail. John was an easy target as an elderly man in old clothes, evidently past working age. His meticulous sorting of money between purse and pocket suggested the purse held a reasonable withdrawal if the pocket would suffice to take the small change. When a stolen purse was found, it was often used as evidence, giving it an afterlife as an article of judiciary interest. In this storyline, the thieves abandoned John's purse, making it part of the flotsam of urban waste or, for an eagle-eyed opportunist that found it, a hopeful possibility of some lucky money.

Losing a purse had significant consequences whether the owner was someone with savings, like John Dove, or a lone woman looking for lodgings for the night. If John's savings represented a degree of independence in being able to pay towards his maintenance, the theft of his purse exposed his vulnerability as an 'old' man without work and dependent on his daughter. In the absence of state pensions, John could easily be rendered homeless or forced to turn to the poor law if his relationship with his daughter broke down. John's assailants clearly selected their victim, but most thefts were opportunistic with a less certain haul. One of Henry Mayhew's London interviewees noted that the 'best' purse he ever stole contained just 2 shillings.[20] Overseas sailors that were paid on docking and migrants who travelled with their entire savings were especially vulnerable to theft, particularly when they did not speak English and had little knowledge of how to seek redress. Organisations like the 'Strangers Home' for 'Lascar' sailors, the Society for Friends of Foreigners in Distress and refuges for Jewish women from Eastern Europe helped new arrivals to Britain navigate the economic landscape, including what to do in the event of their purse being stolen. Women who sold sex had to be careful how they stored money on their person and how much they carried; they were more likely to be accused of crime than taken seriously as victims. Itinerant people or those who relied on nightly lodgings tended to have all their money on their person, a few coppers representing the difference between a bed for the night or the street.[21] Lodging houses sometimes operated an overnight banking system whereby purses (or coins) could be docketed and kept secure overnight.

If purses enabled the sorting and storing of money and felt more secure than the pocket, the fear and anxiety of purse theft was factored into purse design. Beaded purses were relatively heavy, even when empty. The stocking purse in Figure 17.1, which is only one-third beaded, weighs 95 g. The removal of a weightier item from the pocket would, ostensibly, be easier to detect than something light. Many purses incorporated security technology with metal loops to be attached to the belt or a piece of clothing or even, in some cases, to a finger ring. The crochet purse in Figure 17.2 is attached to a small metal hoop. A piece of ribbon or twine threaded through the hoop enabled the wearer to attach the purse to a belt.[22] Some stocking purses had loops at each end that could be tied together and attached to clothing; others were stitched with a 'waist cord' attached.[23]

Aspiration and sentiment

Security features highlight the significance of purses to making ends meet (keep safe what you cannot afford to lose) and speak to the way in which even the most mundane purse could represent hope, dignity and autonomy. When a young married couple with a baby set out from Edinburgh for Mickley (near Harrogate, Yorkshire) in the autumn of 1904, they were hopeful of finding work. The man had been unemployed for several months and money was scarce. They were able to pay rail fare to Carlisle but decided to walk the rest of the way to stretch the little money they had. About eight miles outside Kendal, they lost their purse. Although the contents were paltry, they would have paid for cheap lodgings and food. The loss of the purse spelt catastrophe: they had nothing but the clothes on their backs and some biscuits for the baby. They were still two days' walk from their destination. Probably victims of a theft, the police paid for one night's lodgings while they applied to the local Charity Organisation Society (COS) for a loan to get them to Harrogate, where they had family. This was not the end of the trauma. The loss of the purse haunted them for several years as Kendal COS pursued them for repayment of the emergency loan despite the couple's protests that poor health and irregular work prevented them from repaying the debt.[24] In this sense, if the purse was a technology and emblem of hope, its loss or theft became part of a process of stigmatisation whereby seeking financial help could end in accruing debt. Such stigmatising processes operated as badges of dependency, enabling welfare agencies to transform (even temporary) need into an indicator of belonging to the 'undeserving' poor.

In ideal circumstances then, a purse operated as a signifier of being 'deserving'; it was an 'object of respectability'. From the beginning of the nineteenth century, working-class people were encouraged to save money as a buffer against economic catastrophe when sickness, death or unemployment hit. John Dove is a prime example of this. 'Savings' and 'penny' banks, begun in the late eighteenth century, catered for a working-class savings market. They ranged from high-profile organisations with local dignitaries at the helm, to banks run by institutions that were embedded in working-class everyday life (from Co-ops to Lyons teahouses) to much more ad hoc savings schemes run by workplaces, chapels, pubs and schools.[25] Recent research suggests that savings banks had a diverse clientele, from the affluent working classes (the group often associated with such schemes) to migrants, servants, unskilled labourers, children and women engaged in low-paid or irregular labour.[26] Some people kept accounts open for many years, making regular deposits and occasional withdrawals or saving towards a specific goal, while others made an initial deposit and never used their account again.[27] The principle of saving – whether for a rainy day or to buy necessaries like clothing or furniture – was deeply entwined with a moral narrative of thrift, independence and aspiration.

Penny banks specialised in small change deposits but even here, a purse was often the object in which people set aside their small change or small monies before accruing a sum worth depositing (though if home was secure, teapots, old stockings and inside chimneys were likely repositories for savings until they could be deposited in the bank). The purse was used, as in John Dove's case, to transport monies to and from the savings bank. In this sense, alongside the savings bank passbook, the purse operated as an object of aspiration. For some, the purse *was* the savings bank and had pragmatic and symbolic value. At the Clergy Orphanage in 1880s St John's Wood, London, each child was allocated a purse into which they were encouraged to put savings. The purses were kept together in a locked box in the governess's sitting room, a reflection that saving (thrift) was a key component of their moral education. When a child left the orphanage, they were given the purse containing their savings.[28] The inquest into the death of an elderly woman, a retired cook, in 1893 revealed that she had nineteen purses of 'different shapes, sizes and colours' in the single room she occupied. She had a savings bank account but the purses contained savings too, different amounts suggesting a logic at work in separating the monies. Newspaper commentary deemed the practice 'eccentric' but working-class people's suspicions about the security of banks (not entirely unfounded, even in 1893) combined with the reassurance of being able to sort, see, touch and count savings at will meant keeping purses, sometimes in multiples, as saving repositories was not uncommon.[29] Purses were the ideology of respectability made material but, also, representative of some working-class people's circumspection regarding the trustworthiness of capitalist institutions.

Many of the everyday purses in Beamish's collection appear to have been home-made. Crafting a purse offered children opportunities for simultaneously learning lessons in handicrafts and thrift. Many girls probably learned to crochet or knit a stocking purse in their youth. Elaborate patterns for purses regularly featured in women's magazines (and could easily be adapted by teachers or Sunday School teachers for lessons), but the simplicity of some purses suggests that most people with basic skills would have been able to make their own purse. Knitted and crocheted purses were popular and, even when plain in design, demanded a range of techniques in making them secure, as demonstrated in the purses pictured here. Some purses had beading, multiple colours or decorative stripes, flowers, stars or paisley shapes worked in.[30] Purses made of plaited straw or from seeds and pulses suggest more elaborate craft skills, creativity and ingenuity (dried seeds were cheaper than beads).[31] The ability to fashion a beautiful purse also made them objects to be given as gifts. When John Hammond, aged twenty-five, was apprehended on suspicion of picking pockets, he had four purses on his person. Two of the purses, he protested, had been made and gifted by his mother, who brought the purse pattern to court as evidence.[32] A handmade lentil-and-seed purse (Figure 17.4) made of five panels with decorative features was given as a gift from a merchant navy seaman to his sister.[33] Some women and girls included their names and the date in the design (much like samplers). Again, these purses could be given as gifts.[34] The home-made

Figure 17.4 Seed purse, c. 1900. Image by author; permission to reproduce by kind permission of Beamish: The Living Museum of the North.

qualities of some purses alongside their status as potentially gifted objects could invest them with sentimental significance. While many surviving everyday purses show signs of use, home-made examples in excellent condition imply an object reserved and retained for its abstract qualities, whether sentimental, as an exemplar of skill or, in some cases, because it was superfluous to everyday use. Some purses might have been retained long after their functional use ended. My mother kept my great uncle's purse after he died because she had childhood memories of him engaging her in play with its small change contents. The status of the purse as an object made to keep something precious (money) safe also made it a candidate for holding keepsakes, such as a lock of hair.[35]

Conclusion

What do purses tell us about the identity and experiences of the poor in the Victorian and Edwardian period? As an object for holding money, sometimes all the money to one's name, the purse was simultaneously an object of anxiety and security. The purse could hold the entirety of a week's wages, a life's savings or the handful of coppers that stood between an individual and loss of autonomy. This had practical repercussions but symbolic ones too. Often of little financial value, the purse epitomised independence: to have a purse was to aspire to self-sufficiency, something reflected in the popularity of purses as gifts for children. To lose a purse was, potentially, to tumble into the abyss of debt and dependency. The extent to which these fears were real was written into the design of some purses. Similarly, the need to keep running accounts was embedded in purse technologies that facilitated the separation of money according to value and purpose. In many ways, the purse echoes the value Victorian moralists placed on thrift and, by extension, other character traits associated with it (such as temperance and independence) to make the purse an object of 'respectability'. But this is to privilege a moral framework created by the Victorians to sift the poor into arbitrary categories of deserving and undeserving, the respectable and the rough. While acknowledging the power this model retains (often implicitly) in modern scholarship, it is also possible to see the purse as a material emblem of the violence of capitalism and the precarity of working-class lives. The loss or theft of a purse and the spending of a purse's contents exposed its owner to scrutiny and potentially pitched them into stigmatisation and dependency with long-term consequences. The purse points to the importance of safe places – whether that was secure housing or being able to move through public space with confidence – and the imperative of even small monies to retain individual agency and dignity.

Notes

1   Barbara Burman and Ariane Fennetaux, *The Pocket: A Hidden History of Women's Lives, 1660–1900* (New Haven: Yale University Press, 2020).
2   See, for instance, Emma Griffin, *Breadwinner: An Intimate History of the Victorian Economy* (New Haven: Yale University Press, 2020). Notable exceptions to this trend are Paul Johnson, *Saving and Spending: The Working-Class Economy in Britain, 1870–1939* (Oxford: Oxford University Press, 1985) and Melanie Tebbutt, *Making Ends Meet: Pawnbroking and Working-Class Credit* (Leicester: Leicester University Press, 1983).
3   Emma Griffin, '"Things I Can Remember about My Life": Autobiography and the British Industrial Revolution', *Journal of British Studies*, 61:1 (2022): pp. 26–49.

Objects of Poverty

4 Henry Mayhew, *London Labour and the London Poor: The Condition and Earnings of Those That Will Work, Cannot Work, and Will Not Work*, vol. I (London: Charles Griffin and Company, 1864–5), pp. 346, 373, 470–1.
5 Beamish, the Living Museum of the North, Chester-le-Street, County Durham.
6 See, for instance, Beamish Museum Collection (hereafter BMC), Accession No: 1969–188.9.
7 See, for instance, *Newcastle Guardian*, 1 January 1848, p. 8; *Newcastle Guardian and Tyne Mercury*, 8 January 1848, p. 5; *Old Bailey Papers* (hereafter *OBP*), t18480103-542, Trial of Elizabeth Haws and Maria Brown, 3 January 1848 (https://www.oldbaileyonline.org/).
8 BMC Accession No: 1978–185.
9 BMC Accession No: 1977–1339.
10 BMC Accession No: 1973–202.3.
11 BMC Accession No: 1977–1210.
12 BMC Accession No: 1978–182.
13 BMC Accession Nos: 1977–1383; 1977–1384; 1977–1385; 1405.1.
14 See, for example, BMC Accession No: 1977–1209.
15 BMC Accession No: 1976–96.63.1; 1976–96.93; 1977–183.
16 BMC Accession No: GS 02/04/1987.6.
17 Cumbria Archive Centre (Whitehaven), Whitehaven Colliery DBH/25/11/17/1-3; DBH 25/11/20/1-2. Evidence produced for Inquest into Wellington Pit Disaster, 1910. The objects were used to identify remains, many of which were disfigured. Loose coins could have been removed (or stolen) from contents as too generic but purses were readily identifiable and much less likely to have been removed.
18 See *OBP*, t19081020-60, Trial of Thomas Price, 1908 and t18490820-1623, Trial of Joseph Ward and Mary Myer, 1849 for references to the sound of coins.
19 On differentiating between kinds of money, see Viviana Zelizer, *The Social Meaning of Money* (Princeton: Princeton University Press, 1997).
20 Mayhew, *London Labour and the London Poor*, p. 411.
21 A survey of the Old Bailey online indicates manifold examples of all these scenarios. See https://www.oldbaileyonline.org/.
22 See, for instance, BMC Accession Nos: GS 297-2016.19; 1968–42; 1977–1350.
23 BMC Accession No: 1978–183.
24 Cumbria Archives Centre (Kendal), WDSO Charity Organisation Society, Case 870, 16 November 1904.
25 See Duncan Ross, 'Penny Banks in Glasgow, 1850–1914', *Financial History Review*, 9:1 (2002): pp. 21–39; Julie-Marie Strange and Sarah Roddy, 'Banking for Jesus: Financial Services, Charity and an Ethical Economy in Late Victorian and Edwardian Britain', *Capitalism: A Journal of History & Economics*, 3:1 (2022): pp. 106–35.
26 Jared Day, 'Credit, Capital and Community: Informal Banking in Immigrant Communities in the United States, 1880–1924', *Financial History Review*, 9:1 (2002): pp. 65–78.
27 Linda Perriton and Josephine Maltby, 'Working-Class Households and Savings in England, 1850–1880', *Enterprise and Society*, 16:2 (2015): pp. 413–45.
28 *OBP*, t18840317-400, Trial of George William Holmes, 17 March 1884, accused and convicted of stealing the purses.
29 *Cornish Post and Mining News*, 29 September 1893.
30 BMC Accession Nos: 1977–1383; 1977–1384; 1977–1385; 1077–1405.1.
31 BMC Accession Nos: 1977–1339; GS 462 2014 -2.
32 *OBP*, t18880423-489, Trial of John Hammond, 23 April 1888.
33 BMC Accession No: GS 462 2014 -2.

34 BMC Accession Nos: 1977–1209; 1977–1211; 1977–1212; 1977–1213, all made by Alice Ames; and 1978–176.
35 BMC Accession No: GS 08/05/2000.9.

Further reading

Burman, Barbara, and Ariane Fennetaux. *The Pocket: A Hidden History of Women's Lives, 1660–1900* (New Haven: Yale University Press, 2020).
Day, Jared. 'Credit, Capital and Community: Informal Banking in Immigrant Communities in the United States, 1880–1924'. *Financial History Review*, 9:1 (2002): pp. 65–78.
Johnson, Paul. *Saving and Spending: The Working-Class Economy in Britain, 1870–1939* (Oxford: Oxford University Press, 1985).
Perriton, Linda, and Josephine Maltby. 'Working-Class Households and Savings in England, 1850–1880'. *Enterprise and Society*, 16:2 (2015): pp. 413–45.
Ross, Duncan. 'Penny Banks in Glasgow, 1850–1914', *Financial History Review*, 9 (2002): pp. 21–39.
Strange, Julie-Marie, and Sarah Roddy. 'Banking for Jesus: Financial Services, Charity and an Ethical Economy in Late Victorian and Edwardian Britain'. *Capitalism: A Journal of History & Economics*, 3:1 (2022): pp. 106–35.

PART VII
WORKHOUSE OBJECTS

CHAPTER 18
GOING TO BED IN THE WORKHOUSE: FACILITIES, PRACTICES AND IMPLICATIONS IN THE 1790S
Alannah Tomkins

Introduction

In 1795, the self-appointed social investigator Frederic Morton Eden judged the workhouse in Newark, Nottinghamshire, to be one of the best in the country. The excellencies of this institution were found partly in the layout, namely the separation of lodgings for men and women, and in the provision of additional rooms for those who had descended from prosperity to humiliating poverty. In terms of management, the workhouse's merits included being 'sufficiently capacious', 'well aired' and 'well supplied with vegetables from a good garden'.[1] Eden's judgement on the good order and cleanliness of the workhouse, however, was also based on its bedding. Newark placed between two and five beds in each room, with the majority of mattresses being stuffed with feathers. Virtue in workhouse management (and in line with cleanliness being next to godliness) resided partly in featheriness.

This chapter will consider the wider presence of workhouse beds in Eden's compendious survey of poor-relief arrangements. It will discuss the physical location and composition of the beds as a prelude to reviews of the less tangible aspects of institutional beds, bedrooms and sleep, drawing periodically on additional source material from the 1750s to the 1820s, such as medical publications and life writings. Sasha Handley's research on sleep in the early-modern period has underscored our understanding that beds represented cleanliness, health and aspects of emotional meaning for householders.[2] In the work of other researchers, the marital bed held particular significance.[3] Here, ideas about domestic beds will be translated to the context of a residential institution, common throughout England by the 1790s, to reflect on the importance of beds for the cleanliness and health of inmates, but also their roles in neat management and discipline. It argues that, seen through Eden's eyes, good practice in terms of workhouse governance aligned exactly with the prospect among paupers of a decent night's sleep.

This analysis is valuable because it places poor-law institutions into context in relation to the homes of the poor. Much of the existing literature about beds (and household goods more generally) has focused on the inventories of the middling and wealthy sections of society. Joseph Harley's book about the household contents held by the poor provides an opportunity to evaluate the sleep experiences of paupers who moved between their own rented accommodation and the facilities of a parochial institution. Since beds had been 'ubiquitous' in the homes of the poor for at least a century by the 1790s, and since the value of these beds rose, the absence of a bed in either location would have signalled wretched deprivation.[4] Consequently, the character of the beds, bedding and bedrooms that existed in workhouses are a litmus test for the extent and limits of contemporary welfare before the onset of the designedly-punitive reformed poor law in 1834. At the same time, beds and sleep were tied to ideas about ventilation in contemporary concepts of healthiness. The state of workhouse beds was also, therefore, a proxy for evidence of local awareness and engagement with nascent public health agendas.

Beds, bed-sharing and bed bugs

Eden was a baronet with a keen interest in populations that was both theoretical and practical. He was a founder of the Globe Insurance Company, but not content to let matters rest with this financial investment, he embarked on an investigation of the poor (with the help of sundry 'respectable clergymen' and a paid investigator).[5] This resulted in his three-volume work, *The State of the Poor*, which considers the experiences of the poor in their own homes and as clients of the poor-relief system.

Volumes 2 and 3 of Eden's publication contained reports of 126 workhouses across England, from Cornwall to Northumberland. Only the county of Cambridge was omitted. Fifty-nine of these houses were noticed for some aspect of their sleeping arrangements across workhouses with populations ranging from 5 to 1,406. Reports could cover counts of beds per dormitory room, the number of paupers typically resting in each bed, the composition of bedframes and mattresses, plus the presence, quality and quantity of sheets, blankets and other linen. The properties of the beds were not noticed for every institution, but a general picture emerges about institutional infrastructure. Moreover, the annotations about beds were usually recorded in close proximity to any summaries of the workhouses' tendency to cleanliness/dirt or to ventilation/airlessness, permitting an analysis of the role of beds in ensuring a clean house and healthy residents. Finally, the materials of bedding (as generated by workhouse labour) and times of going to bed (which emerged in compilations of workhouse rules) speak to the place of the bed as the spur to domestic manufacture, and potentially to their holding a carceral role as well as a nurturing one.

In twenty-six workhouses, Eden's data contains counts of beds per room in locations for which he also enumerates the total workhouse population. The figures suggest a firm but not rigidly predictive correlation between the scale of the institution and the magnitude of the dormitories.[6] At opposite ends of the spectrum, the very modest workhouse at Hampton in Middlesex arranged two beds per room for its seventeen inmates, while Norwich in Norfolk consigned forty beds to each of its (regrettably unnumbered) rooms for its 1,406 residents. However, the average number of beds per sleeping room is misleading, owing to the distorting effect of a handful of institutions like Norwich: the median, seven, is more apt for a general picture among multiple workhouses. The size of these rooms containing beds was, unfortunately, rarely given.[7]

Some alleviation of crowding was achieved if there was 'a proper distance' between each bed.[8] (Great) Yarmouth workhouse in Norfolk was reproached for the 'many disagreeable circumstances [that] must frequently happen' when beds were too close together.[9] Reflections on other houses suggest that the parameters for these disagreeable consequences related to the sounds and smells of a densely occupied space at nighttime.

Eden did not consider the possible influence of multiple bedsteads on the desire for security during sleep that was prized by those not living in institutions.[10] Theft may have been less of a risk in a workhouse, but physical vulnerability could prove a concern.[11] A vivid illustration of this is provided by the autobiography of William Marcroft, who entered the workhouse at Middleton, Lancashire, with his mother Sally as a small child in the 1820s. His mother was thought to be insane given her post-partum behaviour, so she was initially placed in the same workhouse dormitory as a young man of twenty, also insane, 'to cure her by frightening'.[12] Such a 'solution', however, was not without its dangers, for both mother and child were attacked by their fellow inmate and, on Sally shouting 'murder', they were removed to a different room.[13]

Contemporary medical discourse denounced the crowding of beds together. In relation to children's sleep, Dr William Buchan linked multiple beds in a nursery with unwholesome air and exposure to risk of colds or other disorders.[14] He further reflected on the value of ventilators for hospitals and jails because 'In all places where numbers of people are crouded together, ventilation becomes absolutely necessary', but made no direct comments on workhouse bedrooms.[15] The need to place several beds in the same room (in their own houses) was listed by another author as one of the misfortunes of the poor as likely to compound the ill effects of low ceilings.[16] Ideally, people who heeded their medical advisors would have sought 'lofty, open bed-chambers, daily ventilated by fresh breezes' without multiple beds and, furthermore, chosen 'healthy situations for our place of constant residence'.[17] Medical texts in this period were arguably devising a narrative of 'environmental risk' around the air in domestic spaces for the edification of readers in prosperous households rather than paupers.[18]

These judgements across the second half of the eighteenth century contextualise Eden's frequent juxtaposition of bed details with the airiness of a workhouse's situation. A different subset of twenty-seven workhouses featured comments about ventilation. Fifteen of these houses were described as well-aired, airy, or as being in an open or elevated situation (likely to promote the free flow of air). High-perimeter walls which prevented air circulation was particularly condemned, notably in urban locations including Coventry and Wolverhampton. Eden, himself a member of the upper middling sort, was perhaps applying the emerging medical messages to a new cohort, the parish poor, in the hopes of mobilising parish officers to promote healthful workhouses.

If the proximity of beds was an issue, cohabitation of a single bed was worse. The cleanliness of temporary or multi-occupancy beds was a concern for customers of lodging houses, and that was in facilities that were available for hire (where businesses were wise to consider their reputations among clients).[19] There were no such commercial pressures on workhouses. Seven workhouses were noticed by Eden for the inmates' bed-sharing. This was rarely a confirmed feature of workhouses with smaller populations of ninety or lower. Nevertheless, the space/bed capacity was so pressed at four houses holding 126–539 people that the poor were required to sleep three or even four to a bed.[20]

Bedfellowship was commonplace in poor and even prosperous households, typically involving people of the same sex, similar age and comparable status.[21] In the homes of the poor, people sometimes 'had to share beds in very trying conditions', even if it was undertaken with people they knew well.[22] In public institutions like workhouses there was less choice over one's bedfellows, less likelihood of being related to them, and less prospect of asserting autonomy over bed-sharing, giving rise to a shortened spectrum of bedtime experience from necessity to compulsion. This was in marked contrast to the 'selection of trusted sleeping companions' that was the case in households of any status, and to the sociability inherent in one's choice of bedfellows when away from home on residential visits to the houses of relations and friends.[23] If workhouse paupers had the same preoccupations as their social betters, they may have been more reconciled to their sleeping arrangements if they were fixed (in the same room, on the same bedstead) and if those people sharing the same space were selected by consensus, being predictable rather than subject to frequent change. Contentment or irritation may also have shifted depending on whether beds were shared in winter or summer, giving rise to welcome warmth or overheating, or on the size of the beds concerned. Limited evidence on the size of workhouse beds from beyond Eden's reports suggests they were six feet long by three- to four feet wide.[24] Three adult paupers sharing such a bedframe would have been very cramped, even if the sensation was familiar from their own former homes or experience of lodging houses.[25]

Bed-sharing was regarded as medically problematic when not undertaken exclusively with marital partners. There was an appalled medical reference to the risk of mutual masturbation (with an example being given of bed-sharing in a girls' boarding school rather than a workhouse).[26] Conversely, if people of disparate ages went to bed together, old people with young, the junior person was allegedly liable to be affected by feebleness and even accelerated death.[27] There is no evidence, however, that opinions on these topics from practitioners were sought by parishes, nor that any changes were implemented in workhouses on the grounds of health concerns about bed-sharing.

Beds in households were the location of vital life events, chiefly marital or extramarital sex, childbirth and death.[28] Lying-in and death in the workhouse were both relatively commonplace and would have provided repeated pulse points in the experience of institutional inhabitants and wider communities. Indeed, the deaths of very old paupers provided one of the occasions when workhouses were reliably reported in the eighteenth-century press.[29] In respect of marriage and sex in bed, however, workhouses diverged significantly from household practices and expectations. The provision of accommodation for married couples was a rarity. Still it did exist, and in some cases, marriages took place between inmates (typically endorsed only if the prospective partners were so old that they were unlikely to produce offspring).[30] Reproductive sex in the workhouse was highly problematic, both on moral and pragmatic grounds (arising from the likely generation of additional poverty or the opprobrium directed at promiscuous inmates). Of course, sexual activity in workhouses is only visible if it gave rise to a recorded prosecution or a scrutinised birth.[31] However, it is not inevitable that illicit sex necessarily took place in bed.

The mattresses in Eden's workhouses attracted comment in thirty-nine places. They were stuffed with chaff or straw (in twelve workhouses, representing 30 per cent), flock (nine or 23 per cent), feathers (ten or 26 per cent), or a mixture of these materials (eight or 21 per cent). This pattern is distinctive when compared to that found by Harley in pauper household inventories. In households for the period 1770–1835, most beds were not described by their material, but where noted chaff or straw was used for 19 per cent of mattresses, flock for 25 per cent and feathers for 56 per cent.[32] This suggests that cheap chaff/straw mattresses were ostensibly more common in workhouses than in homes, and that conversely expensive feather mattresses were much less prevalent in workhouses than homes. Nonetheless, the household inventories that were not specific about mattress composition may, in reality, have hidden a similar extent of usage between all materials in both households and workhouses.

Chaff comprised the husks of corn removed by threshing and was the cheapest bedding material of the three, and in Wirksworth, Derbyshire, and Ecclesfield, Yorkshire, both supplying chaff mattresses, the pillows were filled with the same material. The potential disadvantages of plant-based bedding were that it might prickle the skin, make a crackling noise or putrefy (with or without being in contact with human excretions).[33] These risks would have been experienced most vividly by the beds' occupants rather than by daytime visitors to the house. Interesting to note, though, is that chaff and straw were not the most problematic options so far as Eden and his deputies were concerned. Seven houses were criticised in *The State of the Poor* for the presence of vermin or bed-bugs, and in six cases, the mattresses concerned were partly or wholly composed of flock (i.e. stuffed with refuse wool). The connection between infestations and flock beds is made clearer in Wolverhampton, Staffordshire, where the mattresses' composition was blamed specifically for being retentive of bad smells and 'very productive of vermin'.[34]

Bedbugs were the bane of institutional life in the eighteenth century, particularly in the warmer, summer months (Figure 18.1).[35] They subjected victims to bites and ensured that the bedroom atmosphere was tainted by their smell.[36] Infirmaries made repeated efforts to get rid of them.[37] Wood, as well as textiles, was thought to harbour bedbugs, so workhouses as dispersed as Portsea (Hampshire), Coventry (Warwickshire) and Preston (Lancashire) acquired iron bedsteads in an attempt to suppress their presence. It is likely that, elsewhere, bedframes continued to be constructed from wood.

At Louth in Lincolnshire, the bed spaces, in addition to the bedsteads, were partitioned by wooden boards at each end and on one side. This had the advantage of obstructing the occupants' view of each other but was generally regretted for restricting air-flow and harbouring smells.[38] High praise was reserved for Hull in Yorkshire where, uniquely in Eden's reports, the beds were all 'taken down' once a year (presumably being disassembled for the purpose of cleaning each part of the bedframe).[39]

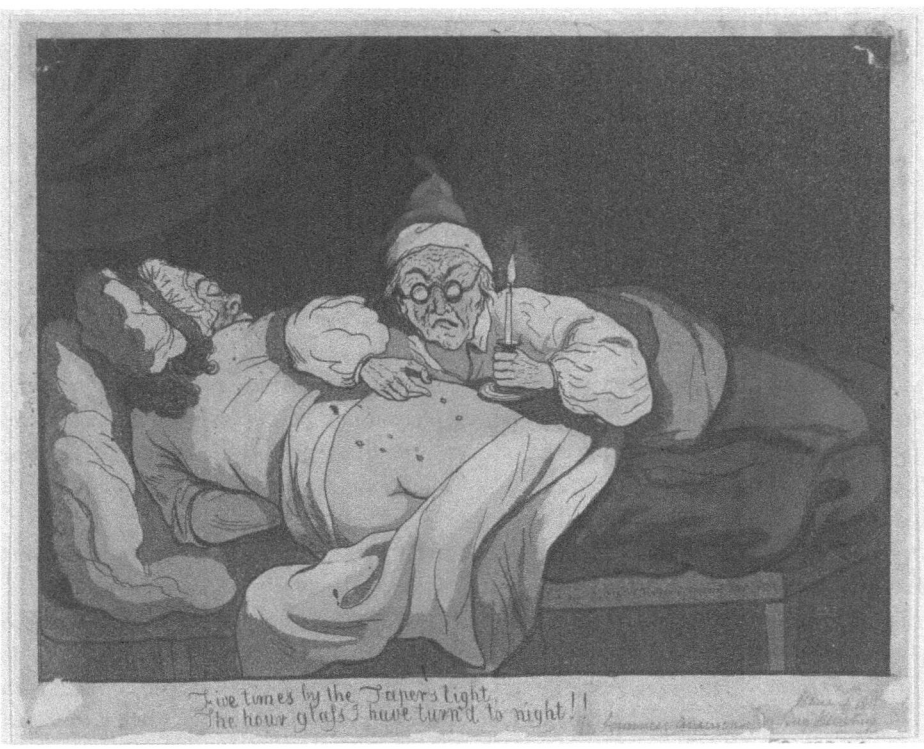

Figure 18.1 Engraving by Thomas Rowlandson, showing a wooden bed frame and the physical presence of bedbugs, 1793. Source: Courtesy of the Metropolitan Museum of Art, New York, 59.533.480. Public Domain Mark.

The most expensive and approved material for mattresses was feathers.[40] It is, therefore, perhaps mildly surprising that any workhouse beds should have made use of this filling. Feather-bedded institutions were notable for yielding few direct criticisms, and instead gaining additional marks of approval. In Bulcamp, Suffolk, along with feather mattresses, the 'nurses' were charged in the workhouse rules with laying wormwood between the sheets, presumably to supply an additional prophylactic against bugs.[41] As the introduction to this chapter suggests, there was a direct relationship in the minds of Eden and his deputies between the adoption of feather beds and aspirations of a workhouse to cleanliness (albeit those aspirations were not always met). Bulcamp in Suffolk was found 'very clean' with its feather mattresses, whereas Spilsby in Lincolnshire, similarly stocked, was 'not as clean as it ought to be'.[42]

Only one workhouse was noted for its bedding being old.[43] It is likely that this sort of refined description would instead be a feature of workhouse inventories, for the purposes of valuation.[44] The resource represented by beds and bedding in the possession of the parish was important both because it had a monetary value and because these were items that could be lent or given to paupers leaving the workhouse (representing an investment in re-establishing a household).[45] Parishes did not necessarily just let bedding fall to pieces or become insanitary, as seen in the purchases of ticking and material for restuffing mattresses, within and beyond Eden's observations.[46]

Far fewer workhouses attracted comment for their bedclothes and bedding, in contrast to the frequent notes about their mattresses. Just fourteen houses were either 'well' or 'tolerably' provided with bed coverings, or were noticed in more detail. A basic provision consisted of two sheets, one blanket and one coverlid, coverlet or rug per bed. These textiles had a retail value, explaining the occasional theft of sheets (for example) from a workhouse. Elizabeth Langham stole eight sheets from the Clerkenwell workhouse in 1784 and on discovery was duly committed to the London Bridewell.[47] Careless thieves even took workhouse textiles bearing the parish mark.[48]

The presence or absence of bed hangings or curtains was not noted by Eden. This is unfortunate, as these soft furnishings became increasingly common in the homes of the poor between 1670 and 1835, offering a measure of warmth, and of privacy if the accommodation was crowded. It seems likely they were valued as sources of security and control, comprising a psychological as well as a physical comfort.[49] It was not inevitable that bed hangings would be missing from the workhouse environment of the 1790s, but preliminary evidence from inventories suggests that they were rare in institutions after 1750, except as a feature of the workhouse master's bedroom. Bed hangings, therefore, provided something of an experiential boundary between domestic and institutional living.[50]

In a well-run workhouse, beds were made up each morning and bedding was aired on a regular basis. Beds were made 'by those who lie in them' at Kendal in Westmorland and by 'nurses' at Leeds.[51] Daily airing was approved at Melton in Suffolk, where bedclothes were turned down, the windows opened, and the doors locked at 10 o'clock each morning, at least in theory.[52] This allowed for an airing in situ rather than taking bed coverings outside, although this latter more strenuous form of airing was carried out at (Great) Yarmouth in Norfolk in 'proper' weather.[53] Routine laundering of bedding was not remarked upon by Eden, although he did notice monthly beatings or annual scourings of bed textiles.[54] It is likely that washing was a mundane, regular and unremarked (female) activity, raising questions about the intersection of beds with workhouse labour and the wider meanings of beds for paupers, staff and workhouse managers.[55]

Significance of workhouse beds

Wherever the pauper inmates were responsible for producing materials, there is the scope to see the textiles in more detail and to construe them as either a source of personal investment or an element of household policing. In Wetheral, Cumberland, female paupers span wool for production of bedclothes, specifically for use in the house.[56] Blanket-making for internal usage was either in progress or planned in three further houses. At Ealing in Middlesex, the work demanded from women and girls included the manufacture of fine flax for sheeting, although whether solely for sale or somewhat for internal use by the house is not specified: on a related note the workhouse's flax and hemp manufacture was projected to make a loss in 1795.⁵⁷

Making, mending and cleaning bedclothes was a routine part of domestic life for poorer women in their own houses, just as the possession of bedding was a basic component of household viability. These activities were also an essential attribute for an institution that was not exclusively or uniformly (at this date) punitive. This raises the question of whether the manufacture of workhouse bedding could possibly have been construed as 'meaningful' work by female inmates.⁵⁸ Did they value the products of their labour if the resulting sheets and blankets were then used by themselves?

In four of Eden's workhouses, all with populations below fifty, the parish made a point of supplying beds and bedding despite the house having been farmed out to a workhouse contractor.⁵⁹ Handley has noted the high cost of bedding in private houses and the prominence of bedding as a proportion of the total value of the inventory.⁶⁰ It seems likely that contractors did not want to be burdened with the costly replacement of worn out or dangerous bedding if they could possibly avoid the liability.⁶¹ Even so, Eden's examples may not have been representative. A variety of contracts survive for parishes brokering arrangements for workhouse 'farmers' that saw the incumbents keeping the existing parish stock of beds in repair or even being entirely responsible for the supply of all beds.⁶² Concerns about financial commitment could cut both ways.

Beyond the material object, beds in workhouses were symbolic of good or bad order: rules made provisions for times of going to bed and behaviour within the bedroom during the proscribed hours of night. Eden focused on giving rules for the larger houses, and in these, the timing of retirement to bed was uniform: nine o'clock in the evening in summer (starting in either March or May), and eight o'clock in winter (from September). In no location is it clear whether the paupers were literally locked into their bedrooms at night or monitored to ensure that they remained in place (although the capacity to lock doors at Melton in Suffolk, mentioned above, suggests that bedroom doors might routinely have been secured).

Going to bed was supposed to be the signal for putting out both candles and fires. This had an immediate application in preventing institutional conflagration and also a health benefit: sleeping bodies were ideally kept cool, and fires even in winter endangered raising the heat in the room beyond the optimum temperature.⁶³ Care in extinguishing flames had to be constant to prevent disaster. When Chester workhouse burned down during one February night in 1767, around seventy-seven of the two hundred inmates were 'burnt to ashes'. Others jumped from windows at the top of the building, which details suggest there may have been some restriction on their egress (although this might have been occasioned by the fire itself).⁶⁴ Perhaps as a result of such fatal examples, there was sometimes a bar on smoking in bedrooms.⁶⁵ In Kendal Westmorland, breach of this rule could result in strict punishment comprising six hours in 'the dungeon'.⁶⁶

One parish offers a telling case study in the overhaul of sleeping arrangements in the years after Eden's surveillance. The workhouse for the parish of St Mary in Nottingham held 168 people in 1795 and did not meet with Eden's approval. Surrounded by high buildings, 'the free current of air is completely obstructed' and vermin 'are found to prevail'. The result was that 'A spotted fever, at this time, rages in the house'.[67] The parish operated on a vast financial scale and in the early nineteenth century rebuilt the workhouse and overhauled its medical relief.[68] In an unusual development, one pauper admitted to the new workhouse in 1814 was so impressed with the accommodations that he wrote a poem in praise of the institution, including its dormitories:

> We from our rooms had a full view
> Of fields, which did our health renew ...
> The beds in them are uniform,
> To keep from winter's cold and storm.[69]

The poet, autobiographer David Love, was as enthusiastic about the workhouse, its beds and its situation, as Eden had been critical of its former incarnation (despite the fact that the two buildings successively occupied the same site).[70] We might infer, therefore, that the new workhouse was built taller than its neighbouring buildings, facilitating views of fields and healthy ventilation for the bedrooms.

Conclusion

Workhouse beds in the 1790s typically comprised wooden bedframes, a mattress equivalent in composition to those in poor households, and bedding of sheets and blankets. It seems likely that the main divergence between domestic and institutional beds was in the provision of bed hangings or curtains: these symbols of security and privacy, valued at home, were not part of the institutional offer. This was perhaps a reflection of status – only the more prosperous or high-status sleepers such as heads of household were able to enjoy them – and perhaps a consequence of bed-sharing. There was less justification for bed-time privacy when the same mattress was being shared by people who were not related by birth or marriage.

Eden's survey was influenced by contemporary medical literature on bedrooms and ventilation, but not all workhouses' sleeping quarters were organised in line with the same advice. Airiness was a commodity that was coincidentally available in some institutions, based on the serendipity of their locations, and could, to some extent, be manufactured by workhouse rules. It was not notably a feature of parochial investment, however, except possibly in the case of Nottingham St Mary.

The meanings that paupers attached to workhouse beds are likely to have been influenced by their permitted level of autonomy in choosing bedfellows, their engagement with domestic tasks like the cleaning and mending of bed textiles and the intensity with which behaviour in bed was controlled. One person's freedom to smoke in bed was another person's exposure to the risk of fire, just as a locked door might represent either constraint or security. The only certainty is that there was a separation between domestic and workhouse beds when it came to authorised sexual activity.

Objects of Poverty

The need for healthy bedding and a good night's sleep during the hours of darkness were probably universal goals. The devil lay in the detail of how these goals might be achieved in the eighteenth-century workhouse.

Notes

1. F. M. Eden, *The State of the Poor*, vol. 2 (London: J. Davis, 1797), p. 571.
2. Sasha Handley, 'Objects, Emotions, and an Early-Modern Bed Sheet', *History Workshop Journal* 85 (2018): pp. 170–1; Sasha Handley, *Sleep in Early Modern England* (New Haven: Yale University Press, 2016), pp. 39–40.
3. Angela McShane and Joanne Begiato, 'Making Beds, Making Households: The Domestic and Emotional Landscape of the Bed in Early Modern England' (pre-publication draft) https://www.academia.edu/39035802/Making_beds_making_households_the_domestic_and_emotional_landscape_of_the_bed_in_early_modern_England_Draft_no_references (accessed 28 January 2025).
4. Joseph Harley, *At Home with the Poor: Consumer Behaviour and Material Culture in England, c. 1650–1850* (Manchester: Manchester University Press, 2024), pp. 85–97.
5. H. C. G. Matthew and Brian Harrison (eds), *Oxford Dictionary of National Biography*, vol. 17 (Oxford: Oxford University Press, 2004), pp. 682–3.
6. The overall correlation coefficient for beds to total population is 0.85, suggesting a high degree of correlation.
7. Just one of the fifty-nine, for Sheffield in Yorkshire, recorded room sizes of nine feet six inches square; Eden, *State*, vol. 3, p. 872.
8. This was the case at Melton in Suffolk: Eden, *State*, vol. 2, p. 687.
9. Eden, *State*, vol. 2, p. 526.
10. Handley, *Sleep*, p. 160.
11. Also see Surrey History Centre QS2/6/1792/Eph/80, Quarter sessions bundles for information and examination regarding James Taylor, a pauper in Lambeth workhouse, accused of steading three shillings and six pence from under the bed of John Grigg, another pauper, as he slept, 1792.
12. William Marcroft, *The Marcroft Family* (Rochdale: E. Wrigley & Sons, 1889), p. 23.
13. Ibid., p. 25.
14. William Buchan, *Domestic Medicine; or, a Treatise on the Prevention and Cure of Diseases by Regimen and Simple Medicines* (London: W. Strahan, T. Cadell, J. Balfour, and W. Creech, 1774), p. 34.
15. Buchan, *Domestic Medicine*, p. 83.
16. Robert Wallace Johnson, *Some Friendly Cautions to the Heads of Families* [1770?], p. 17.
17. John Leake, *Medical Instructions Towards the Prevention and Cure of Chronic Diseases Peculiar to Women, Vol 1 …* (1781), p. 408.
18. Vladimir Jankovic, *Confronting the Climate: British Airs and the Making of Environmental Medicine* (New York: Palgrave, 2010).
19. Handley, *Sleep*, p. 159.
20. At Ealing, Nottingham St Mary, Sheffield and Gressenhall, Norfolk: Eden, *State*, vol. 2, pp. 422, 460, 576, and vol. 3, p. 872. The concentration of bed-sharing could be different for adults and children: National Archives HO 42/62, ff. 45–6 Home Office, domestic correspondence, supplementary 1801 for overcrowding in the workhouse of St Michael Coventry where adults slept three to a bed, children six to a bed.
21. Handley, *Sleep*, p. 176.

22 Harley, *At Home*, pp. 88–9.
23 Handley, *Sleep*, pp. 7, 54.
24 Peter Collinge, Louise Falcini, Tim Hitchcock and Alannah Tomkins (eds), 'Small Bills and Petty Finance', dataset. https://zenodo.org/records/6610414 (accessed 4 June 2024), references GB0169_LD20_6_6_74_6 Lichfield St Mary, Staffordshire 1822 and GB0023_SPC44_2_40_2_7 for Dalston, Cumbria 1827.
25 Henry Fielding, *An Inquiry into the Causes of the Late Increase in Robbers* (London: A. Millar, 1751), pp. 70–1.
26 William Brodum, *A Guide to Old Age, or a Cure for the Indiscretions of Youth* (1799), chapter 22.
27 Anon, *The Medical Museum* (1763), p. 122, in a book allegedly authored by 'gentlemen of the faculty'.
28 Handley, 'Objects', p. 170.
29 *Public Advertiser*, 28 December 1786 for the death in Walsingham workhouse of Ralph Wilson, aged hundred years and four months. *Gazetteer and New Daily Advertiser*, 14 September 1787 for the death in Bath workhouse of Anne Bishop aged hundred and three, who retained her senses to the last. *London Chronicle*, 13–15 August 1793 for the death in Whitehaven workhouse of Ann Bulger aged ninety-three, who made lace without the need for spectacles until a month before her demise.
30 *Lloyds Evening Post*, 3–6 December 1762; *Gazetteer*, 11 September 1772; *Lancaster Gazetteer*, 25 July 1807.
31 Case of suspected sexual assault upon a child in Pangbourne workhouse Berkshire in 1771: *Middlesex Journal*, 7–10 December 1771. Attempted rape of a child at Aldgate workhouse London: *Courier*, 30 August 1800. Accusation of rape in North Walsham workhouse: *Whitehall Evening Post*, 27–30 September 1800. Dorset History Centre (hereafter DHC) PE-BF/OV/7/3/19, Bastardy examination of Leah Norris, 1785; DHC PE-PL/OV/4/3/1, Bastardy Warrant for Samuel White, 1767.
32 Figures calculated from Harley's database and not published. But see: Harley, *At Home*, pp. 86–8.
33 Holly Fletcher, 'Making Beds in Early Modern England: Sleep, Matter and Environmental Change', *Historical Research*, 20 (2024): pp. 17–19.
34 Eden, *State*, vol. 2, p. 678. See also p. 185.
35 John Southall, *A Treatise of Buggs* (London: J. Roberts, 1730) pp. 27–8; Louise Falcini, 'Cleanliness and the Poor in Eighteenth-Century London', PhD thesis (University of Reading, 2018), pp. 165–8.
36 Lisa Sarasohn, '"That Nauseous Venomous Insect": Bedbugs in Early Modern England', *Eighteenth-Century Studies*, 46:4 (2013): pp. 513–30.
37 Alannah Tomkins, *Nursing the English from Plague to Peterloo, 1665–1820* (Manchester: Manchester University Press, 2025), chapter 4.
38 Eden, *State*, vol. 2, p. 396.
39 Eden, *State*, vol. 3, p. 837.
40 Some feathers were more suitable for bedding than others: Fletcher, 'Making Beds', pp. 8–13.
41 Handley, *Sleep*, pp. 60–1.
42 Eden, *State*, vol. 2, pp. 402, 680.
43 Eden, *State*, vol. 2, p. 616 [at Bishop's Castle in Shropshire].
44 For example, Gloucestershire Record Office (hereafter GRO) P227/OV/9/3, Newland workhouse correspondence and inventory, 1788, featuring old bedding; Harley, *At Home*, p. 93 for the frequent use of 'old' in describing sheets in pauper inventories.
45 DHC PC/SN/2/4/1, Sturminster Newton Inventories, 1801–24, plus memoranda of bedding lent out 1803–5. Shropshire Record Office P297/C/2/3, Westbury Parish Work Book,

Objects of Poverty

1799–1805, including workhouse inventory listing bedding given to Jos Vaughan and other paupers 1805.
46 Eden, *State*, vol. 2, pp. 490–519 [for the purchase of flock, and bed ticking, the cloth that encased the mattress stuffing, at Norwich in Norfolk]. Cornwall Record Office X 1056/(28), St Euny's parish Redruth, bill for twenty-five bundles of straw for the workhouse beds, 1782. Somerset Heritage Centre D/P/tau.m/9, St Mary Taunton Vestry Minute Book, 1774–1804, including purchase of new beds for the workhouse 1781.
47 *Public Advertiser*, 3 November 1784.
48 *Old Bailey Proceedings Online* (www.oldbaileyonline.org, version 9.0) t17570114-24, Trial of Martha wife of William Perry, January 1757.
49 Harley, *At Home*, pp. 89–90.
50 Cheshire Record Office P51/22, Chester St John Poorhouse Book, 1731–1756, inventory of 1737; GRO P227/OV/9/3, Newland Workhouse Correspondence and Inventory, 1788.
51 Eden, *State*, vol. 3, pp. 755, 852.
52 Eden, *State*, vol. 2, p. 690.
53 Ibid., p. 345.
54 At Leeds and Manchester: Ibid., p. 345 and vol. 3, p. 848.
55 Falcini, 'Cleanliness', pp. 149–51, 161–3, 170–4.
56 Eden, *State*, vol. 2, p. 95.
57 Ibid., p. 424. The poor in the workhouse at Richmond, Surrey, spun flax for use in the house as clothing and bed linen: Parliamentary Papers, *Abstract of the answers and returns made pursuant to 'An act for procuring returns relative to the expense and maintenance of the poor in England'* (1804), p. 507.
58 Knut Laaser and Jan Karlsson, 'Towards a Sociology of Meaningful Work', *Work Employment and Society*, 36:5 (2022): pp. 798–815.
59 Bedfordshire Archives X250/3, Leigh-Lancaster collection, workhouse agreement for Woburn 1762 where the parish officers agreed to pay a yearly sum to the contractor and to supply household goods including beds and bedding.
60 Handley, 'Objects', p. 172.
61 P. P., *Abstract*, p. 220, describes bedding at Kent workhouses being burned following outbreaks of low malignant fever.
62 Collinge, Falcini, Hitchcock and Tomkins, 'Small Bills' database, see Brampton Cumbria 1828; P. P. *Abstract*, p. 634; Huntingdonshire Archives HP72/18, All Saints Parish St Ives Overseers' Correspondence and Papers including an Agreement to Farm the Poor, 1792.
63 Handley, *Sleep*, p. 47.
64 *London Evening Post*, 26–28 February 1767.
65 Alannah Tomkins, *The Experience of Urban Poverty 1732–82: Parish, Charity, and Credit* (Manchester: Manchester University Press, 2006), pp. 63–4.
66 Eden, *State*, vol. 3, p. 756.
67 Eden, *State*, vol. 2, p. 576.
68 Nottingham Archives PR Addit 9739, Nottingham St Mary Vestry Minutes, 1807–33.
69 David Love, *The Life and Adventures of David Love* (Nottingham: Sutton and Son, 1823), p. 140.
70 For a fuller consideration of Love's experience of the Nottingham workhouse, see Alannah Tomkins, 'Workhouse Medical Care from Working-Class Autobiographies, 1750–1834', in Jonathan Reinarz and Leonard Schwarz (eds), *Medicine and the Workhouse* (Rochester: University of Rochester Press, 2013), pp. 91–4.

Further reading

Falcini, Louise. 'Cleanliness and the Poor in Eighteenth-Century London', PhD thesis (University of Reading, 2018).
Fletcher, Holly. 'Making Beds in Early Modern England: Sleep, Matter and Environmental Change'. *Historical Research*, 20 (2024): pp. 1–22.
Handley, Sasha. 'Objects, Emotions, and an Early-Modern Bed Sheet'. *History Workshop Journal*, 85 (2018): pp. 169–94.
Handley, Sasha. *Sleep in Early Modern England* (New Haven: Yale University Press, 2016).
Harley, Joseph. 'Material Lives of the Poor and Their Strategic Use of the Workhouse during the Final Decades of the English Old Poor Law'. *Continuity and Change*, 30:1 (2015): pp. 71–103.
Harley, Joseph. *At Home with the Poor: Consumer Behaviour and Material Culture in England, c. 1650–1850* (Manchester: Manchester University Press, 2024).
Jankovic, Vladimir. *Confronting the Climate: British Airs and the Making of Environmental Medicine* (New York: Palgrave, 2010).
McShane, Angela, and Joanne Begiato. 'Making Beds, Making Households: The Domestic and Emotional Landscape of the Bed in Early Modern England' (pre-publication draft).
Sarasohn, Lisa. '"That Nauseous Venomous Insect": Bedbugs in Early Modern England'. *Eighteenth-Century Studies*, 46:4 (2013): pp. 513–30.
Tomkins, Alannah. *The Experience of Urban Poverty 1732–82: Parish, Charity, and Credit* (Manchester: Manchester University Press, 2006).

CHAPTER 19
SCRAPS AND SAMPLERS: THE FORM AND FUNCTION OF TEXTILE ARTEFACTS IN THE NINETEENTH-CENTURY WORKHOUSE
Karen Thompson, Peter Jones and Steven King

Introduction[1]

It is hard to think of a more iconic setting to explore 'objects of poverty' than the Victorian workhouse. Ever since George Cruikshank depicted Oliver Twist asking for 'more' with an empty bowl in one hand and wooden spoon in the other (Figure 19.1), a clear image of the material life of paupers has been indelibly etched on the public's imagination. Cold stone floors and hard wooden forms, the rough un-windowed wall and ill-fitting uniforms came to symbolise the workhouse experience for the contemporary public. Cruickshank and Charles Dickens were merely the first, and the most successful, social commentators to tackle the 'workhouse question' in Victorian Britain. Across newspapers, journals and popular fiction, all aspects of workhouse life were acceptable to those who wished to challenge the iniquities of the new poor law and in particular the 'incarceration' (as it was so often characterised) of the poor.[2] In turn, their views have had an extraordinary traction on modern work relating to the lives and experiences of workhouse inmates.[3] Much of this is undoubtedly due to the narrative power of works like *Oliver Twist*, but arguably it has as much to do with the fact that, just like contemporaries, modern readers are highly receptive to such desolate depictions of workhouse life. It really is no surprise that, crafted early and constantly reinforced both pictorially and in print, the reputation of the workhouse as a 'pauper Bastille' has deep roots in our collective imagination.

In terms of the materiality of workhouse life, it is easy to fall into Dickensian inertia: we *know*, because we have consistently been told, that the material lives of inmates were spartan and drab; personal belongings were strongly discouraged if not entirely forbidden; inmates' clothes were removed on entry and replaced with rough and ill-fitting institutional dress; and the accumulated ephemera that gave shape to domestic life on the outside was substituted with the dreary, formless monotony of institutional necessities.[4] Emerging evidence of workhouses as complex sites of interaction, exchange, resistance and agency should lead us to challenge such a one-dimensional view.[5] Yet in terms of everyday material life this is not as easy as might be imagined for three reasons. First, much of the current evidence base consists of official commentaries, heavily informed by the intentions and aspirations of those who crafted the new poor

Figure 19.1 *Oliver Twist Asking for More*, George Cruikshank, 1838. Wellcome Collection, 28956i, Public Domain Mark.

law, combined with the often jaded recollections of those who had been inmates themselves and the observations of commentators who were never truly objective on the 'workhouse question'.[6] Indeed, it can be argued that there is, and always was, a feedback loop in operation with regard to the workhouse: we know that those who established the new poor law intended it to be a place of discipline and hardship, a deterrent to the undeserving poor; we know that paupers resented being sent there as opposed to having relief in their own homes; and we are consistently told by what we have identified here as the Dickensian view that this is how it operated in practice. It is therefore a short step, in the absence of compelling evidence to the contrary, to conclude that the material lives of inmates *must* have been dour and utilitarian.

A second issue is that very few workhouse objects (particularly those which held any significance for paupers themselves or which shaped and embodied their everyday experiences) remain in collections. Those that do are very often of uncertain and, at times, even doubtful provenance. In relation to workhouse clothing, for example, Claire Rose noted that there is 'little [surviving] material evidence for workhouse garments'; and as the authors discovered during research for this chapter even what we think we know about those few items that do exist in museums and other collections is often based on hearsay or anecdotal evidence and can be misleading. One example of this relates to a woman's smock or work shirt in the Southwell Workhouse Museum collection (Nottinghamshire). When gifted it was described by the donor as having been made from a flour sack because, at Shardlow, 'all females had to make their own uniform by unpicking the flour bags and making them into [a] dress'.[7] On closer inspection, this 'white cotton workshirt' seems far from a refashioned flour sack. It appears to have been made from fine bleached linen, unlikely to have been used for sacking, and although it is almost certainly hand-stitched, the needlework is of a very high quality. Crucially, there is no workhouse mark on any part of the garment – no stamped initials to indicate that it was workhouse property[8] – and instead, the initials 'J S' are delicately embroidered inside the neckline. Given what we now know about the nature and function of workhouse clothing, if this garment was ever worn in the workhouse it may well have a different story to tell than the one which came with it into the museum collection and that fits too neatly with the Dickensian view.[9]

The final issue is, of course, that little of the material culture of the workhouse remains because little was *meant* to survive. Former workhouse buildings were, in the twentieth century, 'stripped and skipped' to make way for the new priorities of the National Health Service or to disguise their origins when other purposes were envisaged. Some workhouse furniture and tools, even some clothing items, were garnered from the possessions of those obliged to enter the doors of the institution. Many aspects of the material culture of institutional life were represented by the sturdy and the functional, and such mundane items were rarely considered worth saving. In this sense it is inevitable that we must write the material history of the new poor law institution from fragments and snatches, much as we are now beginning to write the history of the poor themselves from the fragments they left behind.[10]

It is these fragments and the stories they tell that inform the following discussion. If we accept that material evidence is sparse and that its provenance will often be sketchy, such evidence is unlikely to offer a definitive interpretation of how paupers experienced workhouse material culture. Indeed, it is axiomatic that, regardless of what we are able to find out about them, the objects that the workhouse poor encountered would have meant very different things to inmates depending on their age, status, life history and at what point in the life cycle of the new poor law they came into contact with them.[11] We thus need to embrace complexity in our dealings with objects that we can be certain have a workhouse provenance. We also need to explore alternative ways of placing them in our welfare histories, both as artefacts and as evidence. With this in mind, what follows is a brief exploration of two sets of textile objects that are known to have played a role at two different Norfolk workhouses.[12] The first is a collection of five small balls made from scraps of material which were discovered in the attic space of the former Mitford and Launditch workhouse (itself an old poor law institution) near Gressenhall. As we shall see, the scraps were wrapped in rough, hand-stitched outer coverings and the balls show signs of significant use. Aside from their existence in the workhouse, however, we know nothing about who made or used them, or how long and in what ways they were part of workhouse life. Yet, by bringing an analytical eye to the balls, exploring their construction and the materials used, and placing this evidence alongside more traditional archival sources, we demonstrate that it is possible to allow these objects to 'speak' and enable us to situate them more firmly in the history of workhouse material culture.

The second collection of objects is altogether more eloquent and its history more assured. It consists of three 'samplers' or textile narratives that were embroidered by Lorina Bulwer, an inmate in the workhouse at Great Yarmouth in the 1890s and early 1900s. They are as remarkable as the Gressenhall balls are mundane. Each of the 'samplers' is made up of multicoloured scraps of textile sewn onto a base layer of quilting and then embellished by Bulwer with long and seemingly confused embroidered narratives. Here and there, figures (of men, vegetables etc.) were sewn appliqué onto the samplers, the most substantial of which is sixteen feet long and more than a foot wide. They are, in themselves, compelling objects and far from unknown in the literature on needlecraft and in popular culture, having been the subject of local studies and even a BBC television feature, as well as appearing in, for example, histories of written and material culture.[13] However, King and Jones recently argued that, both as narratives and as textile artefacts, the Bulwer samplers cannot be fully understood unless we embrace the complex historical context within which they were created (of Great Yarmouth workhouse, of the treatment of the lunatic poor, and of the epistolary culture of paupers under the new poor law).[14] Section three, below, revisits and extends this discussion, looking again at how Lorina might have sourced the scraps and swatches which she worked up so meticulously into her textile legacy, and what this and the very survival of the objects might tell us about the nature and purpose of the workhouse more generally.

The clear link between these two different sets of workhouse objects is that they were created from scraps and offcuts of textiles that were, presumably, readily available to paupers. This, in itself, is fundamental when thinking about them as 'objects of poverty' and as remnants of workhouse material culture. By getting up close to them, exploring their constituent parts and how they were constructed, we can begin to offer some suggestions about their place in the complex and contested history of the workhouse, and knowing more about them as *objects* may even lead us to reconsider the material world of the workhouse more widely.

The Gressenhall workhouse balls

On first encountering the balls, one is struck by their makeshift construction and the roughness of the outer coverings (Figure 19.2). Nothing about their surface appearance suggests a rich or complex history. Out of context they might easily be passed over or ignored. However, when we delve more deeply into them (quite literally) a different story emerges. The process of investigation was facilitated by the fact that the outer covering

Figure 19.2 Four of the five balls found at the former Mitford and Launditch workhouse, Norfolk. Source: Gressenhall Farm and Workhouse collection, GRSRM 2014.9.1.

of one of the five balls had already started to unravel long before they were discovered in the workhouse attic. Norfolk Museum Service took this opportunity to disaggregate the degraded ball and see what was inside (Figure 19.3). What they found was a further five scraps consisting of very different materials: a veritable cornucopia of textiles contained in one small (approximately 5cm diameter) ball.

With the consent of Gressenhall Farm and Workhouse Museum's curatorial staff, co-author Thompson took a closer look at the scraps and we now know that the ball contained a wide range of yarns, weaves and qualities of textile which, it is likely, would have had an even wider range of uses, either within or beyond the workhouse (see Figure 19.4 for basic descriptions).[15] This raises important questions about the balls' provenance, and in particular how the textiles from which they were constructed were sourced. In the Dickensian view it would be hard to reconcile even this limited diversity with what, in general, we think we know about workhouse textiles and workhouse life. Hitherto, for example, pauper clothing has predominantly been assumed to have been rough, plain, drab and uniform, not merely as a result of necessity or economy but also to drive home the message that the workhouse was a place to be avoided at all costs.[16] Here, however, we have examples of cotton twill, multicoloured fabric and even silk. One explanation might be that at least some of these scraps were not part of the workhouse's stock of fabrics but were brought in from elsewhere – the Matron's rag bag, perhaps, or from paupers' own domestic stocks – but until we discover what textiles were actually being brought into the workhouse this must remain conjecture.

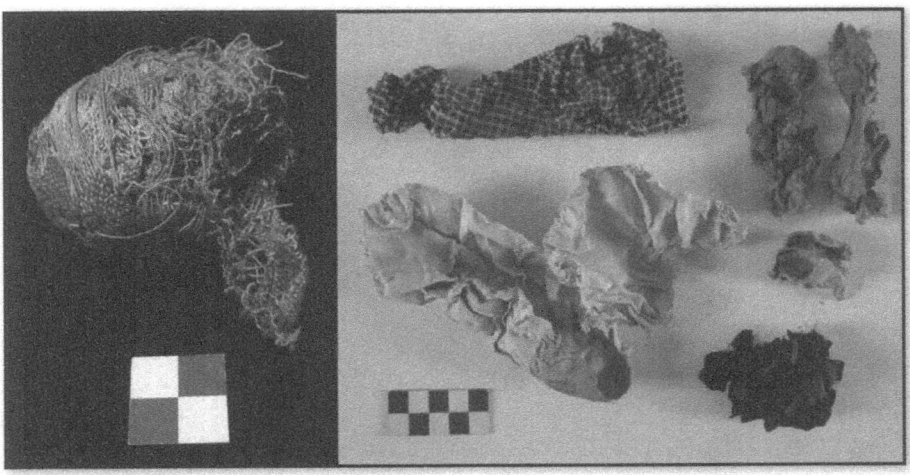

Figure 19.3 Deconstructed ball from the former Mitford and Launditch workhouse, Norfolk. Source: Gressenhall Farm and Workhouse collection, GRSRM 2014.9.2 & 6.

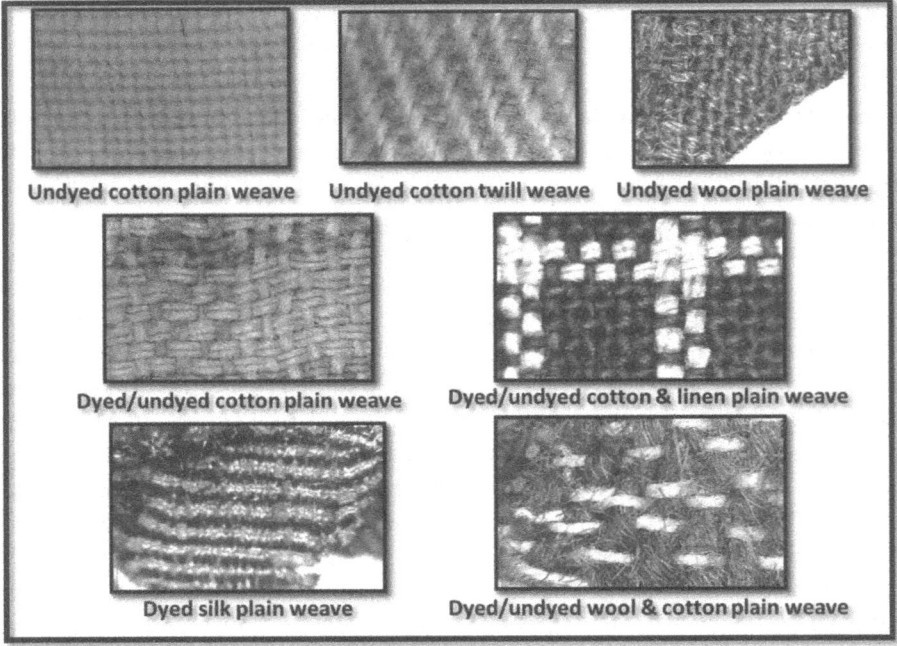

Figure 19.4 Initial findings of investigation into textiles contained in the Mitford and Launditch workhouse ball. Source: Gressenhall Farm and Workhouse collection, GRSRM 2014.9.2 & 6.

One way forward is to look at the evidence of workhouse tenders – newspaper adverts calling for local suppliers to tender for contracts. Through a detailed survey of these tenders it is possible to get a more balanced view of the kinds of textiles which were brought into workhouses in the nineteenth century and, therefore, some notion of whether or not these scraps are likely to have been typical of workhouse stock.[17] It has only been possible to find one early tender for the Mitford and Launditch poor law union (from 1838), which lists a very limited range of required textiles. This tender, published in the *Norfolk Chronicle*, tells us that the union authorities were seeking hard-wearing and practical materials: blue, grey and 'white twist' calico; cotton checks;[18] flannel; drabbett; and serge.[19] This account gives no indication that anything other than utilitarian textiles were being brought into the workhouse; but when we expand the search beyond this single case a very different picture emerges. In more detailed tenders for a further six Norfolk workhouses, for example, we find a much wider range of textiles such as chambray ('plain, light woven dress goods'), jean, moleskin, worsted, serge, beaverteen ('a lighter grade of moleskin'), swanskin ('a thick, closely woven, English woollen cloth similar to flannel') and even some higher-grade textiles like camblet (a quality mixed fabric, usually twill-weave, used for cloaks and other outer garments), gingham and printed cotton.[20] Elsewhere, although no pure silk has been found in union and workhouse tenders, unions beyond Norfolk sought grogram (another cloaking fabric made from a mix of silk and mohair), nankeen (yellow cotton used for medium- and high-quality men's breeches) and velveteen.

Of course, none of this tells us anything specifically about the Gressenhall balls. Without further and deeper investigation far beyond the scope of this chapter, a number of questions are raised but not answered. For example, from the tenders alone it is difficult to know precisely how the listed textiles would have been used. Perhaps more importantly, almost three quarters of all of tenders so far identified do not specify whether the required fabrics were to be used in workhouses or for other poor law union purposes. However, within the twenty-eight advertisements which do make it clear that textiles were for workhouse use, we still find tenders for gingham (Ormskirk, Nottingham, Glanford, Peterborough and Caistor), grogram (Hungerford, Wantage and Peterborough) and even nankeen (Kingsbridge in Devon). This in itself should make us think again about the nature of the textiles that may have been encountered by workhouse paupers, even if we still cannot yet be absolutely certain of the ways they were intended to be used. In particular, this kind of evidence suggests that whoever made the Gressenhall balls, and whoever played with, used or cherished them, may well have had access to a much wider range of fabrics and textile materials than would have been considered likely in the past. Even without a clear provenance the balls provide us with a starting point from which to consider the material culture of the workhouse and the material lives of paupers. The sheer range of textiles involved point strongly to workhouse environments in which fabrics and fragments circulated in considerable volume and, also, to fabric itself embodying multilayered values over and above its use for clothing or covering. The next step is to discern more of the usage history of such material. For this we need to go back to the balls themselves for further technical analysis and dig even deeper into issues like the extent and nature of soiling and the quality of the

Objects of Poverty

weave and thread counts in the scraps they contain. By placing this information within the broader context of the recorded history of the workhouse, it may then be possible to narrow down still further the part that these mundane but intimate objects played in the material life of the workhouse poor. In the meantime, the textile samplers of Lorina Bulwer provide additional perspectives on workhouse scraps and fragments which may also help us to further interpret the Gressenhall balls.

The Bulwer samplers

As we note above, the samplers from Great Yarmouth workhouse are also made from textile scraps and offcuts; but in some ways they could not be more different from the Gressenhall balls. By their very nature, as textile narratives, they literally have their own story to tell. Figures 19.5–19.7 reproduce three sections of the samplers. The monochrome reproductions here do no justice to these brightly coloured, highly patterned and, at times, richly decorated objects. The reds, greens, yellows, blues, pinks, browns and blacks of the background quilting and edging cannot be fully appreciated, and neither can the multiple colours, weights and textures of the threads that form the lettering and the constant underlining of the words. For the purposes of this chapter, however, more important motifs and themes are still clear.

For one thing, there is an astonishing diversity of textiles and weave types in the samplers, and in the sizes of the scraps, running from tiny fragments, such as the one at the bottom of Figure 19.5, through to large swatches and panels. The level of skill involved in making them (particularly in appliqué pictures as illustrated in Figure 19.7) suggests they were completed by an accomplished (not to say highly literate) seamstress and craftswoman. Given these observations, it is unsurprising that Lorina came from a relatively well-to-do family. Her father was a grocer and lodging house keeper in Great Yarmouth, one of four brothers all of whom were local businessmen. Yet within four years of her widowed mother's death in 1893 Lorina found herself in the workhouse. Thanks to the work of genealogists, museum professionals and historians (including co-authors King and Jones) we know quite a lot about Lorina's life and family. At their parent's death her brother Edgar (also resident in Great Yarmouth) took Lorina into his own household. On being widowed himself soon after, Edgar then caused Lorina to be committed to the workhouse on grounds of insanity.[21] For many commentators, it is this simple fact which explains the complexity of the narratives contained in the samplers. They are at times fractured and fragmented, often scatological and sometimes comedic, intentionally or otherwise (see Figure 19.6). For King and Jones, however, they are also part of a much wider and more significant epistolary tradition of complaint, commentary and negotiation that reaches back to the old poor law and the last decades of the eighteenth century.[22]

For the purposes of the present discussion, it is not the narratives that they carry so much as the objects themselves and their constituent parts that are of interest. Thus, a close look at Figures 19.5 and 19.6 reveals numerous fragments of material both sewn into the main panels, almost in the way of patches, and into the borders which serve to

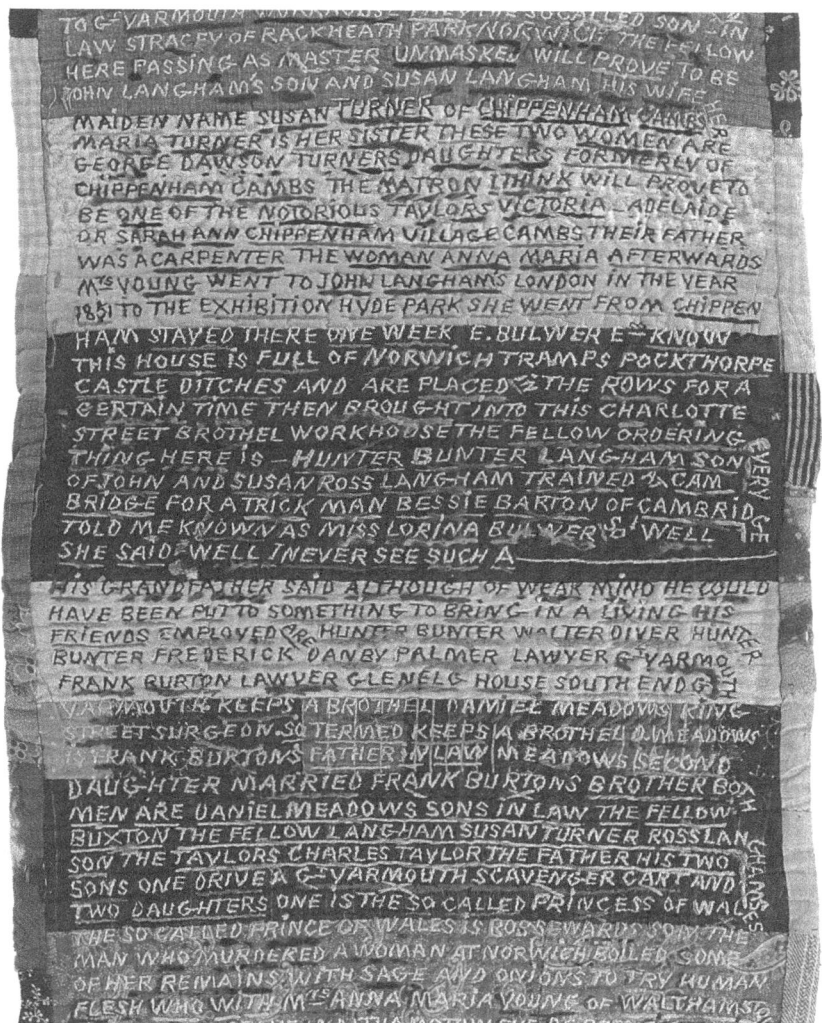

Figure 19.5 Section of a sampler by Lorina Bulwer. Source: Norfolk Museums Service (Norwich Castle Museum & Art Gallery), NWHCM: 2004.824.2.

anchor the object as a fabric and to frame the text, like the margins of a letter. In terms of size, variety of fabric types, colours and the roughness of the cut edges, these small pieces resemble the contents of the Gressenhall balls. Indeed, had Lorina Bulwer not 'hoovered up' scraps for these samplers, it is easy to imagine the fragments might have ended up as Great Yarmouth workhouse balls.

Some further and very obvious issues around the materiality and survival of these objects take us deep into questions about the nature and meaning of the workhouse experience. For example, like the fabric balls, where did Lorina Bulwer get this volume and diversity of fabrics and thread from? It is rather too easy to assume that this was

Objects of Poverty

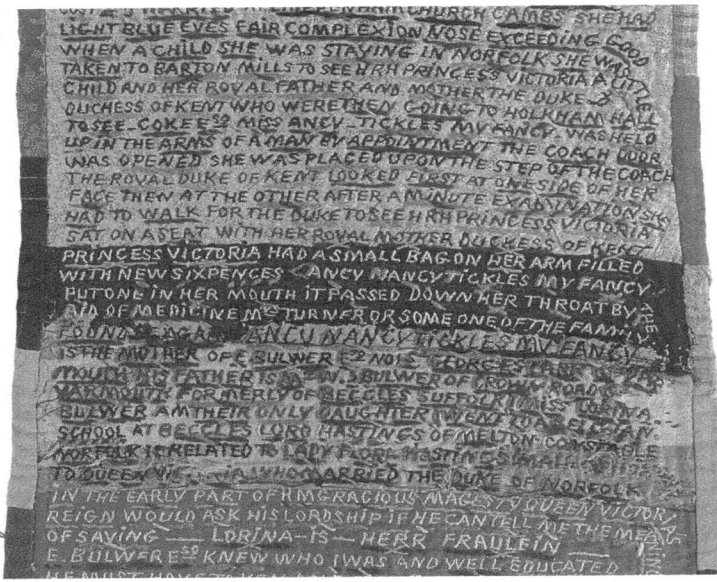

Figure 19.6 Section of a sampler by Lorina Bulwer. Source: Norfolk Museums Service (Norwich Castle Museum & Art Gallery), NWHCM: 2004.824.2.

garnered from old clothing, sacking or leftover textiles and objects hanging around the workhouse. As with the tenders analysed earlier, some of the material was of very high quality and there is no evidence (such as wear and tear and staining) that Lorina simply recycled old clothing. Like the balls, it is possible that the material for the samplers was garnered from a wide variety of sources such as workhouse visitors, workhouse staff or (as seems most likely) from her brother Edgar Bulwer, who was himself a draper. It may even have been purchased for the purpose; some of the fabric squares have a quality and vibrancy that seems to indicate 'newness'. These speculations are important for understanding the material objects themselves, but they also take us into a much wider realm of interpretations of workhouses and workhouse environments, suggesting that these were not closed and inward looking institutions and that there was a traffic of commodities between inmates and the communities from which they were drawn.

A further question also tends in this direction: needlework of this scale and intensity needed time and space. Where was this found in what we are so often told was a regimented and tightly controlled workhouse system?[23] We can think of the poor inmate confined in workrooms, undertaking unpleasant and monotonous tasks, but the evidence of Great Yarmouth gives the lie to this view. It seems likely that Lorina Bulwer had a regular, even designated, space of adequate proportions to undertake her great work, which speaks to a more humane workhouse regime than a Dickensian inheritance might suggest. Finally, we might ask why Lorina was even allowed to produce these objects and why they were subsequently preserved? It is too easy to conclude that, because she was insane, the work was facilitated as a distraction to keep her quiet, and

Scraps and Samplers

Figure 19.7 Appliqué figures on a panel by Lorina Bulwer. Source: Norfolk Museums Service (Norwich Castle Museum & Art Gallery), NWHCM: 2014.29.2.

that these objects were preserved simply because they were so unusual. Looking in more detail at Figure 19.7 might suggest an alternative reading. Authors Jones and King have argued that much of the Bulwer text is fact-based and, this being so, it seems likely that the two men in this section of the sampler were depictions of real people and, given their dress, that they were of relatively high social status (perhaps Guardians or visitors). It is even possible that onlookers may have known who they were. In a similar fashion, anyone looking over Lorina's shoulder might have recognised themselves in her text. The samplers were innately controversial; yet still, they were facilitated and preserved.

Objects of Poverty

This rather different interpretation speaks to the power of pauper agency and, potentially, to the *limitations* on the power of workhouse staff. It also speaks to the growing professionalisation of the staffing base and perhaps to a softening of the workhouse regime after the democratisation of Guardian elections in 1896.[24] The storage, preservation and (presumably, given the fact that all of these items were subsequently purchased at auction) dissemination of the objects into the outside world also, of course, speaks to a new consideration for the poor and their family connections that we do not see in the conventional literature. Thus, objects like these not only tell us about (and make us rethink) the material lives and experiences of the poor, but they are a vehicle, however fragmentary, for a wider reconsideration of the nature and purpose of the new poor law.

Conclusion

What we have presented here are merely fragments of the histories of already fragmentary objects. This does not mean that they are without meaning, either as artefacts or as evidence. The fact that these 'objects of poverty' were made from textile scraps which had led very different lives beforehand offers threads of evidence which can lead us in some unexpected directions. For example, the sheer variety of textiles, weave types, colours and qualities begs a host of questions about how they were sourced and how paupers might otherwise have encountered them inside or outside the workhouse. The very existence of these objects leads us to ask questions about leisure, recreation and the pursuit of personal interests in the workhouse that in some ways run counter to many of our most stubborn beliefs about institutional life. But perhaps the strongest lesson to be drawn from these objects is that there is a whole world of evidence that exists beyond the conventional sources which have so far been used to describe the experiences of the workhouse poor. Most importantly, historians have been increasingly successful in finding and analysing the writing of poor people themselves, rather than simply writing *about* them. A substantial number of these first-hand narratives originated in the workhouse and they too are, or convey, fragments: letters record fragments of conversations and dialogue between paupers and poor law officials, while autobiographies record fragments of lives. Equally they are part of the material life of the poor and must be considered as 'objects of poverty'. The pens and ink that were used and the paper on which text was written would often have been sourced in, or around the apparently unpromising setting of the workhouse in very similar ways to the scraps of fabric and cotton thread that made up the Gressenhall balls and Lorina Bulwer's samplers.[25] Perhaps the time has come to give the same kind of attention to other material aspects of workhouse life, other 'objects of the poor'.

Notes

1 Work on the objects in this chapter was possible with the kind permission and cooperation of curatorial staff at Gressenhall Workhouse and Farm, Norfolk (Norfolk Museums Service),

and Southwell Workhouse, Nottinghamshire (National Trust). Special thanks to Megan Dennis at Gressenhall, and Fiona Lewin at Southwell, for allowing us supervised access to textile artefacts in their collections.

2   Peter Jones and Steven King, *Pauper Voices, Public Opinion and Workhouse Reform in Mid-Victorian England: Bearing Witness* (Cham: Palgrave, 2020), pp. 13–23.

3   See, for instance, the two-part ITV series, *Secrets of the Workhouse* (2013), in which well-known celebrities were alternately shocked and horrified to discover the terrible treatment their ancestors suffered in workhouses as far apart as Glasgow, Ripon (Yorkshire) and Lambeth (London). For further discussion of this tendency, see Alannah Tomkins, 'Poor Law Institutions through Working-Class Eyes: Autobiography, Emotion, and Family Context, 1834–1914', *Journal of British Studies*, 60:2 (2021): pp. 294–5.

4   Especially at moments of changed national thinking. See, for instance, Elizabeth Hurren, *Protesting about Pauperism: Poverty, Protest and Poor Relief in Late Victorian England 1870–1900* (Woodbridge: Boydell, 2007).

5   Steven King, 'Thinking and Re-thinking the New Poor Law', *Local Population Studies*, 99:1 (2017): pp. 104–18; Paul Carter, Jeff James and Steven King, 'Punishing Paupers? Control, Discipline and Mental Health in the Southwell Workhouse (1836–71)', *Rural History*, 30:2 (2019): pp. 161–80; Peter Jones, Steven King and Karen Thompson, 'Clothing the New Poor Law Workhouse in the Nineteenth Century', *Rural History*, 32:2 (2021): pp. 127–48.

6   Jones and King, *Pauper Voices*, pp. 13–23.

7   Acquisition notes for a white cotton workshirt, National Trust (NT) 493213.

8   This common practice in workhouses was explicitly encouraged by the central authorities. Jones, King and Thompson, 'Clothing', p. 136.

9   For an illustration of the workshirt, see Southwell Workhouse Museum collection catalogue, at http://www.nationaltrustcollections.org.uk/results?Collections=2c13873ffffffe0722480241b4d2a4dd&Page=2 (accessed 14 September 2021). On established historiographical views of workhouse dress, see Jones, King and Thompson, 'Clothing', pp. 127, 130.

10 Peter Jones and Natalie Carter, 'Writing for Redress: Redrawing the Epistolary Relationship under the New Poor Law', *Continuity and Change*, 34:3 (2019): pp. 375–99.

11 Jones, King and Thompson, 'Clothing'; Tomkins, 'Poor Law'.

12 This focus on Norfolk is not accidental. Of all English counties it had the most continuous engagement with workhouses under the old poor law, while under the new poor law its complex history of Gilbert unions and other forms of incorporation had important consequences well into the 1870s.

13 Martyn Lyons and Rita Marquilhas, 'Introduction', in Martyn Lyons and Rita Marquilhas (eds), *Approaches to the History of Written Culture: A World Inscribed* (Cham: Palgrave, 2017), pp. 1–3. The BBC focus was part of the 2015 *Antiques Roadshow Detectives* series: https://www.bbc.co.uk/programmes/b05qtc6g (accessed 14 December 2021).

14 Steven King and Peter Jones, 'Fragments of Fury? Lunacy, Agency and Contestation in the Great Yarmouth Workhouse, 1890s–1900s', *Journal of Interdisciplinary History*, 51:2 (2020): pp. 235–65.

15 Further and deeper analysis is being undertaken on the scraps, which is likely to reveal even deeper levels of meaning and usage, and will be the subject of further future publications.

16 Jones, King and Thompson, 'Clothing', pp. 127, 130.

17 An extensive keyword search was undertaken for the period 1834–1900 using the British Library's online newspaper archive: https://www.britishnewspaperarchive.co.uk/ (accessed 05 November 2021). The resulting dataset (from which the following evidence is drawn) is incomplete, but so far contains tenders from ninety-four poor law unions published between 1838 and 1899.

18 Cotton (originally linen) check, and in particular blue check, was one of the most common light fabrics for working dress in the eighteenth and early-nineteenth centuries, used in a

variety of settings and for many different purposes, including the clothing of slaves. Vivienne Richmond, *Clothing the Poor in Nineteenth-Century England* (Cambridge: Cambridge University Press, 2013), pp. 116, 224; Alison Toplis, *The Clothing Trade in Provincial England* (Abingdon: Routledge, 2015), p. 105; David McCord (ed.), *The Statutes at Large of South Carolina* (Columbia: A. S. Johnson., 1840), p. 412.
19 *Norfolk Chronicle*, 8 September 1838. Substantial tenders were usually made for annual/biannual workhouse stocks. Occasionally they were published intermittently as stocks dwindled. Given the unusually limited nature of this particular tender it is likely that it falls into the latter category.
20 Tenders were found for the following Norfolk union workhouses: Mitford and Launditch (1838), Loddon and Clavering (1838), Henstead (1838), Thetford (1838), Swaffham (1849), Depwade (1860), East and West Flegg (1864). All descriptions and descriptive quotations come from Louis Harmuth, *Dictionary of Textiles* (New York: Fairchild, 1915).
21 For details, see King and Jones, 'Fragments of Fury', p. 248 (n.18), 250 (n.23).
22 Ibid., pp. 235–65.
23 Margaret Crowther, *The Workhouse System 1834-1929: The History of an English Social Institution* (Cambridge: Polity, 1981), pp. 196–201.
24 Steven King, *Women, Welfare and Local Politics, 1880-1920: 'We Might be Trusted'* (Brighton: Sussex Academic, 2005).
25 On autobiographical texts, see Tomkins, 'Poor Law Institutions', pp. 285–309, and on letters Natalie Carter and Steven King, '"I Think We Ought Not to Acknowledge Them [Paupers] as that Encourages Them to Write": The Administrative State, Power and the Victorian Pauper', *Social History*, 46:2 (2021): pp. 117–44.

Further reading

Jones, Peter. 'Clothing the Poor in Early-Nineteenth-Century England'. *Textile History*, 37:1 (2006): pp. 17–37.
Jones, Peter. '"I cannot keep my place without being deascent": Pauper Letters, Parish Clothing and Pragmatism in the South of England, 1750-1830'. *Rural History*, 20:1 (2009): pp. 31–49.
Jones, Peter, Steven King and Karen Thompson, 'Clothing the New Poor Law Workhouse in the Nineteenth Century'. *Rural History*, 32:2 (2021): pp. 127–48.
King, Steven. 'The Clothing of the Poor: A Matter of Pride or a Matter of Shame?', in Andreas Gestrich, Steven King and Lutz Raphael (eds), *Being Poor in Modern Europe: Historical Perspectives, 1800-1949* (Bern: Peter Lang, 2006), pp. 365–88.
King, Steven. '"I Fear You Will Think Me Too Presumptuous in My Demands but Necessity Has No Law": Clothing in English Pauper Letters, 1800-1834'. *International Review of Social History*, 54:2 (2009): pp. 207–36.
King, Steven. 'Reclothing the English Poor 1750-1840'. *Textile History*, 33:1 (2002): pp. 37–47.
Richmond, Vivienne. *Clothing the Poor in Nineteenth-Century England* (Cambridge: Cambridge University Press, 2013).
Styles, John. *The Dress of the People: Everyday Fashion in Eighteenth Century England* (New Haven: Yale University Press, 2007).
Toplis, Alison. *The Clothing Trade in Provincial England, 1800-1850* (Abingdon: Routledge, 2011).

CHAPTER 20
INVESTIGATING ALL THEY POSSESSED: DEPREDATION, DAMAGE AND DEFIANCE IN THE VAGRANT WARD FROM 1834 TO 1900
Megan Yates

Introduction

On 11 July 1884, Thomas Chamberlain stood before the court magistrate charged with vagrancy. He was described as

> a half-savage looking fellow, who was brought into Court almost in a state of nudity ... It seemed that this fellow had persisted in attempting to expose his clothing, in the Knighton-road in the presence of some females – ordered to the send to the Union.[1]

Demonised for his appearance, the poverty and deprivation that his scantily clad body showed in court was manufactured into something grotesque and dangerous. Nakedness, particularly for a poor person in the nineteenth century, was considered a social taboo.[2] Chamberlain's underlying issues of being too poor to afford decent clothing and potentially having mental illness as he 'exposed' himself in public were ignored by the press.[3] Such a narrative of criminalising and ostracising vagrants due to their appearance remained prominent in the courts and press.[4] In this case, clothing represented poverty, both in the moral and societal depiction of nakedness and deviancy, through the exposure of his body to females.

For many vagrants, the material possessions that included their clothing are an important lens through which historians can assess the everyday experience, stigmas and life cycles of the vagrant population in the nineteenth century. This chapter will, therefore, seek to ask what evidence of material possessions detailed in workhouse records can reveal about a vagrants' sense of self and how they also expressed individual agency through their possessions, deploying them as tools for negotiating poor relief in the workhouse setting.

There is a spectrum of definitions relating to vagrants in the nineteenth century. Encompassing abject poverty and desperation but also extending to reckless deviance and criminality, the records of their possessions on entry to the workhouse add another dimension to understanding their character. For workhouse staff – often required to decide on the spot whether a vagrant applicant was sufficiently desperate for relief or a criminal trying to deceive them – appearance was paramount. It was expected that vagrants experiencing extreme poverty would have few material possessions on entry to the workhouse.[5] These vagrants moved around a lot, were typically unemployed or in search of work, did not have an official place of residence and, in turn, did not have somewhere to house their belongings. However, records also suggest that some vagrants took the time to pack, carry and collect trinkets, teapots, knives, pipes and other miscellaneous items while travelling between poor law unions. These applicants required a broader judgement from the workhouse staff on entry to a workhouse. They might have carried a knife, but that did not necessarily indicate that they were violent or intended to cause trouble once inside. Knives had multiple other purposes such as cutting up food. This chapter explores how material possessions can help us to deepen interpretations of the complex lived experiences of vagrants as we begin to unpick their sense of selfhood through this evidence.

The first section discusses the extent to which vagrants used clothing to demonstrate their agency in the workhouse. Clothing was a valuable social capital through which to steal, sell, negotiate and rebel. The short and fragmented but nonetheless vivid case studies in this chapter show that even in areas with a strict regime which disqualified vagrants from receiving workhouse relief, they were able to weaponise their clothing and use it to negotiate poor relief. The second section emphasises that although vagrants understood their agency, challenged authority and had a deep knowledge of how to circumvent the law, they were also destitute and disenfranchised. Drawing on evidence from four workhouses in the Midlands (Stourbridge and Stoke-upon-Trent in Staffordshire, Kidderminster in Worcestershire and Southwell in Nottinghamshire), we observe the ways in which the myriad of possessions vagrants had on entry to a workhouse mirrored the multifaceted population. Due to the often-transient nature of vagrant lives and because most workhouse records were written by officials, their first-hand voices are omitted from these poor law records. Nevertheless, by reading between the lines, we encounter a complex picture of complaints and sensationalised press reporting that show vagrants used material possessions in unique and interesting ways.

Agency and deviance

Vagrants have often been dismissed as a rootless group of people, outsiders to the close-knit communities of the nineteenth century.[6] The wide-ranging, all-encompassing legal definition of vagrants under the 1824 Vagrancy Act meant that a vagrant was typically unemployed, wandering aimlessly or in search of work, not known to the community and homeless. Tim Hitchcock has shown that although earlier legislation around vagrancy was comprehensive, there were also 'a range of caveats and exceptions … which effectively permitted a large number of men and women to live on the roads' while simultaneously criminalising this act of wandering.[7] In addition, trickery – faking diseases or disabilities, professing to tell fortunes or reading palms – fed into this definition of vagrancy, adding to the overarching perception that vagrants were devious characters: the archetypal 'undeserving' poor.[8]

Deviancy was a label often attached to groups of people who defied social norms and they were routinely chastised in the popular press. In Stanley Cohen's work focusing on the 'mods and rockers' of the twentieth century, he identifies that deviant subgroups were often identified by the press as a 'folk devil', a demonstration to the wider population of 'what we [society reading the press reports] should not be' or do.[9] This negative perception was perpetuated in the vagrancy literature of the nineteenth century as well, with vagrants identified generally by the press as people to be feared and reprimanded by local, tight-knit communities.[10] The perception was that vagrants were criminals and they were dirty. Although vagrants were feared to be also cunning and crafty, their transience and status as a sub-stratum of the poor conversely meant that they were powerless to change or affect their own position within society. In consequence, the lack of authority over their own lives that vagrants experienced daily meant that they often resorted to expressing their individuality in different ways. They could complain against the rules imposed on them or display their knowledge of the law or their rights by misbehaving under poor relief.

Vagrants were further defined during this century by their appearance: the often shabby, worn-out and dishevelled clothing of one vagrant played a significant role in defining and stigmatising the entire population (Figure 20.1). Their dress was typecast as a reflection of their lack of social status and moral character, contributing to the negative stereotypes and prejudices that were associated with the vagrant population.[11] Across the Midlands corpus studied for this chapter, approximately 25 per cent of the poor law records pertaining to vagrants mentioned their clothing. Their shoes, trousers and jackets were all tools for vagrants to potentially negotiate with or complain about to local poor law authorities. They could set fire to, tear apart and damage their own clothing or the workhouse uniform (if provided with one), and such a form of resistance came at significant cost and annoyance to the workhouse authorities. As explored by James Scott, lower-ranking societal groups expressed their agency using small acts of rebellion 'behind the scenes', whereby they created their own rhetoric of dissent when not directly in front of the person with perceived power.[12] Secret displays of dissent for vagrants in the Midlands occurred most often at night when locked in the ward to sleep. In the morning, the workhouse authorities would sometimes find the vagrant bedroom in disarray and the vagrants' clothes torn to shreds to express dissatisfaction. However, such covert behaviour was also indicative of other emotions such as anxiety, boredom or frustration. Indeed, it was perhaps the case that most vagrants did not perceive themselves as rebellious when they took to tearing their clothes.

In another example, on 31 May 1867, it was reported in the *Staffordshire Sentinel* that Richard Williams had entered the vagrant ward at Stoke workhouse.[13] He was provided with a set of clothes from the workhouse staff and told to reside in the vagrant bedroom. Overnight, Williams tore his shirt into threads and, on his appearance in court the next day, told magistrates that the shirt and trousers were 'too filthy to wear'. An unnamed witness was also quoted in the report confirming that the clothes provided to Williams

Figure 20.1 A widely shared image of a 'typical vagrant', 1887. Source: Charles Ribton-Turner, *A History of Vagrants and Vagrancy and Beggars and Begging* (London: Chapman and Hall, 1887). Wellcome Collection, Public Domain Mark.

had been 'rather impure', while adding the caveat to say that had he complained directly to the workhouse staff, the clothes 'would have been cleaned and disinfected'. When asked to explain his conduct, Williams said he would be 'ashamed to go along the streets' in those clothes and so he destroyed them.[14] He was subsequently found guilty and sentenced to seven days' hard labour in prison.

It is evident from this example that Williams saw himself as someone who was not unclean and could demonstrate a sense of personal agency, deciding for himself what he should and should not put on his body. His dissent behind the scenes, tearing the uniform to shreds overnight because he did not want to wear them any longer rather than complaining face to face with the workhouse authorities, confirms that vagrants could engage in veiled acts of rebellion resulting from a strong sense of their self-worth. Williams did not shout or endanger others; instead, he rebelled by pulling apart his clothing out of view from the workhouse authorities. Although he was punished for this behaviour, his complaint was valid and his expression of agency was clear for all to see.

We can, therefore, observe two key points from this press report. Firstly, the destruction of the clothes signals Williams's sense of self and identity, wanting to appear respectable in public and not be perceived as someone downtrodden or, worse, a criminal threat. Secondly, it was routine for vagrants to be given a set of clothes from the workhouse staff, but the clothes were usually old and worn by several paupers beforehand.[15] The evidence in this case thus demonstrates that clothes for vagrants could be entirely unsuitable for wear. Rhetorical evidence written in further complaints to the poor law authorities in Central London shows that regularly washing clothing intended for vagrants was not a widely adopted practice.[16] Stoke workhouse, it seems, was no different.

A related example occurred in Kidderminster workhouse.[17] In 1848, the Assistant Poor Law Commissioner inspected the workhouse and had, unusually, recorded the grievances raised by vagrants, including 'insufficient changes of stockings, and of other matters'.[18] A follow-up report later confirmed that the workhouse did not provide new stockings on a regular basis. The evidence here is patchy and fragmented in different conflicting reports. Certainly, it appears that Kidderminster did not respond – or did not keep the records – to further official enquiries surrounding this hygiene issue.[19] A variety of inspection reports carried out over this period did, however, show that in neither of the two separate vagrant wards at Kidderminster intended for men were any bathing facilities, although authorities did supply wooden buckets, soap and towels for washing on recommendation from the central authorities.[20] The Kidderminster workhouse and these inspection reports provide a prerequisite to our understanding of the lived experience of vagrants, demonstrating that in this workhouse, at least, the facilities were unclean and unkept, providing foundation to the complaints. The vagrants that complained about the stockings did not rebel in silence as was the case with cloth tearing. Instead, they spoke up about their experience, complaining to a senior poor law official when given the opportunity on a routine inspection.[21] Clothing was deployed here then as a powerful tool for the negotiation of poor relief treatment that began wider conversations around the cleanliness of vagrants in Kidderminster workhouse.

Objects of Poverty

While vagrants knew their rights, the law and their own sense of self, workhouse authorities generally ignored their complaints. Workhouses were not obligated to provide vagrants with poor relief and it was often the case that vagrants were limited to a maximum of two nights at the workhouse.[22] As a result, they were easy to dispense with if they complained or rebelled against the workhouse rules. However, that was not the case with the poor law inspectors for Kidderminster, who showed an unusual display of tolerance towards vagrants based on the perceived legitimacy of their complaints about the standards of clothing. Any concern around cleanliness or insufficient workhouse supplies was reputationally damaging for the poor law authorities, but unlike other poor law unions, the Kidderminster vagrants were listened to. Attitudes towards vagrants could, like the overall administration of the poor relief, vary on location. Therefore, the everyday experience of a vagrant was different place by place and the expectations that vagrants had for their workhouse stay were compiled using a jigsaw of mismatched and localised experiences. This complaint also provided evidence to reveal the lack of uniformity across poor law rules and regulations. The varied experiences of vagrants symbolised the fragmented nature of the poor relief system in the nineteenth century. While in Kidderminster, complaints were taken seriously with follow-up reports commenced, in other areas, such as in the Southwell example detailed below, the attitude was to ignore and criticise the vagrant rather than listen and respond to their complaints.[23]

Life was tough for vagrants seeking refuge in a workhouse and their material environment added to the strain. The Southwell workhouse vagrant ward was small, but the accommodations were far more comfortable than in other areas. For example, there were only eleven beds, but instead of a bedroom consisting of a hard wooden floor strewn with rough, short and spiky straw like some workhouses across the Midlands, Southwell's individual wooden bedsteads were filled with fine and soft straw.[24] Nonetheless, as with all vagrant wards, Southwell vagrants were required to bathe on entry, given a workhouse uniform and, after a night's sleep, forced to break stones with pickaxes for four hours before their breakfast.[25] Such strenuous labour on an empty stomach unsurprisingly led to rebellious behaviour from vagrants. In 1848, the Southwell Board of Guardians wrote to the central authorities in London to complain about the increasingly dangerous behaviour of vagrants staying in their ward, compounded by the sheer number of vagrants passing through their doors.[26] While they could only sleep eleven vagrants at a time, according to workhouse records in 1848, 1854 and 1897, overcrowding was present.[27] For instance, in 1848, it was reported that over the course of three months, 796 vagrants had been relieved at Southwell workhouse. Southwell was not set up to cope with the volume of vagrants it received and struggled to manage 'deviant' behaviour.[28] In one example, the board described four vagrants who had started a fire which destroyed the bedding. On this day, twelve other vagrants had been admitted to prison for destroying their clothes by pulling the fibres apart and four more had intentionally set fire to their clothing.[29] Although Southwell authorities raised several complaints of a similar nature to central London, few responses or actions related to dealing with vagrants are recorded in the archives.[30]

Investigating All They Possessed

Across the corpus of stories in this chapter, we find that there was a tipping point for vagrants, such as with the ripping of poor-quality clothing to shreds or grumbling in complaint at the standards of sanitation around the wards, coalesced into blatant rebellion accompanied by fire and endangering the lives of themselves and others in the workhouse.[31] Vagrants could be quick-tempered people because their lives were often hostile. As such, the harsh regime and limited freedom at Southwell was not successful in keeping vagrants in line but, in fact, pushed them across a threshold into criminality. The lack of material possessions that vagrants had meant that they often had nothing to lose when unhappy with workhouse conditions. Instead, their clothing was a symbol of the power that they could individually and collectively assert in an environment within which they had very limited choices.

Possessions

Beyond clothing, it is rare that historians of nineteenth-century vagrancy can find evidence of the material possessions vagrants kept. This is partly because workhouses were under no obligation to record entry to the vagrant ward in the same way as the settled poor. Stourbridge workhouse, however, was an exception to this rule as it maintained comprehensive admission records for its vagrant ward in the late nineteenth century. On entry, vagrants were asked several questions, searched, and sometimes given a bath and a new set of clothes. As part of this routine, they were asked their names, dates of birth, occupations, locations (where they have come from and where they were going to) and, crucially, the items they brought with them. From these registers, we can observe the material possessions that vagrants carried into the workhouse. Between 1870 and 1886, 6,645 vagrants entered the Stourbridge vagrant ward. Out of this, 2,448 vagrants had no possessions with them, but many others carried with them items to be returned to them on leaving the workhouse (Table 20.1).[32]

By far, the two most common items were tobacco pipes and knives. The tobacco pipe was an important symbol in the nineteenth century, used as an affordable pastime for the poor and, in some cases, was the only possession of the vagrants save the clothes on their backs.[33] For example, John Jones and George Williams, 29- and 28-year-old labourers, had travelled a significant way from Worcester to Stourbridge (21 miles) and applied to the vagrant ward with a pipe each in their possession. Evidently, despite their impoverishment, vagrants still participated in social pastimes like smoking a pipe with friends as the settled poor did.

Across the corpus, the second most common item carried in by the vagrant was a knife. Knives had multiple purposes, such as self-protection or fighting, and for practical uses, such as eating and opening food packages. French Polisher Henry Pritchard, for example, aged twenty had entered the vagrant ward in 1871 with apples and a knife on his person. There was, of course, the fear that among the characters genuinely travelling from place to place in search of work, there were people on the streets with knives looking for a fight or the opportunity to steal.[34] Importantly, however, the individuality and sense

Objects of Poverty

Table 20.1 Most Common Entries for Vagrants in the Stourbridge Admissions Register, 1870–86. Sources: SRO D585/1/4/21; SRO D585/1/3/22; SRO D585/1/4/23

Entries	Number
'Nothing'	2,448
Pipes	2,197
Knives	961
Bundles	738
Tin cans	69
Parcel of clothes	59
Bags	29
Baskets	22
Teapots	16
Razors	10
Basket of clothes	10
Apples	9

of selfhood from vagrants who chose to carry knives into the workhouse illustrates that vagrants as a group were complicated people. No one definition can cover them as their motivations remain unknown.

Sixteen vagrants brought a teapot with them to the Stourbridge vagrant ward; however, no teapots were identified by their colour, design or markings. The practice of carrying a teapot was rooted in the fact that tea was a relatively cheap and widely available commodity, providing a source of warmth and comfort for those who were living most of their lives on the streets.[35] To have a teapot was therefore a strategy for granting themselves a reminder of their home, a place in society and belonging to nineteenth-century communities.[36] Carrying a teapot allowed vagrants to brew and drink tea wherever they happened to be, without relying on the hospitality of others or spending money in a coffeehouse or tavern. Teapots could be filled with water from public fountains and other sources. Tea leaves or other flavourings could be easily acquired through formal or informal economies.[37] Living what could be a rough and demoralising lifestyle, it is important for historians to try to zoom in on items carried by vagrants, like the teapots above, to reveal vagrants' attachments to 'home' and their sense of belonging within the community, as well as a comforting reminder of smoking by a warm fire at home of an evening.

Although the records for vagrant possessions are often thought of as scant, historians can use poor law sources to reveal a mosaic of vagrant material life, which is typically opaque in other histories. This chapter serves as a building block for piecing together the fragments of vagrant stories, creating a mismatched but altogether illuminating mosaic of life on the front lines of nineteenth-century welfare, from the perspective of the people who were officially denied the benefits of indoor poor relief.

Conclusion

Material possessions were powerful tools of negotiation and identity expression for vagrants. They provided a sense of validation and a platform for complaints against harsh workhouse regimes because vagrants knew the rules of the new poor law well. In this chapter we see that vagrants were not passive characters. Their homeless and potentially rootless identities did not rule their thoughts and behaviours. Rather, their possessions amplified their feelings of belonging and put a spotlight on the injustices of the law applying to their poor relief. Their material possessions are, therefore, a useful lens through which to explore the everyday experience of vagrants within a workhouse setting.

Clothing was much more than an item to cover their naked bodies. Vagrants weaponised their clothing. Pulling apart the fabric of the workhouse uniform and setting fire to dirty garments were staples of vagrant disorder found in workhouse records. Identifying the nuances of the everyday workhouse experience of a nineteenth-century vagrant thus reveals a multifaceted picture. We cannot assign one definition to these vagrants, nor can we see them as lacking in agency, and so we instead must delve into the sources and peel back the layers on which a snippet captured in the archives can highlight the complexity of vagrant lives. While this chapter recognises common tropes of violence and self-defence by vagrants following their possession of knives, other items suggest a sense of comfort, homeliness and convenience of carrying a teapot and tobacco pipes from place to place. This evidence presented here puts a spotlight on vagrant experiences in the workhouses and shows a rich tapestry of lived identities from the material possessions of vagrants.

Notes

1 *Leicester Chronicle*, 11 July 1874, p. 10.
2 Phillipa Levine, 'States of Undress: Nakedness and the Colonial Imagination', *Victorian Studies*, 50:2 (2008): p. 189.
3 Alison Smith, *The Victorian Nude: Sexuality, Morality and Art* (Cambridge: Cambridge University Press, 2009).
4 Alexander L. Beier, *Masterless Men: The Vagrancy Problem in England 1560–1640* (London: Methuen, 1987), pp. 1–4.
5 Alexander L. Beier, *Cast Out: Vagrancy and Homelessness in Global and Historical Perspective* (Ohio: Ohio University Press, 2008), pp. 1–10.

6 See Paul Slack, *Poverty and Policy in Tudor and Stuart England, Themes in British Social History* (London: Longman, 1988).
7 Tim Hitchcock, 'Vagrant Lives', in Joanne McEwan and Pamela Sharpe (eds), *Accommodating Poverty: The Housing and Living Arrangements of the English Poor, c. 1600–1850* (Basingstoke: Palgrave Macmillan, 2011), pp. 125–44.
8 Ibid.
9 Stanley Cohen, *Folk Devils and Moral Panics: The Creation of the Mods and Rockers* (Abingdon: Routledge, 2011), pp. 1–15.
10 Paul Lawrence, 'The Vagrancy Act (1824) and the Persistence of Pre-Emptive Policing in England since 1750', *British Journal of Criminology*, 57:3 (2016): pp. 513–31.
11 Charles J. Ribton-Turner, *A History of Vagrants and Vagrancy, and Beggars and Begging* (Montclair: Patterson Smith, 1972), pp. 162–83.
12 Scott, *Domination*, pp. xvii–2.
13 The National Archives (hereafter TNA) MH12/9363/30.
14 *Staffordshire Sentinel*, 1 June 1867, p. 3.
15 Peter Jones, Steven King and Karen Thompson, 'Clothing the New Poor Law Workhouse in the Nineteenth Century', *Rural History*, 32:2 (2021): pp. 127–48.
16 Ibid.
17 TNA MH12/14024/156, Workhouse Inspection Report, 1868.
18 TNA MH12/14019/204, Assistant Commissioner's Report, 1848.
19 Several pieces of correspondence around the stockings at Kidderminster exist. See TNA MH12/14019/200, Covering note from Poor Law Board Inspector, 1848; TNA MH12/14019/195, Letter from inmate of Kidderminster workhouse, 1848; TNA MH12/14019/199, Letter from inmate of Kidderminster workhouse, 1848.
20 Ibid.
21 TNA MH12/9528/240, 1848.
22 Sidney Webb and Beatrice Webb, *English Local Government: English Poor Law History. Part 1: The Old Poor Law* (London: Frank Cass, 1927), pp. 314–50.
23 Ibid.
24 TNA MH12/9528/240, 1848.
25 Paul Carter, Jeff James and Steve King, 'Punishing Paupers? Control, Discipline and Mental Health in the Southwell Workhouse (1836–71)', *Rural History*, 30:2 (2019): pp. 161–80.
26 TNA MH12/9528/227, Letter to the Guardians of Southwell Union, 1848.
27 For a breakdown of the yearly figures leading up to 1848, see TNA MH12/9527/355, Form from Thomas Marriott, Clerk to the Guardians of the Southwell Union, to the [Poor Law Commission], giving the numbers of vagrants given entry to Southwell workhouse, 1841–5.
28 Ibid.
29 Ibid.
30 Ibid.; TNA MH12/9532/225, Report of the Poor Law Board Inspectorate, 1863.
31 See also: Megan Yates, 'Rebellious Vagrants: Fires, Fights and Fisticuffs at the Mansfield Union in the Mid-Late Victorian Period', *Midland History*, 46:3 (2021): pp. 301–17.
32 Staffordshire Record Office (hereafter SRO) D585/1/4/22, Vagrant Admissions and Discharge Book, 1873–4. See also SRO D585/1/4/23, Vagrant Admissions and Discharge Book, 1886–9.
33 Jacqui Pearce, 'Living in Victorian London: The Clay Pipe Evidence', Arts and Humanities Research Council study, 2007. https://www.academia.edu/737367/Living_in_Victorian_London_The_Clay_Pipe_Evidence, pp. 3–5 (accessed 28 January 2025).
34 In Southwell, concern was expressed regarding 'locking up' two male vagrants together, for fear that they would attack each other. See TNA MH12/9536/239, Form of Architectural Notes, 1874.

35 For an overview of the increasing popularity of tea in England, see Francisca Antman, 'For Want of a Cup: The Rise of Tea in England and the Impact of Water Quality on Morality', *Review of Economics and Statistics* (2022): pp. 1–40.
36 Aileen Connor and Rachel Clarke, 'At the Centre of the Web: Later Eighteenth and Nineteenth-Century Ceramics from Huntingdon Town Centre in an International Context', in Alasdair Brooks (ed.), *The Importance of British Material Culture to Historical Archaeologies of the Nineteenth Century* (Nebraska: University of Nebraska Press, 2015), p. 29.
37 See, for example, the memoir from a vagrant's perspective. William Davies and Bernard Shaw, *The Autobiography of a Supertramp* (reprinted online version by Helene de Minkand, Project Gutenberg, 2016). https://www.gutenberg.org/ebooks/51425 (accessed 28 January 2025).

Further reading

Althammer, Beate. 'Roaming Men, Sedentary Women? The Gendering of Vagrancy Offenses in Nineteenth-Century Europe'. *Journal of Social History*, 51:4 (2018): pp. 736–59.
Carter, Paul, Jeff James and Steve King. 'Punishing Paupers? Control, Discipline and Mental Health in the Southwell Workhouse (1836–71)'. *Rural History*, 30:2 (2019): pp. 161–80.
Green, David R. *Pauper Capital: London and the Poor Law, 1790–1870* (Farnham: Ashgate, 2010).
Hitchcock, David J., and Julia McClure (eds), *The Routledge History of Poverty, c. 1450–1800* (London: Routledge, 2021).
McEwan, Joanne, and Pamela Sharpe (eds). *Accommodating Poverty: The Housing and Living Arrangements of the English Poor, c. 1600–1850* (Basingstoke: Palgrave Macmillan, 2011).
Scott, James C. *Domination and the Arts of Resistance: Hidden Transcripts* (New Haven: Yale University Press, 1990).
Snell, K. D. M. *Parish and Belonging: Community, Identity and Welfare in England and Wales, 1700–1950* (Cambridge: Cambridge University Press, 2009).
Vorspan, Rachel. 'Vagrancy and the New Poor Law in Late-Victorian and Edwardian England'. *English Historical Review*, 92:362 (1977): pp. 59–81.

PART VIII
OBJECTS OF INJURY AND DEATH

CHAPTER 21
'OUGHT I NOT TO HAVE BEEN GRATEFUL?': WOODEN LEGS AS MILITARY CHARITY, 1800–1850s
Caroline Louise Nielsen

Introduction

In 1815, Thomas Jackson experienced what he perceived to be one of the most humiliating moments in his life. As part of his discharge from the British Army, Jackson was gifted a wooden 'peg leg'. His account, written over thirty years later, leaves no ambiguity about his feelings towards his new state-funded 'leg':

> Never shall I forget my unceremonious installation into this novel piece of furniture; this curiously wrought, though ill-shaped, piece of timber – this 'National Testimonial' – this trophy of war … When fitted on, strapped at the knee and girt at the waist to painful annoyance, I looked down in sullen silence at the hated appendage, with about the same kind of satisfaction which a dog does when he gets a tin-kettle tied to his tail.[1]

He went on to state, 'this new appendage … was to be free of cost – without money – without price; a free, gratuitous, national gift. Ought I not to have been very grateful? Somehow or other, at that time, I was not grateful.'[2]

A sergeant in the prestigious Coldstream Guards, Jackson was injured in March 1814 while campaigning in the Netherlands. A bullet shattered his lower leg during the bloody siege of Bergen-op-Zoom, a battle which claimed around a third of the British attacking force. His leg was amputated while he was a prisoner of war.[3] He was soon repatriated and spent eighteen months recovering in British army hospitals and barracks. This was when he was given the object which he felt came to define him: his wooden leg.

To the then thirty-year-old Jackson, this mass-produced military object was not only a mark of 'personal deformity, from which the eye of the proud recoils in scorn', but it made him 'the coarse joke of the vulgar; and the sport of impudent children'. He thought he had become a 'useless' man and therefore an emotional and economic drain on his wife – a view shared by his father-in-law.[4] Jackson thought he would only ever be seen, and indeed see himself, in the 'humiliating condition of a cripple'. After all of the horror

Objects of Poverty

of his military service and operation, he was now forced to wear what he viewed to be an inescapable 'object of poverty'.

What follows is an interconnected history of two objects: Jackson's now-destroyed 'national testimonial' wooden peg-leg and the memoir reputedly sold to support him in his old age decades later. Jackson's mobility and assistive aids, once so key to his sense of personal independence and manliness, now only exist for us through his memoir, written around thirty-four years after his initial injury.

Poverty, disability and memoir

Disability is a relational identity that is tied intrinsically to material culture. The social model of disability affirms that it is not physical or intellectual impairment or physiological difference that disables a person but wider society's emotional, cultural, economic and material responses to their condition(s) or appearance. Disability scholars like Katherine Ott have demonstrated responses to disability – and objects associated with it – to be dynamic and dependent on the immediate context of the individual and the communities to which they belong; one's relationship with the object becomes a measure of disablement.[5] A person's age, gender, race, ethnicity and communication and sensory skills interact with a myriad of other societal factors to determine the extent to which someone experiences disability due to physical or mental health condition(s) in their historical context.[6]

Disability as a concept was understood at the time of Jackson as a sustained inability to figuratively or literally 'earn one's bread' and to perform the expected social roles according to age, gender and social status through loss of bodily or mental function.[7] Individuals of lower social status, like Jackson, did not face the same overt pressure to disguise physical or sensory impairment(s) as their elite contemporaries. Scholars of eighteenth-century disabled people and their families have suggested that those of higher social status could be more societally disabled by their physical impairments than their lower-class peers. Faced with cultural ideals that linked bodily integrity and beauty to fertility and the need to maintain a dynastic line of inheritance, there was considerable pressure on both elite men and women to disguise any physical, sensory or communication impairment. It could affect their desirability in the marriage market, their ability to become parents and to maintain social networks and business interests.[8] The poor did not usually have much choice and, indeed, may have had more incentive to disclose poor health.[9] Extensive medical treatment and periods of hidden convalescence were not an economic option for men like Jackson. Injury and illness were frequent visitors to all households, especially the poorest. Jackson experienced this multiple times in the latter part of his life. Cholera left him in such a state of debility in 1832 that it was six months before he could go out in public and about a year before he fully recovered.[10] Although he went on to be prosperous in his forties and early fifties working as a teacher and in a small workshop, any period of illness left him 'suffering in anxiety' about his finances.[11] When a lung disease forced him to retire in 1845, he was left with 'visionary thoughts such as poverty, misery and death, with a thousand other illusive thoughts calculated to still depress the drooping spirit'.[12]

Sustained periods of poor health pushed many in already precarious situations to desperation. Public questioning of those unable to work due to illness was institutionalised within the English poor laws. Anyone who could not give a good account of themselves to officials was liable to be denied welfare and could be forcibly removed from an area.[13] Vagrant or begging ex-soldiers were expected to prove their claimed medical histories both visually and verbally, frequently with the public display of scar tissue and accompanied by a verifiable history of their campaigns.[14] Jackson and other military pensioners had an additional means of legitimating their disablement to contemporaries: the state-issued wooden peg leg. Jackson's 'Chelsea timber toe' visually confirmed the legitimacy of his injury to his immediate peers.

Jackson's memoir as an object should be viewed within this societal expectation that people should prove their status as fitting 'objects of charity', a term widely used for those in receipt of alms. The publication of Jackson's memoir was itself an act of charity. The exact publication history of the book is difficult to determine, but we know that Jackson's forced retirement led him to write his memoir in 1846 while 'under the pressure of much nervous and bodily debility'.[15] He claimed all he wished to do was 'to leave a record of my history to my children and their descendants, as a remembrance of their ancestry, at least as far back as my day'.[16] When the memoir was published, it became an additional signifier of Jackson's honesty and disablement. Those who viewed begging ex-soldiers in the street had to rely on their own knowledge of a person or a specific military campaign to verify the truth of their claims about their injury and honesty. The gentleman who sponsored the printing of Jackson's memoirs effectively did this for his readers, endorsing both his military life and civilian one and the catastrophic nature of his injuries through both the presence of military men and local notables.[17] It is unclear how far Jackson himself financially profited from his memoir. Some soldier-authors used their memoirs as income streams, selling copies themselves on the streets or through subscribers or churches, a practice aided by the evangelical nature of many of the accounts.[18] Most military authors gave little indication in their texts of publication processes, possibly as it was seen as unseemly to do so, with most focusing on their wish to preserve their family legacy and connection with the defining conflict of the time.[19]

Jackson's 'Chelsea slow-time traveller'

Reading Jackson's narrative of his long convalescence forces sustained engagement with someone whose life experiences and finances were entirely dependent on his ability to manage his health through objects. He used multiple assistive objects to simultaneously manage and support his remaining limbs and wounds and to adapt to his changed body shape. Jackson's aim was the same as the surgeons and prosthetic makers of the time: to be able to walk unaided by another person while keeping the weakened tissues of his leg supported and medically stable. Some bulky items he explicitly mentioned to his readers,

Objects of Poverty

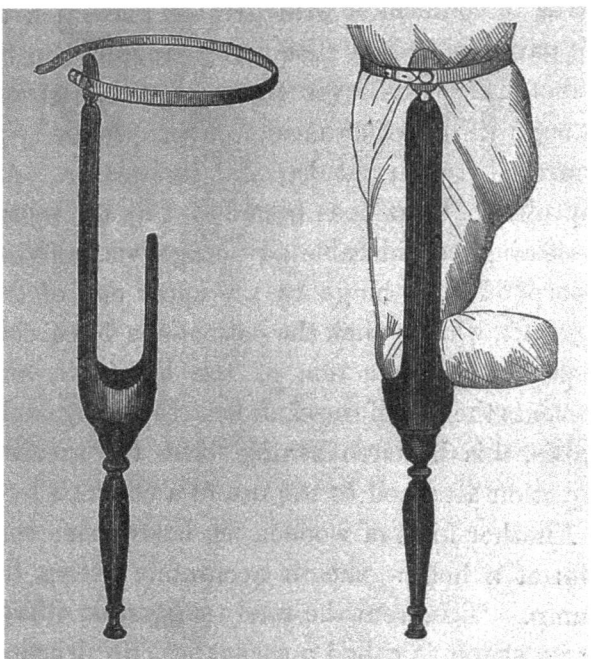

Figure 21.1 Henry Heather Bigg. Simple wooden leg, 1855. Source: Wellcome Collection. Attribution 4.0 International (CC BY 4.0).

such as his 'knee-crutch' or wooden 'peg-leg'; others as equally important in the daily lives of amputees like Jackson went unmentioned.

The medical nomenclature for Jackson's wooden leg was a 'box-leg', 'bucket' or 'knee-crutch' leg.[20] This was the main form of mobility aid for amputees of lower social status. The ubiquity of these items among veterans like Jackson led to them being nicknamed 'government appliances'.[21] These had three core components: the pin, the tread and the bucket or box. A rounded 'bucket' or box shape was attached to a wooden round dowl (the 'pin') with a flattened foot piece (the 'tread'). Bucket or box-type legs were used by those whose tibia had been removed entirely at or above the knee joint. They had to be adapted to accommodate the shape of the person's remaining limb and knee joint. Socket-legs were a variant of the bucket leg designed for those who had lost their foot and ankle alone but retained most of their tibia and knee joint. The rounded part for the remaining tibia was smaller. The remaining limb was fitted into the bucket or socket shape and fixed with leather straps or ties. Metal spinal or waist supports were sometimes added to support the 'shape and carriage' of users with shorter or more unstable femoral stumps, who were at more risk of falling over.[22] The wooden elements were usually made of hardwood timber.[23] Lighter woods like cork were sometimes used for the pin, giving the object an additional moniker of 'Cork legs', a name which sometimes led to the misconception that they were manufactured in Ireland.[24]. The standard 'government appliance' leg was planed smooth, but other images suggest that

Wooden Legs as Military Charity

Figure 21.2 I. Cruikshank, An old sailor with wooden leg and a man with no arms drinking in a tavern, 1791. Source: Wellcome Collection, 26889i, Public Domain Mark.

shaping was sometimes added to suit the wearers' needs, tastes and pocket. In the words of artificial limb entrepreneur and surgeon Robert Heather Bigg, these basic peg-legs 'answer their purpose excellently, for though no attempt is made to replace the lost parts, still use and function [i.e. balance and basic mobility] are fairly well restored'.[25]

Utility determined form. These mass-produced items were focused on their economy, strength and durability rather than appearance. Bigg and the military may have preferred the economy of the basic design, but users were not convinced, as evidenced by Jackson's multiple nicknames for the item. Jackson never used the common names 'cork-leg' or 'appliance' in his memoir, instead preferring terms that described its effects on his life.[26] He'd been 'logged by the leg for life to an ugly, odious piece of timber'; he wore a 'timber toe', a 'Chelsea slow time traveller'. It caused him to 'move forever in slow time'.[27] Jackson felt his slow movements adversely affected his ability to fulfil his role as provider for his family and care for his children. When his first wife died, he experienced 'great trouble, more so than otherwise, owing to the loss of my limb, in doing a mother's part for two little children … Worse of all, I had no time but in the night to nurse them in their little illnesses'.[28] He complained that as he could not do the same level of work as other men due to being 'logged', forcing him to work extra hours at night.[29]

Irrespective of type, external clothing was necessary for many amputees to wear wooden legs. Images of wooden leg and knee-crutch wearers of the time highlight that

293

the supporting straps were worn on the outside of breeches or trousers, with the ties and buckles clearly visible (Figures 21.1 and 21.2). Knee-breeches were sometimes drawn in close to the bottom of the bucket or socket to help protect the remaining leg from the dirt of the road. The extra layers of cloth offered additional protection from uncomfortable rubbing straps and wood. Jackson described the process of putting on his wooden leg for the first time as being 'girted' at the knee and waist.[30] This early modern phrase meant to have something heavy added or tied to one's everyday clothing or to tie the clothes themselves around the lower torso in actual or ceremonial preparation for strenuous movement or violence.[31] Outer clothing and the straps made these objects easier to wear for prolonged periods and prevented them from slipping off and causing the wearer to fall.

Walking with a wooden leg came at a considerable physical cost. Just resting on a wooden leg caused muscle strain, and lack of balance caused users to unintentionally thrust their hip joints forward when standing.[32] The straps and wooden sections of the leg further altered the stance and gait of the wearer, forcing uneven weight distribution onto their remaining joints. Users adopted an exaggerated hip rotation when they walked with increased side movements; the pin had to first be lifted off the ground, and the hip then rotated to 'swing' it round in an outward arc towards the front of the body.[33] The pin caught on the ground if the limb was not raised high enough or the outward arc was not completed, causing the wearer to fall.[34] The tread and pin could not replicate the stabilising effect of the heel or foot. This, in effect, meant forcing their entire body weight suddenly onto the end of their operative stump. This method of walking became known as 'stumping', partly due to the pressure placed on the stump but also due to the noise the pin made on the ground. While all wooden leg users were potentially 'stumped', this movement particularly became associated with ex-soldiers and sailors. Artificial limb designer Bigg believed that all military and naval amputee pensioners 'stumped' rather than walked, losing most of 'their locomotion or handiness' in the process.[35] It was an inevitable product of the nature of their 'national gift', the wooden leg.

Unusually for a man of his social class, Jackson owned both a prosthetic limb and a wooden leg. While the wooden leg served only as a balancing and mobility aid, a prosthetic or artificial limb had the additional function of disguising the missing body part. Jackson's wooden leg was designed to work with outer clothing, while his artificial leg was designed to be worn underneath. Breeches, trousers and undergarments would be rolled down over it. A prosthetic or artificial limb, therefore, had the key function of limiting the amount of societal disablement the user experienced.

Practicality was often an afterthought to appearance in prosthetic and artificial limb design. The most widely used commercial limb of the time was James Potts' 'Anglesey leg', reputedly designed for Henry Paget, the first Marquess of Anglesey.[36] It may have replicated the shape of the leg under clothing, but it was quickly nicknamed 'the Clapper' because the foot components 'clapped' together loudly if the user moved too vigorously, spoiling the desired illusion of bodily integrity.[37] Despite this issue, the Anglesey design remained popular. Most artificial limbs were beyond the financial reach of men like Jackson; his was a gift from his former officer and a London-based Humane Society.[38] We do not know if Jackson's artificial limb was an Anglesey type, but he made his views on it clear. It may have been a 'real, handsome, well shaped, rightabout leg, yet the Chelsea timbertonian is a far better thing to get about with!'[39]

Supporting materials

Wooden legs were rarely worn alone. Most users wore them with other supports to improve their balance and lessen the risk of falling. Jackson's limited descriptions of his movements suggest that he used axillary (shoulder) crutches for balance. Axillary crutches were light wooden tapered frames with a cushion or padded bar.[40] Users propelled their body weight forward in a characteristic 'swinging' motion, resting on the padded bar in their armpit for stability. 'Swinging' became the standard phrase used to describe the exaggerated movements of crutch users, irrespective of whether the user was an amputee or not.[41] 'Swinging' came with substantial cost. The swing movement meant the user's weight was unevenly distributed in the upper torso, causing nerve and muscle damage in the arms and shoulders after long-term use, further exacerbating the effects of the gait change.[42] Other items then had to be used for 'improving the shape and carriage', including spinal 'crutch' supports, worn under a cloak or great coat.[43] Poorer people faced the additional challenge of the expense of keeping their supports padded and clean.

Crutches and box legs were given to convalescent soldier-amputees as part of their recovery and rehabilitation. The swinging motion of moving the pin backwards and forwards was thought to promote gentle exercise in the damaged limb.[44] Jackson recounted the sense of freedom he felt when he was first given crutches, mainly as it enabled him to spend more time out of the hospital with his wife and to begin work as a military clerk. His joy was short-lived. He soon found that 'even a little exertion' on his crutches caused his wound to become 'exceedingly painful and frighteningly inflamed'.[45] Subsequent infections nearly proved fatal on more than one occasion.[46] This did not put him off using them, especially once he realised he could move around faster and more comfortably 'swinging on his crutches' without the weight of his wooden leg.[47]

Jackson probably used other assistive objects which he considered too mundane or unsuitable for sustained public comment in his memoir. These may have included bandages, stockings, leather trusses and cushioned pads that enabled amputees to use their crutches and wooden leg. Military memoirs tend to give only the briefest accounts of the long months of convalescence following a traumatic operation like amputation. Amputations were not one-off interventions, with even the most straightforward amputation requiring months (if not years) of painful interventions.[48] Wounds were regularly reopened to remove infected tissue and bone fragments in a process known as debridement. Ligatures were left hanging out of wounds in the first weeks of an amputation to facilitate this. Jackson had 'excruciating' flax seeds placed into his ligatures to drain pus away.[49] Healed stumps had to be carefully prepared before a wooden leg could be worn. The stump would be strapped with bandages and then covered with a

Objects of Poverty

soft woollen sock, stocking or pad.[50] 'Plasters' were sometimes used; bandages soaked in chemicals, poultices or plaster to create a hard scab covering for an irritated wound. Straw, wool, rags or leather was then used to pad the inside of the bucket or socket element of the wooden leg directly under the stump. It was impossible to keep these clean, so users ran the constant risk of infection.

The unremarkable normality of such items is further confirmed by Jackson's choice of when to discuss these items in his memoir. He only mentioned his bandages and supports to convey the sense of emergency and horror of managing a dangerously infected wound or of surgical intervention. The description of his first debridement illustrates this approach:

> what with tearing off the bandages, which were by this time soldered together with the dried clotted blood, and after them the cross strappings of sticking plaster, which had, as it were, grown into the flesh; the opening of the wound afresh; trying of the ligaments of the arteries; cleansing and new strapping and bandages ... I always thought the cutting off was a minor suffering to the first dressing.[51]

Presumably, he felt it unnecessary to describe the role of these items any further to his readers. Such items would have been part of the daily lives of any member of their family and friends who were disabled, chronically ill or who had had the misfortune to need surgery.

Conclusion

Jackson's narrative illustrates some of the complexities of how we conceptualise the experiences of historical poverty and disability through objects. His account reminds us about the need to focus on destroyed material culture and objects long destroyed. Jackson's assistive supports, bandages and padding were part of his family's everyday life and core to his sense of identity, not always in a positive way. These items gave their owner (some) physical comfort and mobility even if they also increased his risk of infection. Jackson's crutches and wooden legs were not designed to be treasured heirloom objects or to be assessed for their aesthetic potential; they were probably destroyed when they became soiled and had outlived their usefulness.

It would be easy for us to categorise Jackson's wooden leg in terms of our own understandings of, and aspirations for, medical technologies and prosthetics; for example, to display Jackson's memoir and a box leg alongside a surviving example of a more aesthetic 'advanced' Anglesey-style artificial legs in a museum, to narrate an uncomplicated story of ever-improving prosthetics design over time. The public material histories of amputees like Jackson more generally tend to be displayed through the prosthetic technology histories. This is, in part, due to past historiographical trends in the history of amputees and their assistive devices. Prosthetics history is one of the most prominent areas of disability history scholarship, with research covering areas as diverse as medical manufacturing and advertising, veterans' experiences, disability aesthetics and the portrayal of disabled characters.[52] The market for more innovative artificial limbs boomed in the nineteenth century with parallel markets for disguising cosmetics, tailored fashions, wigs and epitheses (facial prosthetics). The importance of these industries in shaping peoples' ideas about what constituted a desirable and healthy or normative body shape and how they could achieve this cannot be understated.[53] This historiographical prominence has transferred into the public history and heritage education setting, with prosthetics being one of the most iconic or emblematic items used to display historic disabled peoples' everyday lives, excluding the more basic or mundane forms of balancing aid or supports.[54] This is starting to change, as evidenced by the ethical discussions initiated by the UK Science Museum Group, Curating for Change and the Museums Strategic Disability Network, which pioneer user-led narratives around assistive devices and bodily difference over more traditional manufacturer-led or solely medicalised histories of disability.[55]

Jackson did not describe his wooden leg, his crutches and his heavier prosthetic in terms of medical innovation, preferring to focus on moments where it had a substantial effect on his domestic life and his ability to financially provide for his family. Jackson's narrative reminds us that we should consider all objects as having multiple layered histories. It presents both the most shocking and the more mundane experiences of living with 'timber toe', from his feelings about learning to walk on crutches and then the wooden leg through to his community's view of his injury and his family's personal nicknames for his wooden leg. His memoir tells us about his experience of stumping and his contemporaries' often cruel responses to it. Let us hope there are many more as-yet-undiscovered narratives in archives and libraries like Jackson's.

Notes

1   Thomas Jackson, *Narrative of the Eventful Life of Thomas Jackson, Late Sergeant of the Coldstream Guards Detailing His Military Career During the Twelve Years of the French War... Written by Himself* (Birmingham: Josiah Allen and Son, 1847), p. 119. Due to rarity of the original, pagination is given for Eamonn O'Keeffe (ed.), *Narrative of the Eventful Life of Thomas Jackson, Militiaman and Coldstream Sergeant, 1803–15* (Solihull: Helion, 2018).
2   O'Keefe, *Narrative*, p. 100.
3   Ibid., pp. 61–80.
4   Ibid., pp. 93, 98.
5   Katherine Ott, 'The Sum of Its Parts: An Introduction to Modern Histories of Prosthetics', in Katherine Ott, David Serlin and Stephen Mihm (eds), *Artificial Parts, Practical Lives: Modern Histories of Prosthetics* (New York: New York University Press, 2002), pp. 1–42; Katherine Ott, 'Disability Things: Material Culture and American Disability History, 1770–2010', in Susan Burch and Michael Rembis (eds), *Disability Histories* (Urbana: University of Illinois Press, 2014), pp. 119–35; Katherine Ott, 'Material Culture, Technology and the Body in Disability History', in Michael Rembis, Catherine Kudlick and Kim Nielsen (eds), *The Oxford Handbook of Disability History* (Oxford: Oxford University Press, 2018), pp. 125–40.

6   Rembis, Kudlick and Nielsen, 'Introduction', in Rembis, Kudlick and Nielsen, *Oxford Handbook of Disability History*, pp. 1–18; David Turner, *Disability in Eighteenth-Century England* (London: Routledge, 2012), pp. 1–4.
7   Turner, *Disability*, pp. 127–30; Iain Hutchison, 'Disability in Nineteenth-Century Scotland: The Case of Marion Brown', *University of Sussex Journal of Contemporary History*, 5 (2002): pp. 1–2.
8   Elizabeth Foyster, 'Parenting the Disabled Child in Early Modern England', research paper (University of Northampton, 2022). On marriage, see: Hannah Barker, 'Soul, Purse and Family: Middling and Lower-Class Masculinity in Eighteenth-Century Manchester', *Social History*, 33:1 (2008): pp. 12–35; Helen Deutsch and Felicity Nussbaum, 'Introduction', in Helen Deutsch and Felicity A. Nussbaum (eds), *Defects: Engendering the Modern Body* (Ann Arbor: University of Michigan Press, 2000), pp. 1–28; Stephen Mihm, '"A Limb Which Shall be Presentable in Polite Society": Prosthetic Technologies in the Nineteenth Century', in Ott, Serlin and Mihm, *Artificial Parts, Practical Lives*, pp. 287–90.
9   O'Keefe, *Narrative*, pp. 113, 114–15, 120.
10 Ibid., pp. 113–16.
11 Ibid., p. 120.
12 Ibid., pp. 120–1.
13 Tim Hitchcock, *Down and Old in Eighteenth-Century London* (London: Hambleton Continuum, 2007), pp. 125–80.
14 Ibid., pp. 108–17; Turner, *Disability*, p. 24.
15 O'Keefe, *Narrative*, p. 122.
16 Ibid. This claim can be contested. Matilda Greig, *Dead Men Telling Tales: Napoleonic War Veterans and the Military Memoir Industry, 1808–1914* (Oxford: Oxford University Press, 2021), pp. 118–41, 166–9.
17 Ibid., pp. xii, xiv; Greig, *Dead*, p. 38.
18 Neil Ramsay, *The Military Memoir and Romantic Literary Culture, 1780–1835* (London: Ashgate, 2011), pp. 41–50.
19 Greig, *Dead*, pp. 118–87.
20 Turner, *Disability*, p. 50; Turner, 'Disability and Prosthetics in Eighteenth and Early Nineteenth-Century England', in Mark Jackson (ed.), *The Routledge History of Disease* (London: Routledge, 2016), pp. 311–12.
21 Vanessa Warne, 'Artificial Leg', *Victorian Review*, 34:1 (2008): p. 31; Charlotte Waller-Cotterhill, 'Experimental Reconstruction of a Nineteenth-Century Lower Limb Prosthetic Peg Leg – the Box Leg', *EXARC*, 3 (2018), n.p.; Henry Heather Bigg, *On Artificial Limbs: Their Construction and Application* (London: John Churchill, 1855), p. 27.
22 A. F. Crell, *The Family Oracle of Health; Economy, Medicine and Good Living adapted to All Ranks of Society from the Palace to the Cottage*, vol. 3 (London: J. Bulcock, 1826), pp. 272, 278; Bigg, *On Artificial Limbs*, p. 106.
23 Waller-Cotterhill, 'Experimental'.
24 Warne, 'Artificial Leg', p. 29.
25 Bigg, *Artificial Limbs and the Amputations Which Afford the Most Appropriate Stumps in Civil and Military Surgery* (London: J. Adlard, 1885), p. 104.
26 O'Keefe, *Narrative*, p. 100.
27 Ibid., p. 117.
28 Ibid., p. 110.
29 Ibid., pp. 117–18.
30 Ibid., p. 100.
31 Edward Ward, *Nuptial Dialogues and Debates* (London: 1710), p. 353; Johann König, *A Royal Compleat Grammar* (London: 1715), p. 89.

32 Charlotte Waller-Cotterill, 'An Experimental Examination into the History and Perception of Two Nineteenth-Century Military Lower-Limb Prostheses with a Biomechanical Analysis of Their Functionality and Long-Term Effects', PhD thesis (University of Sheffield, 2021), pp. 31–3, 54.
33 Ibid.
34 Bigg, *On Artificial Limbs*, p. 22; Waller-Cotterill, 'An Experimental', pp. 31–3, 54.
35 Bigg, *Artificial Limbs*, pp. 102–3.
36 Warne, 'Artificial', pp. 29–32.
37 Alan Thurston, 'Paré and Prosthetics: The Early History of Artificial Limbs', *ANZ Journal of Surgery*, 77:12 (2007): p. 1118.
38 O'Keefe, *Narrative*, p. 99.
39 Ibid., pp. 99, 101.
40 Bigg, *Artificial Limbs*, p. 272.
41 William Spavens, *The Seaman's Narrative* (Louth: Sheardown, 1796), p. 98; O'Keefe, *Narrative*, p. 94; Thomas Dun, *A Compleat History of the Lives and Robberies of the Most Notorious Highway-Men, Foot-Pads, Shop-Lifts and Cheats*, vol. 1 (London: Sam Briscoe, 1719), p. 18; Joseph Amesbury, *Observations on the Nature and Treatment of Fractures of the Upper Third of the Thigh-Bone and of Fractures of Long Standing* (London: T. & G. Underwood, 1829), p. 48.
42 Phillippe Hernigou, 'Crutch Art Painting in the Middle Ages and Orthopaedic Heritage Parts I and 2', *International Orthopaedics*, 38 (2014): pp. 1329–35, 1535–42.
43 Crell, *Family*, pp. 272, 278.
44 Amesbury, *Observations*, pp. 46, 48, 320.
45 O'Keefe, *Narrative*, pp. 93–5.
46 Ibid., pp. 93–6.
47 Ibid., pp. 82–6, 93–9, 117.
48 Turner, 'Prosthetics', p. 307.
49 O'Keefe, *Narrative*, pp. 82–6, 93–9.
50 Waller-Cotterill, 'An Experimental', pp. 79–80, 251.
51 O'Keefe, *Narrative*, p. 83.
52 See Ott, Serlin and Mihm, *Artificial Parts*.
53 Sarah Chaney, *Am I Normal? The 200-Year Old Search for Normal People and Why They Don't Exist* (London: Wellcome, 2022), pp. 42–80; Warne, 'Artificial', pp. 29–33; Mihm, 'A Limb', pp. 287–90.
54 Ott, 'Sum', pp. 7–16.
55 Sophie Goggins, Tacye Phillipson and Samuel J. M. M. Alberti, 'Prosthetic Limbs on Display: From Maker to User', *Science Museum Journal* (Autumn 2017), n.p.; for archival responses, see Penny Richards and Susan Burch, 'Documents, Ethics and the Disability Historian', in Rembis, Kudlick and Nielsen, *Oxford Handbook of Disability History*, pp. 161–74; Sarah White, 'Crippling the Archives: Negotiating Notions of Disability in Appraisal and Arrangement and Description', *American Archivist*, 75:1 (2012): pp. 109–24; Curating for Change.org. https://curatingforchange.org/collections (accessed 01 March 2024); Kudlick, 'Social History of Medicine and Disability History', in Rembis, Kudlick and Nielsen, *Oxford Handbook of Disability History*, pp. 105–24.

Further reading

Burch, Susan, and Michael Rembis. 'Re-Membering the Past: Reflections on Disability Histories', in Susan Burch and Michael Rembis (eds), *Disability Histories* (Urbana: University of Illinois Press, 2014), pp. 1–13.

Goggins, Sophie, Tacye Phillipson and Samuel Alberti. 'Prosthetic Limbs on Display: From Maker to User'. *Science Museum Journal* (Autumn 2017): n.p.

Mihm, Stephen. '"A Limb Which Shall Be Presentable in Polite Society": Prosthetic Technologies in the Nineteenth Century', in Katherine Ott, David Serlin and Stephen Mihm (eds), *Artificial Parts, Practical Lives: Modern Histories of Prosthetics* (New York: New York University Press, 2002), pp. 282–99.

O'Keefe, Eamonn. *Narrative of the Eventful Life of Thomas Jackson, Militiaman and Coldstream Sergeant, 1803-15* (Solihull: Helion, 2018).

Ott, Katherine. 'The Sum of Its Parts: An Introduction to Modern Histories of Prosthetics', in Katherine Ott, David Serlin and Stephen Mihm (eds), *Artificial Parts, Practical Lives: Modern Histories of Prosthetics* (New York: New York University Press, 2002), pp. 1–42.

Rembis, Michael, Catherine Kudlick and Kim Nielsen (eds). *The Oxford Handbook of Disability History* (Oxford: Oxford University Press, 2018).

Turner, David. *Disability in Eighteenth-Century England* (London: Routledge, 2012).

Turner, David. 'Disability and Prosthetics in Eighteenth- and Early Nineteenth-Century England', in Mark Jackson (ed.), *Routledge History of Disease* (London: Routledge, 2016), pp. 301–19.

Warne, Vanessa. 'Artificial Leg', *Victorian Review*, 34:1 (2008): pp. 29–33.

CHAPTER 22
MEDICAL OBJECTS: THE SICK POOR AND THEIR RELIEF IN THE LONG NINETEENTH CENTURY
Steven King and Peter Jones

Introduction

Across the nineteenth century, sickness (widely defined so as to include physical, sensory and mental conditions and impairments) was arguably *the* key experience that drove people into dependence. Certainly, relief of sickness and infirmity was a major preoccupation for officials under the old poor law welfare system and their single biggest category of spending.[1] The legislation for the new poor law in 1834 had little to say about sickness and medicine, but the newly formed poor law unions soon discovered that both their workhouses and outdoor relief lists filled up with the sick, infirm, mentally-ill and dying poor. Officials were thus in constant catch-up mode, having to spend both on medical relief and episodic changes to the fabric of workhouses in terms of new wards, staff and infirmaries.[2] In turn, the historiography on health and medicine for the poor is growing all the time. We now have a much better understanding of issues such as the evolution of annual contracts to treat paupers under the old poor law and professionalisation of nursing under the new poor law; the fight for control of medicine by new poor law medical officers; and the conditions that led to mad poor being transferred to asylums.[3]

Stepping aside from these 'big' issues, however, we know surprisingly little about the everyday treatments applied to the sick poor outside of the medical scandals that have become a preferred lens for most nineteenth-century studies. In part, this reflects the fact that much 'medical relief' under both old and new poor laws was given outside of institutions like workhouses or hospitals in the form of extra cash for general support or to allow people to buy their own medical care and pay off bills they had already incurred. Such cash payments tell us little about the nature of treatments, though almost all of the historiography concurs that some were used to buy unofficial or untested (often known as 'quack') remedies and to engage informal practitioners. There were also problems of process, with doctoring contracts under the old poor law and medical officers' contracts under the new, often specifying that medical men had to provide everyday medicines and treatments from the fees and salaries paid to them.[4] Even so, in the context both of workhouse medicine and outdoor relief, treating the sick was inextricably tied up with the acquisition, use or renewal of devices and other physical objects. These run on a spectrum from the ephemeral (bandages or the paper wrappings of medicines and

Objects of Poverty

poultices) to heavy-duty items such as false limbs which are the subject of other entries in this volume. Pills, lotions, potions and salves were also part of this canvas. Indeed, we can be relatively certain that the number and range of these items expanded exponentially in the nineteenth century, as the range of what could be cured or ameliorated expanded and as expectations of medical interventions grew. Yet it is rare in the literature to focus on what surviving material items can tell us about how the poor experienced various forms of 'sickness', the nature and meaning of welfare, the obligations of communities and the standard of medical care the poor got and expected. This chapter will thus investigate medical care through a detailed analysis of two objects – chosen for their everydayness on the one hand and their durability on the other.

Patent medicines

Medicines were the most requested and supplied element of medical relief next to cash. Parish collections under the old poor law sometimes carry detailed bills for pills, salves and draughts where doctors were brought in on an *ad hoc* basis rather than contracted. We know little about what these items looked like or contained, though we can be relatively sure that the medicine was ineffective.[5] Such archival material is rarer for the new poor law, though the propensity of the poor to visit chemists or apothecaries (and sometimes to die from the medicines taken) provides a window into everyday medical experiences. After all, the sick poor were generally only under the care and confinement of the poor law authorities at certain points in their life cycle. At other times they would have been consumers of quack remedies, patent medicines, herbals and home-made treatments. In one sense, then, the poor formed expectations both of what sorts of treatments should be provided by medical men under the poor law, as well as the quality of those treatments.

Figure 22.1 provides a window into those expectations. From one angle, it represents something quite ordinary. Owbridge's Lung Tonic was a well-known and widely circulated patent remedy claiming to cure everything from tuberculosis to sore throats. The ingredients were a closely guarded secret, but it is reputed to have contained a high concentration of opium, which may go some way towards explaining its commercial success.[6] Such remedies were a staple of the informal and quack medical marketplace of the nineteenth century as postal services and advertising media both became more sophisticated. Placed in a wider context, however, it is extremely revealing. The bottle was dug up by Steven King's father when he was a contractor involved in the conversion of the Cerne Abbas workhouse (Dorset) into a care home for the aged. Discovered with other ephemera – clay pipes, pitchers, bricks, oilcloths, scraps of cloth, clinker, animal bones and manacles – this bottle had clearly been discarded into the workhouse refuse heap rather than being reused.[7] In this instance, the Cerne Abbas context is important. Located between Dorchester and Sherborne, it remained well into the nineteenth century a rural backwater dominated by a single family and, of course, physically dominated by the Cerne Abbas Giant cut into the hillside.[8] The village is also the location of St Augustine's Well (originally The Silver Well), a healing spring that remains well-used to this day.

Figure 22.1 Empty bottle found at Cerne Abbas workhouse, Dorset. Source: Steven King. Authors' personal collection.

Given this backdrop, we might ask three questions which are important to an understanding of the treatment and expectations of the sick poor. First, how did a bottle of Owbridge's mixture get to this relatively remote rural poor law union? The obvious answer is that it was brought or sent by the union medical officer from Sherborne or Dorchester.[9] Such a conclusion would reinforce a common complaint on the part of both the poor and ratepayers that medical officers were appointed who lived at a considerable distance from the workhouses they were meant to serve and, as a result, might neglect their duty.[10] On the other hand, the very presence of the bottle might be read as indicating that Cerne Abbas and its poor were tied firmly into the expanding urban medical marketplace of the nineteenth century.[11] A second question – why was Owbridge's mixture prescribed? – points in the same direction. Thus, it would have been possible for the medical officer to order that his patients should receive extra alcohol or food, both of which would have been supplied by the workhouse at no expense to himself. Similarly, he could have simply made up his own mixture or other remedy and supplied it at little cost.[12] Certainly, many workhouse medical scandals referred in passing to unnamed draughts and mixtures being made up for the indoor and outdoor poor by such medical officers.[13] However, an alternative reading might be that Owbridge's was prescribed because the poor population knew it and trusted it, and had even purchased it themselves before they went into the workhouse.[14]

One final question is, why the bottle was discarded rather than being repetitively reused until it broke? Owbridge's Lung Tonic was in the medical market from 1874, and this particular bottle appears to be of nineteenth-century origin, given the colour of the glass and the style and labelling of the bottle changed radically from the early 1900s. Perhaps the object ended up in a refuse pit by accident. Alternatively, its destination may speak to the idea that medicine bottles in the workhouse were seen as disposable even at a time when it would have been normal to reuse and repurpose all sorts of glassware in the domestic environment.[15] The implications of this reading are potentially important: if medical officers were expected to bring or send new bottles in each case, it would not have taken long for this practice to become normative. This shift is likely to have become a point of protest on the part of paupers, and of contention with guardians who wanted value for money. More than this, both the taking of the medicine and the disposal of the vessel would mark out paupers as medical consumers, as much as or even more than other poor people in the communities from which they were drawn.

As so often in consideration of material culture, these ideas are speculative. Nonetheless, it is easy to see how the survival of this object takes us well beyond the interpretations afforded by a paper bill, advertisement or witness statements in a workhouse dispute. King has argued that the sick poor acquired de facto rights to medical care under the old poor law.[16] A single bottle from an out-of-the-way workhouse in the later nineteenth century might suggest that those rights continued post-1834 and that the dependent poor were firmly anchored into a medical marketplace from which many accounts have assumed they were absent.

The truss

Similar perspectives might be garnered from a very different medical artefact. Before the era of gauze-based surgery for hernias, people usually had to just live with 'ruptures'.[17] The truss, in effect a belt with a pad that forces the hernia back in or at least holds, supports and contains it, was the core piece of medical technology in this process of 'just living'. Paupers under both the old and new poor laws requested new and replacement trusses (and cash to buy such things themselves) or repairs to worn-out items with considerable regularity. These items were not cheap. In May 1747, the overseer of East Dereham (Norfolk) paid Mr Donne of Norwich 10s 6d for a truss. By 1803, a 'new truss for Briton' cost exactly the same amount, but the overseers also paid an additional 3s for an unnamed maker to repair an existing truss so that Briton had a spare. Trusses for children cost less, with 8s for a child named Cocker in 1818.[18] Even where trusses were more modestly costed, they were often at the centre of a wider web of very expensive welfare. For instance, the Norfolk parish of Wighton purchased a truss for Richard Bishop in 1797, but in that year alone, also paid him £3 10s 6d in wider medical relief.[19] The need for this web of relief is demonstrated in a letter from Richard Carter of Chelsea to the overseers of Sonning (Berkshire) in January 1822, where he notes that he is totally unable to work due to 'a severe rupture wich is a great trial to me' and in an 1872 entry to the diary of the Reverend John Coker Egerton of Burwash (Sussex) wherein he recounts the story of 'poor Flemming' who was dying because 'He has a bad rupture & has not been wearing a truss'.[20]

In one sense, these paper-based records provide rich testimony to the idea that old and new poor law officials expected to spend significant sums on ameliorating and curing disability. Yet they are also remarkably flat and give little detail of the complexities of getting, fitting and wearing a truss. This is an important gap given that (in the absence of effective surgery until the 1880s) it was a device to be worn for life. Early trusses were generally crude affairs, with one or two pads designed to contain the rupture held in place via ropes, and a belt around the waist and potentially around the groin area. By the nineteenth century, truss technology was becoming more sophisticated, including pioneering sprung and steel trusses and movable padding.[21] In practice, however, designs and materials had a distinctly local feel; each place or area had its makers, and only in counties such as Norfolk or for places close to London do we get a sense from poor law records that regional centres were in existence even by the 1840s.

Trusses could be constructed from a range of materials, but the most common were leather and some form of quilting (probably soft leather or wool) on the pressure pad or pads. These concealed a hard object (wood or metal) or later a spring which applied pressure directly on the hernia itself.[22] Such trusses were neither easy to fit, nor to keep in place. The need to fix the truss directly on the hernia, beneath a patient's clothing, with restraints on other parts of the body would clearly have led to chaffing, sores and infections elsewhere without careful adjustment. Dr John Wood made exactly this point in his clinical lectures as late as 1877.[23] When officials invested in a truss, they were thus committing to fitting, alteration and renewal, such that dealing with ruptures moves from being an event in paper-based records to a process once we look in depth at the material culture. Hence, while early trusses could be let out or drawn in simply by altering the length of the ropes on either side and then knotting or looping them (possibly with the use of another belt or cloth support), the one in Figure 22.2 has a steel

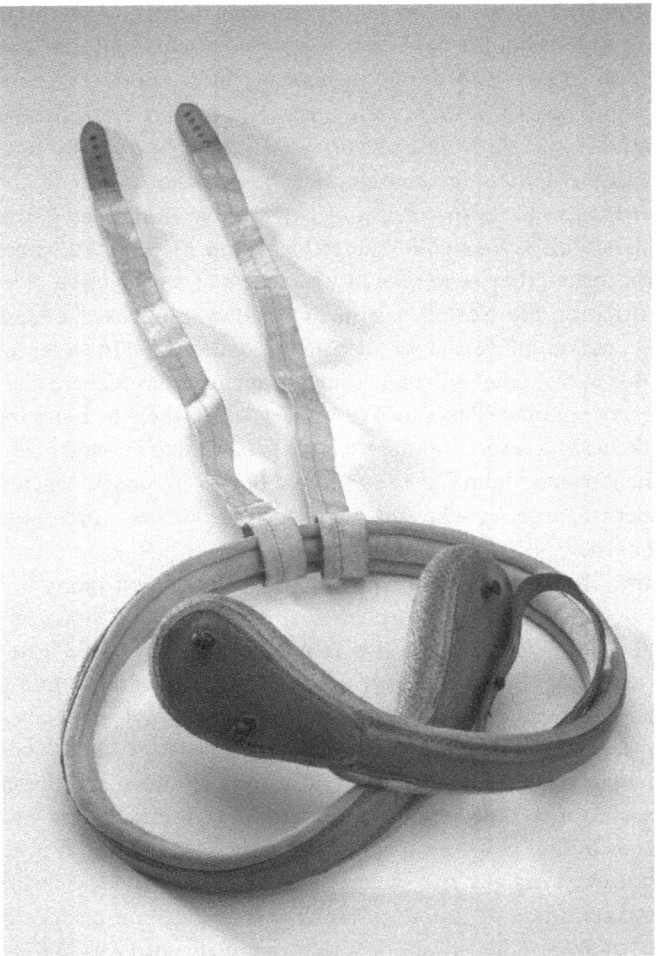

Figure 22.2 Allen and Hanbury Double Truss. Source: Science Museum London, object A635968. Creative Commons Attribution 4.0 Licence.

wire core with fabric surround and would have been made to fit the wearer at least in broad terms.[24] By fusing together archival and material culture records, we can see this process in action. Thus, the truss in Figure 22.2 was probably much like that purchased by the Norfolk parish of Wighton on 19 March 1834. The printed bill head in the parish collection is set out in the following way:

Norwich Truss Manufactory
Bought of George Taylor
112 Pottergate Street
1834 March 19th

1 Common Improved Double Truss (38 inches) £1 5s0d
Paid same time
    Received of Mr C Powell £1 5s0d for ditto John Ladell

The maker, George Taylor, also, however, appended a written addendum to the bill:

The above I hope may suit your workman and as I conclude his Hernia is bad, I have sent two extra springs in case the main springs are not strong enough, which can be applied by sliding off the casen [casing] and letten the extra springs embrace the main one. Also to keep the truss steady, have adjust the under straps to pass under round the thigh and button on the stud in the front pad, these need not be used if the patient can do without. Any alteration shall have the best attention of
Sir, Your obt servt
G Taylor
    Should the patient after a time not be able to get on <u>well</u> with it if he could come up by a carrier for the greater part of the day, I am confident of giving him relief[25]

The implications of this letter are subtle: the overseers must have sent Taylor a detailed description both of the rupture that John Ladell was living with and also some notes regarding his waist size and build. Historiographically, we are unused to thinking of officials getting this close to the everyday lives of the poor people over whom they notionally held power. Thus, although the truss in Figure 22.2 would not have been made *for* Ladell, it would have been made for someone *like* him. The perfunctory spending details in overseers' accounts disguise this lengthy and precise concern for the medical welfare of a single pauper and an active involvement in shaping their medical care.

In some cases, however, this attention to detail and medical process went further. The overseers of Forncett St. Peter (Norfolk) were not content with off-the-peg products but rather sent their distressed paupers to the makers. In November 1777, for instance, they 'Paid Noah Nichols for carrying Wm Kerrison twice to Norwich after a truss', suggesting that the one eventually purchased for 10s 6d involved both an initial measuring and a bespoke fitting in Norwich. James Lyng received the same treatment in July 1796 even though (or perhaps because) parochial spending was spiralling rapidly upwards due to harvest failure and the Napoleonic war.[26] How long trusses might have been expected to last is unclear, but some of the records from the new poor law suggest that paupers were acutely aware of the difference between old and new items both in terms of fit and utility. James Hairs of the Wandsworth and Clapham poor law union, for instance, noted in minutes of evidence before an inquiry that

I had had an old rupture of two years standing on the right side and the pain from the [recent] fall fled at once to that part. I had had an old but very bad Truss for it before, and just before Dr. Leslie first attended me [after the recent fall] I had got a new Truss from Mr. Blaise in Piccadilly. I got that upon an order from a physician in Grosvenor Square.[27]

Objects of Poverty

It is easy to disembody the surviving material culture from its wearer, but the fusion of different sources highlights keenly how what survives was carefully calibrated to users and how much those users relied on this basic technology. This should perhaps not surprise us; the design and nature of truss technology have hardly moved on in centuries, and they remain an everyday coping item for those awaiting hernia surgery. They should be familiar to us, even if we rarely speak of them. In turn, officials knew that providing a well-fitting truss might allow the poor to extend their working lives or at least be less dependent and could even save a life and thus avoid the cost of a pauper funeral. For these reasons, requests for trusses appear almost never to have been turned down by officials under the old and new poor laws. Devices such as those captured in Figure 22.2 thus reflect the emergence of a de facto right for the poor where none existed in law.

Conclusion

Historians have sought to measure the quantity and quality of medical care available to the dependent poor in the eighteenth and nineteenth centuries. Through the lens of medical scandals, we have learned much about the sometimes-casual attitude of officials and doctors to what should have been the most deserving group of paupers.[28] This chapter has had a different starting point, seeking to investigate the everyday realities of the medical lives of paupers. Fusing together documentary and material culture evidence encourages us to see a different old and new poor law, one in which the poor had legitimate expectations of certain kinds and standards of treatment and officials (out of humanity, self-interest or precedent) restrained themselves from exercising the punitive powers available to them. The medical officer who supplied Ownston's Lung Tonic to the inmates of the Cerne Abbas workhouse could have decided not to act or to supply inferior or alternative products, thus saving himself money. He did not do so, as the surviving material culture evidence reveals strikingly. The overseers of several Norfolk parishes could have left the poor suffering with a hernia to their own devices, or purchased generic trusses leaving the poor to manage with them as best they could. Instead, they sent them to Norwich for measuring and fitting, and provided significant cash relief while their physical needs were being attended to. We do not, of course, claim that the sick poor were always treated well. On the other hand, both the surviving instances of material culture here inevitably point to the conclusion that the dependent poor were in sickness, at least, as well provisioned as those who maintained their independence in the communities from which they were drawn, and quite possibly more so.

Notes

1   Steven King, *Sickness, Medical Welfare and the English Poor 1750–1834* (Manchester: Manchester University Press, 2018).

2. Steven King, Paul Carter, Peter Jones, Natalie Carter and Carol Beardmore, *In Their Own Write: A New Poor Law History from Below* (Montreal: McGill-Queens University Press, 2022), pp. 330–60.
3. Samantha Williams, 'Practitioners' Income and Provision for the Poor: Parish Doctors in the Late Eighteenth and Early Nineteenth Centuries', *Social History of Medicine*, 18:2 (2005): pp. 159–86; Carol Helmstadter and Jane Godden, *Nursing before Nightingale, 1815–1899* (Aldershot: Ashgate, 2011); Kim Price, *Medical Negligence in Victorian Britain: The Crisis of Care under the English Poor Law 1834–1900* (London: Bloomsbury, 2015); Leonard Smith, 'Lunatic Asylum in the Workhouse: St. Peter's Hospital Bristol 1698–1861', *Medical History*, 61:2 (2017): pp. 225–45.
4. King, *Sickness, Medical Welfare*, pp. 143–51.
5. Roy Porter, *Bodies Politic: Disease, Death and Doctors in Britain, 1650–1900* (London: Reaktion, 2001).
6. Walter Owbridge's factory in Hull, which built on the success of the tonic, was sold to a subsidiary of the Dutch pharmaceutical company KZO in 1969 for £350,000. *Scottish Daily Mail*, 26 February 2013.
7. He kept it to use as a portable whisky bottle!
8. On the Cerne workhouse, see Edward Cockburn, 'The Cerne Abbas Union Workhouse, 1835–8', *Proceedings of the Dorset Natural History and Archaeological Society*, 94 (1973): pp. 89–95, and more widely on Cerne including the poor, see Mary Jones, *Cerne Abbas: The Story of a Dorset Village* (London: George, Allen & Unwin, 1951).
9. It is also possible that the bottle was brought into the workhouse by a visitor.
10. See Jeanne Brand, 'The Parish Doctor: England's Poor Law Medical Officers and Medical Reform, 1870–1900', *Bulletin of the History of Medicine*, 35:1 (1961): pp. 97–122.
11. David Helm, 'Doctors, Druggists and Patients: The End of the Medical Marketplace in Mid-Nineteenth-Century Gloucester', *Midland History*, 43:1 (2018): pp. 62–81. Trade directories for nearby towns certainly point to the presence of a network of potential sellers. See: https://specialcollections.le.ac.uk/digital/collection/p16445coll4 (accessed 04 March 2023).
12. The medical officer could have reused the bottle for this purpose, but there is no evidence of staining or chipping from multiple uses.
13. King et al., *In Their Own Write*, pp. 330–60.
14. In other building and renovation work in Cerne Abbas, Steven King's father came across five more near-perfect bottles for patent remedies at different locations, clearly indicating a culture of self-dosing and market connectedness.
15. The principle of reuse (and therefore 'recycling' in the broadest sense) was axiomatic in workhouses, although very little dedicated work has so far been published on the subject. See Peter Jones, Steven King and Karen Thompson, 'Clothing the New Poor Law Workhouse in the Nineteenth Century', *Rural History*, 32:2 (2021): pp. 127–48, on the use and reuse of workhouse clothing. For a broad discussion of recycling in history, Emily Cockayne, *Rummage: A History of the Things We Have Reused, Recycled and Refused to Let Go* (London: Profile, 2020).
16. King, *Sickness and Medical Welfare*.
17. The reference to a strangulated hernia is clear. On truss technology, see Liliane Hilaire-Perez and Christelle Rabier, 'Self-Machinery? Steel Trusses and the Management of Ruptures in Eighteenth-Century Europe', *Technology and Culture*, 54:4 (2013): p. 463.
18. Norfolk Record Office (hereafter NRO) PD 86, East Dereham Overseers' Accounts, 1726–1819.
19. NRO PD 533/104, Wighton Outdoor Relief Book, 1793–1814.

Objects of Poverty

20 Berkshire Record Office D/P 113/18/3, Letter; Roger Wells (ed.), *Victorian Village: The Diaries of the Reverend John Coker Egerton of Burwash 1857–1888* (Stroud: Alan Sutton, 1992), p. 127.
21 Hilaire-Perez and Rabier, 'Self-Machinery'.
22 William H. Timbrell, *New Inventions and Directions for Ruptured Persons* (London: Thomas Collins, 1802), pp. 29–32; George Acret, *A Treatise on Hernia Explaining Its Varieties, Situation, Symptoms and Causes; to Which Is Added a Full Description of the Construction and Application of the Most Approved Mechanical Remedies* (London: Houlston and Son, 1835), pp. 59–77.
23 John Wood, *Clinical Lecture on the Application of Trusses to Herniae, Delivered at King's College Hospital* (London: Matthews Brothers, 1877).
24 For this reason, many truss makers also had expertise in corset or staymaking. See Lynn Sorge-English, *Stays and Body Image in London: The Staymaking Trade, 1680–1810* (London: Pickering and Chatto, 2015).
25 NRO PD 553/76, Wighton Miscellaneous Papers, 1793–1814.
26 NRO PD 421/132, Forncett Overseers' Accounts, 1762–1832.
27 The National Archives, MH 12/12701,38932/1868, Letter, 20 July 1868. Mr Balise ran a charity providing trusses for the needy.
28 See Kim Price, '"The shape of the Iceberg": Doctors and Neglect under the New Poor Law, c. 1871–1900', in Jonathan Reinarz and Rebecca Wynter (eds), *Complaints, Controversies and Grievances in Medicine: Historical and Social Science Perspectives* (Abingdon: Routledge, 2015), pp. 129–46.

Further reading

Digby, Anne. *Making a Medical Living: Doctors and Patients in the English Market for Medicine* (Cambridge: Cambridge University Press, 1994).
Hilaire-Perez, Liliane, and Christelle Rabier. 'Self-Machinery? Steel Trusses and the Management of Ruptures in Eighteenth-Century Europe'. *Technology and Culture*, 54:4 (2013): pp. 460–502.
King, Steven. *Sickness, Medical Welfare and the English Poor 1750–1834* (Manchester: Manchester University Press, 2018).
King, Steven, Paul Carter, Peter Jones, Natalie Carter and Carol Beardmore. *In Their Own Write: A New Poor Law History from Below* (Montreal: McGill-Queens University Press, 2022).
Lane, Joan. *A Social History of Medicine: Health, Healing and Disease in England, 1750–1950* (London: Routledge, 2001).
Price, Kim. *Medical Negligence in Victorian Britain: The Crisis of Care under the English Poor Law 1834–1900* (Basingstoke: Palgrave, 2015).
Ritch, Alastair. *Sickness in the Workhouse: Poor Law Medical Care in England, 1834–1914* (Rochester: Rochester University Press, 2019).
Shave, Samantha. '"Immediate Death or a Life of Torture Are the Consequences of the System": The Bridgwater Union Scandal and Policy Change', in Jonathan Reinarz and Leonard Schwarz (eds), *Medicine and the Workhouse* (Rochester: Rochester University Press, 2013), pp. 164–91.
Tomkins, Alannah. "'Labouring on a Bed of Sickness": The Material and Rhetorical Deployment of Ill-Health in Male Pauper Letters', in Andreas Gestrich, Elizabeth Hurren and Steven King (eds), *Poverty and Sickness in Modern Europe: Narratives of the Sick Poor, 1780–1938* (London: Bloomsbury, 2012), pp. 51–68.

CHAPTER 23
INSCRIPTION GRAVESTONES: POVERTY AND COMMEMORATION IN THE LATE NINETEENTH CENTURY

Rebecca Senior[1]

Introduction

On 17 May 1893, the *Yorkshire Evening Post* published a letter about Burmantofts Cemetery in Leeds.[2] The author, identified only as 'The Penman', was responding to another letter the *Post* published several days earlier by Reverend W. H. Stansfield, the vicar of St Agnes Church in the nearby Leeds parish of Harehills.[3] These letters expressed concern that methods used to erect graves in Burmantofts Cemetery were dangerous, particularly 'the peculiar and unusual spectacle' of the shared graves where several coffins were buried in the same grave pit.[4] Stansfield continued, 'On some of the headstones I noticed 10, 12, 14 and 15 names. These are called "guinea graves" but as each name represents a guinea, it would be more correct to say 10 or 12 guineas'.[5] The Penman offered a more detailed description of these graves:

> The so called 'guinea graves' only give you a share in a hole in the ground. But you get a headstone and kerbs, and the handsome allotment of two lines on the former for the record of your name, age and date of disintegration … the holes are made in the exact shape of an adult coffin. When the requisite depth and height are obtained the roof is either planked over or left open with tapes ready to lower the next comer … I see some covered over and half filled up with coffins; the top casket being covered with loose earth and shale. Others stand open.[6]

'Guinea graves' were a type of 'common grave' – a nineteenth-century term used to describe graves filled with the bodies of unrelated people who could not afford to buy private plots of land. Common graves accounted for the majority of burials in Burmantofts Cemetery and were the final resting place for thousands of impoverished people, including inmates from the infamous Leeds workhouse. Burial methods for these graves included 'open graves', such as those described by Stansfield, where a wooden plank was placed on top of each coffin with the hole remaining open until it was filled, and 'public graves', where the hole was filled in after each internment and dug up again for the next.[7] The lowest class of these common graves were unmarked or 'pauper' graves, where bodies were interred at the expense of the state without any form of commemoration such as a coffin or headstone. The Penman described an encounter with the unmarked graves in Burmantofts Cemetery in his letter to the *Yorkshire Evening Post*:

> Over yonder, where the paupers lie, old pickle jars, jampots, and other incongruous receptacles for cut-flowers strike sharply on the sense of the ridiculous ... I learn from a brawny digger, who stands to rest on his shovel for a time, that these wreaths, these bottles, are the only outward indications that underneath are dead bodies buried in rows ... as I walk away I cannot help thinking painfully of those dried wreaths and memorial bottles propped up with clods on the scarred earth; and I cannot help in thinking of the wives and daughters who come here week by week to see when the grave plots are less like a rough stone quarry and shaped into something tangible to weep over.[8]

Once the flowers, pickle jars and jampots were gone, relatives of those buried in unmarked graves were left without any indication of where their loved ones were interred.[9] However, on 15 October 1863, the Leeds Burial Grounds Committee resolved that anyone could pay to have a place in a common grave marked by a gravestone.[10] For the price of a guinea, the stone could be inscribed with their name, age and date of death and each gravestone was mounted on a numbered curb, which ensured those visiting the grave could find it with ease (Figure 23.1).

Figure 23.1 View of 'Guinea Grave Row', Beckett Street Cemetery, Leeds. Photo Credit: The author.

Significantly cheaper than a private plot, these 'guinea graves', or 'inscription graves' as they are formally known, prevented those who could afford it from being buried without commemoration.[11] The inscription grave was the most prevalent mode of commemoration for the poor in Leeds – a fact that did not escape The Penman, who concluded their letter by comparing the lists of names inscribed on inscription gravestones to 'printed scores in a cricket match only here Time and Disease and Poverty are the demon bowlers who knock down their stumps'.[12]

Much attention has been paid to the visual and material culture of middle- and upper-class commemoration in cemeteries from the nineteenth and early twentieth centuries, yet inscription graves saved tens of thousands of people and their bereaved from the indignity of an unmarked grave and allowed the poor to claim ownership of their dead. The common grave is often thought to epitomise the vilification of the poor and the suffering they endured (aided by commentators like The Penman). However, the inscription gravestone should also be seen as a symbol of their agency.[13] Using The Penman's letter as a narrative framework and incorporating visual analysis of the gravestones, I argue that the inscription grave was and still is an important cultural marker of class identity that reveals the agency of poor communities in commemorating their dead.

Inscription graves in Leeds

In 1842, an Act of Parliament authorised Leeds Town Council to open new cemeteries and establish a committee to oversee their management. Paid for with public money, the cemeteries in Armley, Burmantofts and Hunslet were the earliest municipal cemeteries in the country.[14] The new cemeteries were intended to alleviate severe overcrowding in existing burial grounds in the city, including St Peter's Parish Church, which was 'so full in January 1841, that the bodies, when interred in particular places selected by friends, were disinterred after the funeral and the retirement of the friends, and redeposited in some other part of the ground'.[15] Overcrowding was of particular concern to those destined for common graves: the poor. The high number of coffins in these graves and the close proximity of grave pits meant that land subsidence often exposed the remains of those buried last.[16] Fears over the integrity of the corpse were further exacerbated when grave diggers in sites like St Peter's were forced to smash interned coffins and compact the remains to make space for new bodies.[17] The unregulated funeral industry's high prices also forced the working class and poor to endure harrowing conditions upon the death of a family member. Anyone who wanted internment in a common grave as opposed to a pauper grave, which was funded entirely by the local government, had to pay the funeral fees before the body was collected.[18] This practice often meant that rotting corpses were left for long periods of time in cramped residential houses and at high risk of spreading disease.[19] The Burial Act of 1857 addressed some of these issues by establishing reforms aimed at improving conditions for those living in poverty, including making it unlawful to disturb human burials without a license or permission from the Church of England.[20]

Objects of Poverty

Burmantofts Cemetery was the largest of Leeds' new cemeteries. It opened on over ten acres of land outside the city in 1845 and was designed to make burying the city's poor as efficient and dignified as they could afford. The Penman described the cemetery's proximity to other institutions associated with poverty:

> Burmantofts is the Poor Man's Cemetery. It is cheap and fairly approachable. Every day of the year – Sundays, high days, holidays, and working days – you may see mournful processions of weeping relatives winding their way thither behind the remains of those who once were dear to them. Because of this Beckett Street is not the most cheerful thoroughfare in the city. Indeed, what with the Fever Hospital, the Workhouse, with its weary tramps ever slouching towards, the Stoney Rock Smallpox Hospital, the Refuse Destructor and the Cemetery, Beckett Street and its immediate vicinage might fairly be seemed the Place of Gones – bygones and gone wrongs.[21]

Despite The Penman's bleak outlook on the cemetery's location among the tenements of the poor, Burmantoft's inscription graves made it an important commemorative site for the city's poor.[22] Sylvia M. Barnard attributed the first inscription grave to the Reverend Edward Jackson, incumbent of St James Church on York Street in Leeds. Jackson purchased four common graves in Burmantofts Cemetery, which were filled with the bodies of thirty-two people. Each grave was marked by a shared gravestone, which Barnard proposed might have served as the inspiration for the Burial Committee's resolution of 1863.[23] Mostly erected between the 1880s and 1930s, inscription graves offered the working classes and the labouring poor a more desirable alternative to an anonymous burial in a common grave. These graves ensured that the poor were represented in a public space of grief typically reserved for those who could pay for a private grave or memorial.[24] Both the deceased, who avoided the indignity of an unmarked grave, and the bereaved, who could participate in the culture of mourning, benefitted from the reduced price and accessibility of the inscription grave.

The inscription gravestone

In Memory of
Patrick Judge,
Died March 23rd 1895, aged 60 years
Bridget Flanagan,
Died March 24th 1895, aged 23 years
Thomas Sugden,
Died Feb 29th 1895, aged 44 years
James Timlin,
Died March 31st 1895, aged 25 years
Sarah M. Geldard,

Died March 31st 1895, aged 76 years
Charles Foster,
Died April 1st 1895, aged 52 years
William Birmingham,
Died April 4th 1895, aged 25 years
R.I.P.

The above text is reproduced from the gravestone that marks grave 22699 in Burmantofts Cemetery (Figure 23.2). The grave is located in part of the cemetery reserved for Nonconformists, and the burial register records that Patrick Judge (who died on 23rd March 1895) was the first to be interred on the 27th.[25] Though the Burial Register does not offer any in-depth history of those interred in grave 22699, it does record their last address and a brief description of their profession. Patrick lived in Hunslet in Leeds and was described as a 'Labourer'. Bridget Flanagan, who was interred on the same day as Patrick, was listed as a 'Spinster' in the burial records and lived nearby in the area of Holbeck.[26] Both Thomas and James lived in Burley, with the former described as a 'Yeast Dealer' and the latter a 'Labourer'. Sarah, described only as a 'Widow', lived near the cemetery in Burmantofts and Charles was described as a 'Drayman'. William, a 'Moulder' who lived near Holbeck, was the last to be buried before the grave closed on 7th April,

Figure 23.2 Inscription gravestone 22699, Beckett Street Cemetery, Leeds. Photo credit: The author.

Objects of Poverty

meaning it was either 'open' or 'public' for twelve days. Grave 22699 is a typical example of a common grave, as the people interred did not own the plot they were buried in nor share any familial connection to one another. Nonetheless, they were united by their experiences of Leeds as members of the poor community. All those buried in 22699 had resided in poverty-stricken areas of the city yet were able to afford the price of the inscription grave to leave an enduring record of their life and death. Though the stone marking grave 22699 has weathered, the names, ages and dates of death of seven people buried beneath it are still clearly legible due to the deeply carved capital letters. The names of the deceased are engraved in a larger font than the other text and separated out onto different lines, offering a stark counterpoint to the delicate Gothic-style script used for 'In Memory of' and decorative leaf pattern running along the top of the stone.[27] Grave 22699 is engraved centrally on the grave's curb stone to assist recently bereaved and future visitors in locating the grave. Both the gravestone and curb stone have flat edges, and the central sections of each stone have been subtly narrowed to create a more ornate design. The gravestone marking grave 22699 is a stylised and legible memorial. It has stood for over one hundred and twenty years as a place for the bereaved and descendants of seven people, a place to pay their respects and identify their historical connection to the city and its inhabitants.

Despite subtle variations in the shape of the stones, inscription gravestones were largely formulaic in their design and lacked the unique symbolic imagery of more costly memorials.[28] Rows upon rows of inscription graves in Burmantofts Cemetery, now in varying states of repair, were also 'double-sided' (Figure 23.3). The pit for grave 22825 (Figure 23.4), for example, was dug immediately behind that of grave 22699. The names of those in grave 22825 were then engraved on the reverse side of the stone for grave 22699, creating a 'double-sided' gravestone that commemorated fifteen people in total. Some stones, like those marking graves 22699 and 22825, remained located on their original burial site, while others have been moved by human or natural intervention (Figure 23.5).[29] The highest number of accessible inscription graves in Burmantofts are on 'Guinea Grave Row' (Figure 23.1), which cuts through the middle of the cemetery, while others sit among the private graves and on unkempt grassland. Though the overall design of inscription graves was determined by functionality, cost and clarity, the collective visual impact of their gravestones marks the landscape of the cemetery with an important visual representation of historical poverty in the city.

Inscription gravestones were erected on common graves in cemeteries across Leeds throughout the nineteenth and early twentieth centuries. The Leeds General Cemetery was opened in 1835 and accumulated over 97,000 burials before it was closed and reopened by the University of Leeds under its original name, St George's Field, in 1969.[30] Hundreds of people were interred in common graves marked by inscription gravestones in the cemetery, which were subsequently repurposed as decorative pathways surrounding the cemetery chapel (Figure 23.6). This carefully curated display was likely a result of the university's decision to remove the majority of the memorials in the 1960s, however, it raises interesting questions about the visual and material qualities of inscription graves. Using the gravestones as paving slabs prioritises their design over their original function

Inscription Gravestones

Figure 23.3 View of inscription graves, Beckett Street Cemetery, Leeds. Photo credit: The author.

Figure 23.4 Inscription gravestone 22825, Beckett Street Cemetery, Leeds. Photo credit: The author.

Objects of Poverty

Figure 23.5 View of inscription graves, Beckett Street Cemetery, Leeds. Photo credit: The author.

as grave locators, disrupting the idea that they were purely functional, homogeneous objects. It also changes how visitors interact with the grave of the deceased. The Penman briefly described the poor's emotional encounter with inscription graves in Burmantofts Cemetery in his letter:

> The hush and peace of the scene takes you from the pity and incongruity of these common graves. Here are sad-eyed women bending over the earth, putting in plants or arranging new flowers. They own but a selfish interest in this grave, but they will beautify the lot, knowing that relations of others there will come to do the same.[31]

His comments indicated that the inscription gravestone in Burmantofts Cemetery was the site of collaborative mourning for the poor. As a shared object of poverty, it enabled friends and relatives to participate in grieving rituals typically outside their financial reach, and, thanks to the Friends of Beckett Street Cemetery, it continues to provide information about those living in poverty for future generations.[32]

Conclusion

Much attention has been paid to the visual and material culture of middle- and upper-class commemoration in cemeteries during the nineteenth and early twentieth centuries,

Inscription Gravestones

Figure 23.6 Cemetery Chapel and view of inscription grave path, St George's Field, University of Leeds, 2023. Photo credit: The author.

yet inscription graves saved thousands of people and their bereaved from the indignity of an unmarked burial. The inscription gravestone protects the historical records of a community whose possessions were often deemed unworthy of preservation and though the common grave is often thought to epitomise the vilification of the poor and the suffering they endured (aided by commentators like The Penman), the inscription gravestone should also be seen as a symbol of their agency. These objects offer important insights into how those in poverty participated in commemorative practices in this period and enabled people with very little money to claim a significant part of the cemetery for themselves and their bereaved.

Notes

1 This study was supported by the Paul Mellon Centre for Studies in British Art.
2 Burmantofts Cemetery is currently known as Beckett Street Cemetery and is maintained by the Friends of Beckett Street Cemetery – an organisation founded by Sylvia M. Barnard in 1985 to prevent Leeds City Council removing the memorials and grassing over the site. For the sake of continuity, this chapter uses the title Burmantofts Cemetery throughout. For more information, see https://www.beckettstreetcemetery.org.uk (accessed 27 January 2025).

3   The Penman, 'Among the Graves: The State of Burmantofts Cemetery. How New Graves Are Built', *Yorkshire Evening Post*, 17 May 1893.
4   Reverend W. H. Stansfield, 'Burmantofts Cemetery: The State of the Graves', *Yorkshire Evening Post*, 15 May 1893.
5   Stansfield, 'The State of the Graves', p. 3.
6   The Penman, 'Among the Graves', p. 1.
7   The stigma associated with different types of common grave is a complex issue and explored at length in Julie-Marie Strange, *Death, Grief and Poverty in Britain, 1870–1914* (Cambridge: Cambridge University Press, 2005), pp. 131–63.
8   The Penman, 'Among the Graves', p. 1.
9   Before the intervention of the Leeds Burial Grounds Committee, the only alternative was to purchase a private grave with accompanying memorial, something far outside the financial reach of the city's poor inhabitants.
10 Both Stansfield and The Penman used the term 'headstone' to refer to the stone tablet that marks an inscription gravesite. This term was used interchangeably with 'gravestone' throughout the nineteenth century, with the *OED* describing a 'headstone' as 'An upright stone at the head of a grave; a gravestone'. I use the term gravestone throughout to align with its contemporary etymological usage. See James Augusts Henry Murray, *A New English Dictionary on Historical Principles; Founded Mainly on the Materials Collected by the Philological Society* (London: Clarendon Press, 1901), p. 151. For the Leeds Burial Committee, see: Sylvia M. Bernard, *To Prove I'm Not Forgot: Living and Dying in a Victorian City* (Manchester: Manchester University Press, 1990), p. 37.
11 The price of a 'guinea grave' gradually increased throughout the nineteenth and early twentieth centuries. This chapter uses the term 'inscription grave' throughout. See, Bernard, *To Prove I'm Not Forgot*, p. 37.
12 The Penman, 'Among the Graves', p. 1.
13 Strange, *Death, Grief and Poverty in Britain*, p. 133.
14 For more information about the cemeteries in Leeds during this period, see Jim Morgan, *The Burial Ground Problem in Leeds c. 1700–1914* (Leeds: Thoresby Society, 2013) and Antony Ramm, 'A Brief History of the Cemeteries in Leeds', 2019. www.secretlibraryleeds.net/2019/08/23/a-brief-history-of-cemeteries-in-leeds/ (accessed 27 January 2025).
15 Poor Law Commissioners, *Sanitary Inquiry: – England.: Local Reports on the Sanitary Condition of the Labouring Population of England, in Consequence of an Inquiry Directed to be made by the Poor Law Commissioners. Presented to both Houses of Parliament, by command of Her Majesty, July, 1842* (London: W. Clowes and Sons, Stamford Street, for Her Majesty's Stationery Office, 1842), p. 21.
16 Jim Morgan, 'The Burial Question in Leeds in the Eighteenth and Nineteenth Centuries', in Ralph Houlbrooke (ed.), *Death, Ritual and Bereavement* (Routledge: London, 1989), pp. 95–104.
17 A 'rammer' device was described during a Select Committee from 1842 and it was widely known that bodies were regularly packed into common graves as tightly as possible. See Barnard, *To Prove I'm Not Forgot*, p. 35.
18 For a thorough account of the conditions facing those in poverty including body disposal, see Chris Brooks, *Mortal Remains: The History and Present State of the Victorian and Edwardian Cemetery* (Chicago: Wheaton Press, 1989), pp. 33–9 and Strange, *Death, Grief and Poverty in Britain*, pp. 131–63.
19 For a discussion of conditions endured by those living in poverty in Leeds during this period, see: Barnard, *To Prove I'm Not Forgot*, pp. 21–40.
20 Receiving houses for corpses were established by Public Health Acts in the second half of the nineteenth century. Brooks, *Mortal Remains*, p. 40.

21 The Penman, 'Among the Graves', p. 1.
22 Leeds was renowned for its observation of 'great deaths' en masse in this period when thousands of people lined the streets to venerate famous deceased with pomp and ceremony. John Wolffe, *Great Deaths: Grieving, Religion, and Nationhood in Victorian and Edwardian Britain* (Chicago: University of Chicago Press, 2001), pp. 102–10.
23 Bernard, *To Prove I'm Not Forgot*, pp. 37–9.
24 The Friends of Beckett Street Cemetery website records that Burmantofts Cemetery has the highest number of inscription graves in the country. https://www.beckettstreetcemetery.org.uk/events_ww1_page_07.php (accessed 27 January 2025).
25 Yorkshire Archive Service, Leeds, REF LC/CEM (B)/1/9, Digitised Registers, Beckett Street Cemetery Burial Records. Numbers 38801–58640 (Leeds: 1889–1909), 208.
26 Ibid.
27 For information on the stone masons and letter cutters who undertook work on inscription graves in Leeds, see Bernard, *To Prove I'm Not Forgot*, pp. 37–9.
28 Alongside the large-scale commemoration of royalty, political figures and victims of war, those who could afford to pay for a gravestone or memorial at private expense had more scope to incorporate allegorical and symbolic imagery into their design and create unique sculptural monuments. For further information, see Patricia Jalland, *Death in the Victorian Family* (Oxford University Press, 1997), pp. 377–84.
29 Many of the inscription gravestones in Burmantofts Cemetery are in a state of disrepair, with some having moved and/or broken due to subsidence.
30 An Act of Parliament was passed in 1965 that enabled the University of Leeds to acquire the cemetery and create an open public space after it had fallen into disuse. Imogen Gerard and Kelsie Root, 'The Dead and the Living Interconnected on Campus', 2017. https://livingwithdying.leeds.ac.uk/2017/07/28/the-dead-and-the-living-interconnected/ (accessed 27 January 2025).
31 The Penman, 'Among the Graves', p. 1.
32 When I visited the cemetery, I saw that several of the inscription graves were laid with fresh flowers, while some had poppy memorial decals stuck to their surface and someone had gone to the trouble of highlighting the carved letters with white paint.

Further reading

Bernard, Sylvia M. *To Prove I'm Not Forgot: Living and Dying in a Victorian City* (Manchester: Manchester University Press, 1990).
Brooks, Chris. *Mortal Remains: The History and Present State of the Victorian and Edwardian Cemetery* (Chicago: Wheaton Press, 1989).
Gerard, Imogen, and Kelsie Root. 'The Dead and the Living Interconnected on Campus', 2017. https://livingwithdying.leeds.ac.uk/2017/07/28/the-dead-and-the-living-interconnected/ (accessed 27 January 2025).
Morgan, Jim. *The Burial Ground Problem in Leeds c. 1700 – 1914* (Leeds: Thoresby Society, 2013).
Ramm, Antony. 'A Brief History of the Cemeteries in Leeds', 2019. www.secretlibraryleeds.net/2019/08/23/a-brief-history-of-cemeteries-in-leeds/ (accessed 27 January 2025).
Strange, Julie-Marie. *Death, Grief and Poverty in Britain, 1870–1914* (Cambridge: Cambridge University Press, 2005).
Wolffe, John. *Great Deaths: Grieving, Religion, and Nationhood in Victorian and Edwardian Britain* (Chicago: University of Chicago Press, 2001).

SUBJECT INDEX

advertisements 53–5, 66, 67, 191, 192, 232, 267, 304
allotments 190, 191
alternative currencies 34, 90
   tokens 23, 219–29
   trucking 225–6
   see also pawning
animals
   birds 94, 97, 105
   cats 124, 176
   cruelty 97, 170–5
   donkey 94, 97
   rabbits 170, 190–1
   see also chicken coops; dogs; toys
apprenticeships 152
artificial lighting 65, 66, 80, 254

banks *see* purses; savings
beds
   bedframes 56, 248
      iron 251
      old 192
      wooden 251, 280, 290
   chaff 61, 251
   dolls 122–3
   feathers 247, 251, 252
   flock 251
   hay 61
   hygiene 248–53
   makeshift 53–8
   noise of 251
   sexual activity in 250–1
   straw 55–6, 61, 251, 280
   tick 61
   see also cots
bedbugs 251, 255
bedclothes 56, 57, 59, 61, 148, 253–4
   burning of 280
   cleaning and repairing of 253, 254
   pillows 91, 148, 251
   theft of 253
bedsharing 60, 124, 249–50
bedtimes
   institutional 143, 248, 254
bread 17–26, 68, 180
   adulteration 21
   cultures 20–1
   harvest failures 19, 21–2, 28, 30, 307

Parliamentary acts relating to 19
   and the poor law 22–3, 27, 28, 33, 34–5
   and protest/riot 19, 20–4
   regional consumption of 18–20
   and religion 20, 22, 90
   scales (Speenhamland) 22–3
British Army 289
   ex-soldiers 291
   pensioners 291
   veterans 292
   see also disability
burns and scalds 65–73, 81
buttons 105–9, 112, 124, 148, 157–64, 307

cemeteries *see* graves
ceramics *see* teaware and utensils
charity 22, 238
   see also bread; disability; orphans
chicken coops 187–99
   in media 191, 192–4
   in visual imagery 193–4
childhood *see* child neglect; dolls; needlework; orphans; toys
child neglect 56, 67–8, 78–82
Childrens' Act (1908) 68–70
   Colebrooks' Bill (Fireguard Act 1952) 70–1
Christmas 35, 80, 94, 122, 125, 132, 134, 191
cleanliness 93, 142, 193, 209, 247–55
   see also bedbugs; bedding; beds; workhouse
clothing 3–4, 133, 136
   accessories 235
   cleaning of 79, 93
   as credit 205, 212
   and disability 293–5
   donated 124
   flammable 66–7
   home-made 160
   miniature-to-scale garments 143–53
   old 80, 235, 237
   pockets 235–7
   repairing and repurposing 90, 133, 160
   sales of 144
   second-hand 3, 123, 160, 204, 205
   shipboard clothing 92–3
   Sunday best 204

Subject Index

see also needlework; pawning; purses; vagrants; workhouse
coal
   in the bath 75–86
   cooking with 75–82
   consumption of 80
   fires 75–82
conflagration 53, 254, 280
cooking utensils 65, 66
coroners' inquests 17, 53, 56, 58, 60–1, 66–9, 239
cots 56–7, 59–61, 69
council housing 76–82, 187–98

debt 78–82, 225, 226, 238
destitution 93, 99, 122, 220–1, 209, 210, 276
diet *see* bread; food; workhouse
disability 100, 132, 134, 176, 235, 276, 305
   in memoir 289–300
   wooden legs 289–300
dogs 190
   abuse of 170–5
   in autobiographies 175–83
   companionship 169–83
   in poetry 174
   in visual imagery 172–4, 176, 183
dolls
   in autobiographies 119–25
   cheap 121–3
   clothing 122–3, 132
   emergency/slum 115
   luxury 124
   makeshift 115–28
   orphan 143
   in visual imagery 119
domestic service 125, 152
dressmaking *see* clothing; needlework

economies of makeshift 4, 89, 203
   selling possessions 4, 55, 68
   see also pawning
egg boxes 53–65
electric appliances 70, 78, 81
emotional objects 124–5, 134, 148
   see also dogs; dolls; tokens

fabrics
   calico (cotton) 157–64, 267
   cotton 148, 209, 233, 234, 263, 267
   cotton twill 265
   cut-offs 123
   flock 251
   lace 115, 148
   linen 144, 148, 157, 161, 163, 209, 263
   rags 53, 56, 116, 122, 124, 133, 134, 136, 296
   scraps of 233, 234, 235, 264–8

silk 209, 232, 265, 267
twine 234, 263, 267
unspecified 234, 306
wool 94, 122, 123, 124, 134, 148, 251, 253, 296, 305
see also woolworks
fireguards
   absent 65–73, 81
   makeshift 69
   pawing of 66, 68
fire prevention 65–73
firewood 55
food and drink
   alcohol (unspecified) 19, 90, 170, 175, 237
   ale 21, 28, 33–5, 204
   brandy 30, 33–5
   cheese 19, 27, 28, 34, 35
   coffee 30, 33, 48
   crisis 19–23
   food production 4, 187–99
   foodstuffs 18–20, 90
   fruit 30, 33
   meat 18, 28, 32, 33, 90, 115, 180
   milk 27, 28, 33, 39, 81, 111
   as medicine 33
   oatmeal 32
   port 30
   prices 17, 30–2
   rice 22, 30, 32, 33
   rum 30, 33, 34, 90, 236
   spices 28, 30, 33, 35
   street 43
   sugar 28, 30–5, 39, 56
   tea 28–35, 40, 135, 282
   treacle 28, 30, 180
   vegetables 28, 189, 191, 192, 247, 264
   waste 90
   wine 30, 33
   see also bread; chicken coops; saloop stalls; workhouse
fowl *see* chicken coop
friendly societies 225
fuel poverty 79
funerals 28, 34–5, 59
   cost of 313
   see also graves; pauper burials
furniture
   burning of 79
   makeshift 55, 56
   selling of 68

gas appliances 70, 78, 79
gardens 189–97
   see also workhouse
gifts 91–2, 122, 123, 124–5, 132, 239
   see also Christmas

Subject Index

glassware 91, 304, 312
graves
   burial act 313
   coffins 58, 59, 313
   guinea (inscription) 311–21
   non-conformist 315
   unmarked 312
   see also gravestones
gravestones
   as paving slabs 316
   see also graves
grief 148, 314, 318

hawkers 43, 133
health visitors 61, 78, 79, 81
household budgets/expenditure 19–20, 80, 131, 163
   see also debt
housing acts and bye-laws 188–9
hunger 17, 204

infant/child mortality 60–1, 65–9

knives 281
knitting 122, 123, 142–3, 148, 160

literacy 134, 142, 163
lodging house 57, 237, 268
   charitable 57–60, 221–9
lying-in 32–3, 250

material culture 1–4
   defining 5–6
   of the poor 2–4
Medical Officers of Health 77, 80, 190, 191–2, 196
Ministry of Health 188, 190
money see alternative currencies; debt; purses

needlework
   education 141–55, 157–66
   fancy 148, 161
   manuals 163–4
   plain 141–55, 157–64
   prizes for 144, 145
   and religion 142–3, 145–6
   samplers 141–55, 157–66
   sewing machine 123, 163–4
   see also buttons; clothing; fabrics; knitting; woolwork; workhouse
neighbours 53, 54, 55, 67, 122, 170, 180
new poor law 3
   and the lunatic poor 264, 268–72
   medical relief under 301–10
      patent medicines 302–4
      trusses 304–8
   overseers' accounts 307

   and pauper burials 58, 311–2, 313
   relief under 23, 170, 262
   'undeserving' poor 277
   see also vagrants; workhouse
newspapers 53–63, 80, 93–7, 190, 235, 239, 250
   letter to 311, 318
   newspaper campaigns 65–71, 190–3
   see also vagrants

oil appliances 70, 79
old poor law 3, 17–18, 22–3, 27–38
   medical relief under 255, 304–8
   overseers' accounts 27–35, 305–7
   overseers' vouchers 29–35
   pauper inventories 251
   pauper letters 22, 205
   pensions 211
   relief under 17–18, 21–3, 28–35, 170, 176, 203–13
   see also beds; bread; pawning; workhouse
orphans 119, 141–51, 239

pawn brokers 203–18
   casual 203
   ledgers 205
   prosecution of 205–7
   see also pawning
pawning
   of bedding 209
   of clothes 203–18
   of economic tools 43
   and gender 205
   of household possessions 55–6
   lending for 205
   and the Old Bailey 205
   of stolen goods 205–7
   of workhouse property 205–13
   see also fireguards
play 68
   and imagination 121, 123, 134
   space of 135–6, 267
   see also dolls; toys
pledging see pawning

poultry see chicken coops
poverty
   defining 4–5
purses
   as consumer goods 232–3
   as gifts 239–40
   home-made and crafted 239–40
   for keepsakes 241
   mass-produced 234–5
   rudimentary 233–4
   for savings 236–9
   theft of 235–8, 239

Subject Index

rehousing 75–82, 187–98
rent 19, 55, 188
  arrears 79
  council 188
  eviction 55–6
  officers 196–7
respectability 3, 76, 77, 94–8, 100, 212, 231–43, 236–9

sailors
  caricatures of 92–8, 101
  craft 89–101
  and manhood 92–3
  merchant navy 91–2, 239
  Royal Navy 90–4, 101
  wages 92–3, 232, 237
  see also seamen
saloop stalls 39–50
  in Old Bailey records 41, 44, 45, 46
  in visual imagery 40–1, 43–7
  see also teaware and utensils
Salvation Army 57–60, 219–29
savings
  banks 238–9
  concealment of 239
  and penny banks 238–9
  schemes 238
  see also purses
second-hand dealers/sellers 42–3
  see also pawn brokers; pawning
sheds 192
  see also chicken coops
slums 56, 59, 75–7, 79
  practices 187–98
social workers 69–70, 76–82
street sellers 30–50
  women as 45, 47
Sunday school 134, 239

teaware and utensils 41–6, 135, 239, 282
  see also food; saloop stalls
temperance 225
theft 54, 55, 56, 79, 81, 133, 175
  see also money; pawning; purses
thrift 236 see also purses
tobacco 27, 30, 33, 34, 35
  boxes 55, 236
  pipes 281
  pouches 91
  smoking 28, 34, 254, 281
toys
  animals 134
  distribution 133
  in literature 132
  makeshift 122, 132–3, 136

marbles 135
  in Old Bailey records 132–3
  production of 132–3
  religious 134
  tin 133–4
  in visual imagery 133, 135–6
  wooden 134–5
  see also dolls; play
trade directories 133

unemployment 55, 99, 191, 204, 238

vagrants
  acts relating to 276
  agency 277–81
  clothing 277–81
  and disability 291
  possessions 281–3
  press perceptions of 275–81
  in visual imagery 278
  see also workhouse
wages 17–18, 19, 22–3, 55, 56, 80, 131, 223, 225, 232
  see also alternative currencies; sailors
warmth 43–8, 78–9, 80, 81–2, 124, 232, 235, 250, 253, 282
welfare state 75–86
whistles 105–14
  as control 110
  conductor's 108
  cyclists 107, 109–10
  dog handler's 108
  factory overseers' 108
  firefighter's 108
  makeshift 106–8
  policeman's 108, 110, 111
  as protection 110
whistling 107–11
  and crime 111
  nuisances 110–11
woolwork 94–8, 99
workhouse 3, 4
  admissions 210–12, 281
  alternative to 221–2
  in autobiographies 249, 255
  bathing facilities 279
  burials 311
  cleanliness 247–56, 279–80
  clothing 262–3, 277–81
  diet 23, 27–38
  dormitories 34, 248, 277
  ephemera 302
  garden 29, 34, 247
  labour 28, 34, 253, 280
  overcrowding 280
  provisions 27–35, 211